Prentice Hall

Realidades A

Teacher's Resource Book

Para empezar–Tema 4

Boston, Massachusetts Chandler, Arizona Glenview, Illinois Upper Saddle River, New Jersey

Acknowledgements for *Lecturas Teacher's Guide*

Bernadette M. Reynolds
Montbello High School
Denver, CO

Carol Eubanks Wargin

Rudolf L. Schonfeld
Parsippany High School
Parsippany, NJ

ISBN-13: 978-0-13-369251-8
ISBN-10: 0-13-369251-5

PEARSON

1 2 3 4 5 6 7 8 9 10 13 12 11 10 09

Table of Contents

Welcome to *Realidades!*

Realidades is based on the belief that the purpose of learning Spanish is to communicate with the people who speak it and to understand their cultures. It is designed to help your students achieve that goal by getting them to communicate right from the start. This *Teacher's Resource Book* is intended to help you accomplish that goal by giving you the support you need to teach Spanish effectively to all your students.

Organization of the *Teacher's Resource Book*

This *Teacher's Resource Book* is divided into two volumes. Volume A contains the teaching resources to supplement the preliminary chapter, called *Para empezar,* and *Temas* 1–4. Volume B includes the resources needed for *Temas* 5–9. For your convenience, both volumes are also provided electronically on the *TeacherExpress CD-ROM.*

The following resources are provided for each chapter in ***Realidades.***

Theme Project

Each *Tema* has a classroom theme project. These projects span the two chapters within the *Tema* and encourage students to prepare products and presentations directly related to the *Tema* subject matter. These projects help students internalize both vocabulary and grammar, and allow them to use their knowledge of Spanish in a meaningful way. The blackline masters in this section introduce students to the theme project and contain instructions for preparing the project. A rubric is also provided for students so that they will understand how their presentation will be evaluated.

School-to-Home Connection Letter

Parental involvement plays an integral part in student success and in supporting language learning at home. To that end, we provide a model letter for each chapter that you can either photocopy or personalize and send home to parents or guardians. The letter explains what the student will learn: the chapter communication objectives, vocabulary topics, grammar structures, language learning strategies, and video highlights. It also outlines the development of reading, writing, and speaking skills throughout the chapter. A brief activity at the end allows parents to participate in their child's learning.

Resource Checklist

The Resource Checklist is a chart that visually represents where each supporting component appears in the ***Realidades*** program for each section of every chapter. This includes both teacher and student components: the Assessment Program, the Video Program, the Audio Program, the *Leveled Vocabulary and Grammar Workbook,* the *Communication Workbook,* the *Realidades para hispanohablantes Workbook,* and the *TPRS Storytelling Book,* in addition to technology components such as the *ExamView Test Bank CD-ROM* and the *Fine Art Transparencies.* It also highlights where each component in this *Teacher's Resource Book* can be used. This chart serves as a checklist to ensure that you bring to class what you need for any given chapter section. For your convenience, chapter resources are also indicated at point of use within the *Teacher's Edition* of the textbook.

The following abbreviations are used in the Chapter Resource Checklists:

Abbreviation Key

CO	Chapter Opener
APV	A primera vista
VH	Videohistoria
MAN	Manos a la obra
LEC	Lectura
CV	La cultura en vivo
PO	Presentación oral
PE	Presentación escrita
MH	El mundo hispano
REP	Repaso del capítulo
PER	Perspectivas del mundo hispano
PREP	Preparación para el examen
RPH	Realidades para hispanohablantes
CWS	Companion Web Site

A primera vista Input Scripts

Each chapter of ***Realidades*** has a language input section called *A primera vista: Vocabulario en contexto* that introduces vocabulary and lexical uses of grammatical structures to students. The Input Scripts offer a step-by-step approach to presenting the new terms in a contextualized manner that engages students, yet requires minimal production on the learner's part. They can be followed in their entirety or they can be used as a resource for ideas to supplement the suggestions found in the *Teacher's Edition*. The Input Scripts are based on the theory of comprehensible input as a teaching tool. (For more information on how to use the Input Scripts, see the discussion under *Teaching with Input Scripts* on p. vi.)

Audio Scripts

This section contains the complete audio script for that chapter of ***Realidades.*** These include scripts for use with all of the listening activities within the *Student Edition,* as well as for pronunciation, end-of-chapter vocabulary, and assessment. Also included are scripts for the listening activities for the *Communication Workbook: Writing, Audio & Video Activities.* Use these to complement the accompanying audio program or as a student comprehension aid in class. You may want to use them to familiarize yourself with the activities before using them in class, or in cases where you do not wish to play the recording.

Video Scripts

The ***Realidades*** program has a comprehensive video component to support each chapter. The captivating input video for the *A primera vista: Vocabulario en contexto* section, corresponding to the *Videohistoria,* was shot on location in Spain, Mexico, Costa Rica, and Texas, and integrates culture and vocabulary with real-life, often humorous, situational interactions. In addition, ***Realidades*** offers the unique *GramActiva* Videos that explain and practice grammar structures in high-energy, entertaining segments that complement the *Gramática* sections within each chapter. Finally, in Temas 5 to 9, a third video component further engages student interest by means of a suspense-filled mystery thriller called *¿Eres tú, María?* In some cases, you may want to provide copies of the video scripts to students as an aid to comprehension when they view the videos. You may also want to use them to identify specific vocabulary and grammar structures that you want to focus on in the videos before you show videos in class.

Communicative Activities

These Communicative Activities blackline masters focus on student-to-student involvement where students have some control over the communicative elements. They allow for personalization and individualization, and often allow students to share real information. They practice communication and help students become comfortable interacting in a second language. Although a given activity may focus on particular vocabulary or structures, the emphasis is always on using language to give or obtain information. These activities have been designed to complement the ones found within ***Realidades*** and are meant to help students develop better communicative skills. (For more information on these blackline masters and how to use them, see *Teaching with Communicative Activities* on p. vii.)

Situation Cards

The Situation Cards blackline masters are designed to help students build confidence and develop skills as they work toward the goal of communicative proficiency. These guided conversations will provide your students with the opportunity to complete real-life tasks in Spanish. They will build confidence in even the most uncertain or reluctant students, and will enable more talented students to be truly creative with the language. There are a total of 38 pairs of Situation Cards, two per chapter. (For more information on these blackline masters and how to use them, see the section *Teaching with Situation Cards* on p. xi.)

GramActiva Blackline Masters

The GramActiva reproducible masters are templates and graphic organizers to be used in conjunction with specific hands-on activities in the *Student Edition*. These blackline masters require students to create products or to use charts, graphs, and other visual aids such as Venn diagrams, word webs, and surveys. They are referenced at point of use in the *Teacher's Edition*. Depending on the activity, you may want to pass these out the day before so students can fill them in or otherwise prepare for using them.

Vocabulary Clip Art

The Vocabulary Clip Art offers reproducible images of the visualized vocabulary in each chapter of ***Realidades.*** These visuals can be used in a variety of ways to provide students with a hands-on opportunity to work with new vocabulary. Engaging students in activities in which they "see, hear, say, and do," you will be more successful at reaching all students. Due to the thematic organization of ***Realidades,*** these blackline masters are appropriate for any classroom that focuses on language acquisition. (For more information on these blackline masters, see *Teaching with Vocabulary Clip Art* on p. xii.)

Leveled Vocabulary and Grammar Workbook

Answer Key: Core Practice

The Answer Key for the *Core Practice* activities allows you to quickly check the answers so students can have quick feedback. You may wish to reproduce these as a classroom set that you keep in a resource center or hand out so students can check their own work. You can also access pages with the answers displayed on the *PresentationExpress DVD*.

Answer Key: Guided Practice

These are reduced pages of the *Leveled Vocabulary and Grammar Workbook: Guided Practice*. You can use them yourself to check work, or reproduce them in booklet form or on overheads so that students can check their own work. You can also access these pages on the *PresentationExpress DVD*.

Communication Workbook with Test Preparation

Answer Key: Writing, Audio & Video Activities

These are reduced pages of the *Writing, Audio & Video Workbook* with the answers printed on them. You can use them yourself to check work, or reproduce them in booklet form or on overheads so that students can check their own work. You can also access pages with the answers displayed on the *PresentationExpress DVD*.

Answer Key: Test Preparation

This page provides answers for the Reading Skills worksheets and the Practice Test. Please note that answers to the Integrated Performance Assessments will always vary. The rubrics that you can use to assess student performance are given right on the student's page so that the students can see how they are to be evaluated.

Teaching Tips for the *Teacher's Resource Book*

Teaching with Input Scripts

The Input Scripts are based on the notion of comprehensible input. Rather than putting pressure on students to produce complex sentences with their newly acquired vocabulary and structures, they are given opportunities to show their comprehension through minimal responses. These responses range from physical responses (such as pointing to images in their textbook or manipulating the Vocabulary Clip Art images found in this *Teacher's Resource Book*) to short verbal responses (such as answering yes-no questions or questions with a choice of two answers) to short, structured conversations.

Input Vocabulary: This section provides a script for presenting the vocabulary in

Vocabulario en contexto. The vocabulary from both pages may be presented at once, or it may be broken up into two presentations. For example, in the *A primera vista* for *Capítulo 3A,* breakfast foods are presented in the form of a grocery store ad on one page, while lunch and dinner foods are presented in menu form on the facing page. In this case, the Input Scripts present the two sets of vocabulary separately. The emphasis in this section is on presenting the new terms in a creative fashion.

Input Dialogue/Monologue: In the *A primera vista,* grammatical structures are presented in context through dialogues and monologues. Although they are quite short, many key concepts are embedded in the dialogues. The goal of this section of the Input Scripts is to help you present the dialogues in manageable sections that allow you to stop and ask students minimal-response questions that target the key grammatical concepts.

Comprehension Check: This section provides additional activities to help you gauge how well students understand the vocabulary and grammatical structures presented. Additionally, this section reinforces learning through high-interest games and other activities.

Teaching with Communicative Activities

Learning a foreign language does involve learning important linguistic skills, such as grammar, syntax, and spelling, but also involves developing communicative skills, such as the ability to carry on a conversation in the target language, the ability to make a brief oral presentation, and the ability to communicate through written language.

These communicative activities focus primarily on listening and speaking skills—those skills that are more difficult to acquire outside of the classroom. Most of the activities are completed in pairs. One type of activity *(Actividades en grupo)* is intended for small groups of students. Students must communicate with each other to complete the activities. They ask and answer questions, role-play different scenes, share opinions on a variety of topics, and exchange real, but limited, information. In short, they use language in realistic situations that do not involve the teacher or a recording.

Activity Types: There are nine basic types of communicative activities included in this book: *Con otro(a) estudiante* (Partner Practice), *Descubrir …* (Discovery), *Diagramas* (Diagrams), *Entrevista* (Interview), *Hacer un papel* (Role-Play), *Opiniones* (Opinions), *Opiniones y reacciones* (Opinions and Reactions), and *Tres en raya* (Tic-Tac-Toe).

General Guidelines: Because most true communication takes place between two people or in small groups, most of the activities are to be used by pairs of students. You will want to determine the assignment of partners for the activities to be completed by student pairs. Also, you will want to have partners for a week or more, but partners should change at least once a month. Working together for several activities helps students get to know each other and learn to work together; changing partners at least once a month prevents students from getting too comfortable and wasting time. Reassign partners if a partnership simply doesn't work out, for whatever reason. Before students begin an activity, check to make sure that everyone understands the directions. As students complete these activities, keep in mind that most conversation, even in one's native language, involves hesitation, mispronunciation, and errors. These will occur more frequently while learning a second language. Remember that these activities are not intended as grammar practice, but are designed as conversational activities to practice communication. If you notice consistent errors while students are working, make brief notes and review the relevant structures after the activity has been completed. Although difficult, it is best not to comment on errors while students are completing the activities. Students should be focusing on communication, not on structure.

Pair Activities

Con otro estudiante **(Partner Practice)**
Purpose: To practice vocabulary and patterns; to discuss different situations.
For: Two students.
Accountability: Observe students on task and assign oral grades or random questions from the activity to check comprehension. You might use the pictures for an oral quiz.
Copies Needed: An A version for one student, and a B version for the other.
Directions:

1. Divide the class into pairs. All students do this activity simultaneously.
2. Distribute an A and a B version to each pair.
3. Go over the directions and set a time limit. Let students know what they are to do if they finish early.
4. **Steps:**
   a. Students should take turns asking each other the questions on their sheets.
   b. The partner should listen to each question and look at the pictures or information on his or her own sheet and then give an answer.
   c. The questioner should listen to the partner's answer and circle the correct answer or write it on the line provided, or record the answer in the appropriate space on a chart or table. The teacher can decide whether a sentence fragment is acceptable or whether a complete sentence should be written. (Using fragments in note-taking is a useful skill.) Remember that in communicative activities, the process of exchanging information is the most important aspect.
   d. The emphasis here is on providing students with directed practice in a communicative context. Students communicate by exchanging information with a partner. Students get information from and give information to their partner. The listening student is responsible for some activity that requires attention to the partner's answer. You might follow up this paired practice by returning to a large-group format and listening to the answers students give orally. Collect the worksheet only if you want to check spelling skills.
5. To extend the activity, students may exchange papers and do the activity again with the same or different partners.

Descubrir qué ..., cómo ... / Descubrir gustos y preferencias **(Discovery)**
(These two sorts of Discovery activities are somewhat parallel in format but different in content. A slash (/) is used to differentiate between them below.)
Purpose: To practice creating questions and statements to discover the interests, activities, etc., of other students. / To ask and answer personalized questions on a variety of topics.
For: Two students.
Accountability: You may want to observe students on task and assign oral grades. When students hand in completed sheets, you may assign points for the written work. You can verify accurate listening by randomly looking at the sheets and asking students for some questions.
Copies Needed: One per student. / An A version for one student, and a B version for the other.
Directions:

1. Divide the class into pairs. All students do this activity simultaneously.
2. Distribute one copy to each student. / Distribute an A and a B version to each pair. Students should not show their version to their partner.
3. Go over the directions and set a time limit. Let students know what they are to do if they finish early.
4. **Steps:**
   a. Students should first select five items from the list of 20 choices given and create five statements. / Students should themselves first answer each question on their sheet on line A. (This step may be done as homework.) Students then take turns asking each other the questions, reading one question at a time.

b. Students should then take turns asking questions, based on the items listed. The goal is to find out which of the five items the partner has chosen. Students should record the answers given by their partners by writing *Sí* or *No* on the blank spaces numbered 1 *(Juego Uno)*. / Partners should listen attentively to the questions and then respond. You may decide ahead of time if you want students to respond in complete sentences or not.
c. The first person to discover the choices made by his or her partner wins. / The questioner should record each answer in a complete sentence in the third person on line B.
d. The game can be repeated with each student selecting different items according to the suggestion given for *Juego Dos*.
5. To extend the activity, students may continue to ask questions using the items listed until all items have been discussed. / Another way to extend the activity might be for students to write and ask additional questions.

Diagramas **(Diagrams)**
Purpose: To practice sentence-building and listening comprehension.
For: Two students.
Accountability: You may want to observe students on task and assign oral grades. Students may turn in copies of their own and their partner's diagrams; you then can check both papers and assign grades. If students write out the diagrammed sentences, you might assign written grades.
Copies Needed: Two copies per student.
Directions:
1. Divide the class into pairs. All students do this activity simultaneously.
2. Distribute two copies per student.
3. Go over directions and set a time limit. Let students know what they are to do if they finish early. Have students write their own name on the sheets where their own sentences will appear. Have them write their partner's name on the sheets where they will create diagrams of the sentences read to them by their partner.
4. **Steps:**
   a. Each student should first create his or her own sentence by diagramming—drawing lines from items in one column to items in the second column and the third column. No item may be used more than once, and lines may not be drawn straight across. Students should be careful to create sentences that are logical.
   b. One student should read all of his or her sentences to the partner. The partner must diagram on the second copy, according to the sentences heard. The first student may not show the partner the sentences being read aloud.
   c. The other student should then read his or her sentences to the partner.
   d. Finally, the diagrams are compared, to see how well each partner heard the other.
5. To extend the activity, you might ask the class to write out some or all the sentences on one of the copies. Those who do not finish in the time given could complete this task as homework.
6. On another day, the same sheets could be distributed to the class, and you could read a set of sentences to be diagrammed as a class listening activity or quiz.

Entrevista **(Interview)**
Purpose: To ask other students personalized questions on a variety of topics.
For: Two students.
Accountability: You may want to observe students on task and assign oral grades. Students can hand in written papers and you can assign written grades. You can verify accurate listening by looking at collected sheets and asking students some of the questions.
Copies Needed: An A version for one student, a B version for the other.
Directions:
1. Divide the class into pairs. All students do this activity simultaneously.

2. Distribute an A and a B version to each pair. Students should not show their version to their partner.
3. Go over the directions and set a time limit. Let student know what they are to do if they finish early.
4. **Steps:**
   a. Students should take turns interviewing each other, reading one question at a time. They should not show the questions to their partners.
   b. Partners should listen attentively to the questions and then respond. You may decide ahead of time if you want students to answer in complete sentences or not.
   c. The interviewer should record each answer in a complete sentence in the third person.
5. To extend the activity, students can write and ask additional questions.

Hacer un papel **(Role-play)**
Purpose: To practice vocabulary and patterns; to encourage creativity.
For: Two students.
Accountability: You may want to observe students on task and assign oral grades. Students may be asked to role-play in front of the class.
Copies Needed: An A version for one student, and a B version for the other.
Directions: Students are encouraged to be flexible and creative as long as their answers are logical.

1. Divide the class into pairs. All students do this activity simultaneously.
2. Distribute an A and a B version to each pair.
3. Go over the directions and set a time limit. Let students know what they are to do if they finish early.
4. **Steps:**
   a. One student should ask his or her partner all of the questions on his or her version. The partner should answer appropriately, according to the information provided at the bottom of his or her sheet. Answers should be logical, but may be varied and creative.
   b. The questioner should listen to the partner's answer and indicate whether or not it is logical. The questioner should then write down the answer.
   c. After one set of questions has been used, the partners switch to the other version.
5. To extend the activity, students may exchange papers and do the activity again with the same or different partners.

Opiniones **(Opinions)**
Purpose: To express personal opinions and the opinions of others.
For: Two students.
Accountability: You may want to observe students on task and assign oral grades. You can verify accurate listening by randomly looking at the sheets and asking students some of the same questions.
Copies Needed: An A version for one student, a B version for the other.
Directions:

1. Divide the class into pairs. All students do this activity simultaneously.
2. Distribute an A and a B version to each pair. Students should not show their version to their partner.
3. Go over the directions and set a time limit. Let students know what they are to do if they finish early.
4. **Steps:**
   a. Each student should first complete the table with his or her own opinions about the items or activities listed.
   b. Students should then take turns asking their partner to state the opinions on their practice sheet. Students should answer according to the information given on their version of the table. The person asking the questions should fill in the answers on his or her version of the table.
   c. Students continue to take turns asking each other their personal opinions of the items or activities listed and recording information.
5. To extend the activity, students may exchange their papers and repeat the activity with the same or different partners.

Opiniones y reacciones **(Opinions and Reactions)**

Purpose: To express personal opinions.

For: Two students.

Accountability: You may want to observe students on task and assign oral grades. Students can hand in completed sheets. You may then assign written grades.

Copies Needed: An A version for one student, a B version for the other.

Directions:

1. Divide the class into pairs. All students do this activity simultaneously.
2. Distribute an A and a B version to each pair. Students should not show their version to their partner.
3. Go over the directions and set a time limit. Let students know what they are to do if they finish early.
4. **Steps:**
   a. Each student should first complete his or her own statements.
   b. Students should then take turns reading statements from their version to their partner. Partners should listen and react logically using the guided responses on the sheets.
5. To extend the activity, students may exchange their papers and repeat the activity with the same or different partners. They might be encouraged to add original reactions.

Tres en raya **(Tic-Tac-Toe)**

Purpose: To practice vocabulary and patterns.

For: Two students.

Accountability: You may want to observe students on task and assign oral grades or ask random questions from the activity to check comprehension.

Copies Needed: An A version for one student, a B version for the other.

Directions:

1. Divide the class into pairs. All students do the activity simultaneously.
2. Distribute an A and a B version to each pair.
3. Go over the directions and set a time limit. Let students know what they are to do if they finish early.
4. **Steps:**
   a. Students take turns choosing numbered squares. The partner then reads the question or statement that appears in the chosen square from his or her sheet.
   b. The partner who chose the number should listen to the question and give the answer or complete the statement read to him or her.
   c. The partner reading the question should listen to the answer and indicate whether it is correct or incorrect. Correct answers are shown in each numbered square in parentheses.
   d. When one partner answers correctly, both partners should mark the appropriate symbol, *O* for partner A, or *X* for partner B, in that numbered square on their paper. Both partners will have *X*s and *O*s in the same numbered squares. If a partner answers incorrectly, the questioner *does not* tell the correct answer and no marks are made on the game sheet. The partner may choose the same numbered square again later to try to answer that question.
   e. To extend the activity, students may exchange papers and do the activity again, with the same or different partners.

Teaching with Situation Cards

The Situation Cards are designed to focus on the chapter's communicative objectives while integrating the vocabulary and grammar. In addition, they guide an exchange between two students, in which Student A initiates the conversation and Student B responds (both students know what the general topic is, but neither knows exactly what the other one's instructions are). Finally, they provide a structured role-play with opportunities for personalization and open-ended conversation.

Using the Situation Cards: The Situation Cards are most successful when students have already worked with the vocabulary and grammar. You will see the cards referenced in the *Repaso del capítulo* section of the *Teacher's Edition*. There are a variety of ways to use the Situation Cards. You can photocopy them, cut them out, and paste them on 3 x 5 cards. Some teachers copy them directly onto colored paper and use a different color for each level. Other teachers laminate them for use as class sets. Use the cards for extended oral practice at the beginning of the class, as a warm-up, as practice for the speaking section of the *Examen del capítulo* (found in the Assessment Program book that is also part of the ***Realidades*** ancillary program), as informal speaking practice, or as the chapter's formal assessment for speaking proficiency. The Situation Cards also work well as a review for an end-of-quarter or final exam or at the beginning of the following year.

Directions:

1. Organize the students in pairs.
2. Distribute the cards. You can give each pair both situations to work on or you can give one situation to a pair of students and then have them exchange with another pair when completed.
3. Quickly brainstorm vocabulary and expressions that might be helpful in completing the tasks on the Situation Cards.
4. Start the activity. Remember that Student A will always initiate the conversation. Keep the activity within reasonable time limits. Three to seven minutes is ideal.
5. Circulate to verify that students are on task. This is also a good moment to informally assess students' level of comfort with the vocabulary and the speaking task, and to decide whether any reteaching is necessary. Do not correct errors at this point.
6. Signal when students should stop. You may ask them to reverse roles. Or you may devise a "traffic pattern" in which each pair of students puts their two cards together and exchanges them with another pair of students.

Assessment for Situation Cards: The Situation Cards can be used as a tool for informal or formal assessment. Students can act out the conversation with the partner with whom they practiced, with an assigned partner, or with the teacher.

Assessment can be based on a single criterion or on several different ones. For informal assessment, you might want to choose from any of the following criteria: completion of the task, appropriateness, comprehensibility, originality, quality above and beyond base expectations, individual improvement, group improvement, accuracy, or fluency. For a more formal assessment tool, see the *Scale for Evaluating Writing/Speaking Proficiency*, found in the *To the Teacher* section, pp. T1–T9, of the Assessment Program book. Whatever system you use, be sure to share it with your students before the assessment begins so that they will understand how they are to be graded.

Finally, once students have become accustomed to the Situation Cards, you might encourage them to write their own.

The use of these Situation Cards is a motivating and effective tool for guiding students to a level of increased comfort and confidence, and to a quality performance in the very challenging process of developing speaking proficiency.

Teaching with the Vocabulary Clip Art

The following ideas for using the Vocabulary Clip Art are only a sample of the many ways in which it can be used. You will probably devise additional ways to get students physically involved with learning and practicing new vocabulary. You will need to make copies of the art for each student to participate in these activities. You may wish to laminate one or two complete sets for permanent classroom use.

Homework Assignment: Have students use the visuals to create flashcards. They can cut and paste the visuals on cards and write the Spanish word on the back of the card.

Picture Dictionary: Have students write the Spanish word for each picture on photocopies of pages as art of a "picture dictionary." These pages can be kept in a notebook that can be used as a valuable reference or review tool for students.

Assess Listening Comprehension: Begin by simply identifying a word on a page and by having students identify objects. Describe an object and have students point to it. Tell a story using the visual and have students point to vocabulary words in the story or indicate the sequencing through drawing lines or arrows. You might want to make an overhead transparency so that you (or a student) can be at the overhead doing both activities at the same time.

Additional Assessment of Listening Comprehension: Have students work in pairs to use the ideas in the prior bullet item. Circulate to keep the students on task and assess pronunciation and comprehension. Do not correct errors at this point; rather, use this time to determine areas needing further work.

Individual Images: Have students cut out the individual pictures and keep them in their notebook in a large zippered freezer bag that is three-hole punched. Here are some ideas for using the individual images:

1. Repeat the activities in the "Assess Listening Comprehension" section, and have students sort through the individual images to indicate comprehension. For example: If you say the word *lápiz,* students should place the picture for "pencil" in the center of their desks and then continue to add the pictures for objects you call out. Cut up the overhead transparency of the vocabulary art so that you (or a student) are at the overhead manipulating the image simultaneously with the students.
2. Have students work with each other saying the vocabulary words, telling stories, and asking questions. For example, a student might say, *"Dame el libro."* The partner should use the visuals to perform the action. Getting each student to manipulate the vocabulary images is an excellent way to assist learning.
3. Have students draw a background for the visuals, such as a classroom. Have them sit back-to-back, and have one student arrange objects in a certain order. He or she then tells the partner where each item is located. For example, one student can tell the partner, *La silla está delante de la mesa*. The other student can ask questions, but should not see the layout of the objects until he or she thinks the placement is correct. Students can then compare layouts.
4. Encourage students to color in the pictures or personalize them and use them to decorate their compositions.
5. Have students create their own Bingo cards using the visuals. Have each student create a grid of five down and five across. Students then place 25 visuals in any order. Have one student be the "caller" and call out different vocabulary words. Students turn the words over on their grids until one has five down, across, or diagonally. The winning student names the vocabulary pieces he or she turned over and becomes the next "caller."
6. Use the individual pictures as an oral vocabulary quiz. Have students name each image as he or she lays them on the desk in front of you. Students who do not feel confident with all the chapter's vocabulary may select a handful of images and name those visuals for you.

Overview of *Communication Workbook with Test Preparation:* Practice Tests

Standardized Test Preparation for the Spanish Classroom

- **Standards for Foreign Language Learning** Description of the five standards.
- **Correlations of the Practice Tests in the Test Preparation section of the *Communication Workbook* for *Realidades* A, *Temas* 1–4 to the *Standards for Foreign Language Learning***
- **Test Preparation** Overview of standardized tests, scoring rubrics, and suggestions for using the practice tests in the Spanish classroom.
- **Answers** Answers for multiple questions and sample top-score responses for Short and Extended Responses questions.

Correlation of Practice Tests to the *Standards for Foreign Language Learning*

Theme	Practice Test	Standards
Tema 1: Mis amigos y yo	Capítulo 1A: Friendship Among Latin Americans	2.1, 3.1
	Capítulo 1B: ¡Hola! Me llamo Pedro	1.2, 1.3, 3.1
Tema 2: La escuela	Capítulo 2A: The High-School Experience in Latin America	2.2, 3.1, 4.2
	Capítulo 2B: Mi día escolar	1.2, 3.1
Tema 3: La comida	Capítulo 3A: The Hidden Corn: A Mayan Legend	2.1, 3.1
	Capítulo 3B: Pizza, ensaladas y … helado de fresas	1.2, 3.1
Tema 4: Los pasatiempos	Capítulo 4A: Aztec Games and Rituals	2.1, 2.2, 3.1
	Capítulo 4B: Una conversación difícil	1.2, 3.1

Standards for Foreign Language Learning

COMMUNICATION: Communicate in Languages Other Than English

Standard 1.1: Students engage in conversations, provide and obtain information, express feelings and emotions, and exchange opinions.

Standard 1.2: Students understand and interpret written and spoken language on a variety of topics.

Standard 1.3: Students present information, concepts, and ideas to an audience of listeners or readers on a variety of topics.

CULTURES: Gain Knowledge and Understanding of Other Cultures

Standard 2.1: Students demonstrate an understanding of the relationship between the practices and perspectives of the culture studied.

Standard 2.2: Students demonstrate an understanding of the relationship between the products and perspectives of the culture studied.

CONNECTIONS: Connect with Other Disciplines and Acquire Information

Standard 3.1: Students reinforce and further their knowledge of other disciplines through the foreign language.

Standard 3.2: Students acquire information and recognize the distinctive viewpoints that are only available through the foreign language and its cultures.

COMPARISONS: Develop Insight into the Nature of Language and Culture

Standard 4.1: Students demonstrate understanding of the nature of language through comparisons of the language studied and their own.

Standard 4.2: Students demonstrate understanding of the concept of culture through comparisons of the cultures studied and their own.

COMMUNITIES: Participate in Multilingual Communities at Home and Around the World

Standard 5.1: Students use the language both within and beyond the school setting.

Standard 5.2: Students show evidence of becoming life-long learners by using the language for personal enjoyment and enrichment.

Test Preparation

Research shows that students can improve their test scores by (1) reading more in their first language; (2) reading more in a second language; (3) learning test-taking strategies; (4) taking practice tests; and (5) discussing the answers and strategies used to obtain the best responses. School districts across the United States are asking that all teachers incorporate into daily instruction strategies that will enable students to improve their standardized test scores. The Test Preparation pages have been written especially to enable any Spanish teacher to use the Spanish curriculum to help students improve their overall test performance.

Getting to Know the Test

Students are required to take standardized tests several times during their school career. The practice tests in the *Communication Workbook with Test Preparation* contain a variety of readings to reflect the types of passages students might expect to find on a standardized reading test. They also provide practice for the three types of questions students might encounter on such a test: multiple choice, Short Response, and Extended Response.

Multiple Choice Multiple choice questions always have four answer choices. Students pick the one that is the best answer. Answers to the multiple choice questions are included in this *Teacher's Resource Book*.

Short Response This symbol appears next to questions that require short written answers:

This symbol appears next to questions requiring short written answers that are a creative extension based on the reading:

It is suggested that students take approximately 3 to 5 minutes to answer a Short Response question. These types of questions are called "performance tasks" and require that students read all parts of the question carefully, plan their answer, and then write the answer in their own words. A complete answer to a Short Response question is worth 2 points. A partial answer is worth 1 point or 0 points. The Short Response questions on the student test preparation pages are written in either English or Spanish. Students are instructed to respond in English when the question is in English and in Spanish when the question is in Spanish. Sample top-score Short Response answers are included in this *Teacher's Resource Book*.

Extended Response This symbol appears next to questions requiring longer written answers based on information that can be inferred from the reading:

This symbol appears next to questions requiring longer written answers that are a creative extension based on the reading:

It is suggested that students take about 5 to 15 minutes to answer an Extended Response question. These types of questions are also called "performance tasks" because they require that students read all parts of the question carefully, plan their answer, and then write the answer in their own words. A complete answer to an Extended Response question is worth 4 points. A partial answer is worth 3, 2, 1, or 0 points. The Extended Response questions on the student test preparation pages are written in either English or Spanish. Students are instructed to respond in English when the question is in English and in Spanish when the question is in Spanish. Sample top-score Extended Response answers are included in this *Teacher's Resource Book*.

How the Test Will Be Scored

Multiple Choice Questions

Multiple choice answers are either right or wrong. Students receive 1 point if the correct answer is selected.

Performance-Based Questions (Short Response and Extended Response)
Short Response and Extended Response questions, which are called "performance tasks," are often scored with rubrics. Sample rubrics are provided below. These rubrics describe a range of performance and students receive credit for how close their answers come to the anticipated response.

Rubric for Short Response Questions

2 points The response indicates that the student has a complete understanding of the reading concept embodied in the task. The student has provided a response that is accurate, complete, and fulfills all the requirements of the task. Necessary support and/or examples are included, and the information given is clearly text-based. Any extensions beyond the text are relevant to the task.

1 point The response indicates that the student has a partial understanding of the reading concept embodied in the task. The student has provided a response that may include information that is essentially correct and text-based, but the information is too general or too simplistic. Some of the support and/or examples may be incomplete or omitted.

0 points The response is inaccurate, confused, and/or irrelevant, or the student has failed to respond to the task.

Rubric for Extended Response Questions

4 points The response indicates that the student has a thorough understanding of the reading concept embodied in the task. The student has provided a response that is accurate, complete, and fulfills all the requirements of the task. Necessary support and/or examples are included, and the information given is clearly text-based. Any extensions beyond the text are relevant to the task.

3 points The response indicates that the student has an understanding of the reading concept embodied in the task. The student has provided a response that is accurate and fulfills all the requirements of the task, but the required support and/or details are not complete or clearly text-based.

2 points The response indicates that the student has a partial understanding of the reading concept embodied in the task. The student has provided a response that may include information that is essentially correct and text-based, but the information is too general or too simplistic. Some of the support and/or examples and requirements of the task may be incomplete or omitted.

1 point The response indicates that the student has very limited understanding of the reading concept embodied in the task. The response is incomplete, may exhibit many flaws, and may not address all the requirements of the task.

0 points The response is inaccurate, confused, and/or irrelevant, or the student has failed to respond to the task.

Using the Practice Tests

Practice Test and Answer Key Format

There is one Practice Test for each *capítulo* in Level A. For each test, you will find three parts:

- reading selection
- questions
- response sheet

The student tests for *Communication Workbook with Test Preparation* are not reproduced in this Answer Key. You will need to refer to the student workbook for copies of the tests. Answers to each test for *Temas* 1–4 appear in this *Teacher's Resource Book.*

Practice Tests

There are two readings per *tema.* These readings incorporate the themes and content of each *tema* (e.g., school, shopping, leisure activities). The first reading for each *tema* is in English and is similar to the English readings students will encounter on standardized tests. The second reading is in Spanish and is written for beginning-level students.

The convenient correlation chart that appears on p. xv correlates all of the tests to the *Standards for Foreign Language Learning.*

The readings in English expand the cultural theme of the *Realidades temas* for which they were written. These readings can be integrated into instruction during the actual teaching of the *tema* or at some later point during the school year.

The readings in Spanish incorporate the chapter vocabulary and grammar and are most useful after completion of the *temas* or chapters for which they were written. Of course, these selections add the challenge of reading in Spanish to the other strategies used on reading tests. Encourage students to employ the same strategies used when reading in English (see "Tips for Improving Your Score" on pp. 108–111 of the Introduction to the *Communication Workbook with Test Preparation*). You will notice that the multiple choice questions are written in English. This practice is supported by research stating that students can demonstrate reading comprehension more effectively when the follow-up questions are in English and they are allowed to respond in English. The Short Response and Extended Response questions are generally written in English prompting an English response. Responses in English again allow students to demonstrate comprehension and allow them to practice reading skills, such as comparing and contrasting, recognizing cause and effect, and identifying author's purpose, required for success with standardized tests. This practice recognizes that beginning-level students do not have the proficiency in Spanish to respond to such in-depth questions.

Integrating the Practice Tests with Instruction

Decide when you want to use a practice test within your lesson plan. You can use the tests during class time or as homework assignments. Be sure to review with students how the test questions will be scored, including how the rubric is used. Students have a copy of the rubrics on pp. 111–112 of their workbook. Allow approximately 25 minutes for students to take the test. Grade the multiple choice questions as a whole-class activity and discuss the correct responses, or collect the papers and grade them on your own. The answers are provided in this *Teacher's Resource Book*. However, to grade the Short or Extended Response questions, it is suggested that you collect the papers and grade them using the rubrics and the sample top-score responses provided in this *Teacher's Resource Book*. When you return the tests to the students, you might want to share the sample top-score responses and discuss how they could best construct a response that earns the highest score on the rubric.

Preparing Students for Standardized Tests

Teaching Students to be Good Test-Takers

Many students are not successful on standardized tests because they lack the skills and strategies employed by good test-takers. You can use the strategies found on pp. 108–111 of the Introduction to the *Communication Workbook with Test Preparation* to review with students prior to administering the first practice test. It is helpful to remind students of these strategies each time that they take a practice test.

Success for ALL Students

Helping Students Raise Their Test Scores

The *Communication Workbook with Test Preparation* provides each teacher with complete support to prepare students for success on standardized tests. Students learn valuable test-taking tips, practice taking tests and responding to various types of questions, learn why a response was correct, and learn how to better shape their responses in the future. Over time, they will become more comfortable with taking standardized tests. In addition, the high-interest readings will enable students to expand their knowledge and understanding of the cultures of the Spanish-speaking world while building important reading and writing skills.

¡Buena suerte!

Introduction to the *Lecturas Teacher's Guide*

The Teacher's Guide that accompanies the Level 1 Reader provides a variety of information to assist you in your presentation of the reading selections. It contains suggested answers to the postreading questions found in the reader, additional questions for class discussion, teaching suggestions, and cultural information pertinent to the individual reading selections.

Organization of the *Lecturas 1 Reader*

The ***Lecturas*** 1 Reader contains a variety of reading selections, including poems, comic strips, plays, short stories of different types, and recreational activities. It provides students with materials that are interesting, easy to read, age-appropriate, and suitable for a middle school Spanish student. The selections proceed from less difficult to more difficult, thereby allowing students to sample material that gradually becomes more challenging lexically and syntactically.

The reader is designed to be used as a cooperative, combined effort on the part of the instructor and the student. Later selections, however, might be assigned as homework or for independent or recreational reading.

Students are encouraged to read extensively, that is, to read for a general understanding of the author's intent, for main ideas, and to react personally to the reading selections. They are also encouraged to employ the strategies that skilled readers use when they approach a reading selection: guessing at meaning from context rather than looking up every unknown word; skipping words that add little meaning rather than placing equal importance on all words; and recognizing cognates, root words, and synonyms.

Each of the reading selections is accompanied by one or more prereading questions; two or more postreading questions, which appear in a section called *¿De qué se trata?;* and a vocabulary section called *¿Qué quiere decir?*

The prereading questions are designed to help set the scene so that students can focus on the material that follows. They have been personalized in order to draw students into the reading. For example, students might be asked to recall some past experience in their own lives that parallels the experience of the main character(s). In Level 1, these questions are in English so that students will be free to respond and to provide for a more lively and meaningful classroom discussion.

Some unfamiliar words, expressions, and grammatical structures have been incorporated into each reading selection. Many are cognates or other easily decodable words and, therefore, have not been glossed. A limited number of unfamiliar words, expressions, and grammatical structures that students may not so readily understand are explained at the end of each reading. They are not highlighted in the text in order to avoid interrupting students' reading and to encourage them to guess at meaning from context. The unfamiliar material is in the postreading section entitled, *¿Qué quiere decir?* Glosses appear in the order in which they occur in the reading selection. English equivalents are provided and, occasionally, familiar Spanish synonyms or Spanish-language definitions are used.

Each reading is followed by a section called *¿De qué se trata?*, composed of two or more postreading questions that are designed to elicit oral discussion. These questions often invite students to evaluate information given in the reading selection. And they frequently ask students to personalize the information, thereby making it more meaningful for them. In Level 1, these questions appear in English to foster a high level of oral classroom discussion.

When one asks students to respond to questions about a reading, three different kinds of information might be requested: factual, inferential, or information that requires some kind of personal application. In order to test students' comprehension of the selections, you may prefer to ask (or to have students ask) some factual questions first and then proceed with the questions in the *¿De qué se trata?* section. You may use the additional questions provided in the Teacher's Guide as time permits to elicit more in-depth discussion of the readings.

Integrating Technology in the *Realidades* Classroom

Realidades offers teachers and students a wide range of technology tools to plan, teach, practice, assess, and remediate. These tools save valuable teaching time while engaging students in varied learning experiences.

Student Technology in REALIDADES

- **Digital Student Learning Center @ realidades.com** Through the Digital Student Learning Center found at realidades.com, students have access to an unprecedented array of online technology tools to learn, practice, perform, assess, and remediate. The online eBook contains the complete Student Edition plus audio and video. Students also link to a complete suite of tools that includes interactive workbooks, additional online practice with immediate response and built-in remediation, grammar tutorials, audio and video interactivities, and self-tests.
- **Companion Web Site @ realidades.com** Students can access the many additional online practice activities found at the Companion Web Site using the Web Codes in the Student Edition. The Companion Web Site contains activities such as the highly acclaimed *Canciones de hip hop*, Animated Grammar, GramActiva Videos, Reading Worksheets, and four puzzles per chapter. All Companion Web Site activities are linked inside the Digital Learning Center as extra practice, with the exception of the Puzzles.
- **Downloadable audio files @ realidades.com** At the Companion Web Site and within the Student Digital Learning Center, students can download the audio files for all the Student Edition listening activities and the *Canciones de hip hop* to a computer or audio player.
- **MindPoint Quiz Show CD-ROM** The interactive games offer a fun end-of-chapter review while providing students and teachers with detailed reports on how well individual students and/or the class have performed on questions based on the National Standards and chapter objectives.

Student Technology	
realidades.com *Realidades Companion Web Site*	• instant access using Web Codes • tutorial practice for vocabulary and grammar • Internet links and activities • four puzzles per chapter • end-of-chapter self-test
MindPoint™ Quiz Show CD-ROM	• interactive game show format for review • competition against computer, a partner, or entire class • detailed report provides instant overview of student performance against the National Standards and chapter objectives
myeBook Online Textbook	• Student Edition online or on CD-ROM • access to audio and video
Downloadable audio files	• downloadable *Canciones de hip hop* • audio for vocabulary, Student Edition activities, and pronunciation for students to download • Web Codes listed in Student Edition

Teacher Technology in REALIDADES

- **Digital Teacher Center @ realidades.com** Teachers have access to a wealth of support at the Digital Teacher Center at **realidades.com**. Teachers can plan using built-in lesson plans and tools for assigning tasks. Take advantage of the built-in grade book with automatic scoring, as well as complete assessment and remediation support. A teacher User's Guide for **realidades.com** can be downloaded from the Teacher Site at Web Code jck-1001. MyPearsonTraining.com offers additional teacher support and training.
- **PresentationEXPRESS™ CD-ROM** Present vocabulary and grammar using this time-saving teacher presentation tool that integrates audio, images, Fine Art Transparencies, Vocabulary Clip Art, grammar slides, video, answers, and interactive QuickTake Quizzes.

- **TeacherEXPRESS™ DVD** Teach, plan, and assess with this interactive Teacher's Edition. The DVD provides instant access to Lesson Planning, Teacher Edition pages, Teaching Resources, ExamView™ Tests on DVD, Vocabulary Clip Art, and Web resources.
- **Video Program** The innovate videos on DVD or on **realidades.com** accompany each chapter.
- **Videocultura** Students explore culture through an engaging video that connects to the cultural themes of each *Tema*.
- **Audio Program** Audio supports the *A primera vista* language input; pronunciation; Student Edition listening activities; audio activities found in the *Communication Workbook: Writing, Audio & Video Activities*; songs; and the listening tasks from the chapter tests.
- **ExamView™ Tests on DVD** In addition to two chapters tests, two test banks for each chapter are provided, plus a test bank per chapter to use with Heritage Learners and Pre-AP* students. It allows you to edit questions and tests or create new tests.
- **Transparencies** Three different sets of transparencies include Vocabulary and Grammar Transparencies, Answers on Transparencies, and Fine Art Transparencies.

Teacher Technology	
TeacherEXPRESS™ DVD	• Lesson Planner • Teacher's Edition • Teaching resources • Vocabulary Clip Art • Computer Test Bank • Web resources
PresentationEXPRESS™ CD-ROM	• PowerPoint-based teaching tool • Vocabulary images and clip art • Audio and video • Grammar transparencies • Fine Art Transparencies • Answers on transparencies • ExamView™ QuickTake quizzes
Video Program on DVD	• *A primera vista* segments expand each chapter's *Videohistoria* • *GramActiva* segments teach the new grammar using humor and graphics • *¿Eres tú, María?* mystery video
Videocultura on DVD and online	• Theme-based culture videos
realidades.com	• Digital Teacher Center • Built-in lesson plans • Tools for assigning tasks and creating activities • Built-in grade book with automatic scoring • Complete assessment and remediation support
Teacher Homepage	• Teaching ideas accessible via Web Code jck-1001
Audio Program (22 CDs)	• *Vocabulario y gramática en contexto* • *Videohistoria* • Student Edition *Escuchar* Activities • *Pronunciación* • Communication Workbook audio • Listening section of *Examen del capítulo* • Songs
SuccessNet™ Online Access Pack	• Registration code to activate myeBook

Table of Contents

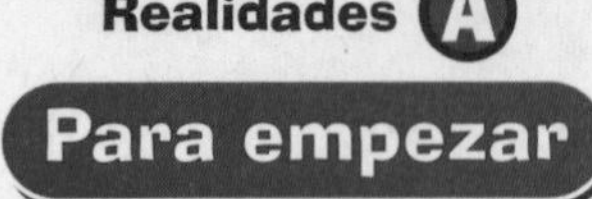

Theme Project

Preliminary Chapter Theme Project
Pronóstico del tiempo

Overview:

You will write a television script and create maps for a weather forecast for four locations in the Western Hemisphere. Then you will videotape your forecast for the class to view.

Materials:

Poster board, markers, video camera, videocassette

Sequence:

STEP 1. Review the instructions with your teacher.

STEP 2. Write a rough draft of your weather forecast. Exchange scripts with a partner for peer-editing. Make corrections based on your partner's comments.

STEP 3. Create one or more maps for your forecast on poster board. After completing your map(s), add drawings or symbols that indicate the weather in each city you plan to talk about and the temperature there.

STEP 4. Rehearse your forecast with a partner. Provide your partner with feedback regarding the content, accuracy, and presentation of the forecast.

STEP 5. Videotape your weather forecast. Show your videotape to the class.

Assessment:

Your teacher will use the rubric on the following page to assess this project.

Preliminary Chapter Project: Pronóstico del tiempo

RUBRIC	Score 1	Score 3	Score 5
Evidence of Planning	No written draft.	Draft was written, but not corrected.	Evidence of corrected draft.
Use of Illustrations	No map included.	Map was difficult to read, incomplete, and/or inaccurate.	Map was easy to read, complete, and accurate.
Presentation	Does not include the majority of the required elements.	Includes some of the following: greeting, name, day, date, weather, and temperature for 4 locations.	Includes all of the following: greeting, name, day, date, weather, and temperature for 4 locations.

Para empezar

School-to-Home Connection

Dear Parent or Guardian,

Thank you for taking the time to review what your child is learning in his or her Spanish class. You can play an integral role in your child's acquisition of Spanish by staying informed of what is being taught in class and supporting language learning at home.

Realidades, your child's Spanish textbook, is designed to promote both written and oral communication. Each theme-based chapter includes vocabulary in context, grammar, and cultural lessons. Also included are pronunciation exercises, detailed language studies, and ways to recognize and use Spanish outside of the classroom.

Upon completion of this chapter, your child will be able to:

- greet people
- introduce themselves to others
- begin using numbers, tell time, and talk about things related to the calendar
- talk about things in the classroom
- describe weather condtions and identify seasons

Also, your child will explore:

- the correct way to address adults
- the different uses of the word "you"
- the correct use of punctuation and accent marks

Additional help is available online at www.realidades.com by using the Web Codes in the Student Edition or in the Leveled Vocabulary and Grammar Workbook.

Check it Out! Have your child use the new vocabulary from this chapter to write a dialogue where two people greet each other and discuss the weather. Then have him or her explain the dialogue to you in English.

Sincerely,

For: Tips to Parents
Visit: www.realidades.com
Web Code: jce-0010

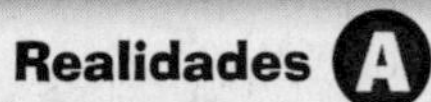

Realidades A

Para empezar

Chapter Resource Checklist

Resources	CO†	En la escuela	En la clase	El tiempo	REP	PREP
Teacher						
Teacher's Resource Book						
Input Script						
Audio Script						
GramActiva BLM						
Communicative Activities BLM						
School-to-Home Connection BLM						
Clip Art						
Situation Cards BLM						
TPR Stories Book						
Fine Art Transparencies Teacher's Guide						
Placement Test: RPH						
Pre-AP* Resource Book						
Student						
Leveled Vocabulary and Grammar Workbook						
Guided Practice						
Core Practice						
Communication Workbook with Test Preparation						
Writing						
Audio						
Video						
Test Preparation						
RPH Workbook						
Lecturas para hispanohablantes						
Grammar Study Guides						
Transparencies						
Answers on Transparencies						
Vocabulary and Grammar						
Fine Art						
Assessment						
Assessment Program						
Quizzes						
Chapter Test						
realidades.com						
ExamView Test Bank CD-ROM						
QuickTake on PresentationExpress						
MindPoint QuizShow CD-ROM						
Alternate Assessment Program						
Performance-Based Writing						
Self-Test on realidades.com & CWS						
Assessment Program RPH						
Technology						
realidades.com						
myeBook						
TeacherExpress CD-ROM						
PresentationExpress DVD						
Video Program DVD						
Culture Video DVD						
Audio Program CD 1						
Assessment CD 20						
Song CD 22						
Canciones de hip hop on realidades.com & CWS						

† *See Abbreviation Key on page iv.*

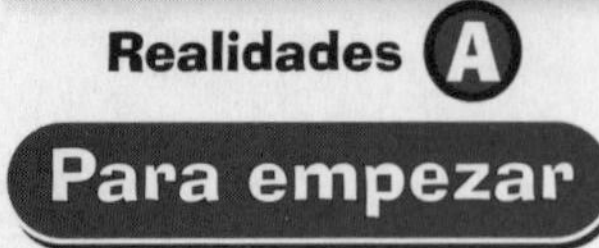

Input Script

Presentation: *En la escuela*

Input *¡Hola! ¿Cómo te llamas?:* Bring to class a woman's hat (or long wig), if you are a man, or a man's hat (or a pair of glasses with fake nose and mustache attached) if you are a woman. Also bring a baseball cap. Present the first dialogue (sporting the man's hat or fake nose and mustache if you are a woman!) and using the male student doll or photo. Circulate around the room and have students greet you with "*¡Buenos días, señor!*" Ask their name and have them respond. Follow the same procedure for the second dialogue. (Don't forget your woman's hat or wig if you are a man!) Point out the time change and the greeting. Repeat the procedure for the third dialogue, this time wearing the baseball cap. Ask for volunteers to act out the dialogues.

Input *¡Hola! ¿Cómo estás?:* Use the props from *¡Hola! ¿Cómo te llamas?* and follow the same procedure to present *¡Hola! ¿Cómo estás?* Use hand signals to convey the meaning of ***bien, muy bien,*** and ***regular.***

Presentation: *En la clase*

Input *La sala de clases:* Hand out copies of the Vocabulary Clip Art and have students tear the images into individual objects. Gesture to students to teach ***el estudiante*** and ***la estudiante.*** Use the male or female prop from the ***En la escuela*** presentation to teach ***el profesor*** and ***la profesora.*** Hold up a pencil and model the first dialogue. Repeat the first line and substitute other classroom objects. Have students hold up the Clip Art as they say the second line. Then have students write the objects' names on the back of each Clip Art image. Hold up a book and model the second dialogue. Repeat the first line again, substituting different objects. Students will say the second line and show you the word.

Input *El alfabeto:* Model the pronunciation of the alphabet. Then say each letter and have students act it out. Model the dialogue, then repeat, with other objects. Have students spell the objects they hear by acting out the letters. Then have them say the word in Spanish.

Presentation: *El tiempo*

Input *El tiempo:* Cut up the weather Clip Art into individual images. Draw a map of the United States on the chalkboard. Give a weather report, taping the images to the map. Have students tear up copies of the weather and seasons Clip Art into individual images. Ask what the weather is like in different parts of the country in different seasons. Students will hold up the season and an appropriate weather condition.

Comprehension Check

- On flashcards, draw three clocks to indicate morning, afternoon, and night. Put on one of the hats from the ***En la escuela*** presentation and show a flashcard. Have students greet you or ask how you are according to the time of day and your age and gender.
- Have pairs of students ask each other "*¿Cómo se dice ___?*" using their Clip Art images of classroom objects from the ***La sala de clases*** presentation as flashcards.
- Tell students the letters that make up one of the classroom objects, only out of order. Students will unscramble their Clip Art letters to spell the word.
- Make true and false statements about the weather in different parts of the United States in different seasons. Have students hold up the Clip Art images if the statement is true.

Realidades A

Para empezar

Audio Script

Audio CD, Capítulo Preliminar

Track 01: ***En la escuela,*** **Student Book, p. 2, (2:00)**

¡Hola! ¿Cómo te llamas?

Read along as you listen to the dialogues.

Male Teen 1: ¡Buenos días, señor!
Adult Male: ¡Buenos días! ¿Cómo te llamas?
Male Teen 1: Me llamo Felipe.

Female Teen 1: ¡Buenas tardes!, señora.
Adult Female: ¡Buenas tardes! ¿Cómo te llamas?
Female Teen 1: Me llamo Beatriz.
Adult Female: Mucho gusto.
Female Teen 1: Encantada.

Male Teen 2: ¡Buenas noches! ¿Cómo te llamas?
Female Teen 2: ¡Hola! Me llamo Graciela. ¿Y tú?
Male Teen 2: Me llamo Lorenzo.
Female Teen 2: ¡Mucho gusto!
Male Teen 2: Igualmente.

Track 02: ***En la escuela:*** **Act. 1, Student Book, p. 3, (1:47)**

Buenos días

Listen as people greet each other. Then point to the clock that indicates the time of day when the greetings are probably taking place. You will hear each dialogue twice.

Male Teen 1: Buenas noches, señor Rodríguez.
Adult Male 1: Hola, Roberto.
Adult Female 1: Buenas tardes, Alicia.
Female Teen 1: Buenas tardes, señora.
Female Teen 2: Buenos días, Señora Gómez.
Adult Female 2: Hola, Ana.
Adult Male 2: Buenos días, Pablo.
Male Teen 2: Buenos días, señor.
Female Teen 3: Buenas noches, Jorge.
Male Teen 3: Hola, María.
Female Teen 4: Hola, Juana.
Female Teen 5: Buenas tardes, Catalina.

Track 03: ***En la escuela,*** **Student Book, p. 4, (1:01)**

¡Hola! ¿Cómo estás?

Read along as you listen to the dialogues.

Adult Male 1: Buenos días, Adela. ¿Cómo estás?
Female Teen 1: Bien, gracias, señor Ruiz. ¿Y usted?
Adult Male 1: Bien, gracias.
Male Teen 1: Buenas tardes, señor Ruiz. ¿Cómo está usted?
Adult Male 1: Muy bien, gracias. ¿Y tú?
Male Teen 1: Bien, gracias.
Male Teen 2: Buenas noches, Miguel. ¿Qué tal?
Male Teen 3: Regular. ¿Y tú, Carlos? ¿Qué pasa?
Male Teen 2: Nada.
Female Teen 2: ¡Adiós, señorita Moreno! ¡Hasta luego!
Female Teen 3: ¡Hasta mañana!
Male Teen 4: ¡Hasta luego, Juan!
Male Teen 5: ¡Nos vemos!

Track 04: ***En la escuela:*** **Act. 4, Student Book, p. 5, (1:39)**

¿Hola o adiós?

Make a chart on your paper with two columns. Label one *Greeting,* the other *Leaving*. Number your paper from 1 to 8. As you hear each greeting or leave-taking, place a check mark in the appropriate column next to the number. You will hear each statement twice.

1. Hola, Juan. ¿Qué pasa?
2. Adiós, Miguel.
3. Buenos días, señor García.
4. Hola, Elena.
5. Nos vemos.
6. Hasta mañana, señor Pérez.
7. Buenas noches, señora.
8. Hasta luego, Ana.

Track 05: Audio Act. 1, Writing, Audio & Video Workbook, p. 1, (1:30)

You are at a party with students visiting from Ecuador. You have practiced several responses to the things they might say when you meet them. Listen to each question or statement and write the letter of the best response in the blank. You will hear each statement or question twice.

1. ¡Hola! Me llamo Roberto.
2. ¿Cómo te llamas?
3. ¿Cómo estás?
4. Hasta luego.
5. Encantado.
6. ¿Qué tal?

Track 06: ***En la escuela,*** **Student Book, p. 6, (0:55)**

¡Atención, por favor!

Read along as you listen to the statements.

¡Silencio, por favor! Abran el libro en la página diez.
¡Atención! Cierren el libro.
Repitan, por favor: Buenos días.
Buenos días.
Levántense, por favor.
Siéntense, por favor.
Saquen una hoja de papel. Escriban los números.
Entreguen sus hojas de papel.

Track 07: ***En la escuela:*** **Act. 7, Student Book, p. 6, (1:05)**

¡Siéntense!

You will hear some classroom commands. Listen carefully and act them out. You will hear each command twice.

Abran el libro.
Levántense.
Repitan: Buenas tardes.
Siéntense.
Cierren el libro.
Saquen una hoja de papel.

Track 08: ***En la escuela,*** **Student Book, p. 7, (3:19)**

Los números

You will hear each word twice. After the first time there will be a pause so you can pronounce it, then you will hear the word a second time.

cero	ocho	dieciséis	cuarenta
uno	nueve	diecisiete	cincuenta
dos	diez	dieciocho	sesenta
tres	once	diecinueve	setenta
cuatro	doce	veinte	ochenta
cinco	trece	veintiuno…	noventa
seis	catorce	treinta	cien
siete	quince	treinta y uno	

Track 09: ***En la escuela,*** **Student Book, p. 8, (1:40)**

¿Qué hora es?

You will hear each phrase twice. After the first time there will be a pause so you can pronounce it, then you will hear the phrase a second time.

Es la una.
Son las dos.
Son las tres y cinco.
Son las cuatro y diez.
Son las cinco y cuarto.
Son las seis y media.
Son las siete menos veinte.
Son las ocho y cincuenta y dos.

Track 10: ***En la escuela:*** **Act. 12, Student Book, p. 8, (1:59)**

La hora

Write the numbers 1–8 on a sheet of paper. Write the times you hear with numerals—1:00, 2:15, and so on. You will hear each sentence twice.

1. Es la una y media. (1:30)
2. Son las diez. (10:00)
3. Son las once y cinco. (11:05)
4. Son las doce. (12:00)
5. Son las seis y media. (6:30)
6. Son las siete y cuarenta y cinco. (7:45)
7. Son las nueve y veinte. (9:20)
8. Son las tres y treinta y cinco. (3:35)

Track 11: Audio Act. 2, Writing, Audio & Video Workbook, p. 1, (2:56)

You have lost your dog, so you put up signs in your neighborhood asking your neighbors to call you if they see him. You will hear six messages on your answering machine from neighbors who have seen your dog. You will not understand everything they say, but listen carefully to find out their house number and what time they called so that you can track down your dog. Write down each house number and time on the chart. You will hear each message twice.

1. Soy la señora Rodríguez, de la casa cuarenta y cinco. Son las seis de la mañana. ¡Buena suerte!
2. Soy el señor Sánchez, de la casa número quince. Son las cinco y cuarenta y cinco. Adiós.
3. Soy Kiko, de la casa treinta y tres. Son las ocho y treinta. ¡Buena suerte!
4. Soy Marta, de la casa cuarenta y dos. Son las siete y cuarto. ¡Buena suerte!
5. Soy el señor Martínez, de la casa veintinueve. Son las seis y media. Hasta luego.
6. Soy la señora Mendoza, de la casa veintiuno. Son las seis y cincuenta. Adiós.

Track 12: ***En la escuela,*** **Student Book, p. 9, (1:44)**

El cuerpo

You will hear each word or phrase twice. After the first time there will be a pause so you can pronounce it, then you will hear the word or phrase a second time.

la cabeza	el brazo	la pierna
el ojo	el dedo	el pie
la nariz	el estómago	¡Ay! Me duele el pie.
la boca	la mano	

Track 13: ***En la escuela:*** **Act. 13, Student Book, p. 9, (1:09)**

Señalen

You will hear some commands. Listen carefully and act out the commands. When you hear the word *señalen,* you should point to that part of the body. You will hear each set of statements twice.

Señalen la nariz.	Señalen la cabeza.
Señalen el estómago.	Señalen el pie.
Señalen la mano.	Señalen el brazo.

Track 14: ***En la clase,*** **Student Book, p. 10, (2:23)**

La sala de clases

You will hear each word or phrase twice. After the first time there will be a pause so you can pronounce it, then you will hear the word or phrase a second time.

el estudiante	la estudiante
el profesor	la profesora

Read along as you listen to the dialogue.

MALE TEEN: ¿Qué quiere decir *lápiz?*
ADULT MALE: Quiere decir *pencil.*
FEMALE TEEN: ¿Cómo se dice *book* en español?
ADULT FEMALE: Se dice libro.

You will hear each word or phrase twice. After the first time there will be a pause so you can pronounce it, then you will hear the word or phrase a second time.

el pupitre	el lápiz	el libro
el bolígrafo	el cuaderno	
la carpeta	la hoja de papel	

Track 15: ***En la clase:*** **Act. 1, Student Book, p. 10, (1:35)**

El libro, el lápiz …

You will hear names of classroom objects. After you hear each word, hold up the object if you have it on your desk or point to it if it is somewhere in the classroom. You will hear each word twice.

1. la hoja de papel
2. el libro
3. la profesora (el profesor)
4. el pupitre
5. el bolígrafo
6. el cuaderno
7. el lápiz
8. la carpeta

Track 16: ***En la clase,*** **Student Book, p. 12, (2:59)**

El alfabeto

You will hear each word or phrase twice. After the first time there will be a pause so you can pronounce it, then you will hear the word or phrase a second time.

a	i	pe	doble ve *or* doble u
be	jota	cu	equis
ce	ka	ere	i griega *or* ye
de	ele	erre	zeta
e	eme	ese	
efe	ene	te	
ge	eñe	u	
hache	o	ve *or* uve	

Track 17: ***En la clase:*** **Act. 4, Student Book, p. 12, (3:47)**

Escucha y escribe

On a sheet of paper, write the numbers 1–8. You will hear several words you know spelled aloud. Listen carefully and write the letters as you hear them. You will hear each word spelled twice.

1. ge-u-ese-te-o (gusto)
2. be-i-e-ene (bien)
3. ere-e-ge-u-ele-a-ere (regular)
4. o-ene-ce-e (once)
5. be-ere-a-zeta-o (brazo)
6. pe-i-e-ere-ene-a (pierna)
7. pe-u-pe-i-te-ere-e (pupitre)
8. ce-a-be-e-zeta-a (cabeza)

Track 18: ***En la clase,*** **Student Book, p. 14, (3:07)**

El calendario y la fecha

los días	domingo	junio
lunes	los meses	julio
martes	enero	agosto
miércoles	febrero	septiembre
jueves	marzo	octubre
viernes	abril	noviembre
sábado	mayo	diciembre

Read along as you listen to the dialogue.

Male Teen: ¿Qué día es hoy?
Female Teen: Hoy es lunes. Mañana es martes.
Male Teen: ¿Cuántos días hay en el mes de agosto?
Female Teen: Hay treinta y uno.

Track 19: ***En la clase,*** **Student Book, p. 15, (0:28)**

El calendario y la fecha

Read along as you listen to the dialogues.

Female Teen 1: ¿Cuál es la fecha?
Female Teen 2: Es el 22 de agosto.
Male Teen: ¿Cuál es la fecha?
Female Teen 3: Es el primero de agosto.

Track 20: Audio Act. 3, Writing, Audio & Video Workbook, p. 2, (1:30)

A new student has come into your Spanish class. He seems lost when the teacher asks the students to take out certain items. As you listen to what the teacher says, help him by identifying the picture that matches the item the teacher is asking the students to get out for class. You will hear each command twice.

Modelo: Saquen el libro.

1. Saquen la carpeta.
2. Saquen un lápiz.
3. Saquen el cuaderno.
4. Saquen una hoja de papel.
5. Saquen un bolígrafo.

Track 21: ***El tiempo,*** **Student Book, p. 18, (1:50)**

¿Qué tiempo hace?

You will hear each word or phrase twice. After the first time there will be a pause so you can pronounce it, then you will hear the word or phrase a second time.

Hace sol.	Llueve.	el verano
Hace calor.	Nieva.	el otoño
Hace frío.	Las estaciones.	el invierno
Hace viento.	la primavera	

Track 22: ***El tiempo:*** **Act. 1, Student Book, p. 19, (1:01)**

El tiempo

You will hear six descriptions of different weather conditions. Write the numbers 1–6 on a sheet of paper. Then, next to each number, write the letter of the weather that is being described in the photo.

1. Hace calor.
2. Llueve.
3. Nieva.
4. Hace frío.
5. Hace viento.
6. Hace sol. No hace calor.

Track 23: Audio Act. 4, Writing, Audio & Video Workbook, p. 2, (1:59)

Your teacher is using a map and an alphabet/number grid to plan a class trip to Spain. The five dots on the grid represent cities in Spain where your group will stop. Listen as you hear the first letter/number combination, as in the game of Bingo. Find that dot on the grid and label it "1." Next to it, write the name of the city. After you hear the second letter/number combination, find the second dot and label it "2," writing the name of the city next to it, and so on for the rest of the dots. Connect the dots to show the route of the class trip. You will hear each phrase twice.

1. Jota-dieciocho, Granada.
2. Jota-nueve, Madrid.
3. Te-seis, Barcelona.
4. Jota-uno, Santander.
5. Efe-siete, Salamanca.

Track 24: Audio Act. 5, Writing, Audio & Video Workbook, p. 3, (4:21)

While on vacation in Uruguay, your teacher visits an elementary school classroom. Each student in the class tells your teacher his or her birthday (cumpleaños) and what the weather is like at that time of the year in Uruguay. Remember, in South America the seasons are the reverse of those in the United States. In the first column write out each student's date of birth, and in the second column what season his or her birthday is in. You will hear sentence twice.

1. **Male 1:** Soy Juan, mi cumpleaños es el veinte de julio. Nieva en julio porque es invierno.
2. **Female 1:** Hola, soy María. Mi cumpleaños es el once de septiembre. Hace frío en septiembre porque es el fin del invierno.
3. **Male 2:** Hola, soy Miguel. Mi cumpleaños es el siete de mayo. Hace viento en mayo porque es otoño.
4. **Male 3:** Hola, me llamo Óscar y mi cumpleaños es el diecinueve de diciembre. Hace calor en diciembre porque es verano.
5. **Female 2:** Hola, soy Carolina y mi cumpleaños es el quince de enero. Hace sol y hace calor en enero porque es verano.
6. **Female 3:** Hola. Soy Marta y mi cumpleaños es el dieciséis de octubre. Llueve en octubre porque es primavera.
7. **Female 4:** Hola, soy Elena. Mi cumpleaños es el treinta y uno de marzo. Hace viento, pero hace calor porque es otoño.
8. **Male 4:** Hola, soy Pedro y mi cumpleaños es el veinticinco de junio. Hace frío en junio porque es invierno.

Track 25: ***Repaso del capítulo,*** **Student Book, p. 22, (4:02)**

Vocabulario y gramática

Listen to these words and expressions that you have learned in this chapter. You will hear each word or expression once.

See Student Book page 22 for vocabulary list.

Track 26: ***Preparación para el examen,*** **Student Book, p. 23, (1:10)**

Escuchar

Practice task.

On the exam you will be asked to listen to and understand people as they greet each other and introduce themselves. To practice, listen to some students greet people in the school halls. Answer these questions about each greeting: Is it in the morning or afternoon? Was the greeting directed to an adult? How did that person respond?

1. **Adult Male 1:** Buenas tardes, Sr. Ruiz. ¿Cómo está Ud?
   Adult Male 2: Bien, señor.
2. **Female Teen 1:** ¡Hola, Elena!
   Female Teen 2: Buenos días. Nos vemos en la escuela.
3. **Male Teen 1:** Julio, ¿qué tal?
   Male Teen 2: Regular, ¿y tú?

Track 27: ***Preparación para el examen,*** **Student Book, p. 23, (1:14)**

Escuchar

You will be asked to listen to and understand someone announcing the current date and time. To practice, listen to the message and answer the questions: What is the time of day? What is the date?

1. Muy buenos días. Es el veintidós de septiembre. Son las ocho y media de la mañana.
2. Muy buenas tardes. Es el ocho de enero. Son las dos y veinte de la tarde.
3. Muy buenas noches. Es el cuatro de noviembre. Son las nueve y diez de la noche.

Realidades A

Para empezar

Nombre ______________________________

Fecha ______________________________

Communicative Activity **P-1**

Estudiante **A**

The International Club is having a party to help new students meet. You and your partner will play the roles of Spanish-speaking exchange students. Both of you must choose a first name and a last name from the chart before you answer your partner's questions. Follow the number sequence throughout the conversation. You will need to provide some information not listed in the chart. Then introduce yourself to your partner and ask him or her the questions below. Write your partner's answers on the lines next to the questions.

1. Hola. Me llamo ______________________ . Y tú, ¿cómo te llamas?

3. Mucho gusto. ¿Cómo estás?

5. ______________________ gracias.

7. ¡Hasta luego! ______________________ . ¡Nos vemos!

Boys	**Girls**	**Last Name**
Andrés	Ana	López
Alejandro	María	García

Realidades A

Para empezar

Nombre ______________________________

Fecha ______________________________

Communicative Activity **P-1**

Estudiante **B**

The International Club is having a party to help new students meet. You and your partner will play the roles of Spanish-speaking exchange students. Both of you must choose a first name and a last name from the chart before you answer your partner's questions. Follow the number sequence throughout the conversation. You will need to provide some information not listed in the chart. Then introduce yourself to your partner and ask him or her the questions below. Write your partner's answers on the lines next to the questions.

2. Hola. Me llamo ______________________ . Encantado(a).

4. ______________________ . ¿Y tú?

6. ¡Adiós!

Boys	**Girls**	**Last Name**
Enrique	Camila	Hernandez
Luis	Berta	Gómez

Realidades **A**

Para empezar

Nombre ______________________

Fecha ______________________

Communicative Activity **P-2**

Estudiante **A**

You are working on a Spanish crossword puzzle. Unfortunately, you only have the picture clues for the vertical words. Using these clues, fill in the vertical words. Then ask your partner for the horizontal clues you need (for example: *Siete horizontal, por favor.*) and write them down. Your partner will also ask you for help filling in the vertical words on his or her puzzle.

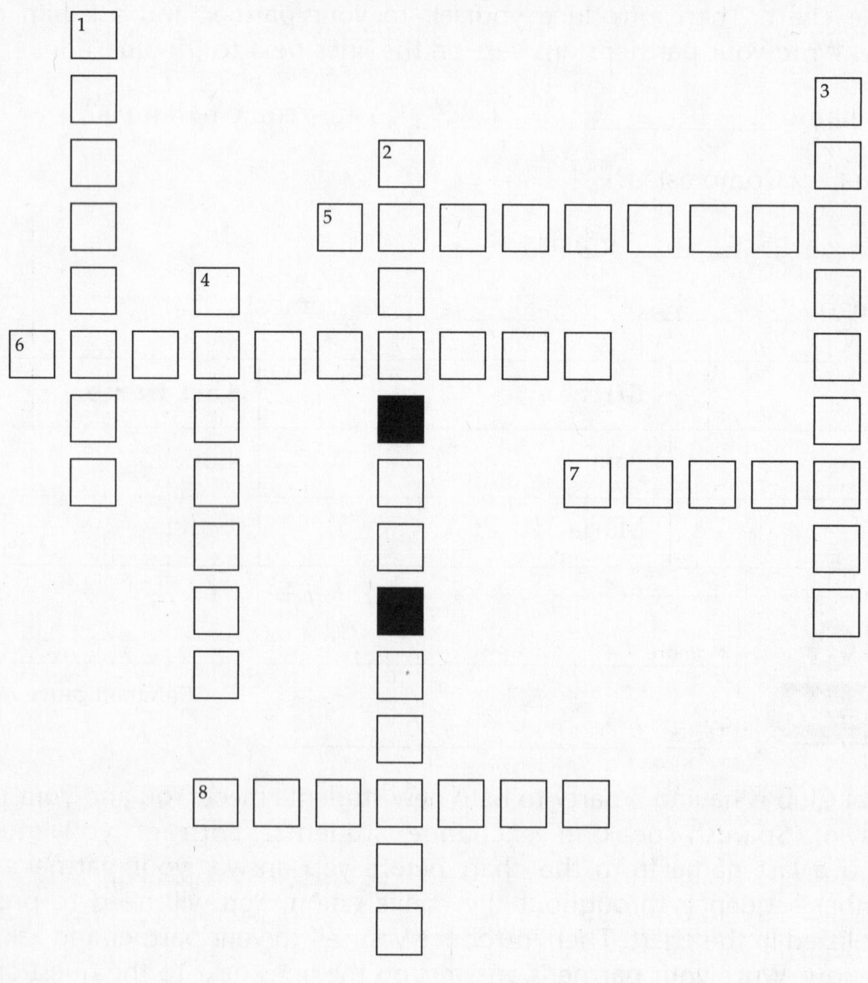

1.

2.

3.

4.

Realidades A

Para empezar

Nombre

Fecha

Communicative Activity **P-2**

Estudiante **B**

You are working on a Spanish crossword puzzle. Unfortunately, you only have the picture clues for the horizontal words. Using these clues, fill in the horizontal words. Then ask your partner for the vertical clues you need (for example: *Uno vertical, por favor.*) and write them down. Your partner will also ask you for help filling in the horizontal words on his or her puzzle.

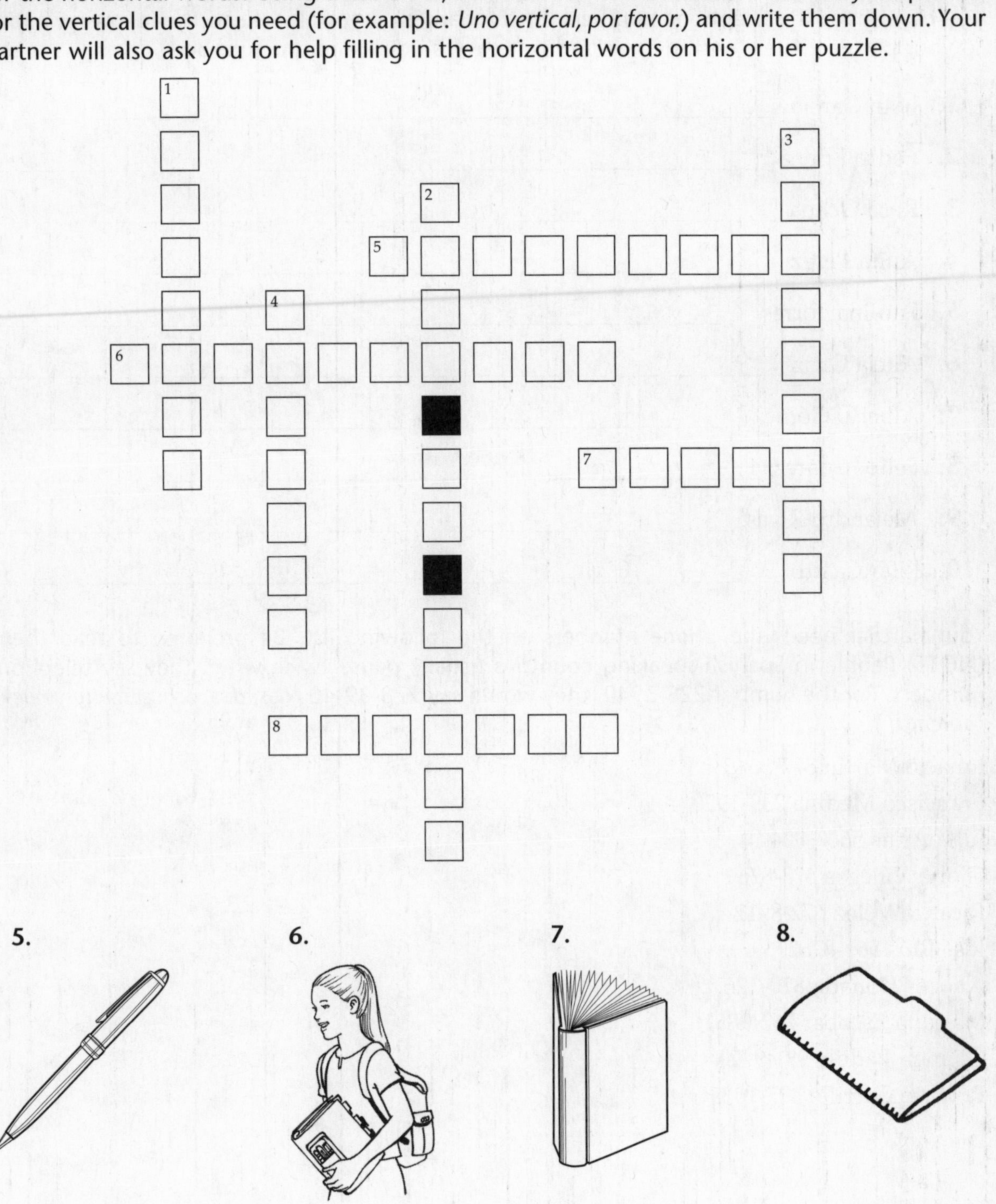

Nombre ______________________________

Communicative Activity **P-3**

Fecha ______________________________

Estudiante **A**

The International Club at your school is hosting a get-acquainted party for the foreign exchange students. Your job is to call some of the students to invite them to the party, but you don't have the telephone numbers for the names on your list. Read the following names to your partner, listen, and then write down each student's phone number.

1. Juan García ______________________________
2. Pedro López ______________________________
3. Rosa Ochoa ______________________________
4. Anita Pérez ______________________________
5. Paulina Torres ______________________________
6. Alicia Ortiz ______________________________
7. Alberto Gómez ______________________________
8. Felipe Suárez ______________________________
9. Alejandro Rivas ______________________________
10. Pilar Castro ______________________________

Your partner needs the phone numbers on the following list. Be prepared to read them. (NOTE: People in Spanish-speaking countries usually pause twice when they say telephone numbers. For the number 228-3940, they would say 228-39-40 *[dos, dos, ocho, treinta y nueve, cuarenta]*.)

Ignacio Martín 877-5645
Francisco Medina 239-1920
Julia Arias 566-1824
Gloria Villegas 673-8761
Ricardo Vélez 672-8712
José Ríos 561-8762
Andrés Donado 870-1267
Mariana Escobar 762-9851
Carmen Padilla 981-9721
Roberto Carrillo 897-1039

Realidades A

Para empezar

Nombre ______________________

Fecha ______________________

Communicative Activity **P-3**

Estudiante **B**

The International Club at your school is hosting a get-acquainted party for the foreign exchange students. Your job is to call some of the students to invite them to the party, but you don't have the telephone numbers for the names on your list. Read the following names to your partner, listen, and then write down each student's phone number.

1. Ignacio Martín ______________________
2. Francisco Medina ______________________
3. Julia Arias ______________________
4. Gloria Villegas ______________________
5. Ricardo Vélez ______________________
6. José Ríos ______________________
7. Andrés Donado ______________________
8. Mariana Escobar ______________________
9. Carmen Padilla ______________________
10. Roberto Carrillo ______________________

Your partner needs the phone numbers on the following list. Be prepared to read them. (NOTE: People in Spanish-speaking countries usually pause twice when they say telephone numbers. For the number 228-3940, they would say 228-39-40 *[dos, dos, ocho, treinta y nueve, cuarenta].*)

Juan García 981-1946
Pedro López 120-3486
Rosa Ochoa 458-2872
Anita Pérez 983-1837
Paulina Torres 249-1937
Alicia Ortiz 192-8732
Alberto Gómez 238-2137
Felipe Suárez 129-1862
Alejandro Rivas 312-1728
Pilar Castro 239-1827

Situation Cards

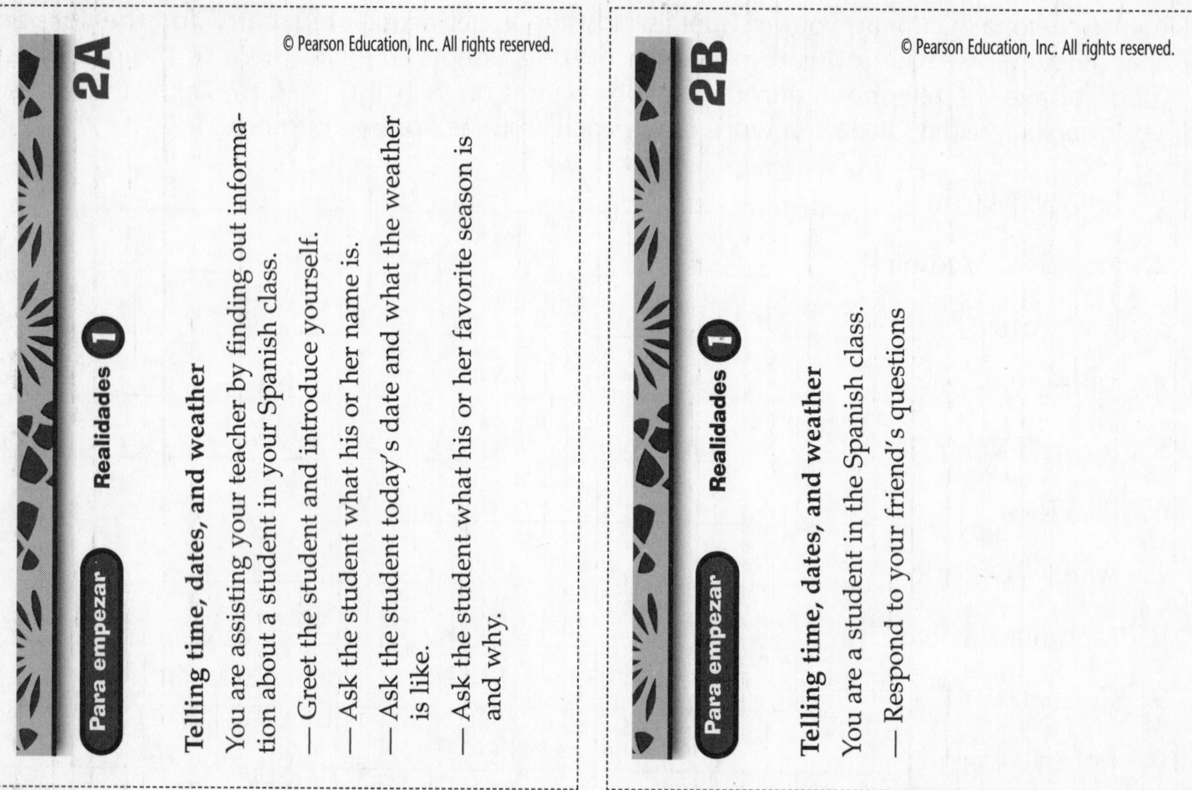

Para empezar Realidades 1 **2A**

Telling time, dates, and weather

You are assisting your teacher by finding out information about a student in your Spanish class.

— Greet the student and introduce yourself.

— Ask the student what his or her name is.

— Ask the student today's date and what the weather is like.

— Ask the student what his or her favorite season is and why.

Para empezar Realidades 1 **2B**

Telling time, dates, and weather

You are a student in the Spanish class.

— Respond to your friend's questions

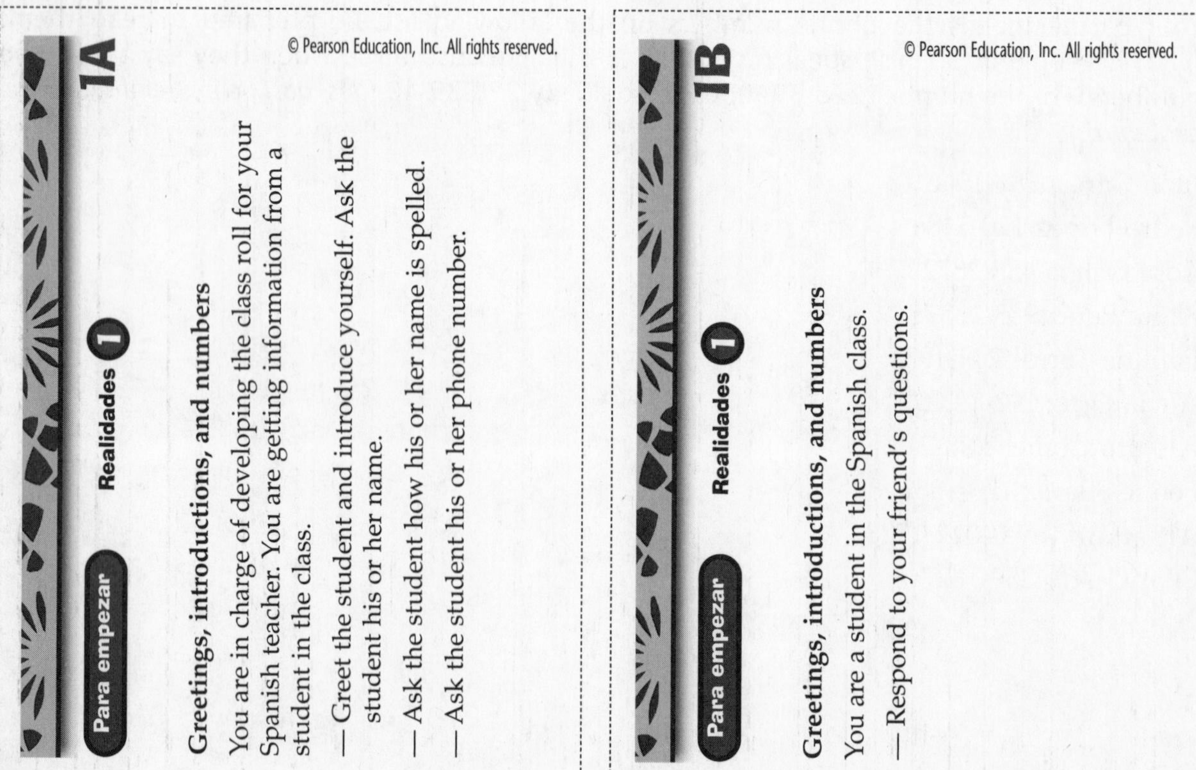

Para empezar Realidades 1 **1A**

Greetings, introductions, and numbers

You are in charge of developing the class roll for your Spanish teacher. You are getting information from a student in the class.

— Greet the student and introduce yourself. Ask the student his or her name.

— Ask the student how his or her name is spelled.

— Ask the student his or her phone number.

Para empezar Realidades 1 **1B**

Greetings, introductions, and numbers

You are a student in the Spanish class.

— Respond to your friend's questions.

Vocabulary Clip Art

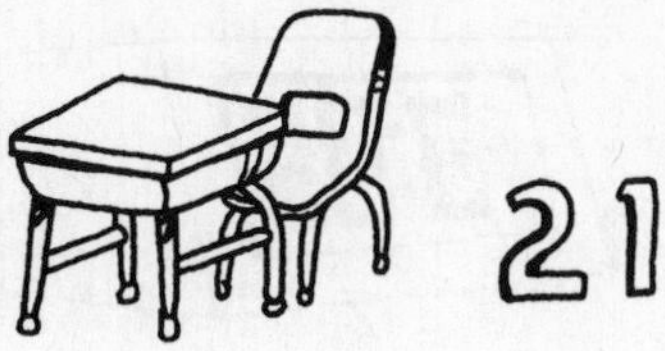

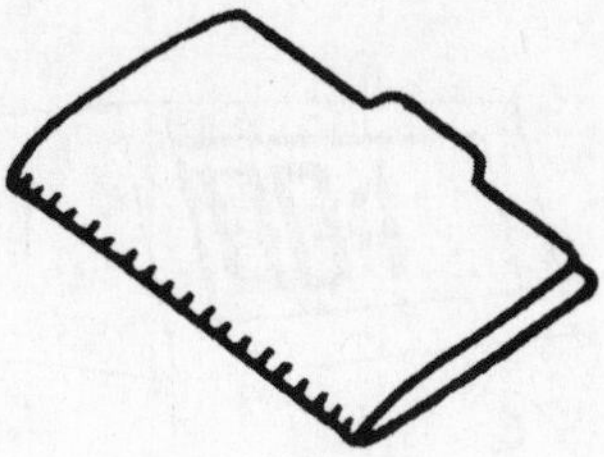

Realidades 

Para empezar

Vocabulary Clip Art

2:00

12:50

3:05

1:00

4:10

Realidades A

Para empezar

Vocabulary Clip Art

Vocabulary Clip Art

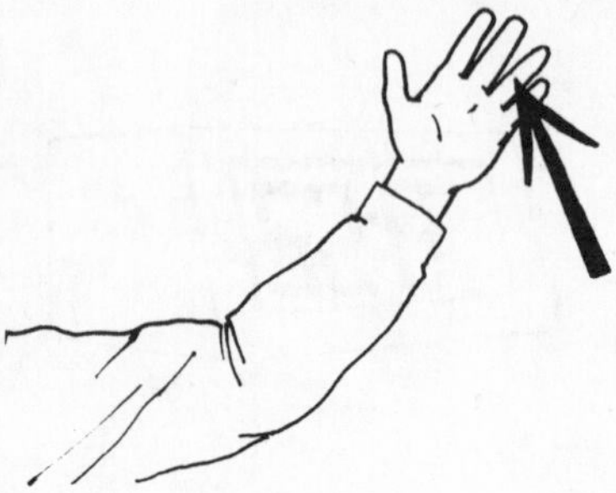

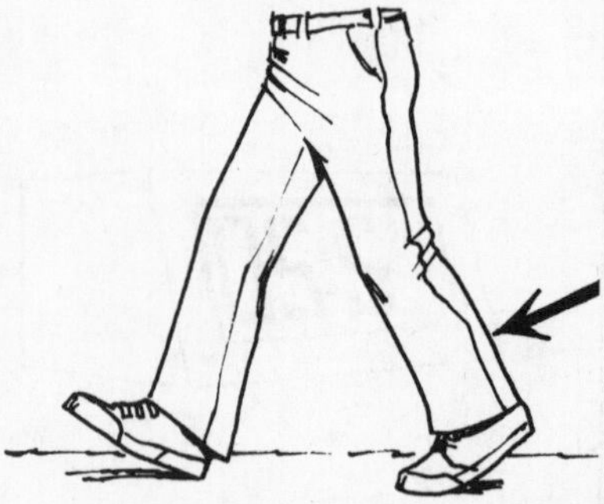

Para empezar

Vocabulary Clip Art

Realidades A

Para empezar

Core Practice Answers

P-1

1. ¿Cómo te llamas?; Mucho gusto.
2. ¡Buenos días!; ¿Cómo estás, Rosalía?; Bien.; ¡Nos vemos!
3. ¡Buenas tardes!; Encantada.; ¡Hasta luego!

P-2

A.

1. **circle:**
   ¡Hola!
   ¿Cómo está Ud.?
   Mucho gusto.
   Buenos días.
   ¿Y usted?
   ¡Hasta luego!
   Buenos días, señor.
   Estoy bien.
2. **underline:**
   ¡Hola!
   Mucho gusto.
   ¿Qué tal?
   Buenos días.
   ¿Cómo estás?
   ¡Hasta luego!
   ¡Nos vemos!
   Estoy bien.
   ¿Y tú?

B.

1. Ud.
2. Tú
3. Tú
4. Ud.
5. Ud.

C.

3, 5, 1, 2, 4

P-3

1. D
2. C
3. E
4. B
5. A

P-4

A.

1. 56 (cincuenta y seis)
2. 30 (treinta)
3. 82 (ochenta y dos)
4. 70 (setenta)
5. 100 (cien)
6. 12 (doce)
7. 48 (cuarenta y ocho)

```
O C H E N T A Y D O S L C T
M O J X U E Y S W H U S S R
O G X L E G I L E C E H M E
G U N V C T B C R T U C G I
O H C O Y A T N E R A U C N
T T C C V A T N W L Y F W T
M B K W C E T U Y O N L O A
E F Q F Q A N B Y F K R L V
H C E E A Y R T D M W D A W
C I N C U E N T A Y S E I S
R E C O J I W C J Y G Q U Q
U L J D I U D G V X D D K G
```

B.

1. 1:30 / 2:30
2. 12:15 / 1:15
3. 10:00 / 10:00
4. 6:15 / 8:15
5. 2:00 / 7:00 (19:00)

P-5

A.

el brazo should point to an arm
la cabeza should point to the head
la nariz should point to the nose
el estómago should point to the stomach
la pierna should point to a leg
la boca should point to the mouth in general
la mano should point to a hand
el pie should point to a foot
el dedo should point to either a finger or a toe
el ojo should point to an eye

B.

Answers will vary. Should look like "Me duele el brazo." for example.

P-6

A.

1. el
2. el
3. la
4. la
5. el
6. la
7. el
8. el / la
9. el
10. el

B.

1. 67 bolígrafo
2. 100 hojas de papel
3. 21 pupitre
4. 19 cuadernos
5. 36 lápices

P-7

1. No, es sábado.
2. No, es miércoles.
3. No, es jueves.
4. No, es lunes.
5. No, es viernes.
6. No, es martes.
7. No, es domingo.
8. No, es domingo.

P-8

A.

el nueve de marzo
el cinco de julio
el cuatro de septiembre
el ocho de noviembre
el primero de enero

B.

1. Answers will vary. Hoy es . . .
2. No, es el catorce de febrero. (No, no es el trece de enero.)
3. Es el primero de enero.
4. No, es el veinticinco de diciembre. (No, no es el veinticinco de noviembre.)
5. Es el diecisiete de marzo.
6. Es el cuatro de julio.
7. Answers will vary. Mañana es . . .

P-9

A.

First Row: febrero / invierno / hace frío, nieva
Second Row: abril, mayo / primavera / hace frío, llueve, or hace calor
Third Row: julio, agosto / ____ / hace sol, hace calor
Fourth Row: septiembre, octubre / otoño / ____

B.

Answers may vary depending on what part of the country you are in.

1. Hace calor en julio.
2. No, hace frío en enero.

3. Hace frío en octubre, noviembre, diciembre, enero, febrero y marzo.
4. Hace calor en el verano.
5. No, no nieva en agosto.

Crucigrama (P-10)
Across:
3. lápiz
7. estación
8. hasta luego
9. llueve
13. hace frío
16. invierno
17. septiembre
19. día
21. cabeza
23. señora
24. pie
25. semana
27. otoño

Down:
1. viernes
2. lunes
4. nieva
5. profesor
6. enero
8. hace sol
10. verano
11. pupitre
12. hace calor
14. primavera
15. fecha
18. mes
20. brazo
22. año
23. sábado
25. señor
26. hola

Organizer (P-11)
I. Vocabulary Answers will vary.
II. Grammar
1. el, la, el, la
2. -o, -a

Realidades A — Para empezar

Nombre ______ Hora ______

Fecha ______ **Vocabulary Flash Cards, Sheet 1**

Write the Spanish vocabulary word below each picture. If there is a word or phrase, copy it in the space provided. Be sure to include the article for each noun.

Buenos días. *Buenos* *días.*	**Buenas noches.** *Buenas* *noches.*	**Buenas tardes.** *Buenas* *tardes.*
¡Hola! *¡Hola!*	**¿Cómo te llamas?** *¿Cómo* *te* *llamas?*	**Me llamo...** *Me* *llamo...*
Encantado, Encantada. *Encantado*, *Encantada.*	**Igualmente.** *Igualmente.*	**Mucho gusto.** *Mucho* *gusto.*

Realidades A — Para empezar

Nombre ______ Hora ______

Fecha ______ **Vocabulary Flash Cards, Sheet 2**

¿Cómo está Ud.? *¿Cómo* *está* *Ud.?*	**¿Cómo estás?** *¿Cómo* *estás?*	**¿Qué pasa?** *¿Qué* *pasa?*
¿Qué tal? *¿Qué* *tal?*	**¿Y tú?** *¿Y* *tú?*	**¿Y usted (Ud.)?** *¿Y* *usted (Ud.)?*
(muy) bien *(muy)* *bien*	**regular** *regular*	**gracias** *gracias*

Realidades A | Nombre ______ Hora ______

Para empezar | Fecha ______

Vocabulary Flash Cards, Sheet 3

nada *nada*	**señor, Sr.** *señor*, *Sr.*	**señora, Sra.** *señora*, *Sra.*
señorita, Srta. *señorita*, *Srta.*	**¡Adiós!** *¡Adiós!*	**Hasta luego.** *Hasta luego.*
Hasta mañana. *Hasta mañana.*	**¡Nos vemos!** *¡Nos vemos!*	**uno** *uno*

Realidades A | Nombre ______ Hora ______

Para empezar | Fecha ______

Vocabulary Flash Cards, Sheet 4

dos *dos*	**tres** *tres*	**cuatro** *cuatro*
cinco *cinco*	**seis** *seis*	**siete** *siete*
ocho *ocho*	**nueve** *nueve*	**diez** *diez*

Realidades A — Para empezar

Nombre ______ Hora ______

Fecha ______ **Vocabulary Flash Cards, Sheet 5**

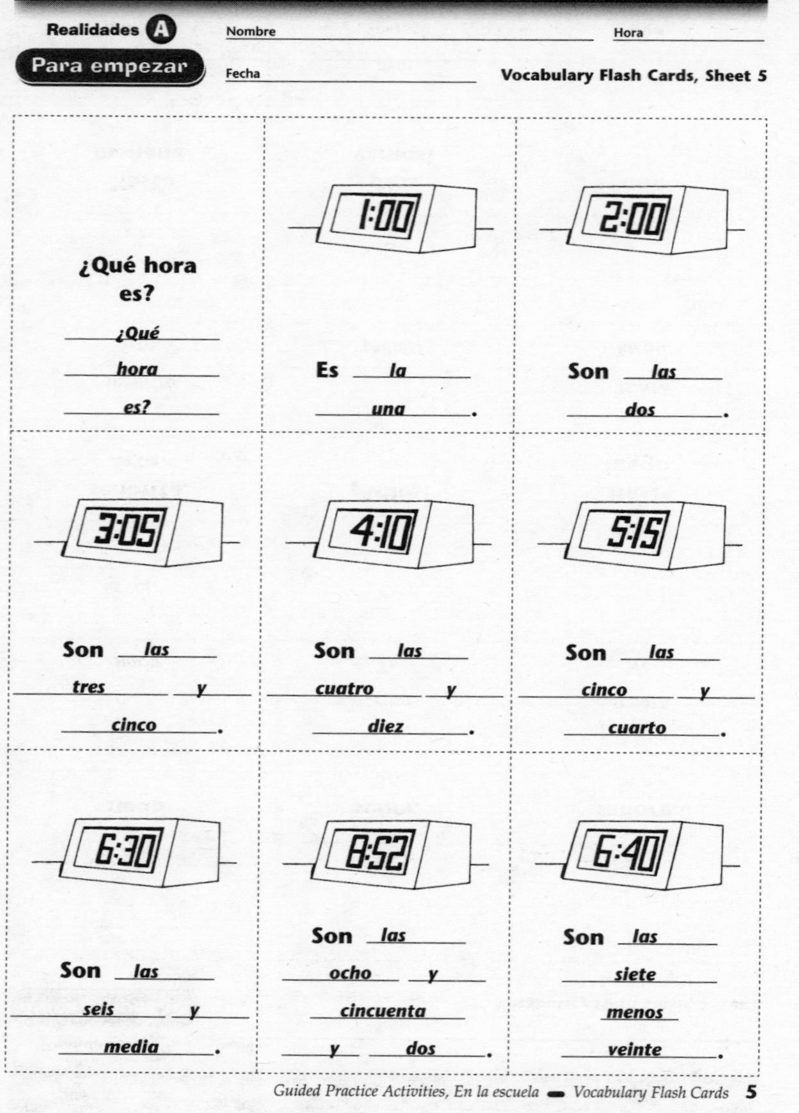

Realidades A — Para empezar

Nombre ______ Hora ______

Fecha ______ **Vocabulary Flash Cards, Sheet 6**

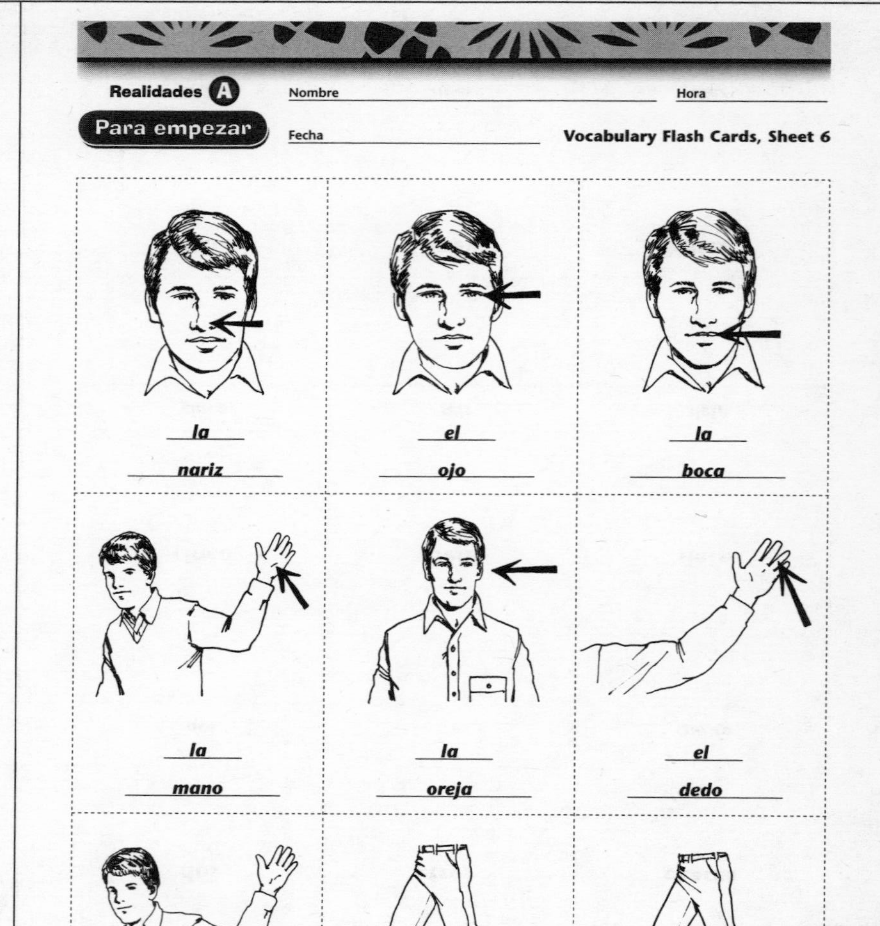

Realidades A

Para empezar

Nombre ______ Hora ______

Fecha ______ **Vocabulary Check, Sheet 1**

Tear out this page. Write the English words on the lines. Fold the paper along the dotted line to see the correct answers so you can check your work.

En la escuela

Buenos días.	***Good morning.***
Buenas noches.	***Good evening.***
Buenas tardes.	***Good afternoon.***
¡Hola!	***Hello!***
¿Cómo te llamas?	***What is your name?***
Me llamo...	***My name is . . .***
Encantado, Encantada.	***Delighted.***
Igualmente.	***Likewise.***
Mucho gusto.	***Pleased to meet you.***
señor, Sr.	***sir, Mr.***
señora, Sra.	***madam, Mrs.***
señorita, Srta.	***miss, Miss***
¡Adiós!	***Good-bye!***
Hasta luego.	***See you later.***
Hasta mañana.	***See you tomorrow.***
¡Nos vemos!	***See you!***

Fold In ↓

Realidades A

Para empezar

Nombre ______ Hora ______

Fecha ______ **Vocabulary Check, Sheet 2**

Tear out this page. Write the Spanish words on the lines. Fold the paper along the dotted line to see the correct answers so you can check your work.

Good morning.	***Buenos días.***
Good evening.	***Buenas noches.***
Good afternoon.	***Buenas tardes.***
Hello!	***¡Hola!***
What is your name?	***¿Cómo te llamas?***
My name is . . .	***Me llamo...***
Delighted.	***Encantado, Encantada.***
Likewise.	***Igualmente.***
Pleased to meet you.	***Mucho gusto.***
sir, Mr.	***señor, Sr.***
madam, Mrs.	***señora, Sra.***
miss, Miss	***señorita, Srta.***
Good-bye!	***¡Adiós!***
See you later.	***Hasta luego.***
See you tomorrow.	***Hasta mañana.***
See you!	***¡Nos vemos!***

Fold In ↓

Realidades A — Para empezar

Nombre ______ Hora ______

Fecha ______ **Guided Practice Activities P-1**

Vowel sounds

- Like English, Spanish has five basic vowels, **a, e, i, o,** and **u**. But unlike English, each Spanish vowel sounds nearly the same in every word, which will help you figure out how to pronounce any Spanish word you see.

A. The letter **a** is pronounced "ah," as in the English word "f**a**ther." Write three Spanish words related to *body parts* (**el cuerpo**) that contain the letter **a**. Say each word as you write it, paying special attention to the **a**.

Possible answers provided:

pierna ***mano*** ***nariz***

B. The letter **e** is pronounced "ay," as in the English word "pay." Write three Spanish *numbers under ten* that contain the letter **e**. Say each word as you write it, paying special attention to the **e**.

tres ***nueve*** ***seis***

C. The letter **i** is pronounced "ee," as in the English word "see." Write two Spanish words used in *greetings* that contain the letter **i**. Say each word as you write it, paying special attention to the **i**.

Igualmente. ***Buenos días.***

D. The letter **o** is pronounced "oh," as in the English word "go." Write three Spanish *numbers over ten* that contain the letter **o**. Say each word as you write it, paying special attention to the **o**.

once ***doce*** ***veintiuno***

E. The letter **u** is pronounced "oo," as in the English word "zoo." Write three Spanish words that you've learned so far that contain the letter **u**. Say each word as you write it, paying special attention to the **u**.

uno ***usted*** ***Mucho gusto.***

Realidades A — Para empezar

Nombre ______ Hora ______

Fecha ______ **Guided Practice Activities P-2**

The letter *c*

- The letter **c** has two different sounds in Spanish. When it is followed by **a, o, u,** or any consonant other than **h**, it is a "hard **c**" and is pronounced like the **c** in "cat." Say these words with a hard **c**:

  cómo **práctica** **encantado**

- When the letter **c** is followed by **e** or **i**, it is a "soft **c**" and is pronounced like the **s** in "Sally." Say these words with a soft **c**:

  doce **gracias** **silencio**

A. Write out the numbers below (which all contain at least one letter **c**) in Spanish on the blanks provided.

1. 4 ***cuatro***
2. 0 ***cero***
3. 13 ***trece***
4. 100 ***cien***
5. 11 ***once***
6. 5 ***cinco***
7. 16 ***dieciséis***
8. 14 ***catorce***
9. 55 ***cincuenta y cinco***
10. 48 ***cuarenta y ocho***

B. Now, say aloud each of the words you wrote, paying special attention to the letter **c**. Go back to the answers you gave in **part A** and underline each hard **c** (as in **c**at). Circle each soft **c** (as in **S**ally). **Ojo**: Some words contain more than one **c**.

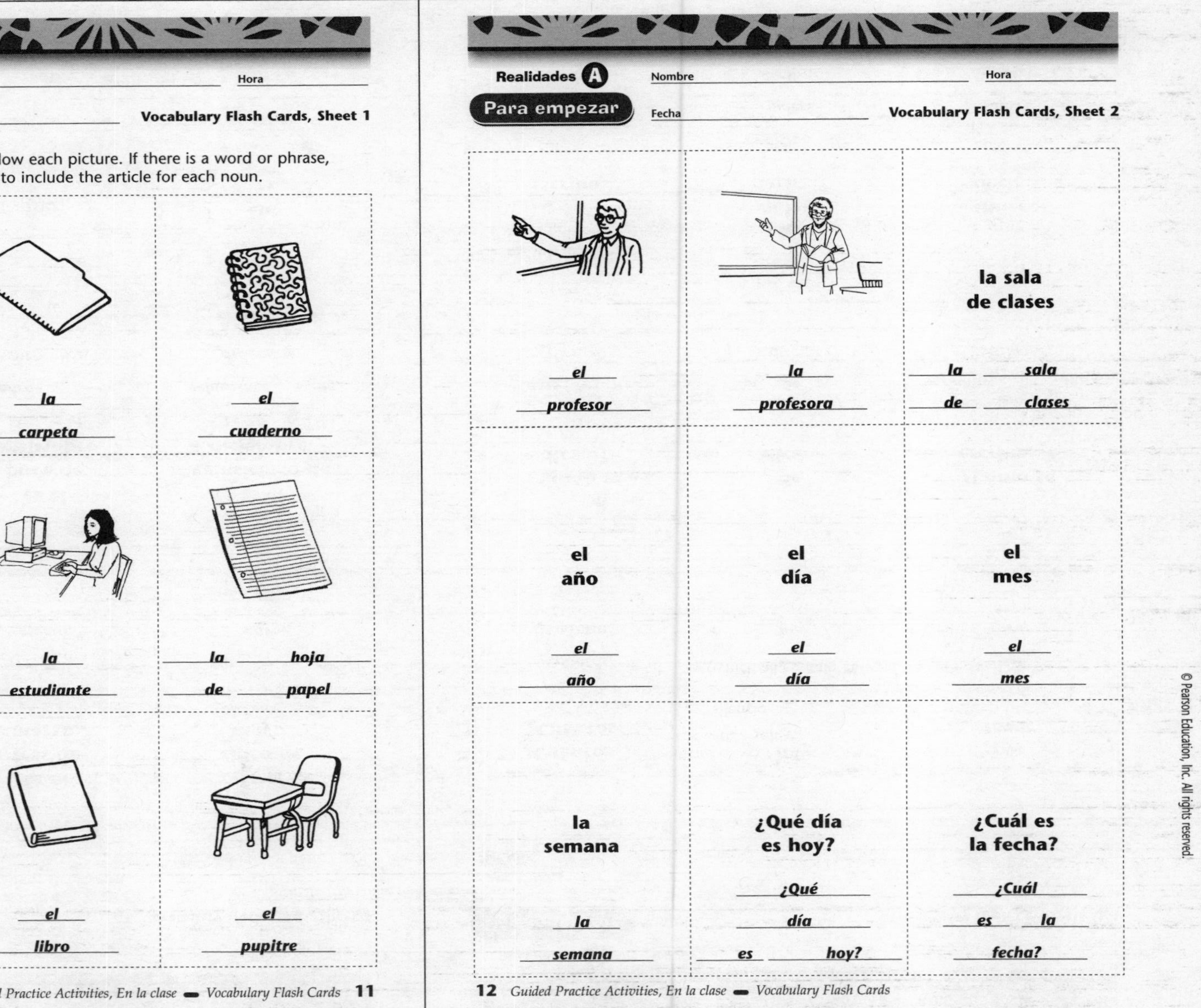

Realidades A — Nombre ______ Hora ______

Para empezar — Fecha ______

Vocabulary Flash Cards, Sheet 1

Write the Spanish vocabulary word below each picture. If there is a word or phrase, copy it in the space provided. Be sure to include the article for each noun.

el bolígrafo	*la carpeta*	*el cuaderno*
el estudiante	*la estudiante*	*la hoja de papel*
el lápiz	*el libro*	*el pupitre*

Realidades A — Nombre ______ Hora ______

Para empezar — Fecha ______

Vocabulary Flash Cards, Sheet 2

el profesor	*la profesora*	**la sala de clases** — *la sala de clases*
el año — *el año*	**el día** — *el día*	**el mes** — *el mes*
la semana — *la semana*	**¿Qué día es hoy?** — *¿Qué día es hoy?*	**¿Cuál es la fecha?** — *¿Cuál es la fecha?*

Realidades A　Nombre ____ Hora ____

Para empezar　Fecha ____　**Vocabulary Flash Cards, Sheet 3**

Es el primero de enero. *Es* *el* *primero* *de* *enero.*	**Es el tres de marzo.** *Es* *el* *tres* *de* *marzo.*	**Es el cinco de mayo.** *Es* *el* *cinco* *de* *mayo.*
Es el catorce de febrero. *Es* *el* *catorce* *de* *febrero.*	**Es el once de septiembre.** *Es* *el* *once* *de* *septiembre.*	**Es el veinticinco de diciembre.** *Es* *el* *veinticinco* *de* *diciembre.*
mañana *mañana*	**hoy** *hoy*	**en** *en*

Realidades A　Nombre ____ Hora ____

Para empezar　Fecha ____　**Vocabulary Flash Cards, Sheet 4**

¿Cuántos?, ¿Cuántas? *¿Cuántos?* , *¿Cuántas?*	**hay** *hay*	**por favor** *por* *favor*
¿Cómo se dice...? *¿Cómo* *se* *dice...?*	**Se dice...** *Se* *dice...*	**¿Cómo se escribe...?** *¿Cómo* *se* *escribe...?*
Se escribe... *Se* *escribe...*	**¿Qué quiere decir...?** *¿Qué* *quiere* *decir...?*	**Quiere decir...** *Quiere* *decir...*

Realidades A | Nombre ______ | Hora ______

Para empezar | Fecha ______ | **Vocabulary Check, Sheet 1**

Tear out this page. Write the English words on the lines. Fold the paper along the dotted line to see the correct answers so you can check your work.

En la clase

el bolígrafo	***pen***
la carpeta	***folder***
el cuaderno	***notebook***
el estudiante, la estudiante	***student***
la hoja de papel	***sheet of paper***
el lápiz	***pencil***
el libro	***book***
el profesor, la profesora	***teacher***
el pupitre	***(student) desk***
la sala de clases	***classroom***
el año	***year***
el día	***day***
el mes	***month***
la semana	***week***
hoy	***today***
mañana	***tomorrow***

Fold In

Realidades A | Nombre ______ | Hora ______

Para empezar | Fecha ______ | **Vocabulary Check, Sheet 2**

Tear out this page. Write the Spanish words on the lines. Fold the paper along the dotted line to see the correct answers so you can check your work.

pen	***el bolígrafo***
folder	***la carpeta***
notebook	***el cuaderno***
student	***el estudiante, la estudiante***
sheet of paper	***la hoja de papel***
pencil	***el lápiz***
book	***el libro***
teacher	***el profesor, la profesora***
(student) desk	***el pupitre***
classroom	***la sala de clases***
year	***el año***
day	***el día***
month	***el mes***
week	***la semana***
today	***hoy***
tomorrow	***mañana***

Fold In

Realidades A | Nombre ____ Hora ____

Para empezar | Fecha ____ **Guided Practice Activities P-3**

More *c* sounds

- In **Activity P-2** you learned that the letter **c** has two different sounds in Spanish: "hard **c**" and "soft **c**." The "hard **c**" sound is also created by the letter groups **que** and **qui**. **Que** is always pronounced like the English "kay" and **qui** is always pronounced like the English word "key." Say these words:

  quince **que** **quiere**

A. Remember that the hard **c** is sometimes spelled with a **c** and sometimes with a **q**. Underline the words in each group below with a hard **c** ("cat") sound. Say each word aloud as you read it.

1. clase / García / doce
2. trece / cien / carpeta
3. equis / cierren / dieciséis
4. gracias / saquen / Cecilia
5. cero / silencio / catorce
6. once / cuaderno / diciembre

B. Circle the words in each group with a soft **c** ("Sally") sound. Say each word aloud as you read it.

1. Ricardo / cuarto / atención
2. diciembre / cómo / octubre
3. carpeta / cuaderno / Alicia
4. qué / quiere / decir
5. cien / Cristina / cuántos
6. saquen / cierren / capítulo

Realidades A | Nombre ____ Hora ____

Para empezar | Fecha ____ **Guided Practice Activities P-4**

The *h* sound

- In Spanish, some letters have different pronunciations than they do in English. For example, the letter **j** is pronounced like the letter *h* in the English word "**h**at," but even more strongly and in the back of the throat. The letter **g**, when followed by **e** or **i**, also has the same "h" sound. However, the Spanish letter **h** is always silent! Say these words aloud:

  Jorge **jueves** **hay** **hasta** **hoja**

A. Circle all of the words below with a *pronounced* "h" sound. Don't be fooled by the silent letter **h**! Say each word aloud as you read it.

julio	hoy	hasta
hoja	Jorge	Juan
junio	Guillermo	hora
José	página	hay
juego	¡Hola!	Eugenia

B. Now, go back to the words in **part A** and draw a diagonal line through every silent **h**. The first one has been done for you. Did you notice that **hoja** has both a silent **h** and a **j** that has a *pronounced* "h" sound?

Realidades A — Para empezar

Nombre ______ Hora ______

Fecha ______ **Vocabulary Flash Cards, Sheet 1**

Hace calor.	*Hace frío.*	*Hace sol.*
Hace viento.	*Llueve.*	*Nieva.*
el otoño	*el verano*	*el invierno*

Realidades A — Para empezar

Nombre ______ Hora ______

Fecha ______ **Vocabulary Flash Cards, Sheet 2**

la primavera	**la estación** — *la estación*	**¿Qué tiempo hace?** — *¿Qué tiempo hace?*

Realidades A Nombre ______ Hora ______

Para empezar Fecha ______ **Vocabulary Check, Sheet 1**

Tear out this page. Write the English words on the lines. Fold the paper along the dotted line to see the correct answers so you can check your work.

El tiempo

Hace calor.	***It's hot.***
Hace frío.	***It's cold.***
Hace sol.	***It's sunny.***
Hace viento.	***It's windy.***
Llueve.	***It's raining.***
Nieva.	***It's snowing.***
la estación	***season***
el invierno	***winter***
el otoño	***fall, autumn***
la primavera	***spring***
el verano	***summer***

Fold In

Realidades A Nombre ______ Hora ______

Para empezar Fecha ______ **Vocabulary Check, Sheet 2**

Tear out this page. Write the Spanish words on the lines. Fold the paper along the dotted line to see the correct answers so you can check your work.

It's hot.	***Hace calor.***
It's cold.	***Hace frío.***
It's sunny.	***Hace sol.***
It's windy.	***Hace viento.***
It's raining.	***Llueve.***
It's snowing.	***Nieva.***
season	***la estación***
winter	***el invierno***
fall, autumn	***el otoño***
spring	***la primavera***
summer	***el verano***

Fold In

To hear a complete list of the vocabulary for this chapter, go to www.realidades.com and type in the Web Code jcd-0099. Then click on **Repaso del capítulo.**

Realidades A | Para empezar

Nombre ______ Hora ______

Fecha ______

Guided Practice Activities P-5

Special letters

- When studying the alphabet, you will notice a few letters that you may not have seen before. In addition to the letters we have in English, Spanish also has **ll**, **ñ**, and **rr**.
  - **a)** **ll** is pronounced like a "y" in English, as in the word "yellow."
  - **b)** **ñ** is pronounced like the combination "ny," as in the English word "ca**ny**on."
  - **c)** **rr** is a "rolled" sound in Spanish. It is made by letting your tongue vibrate against the roof of your mouth, and sounds a bit like a cat purring or a child imitating the sound of a helicopter.

Look at the pictures below and fill in the blanks in the words or phrases with either the letter **ll**, **ñ**, or **rr**. Be sure to say each word aloud as you write it, practicing the sounds of the new letters.

1. Es la se__*ñ*__ora Guité__*rr*__ez.

2. Me __*ll*__amo Gui__*ll*__ermo.

3. Es el libro de espa__*ñ*__ol.

4. __*Ll*__ueve en la primavera.

5. Hace viento en el oto__*ñ*__o.

Realidades A | Para empezar

Nombre ______ Hora ______

Fecha ______

Guided Practice Activities P-6

The letters *b* and *v*

- In Spanish, the letters **b** and **v** are both pronounced with a "b" sound, like in the English word "boy." This makes pronunciation simple, but can make spelling more challenging! Say the following words:

  Buenos días. ¡Nos vemos! brazo veinte bolígrafo verano

The phrases below all contain either **b** or **v**. Pronounce both with a "b" sound, and write the correct letter in the blanks in each conversation.

1. —Hola, profesor.

—__*B*__uenos días, estudiantes.

2. —¿Qué tiempo hace en el otoño?

—Hace __*v*__iento.

3. En fe__*b*__rero hace mucho frío.

—Sí, hace frío en el in__*v*__ierno.

4. —¿Qué tiempo hace en la prima__*v*__era?

—Llue__*v*__e pero hace calor.

5. —¿Qué día es hoy?

—Hoy es el __*v*__einte de no__*v*__iembre.

6. —Le__*v*__ántense, por fa__*v*__or.

—Sí, profesora.

7. —¿Cómo estás?

—__*B*__ien, pero me duele el __*b*__razo.

Realidades A | Nombre ____ | Hora ____

Para empezar | Fecha ____ | AUDIO

Actividad 1

You are at a party with students visiting from Ecuador. You have practiced several responses to the things they might say when you meet them. Listen to each question or statement and write the letter of the best response in the blank. You will hear each statement or question twice.

a. Me llamo ...	1. d
b. Muy bien, gracias.	2. a
c. Regular.	3. b or c
d. Mucho gusto.	4. f
e. Igualmente.	5. e
f. Hasta mañana.	6. b or c

Actividad 2

You have lost your dog, so you put up signs in your neighborhood asking your neighbors to call you if they see him. You will hear six messages on your answering machine from neighbors who have seen your dog. You will not understand everything they say, but listen carefully to find out their house number and what time they called so that you can track down your dog. Write down each house number and time on the chart. You will hear each message twice.

	NÚMERO DE CASA (*House number*)	HORA DE LA LLAMADA (*Time of call*)
1.	45	6:00
2.	15	5:45
3.	33	8:30
4.	42	7:15
5.	29	6:30
6.	21	6:50

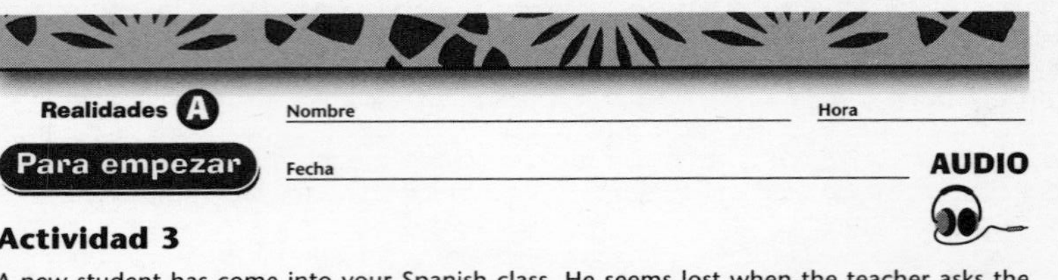

Realidades A | Nombre ____ | Hora ____

Para empezar | Fecha ____ | AUDIO

Actividad 3

A new student has come into your Spanish class. He seems lost when the teacher asks the students to take out certain items. As you listen to what the teacher says, help him by identifying the picture that matches the item the teacher is asking the students to get out for class. You will hear each command twice.

Modelo f 1. b 2. c 3. e 4. d 5. a

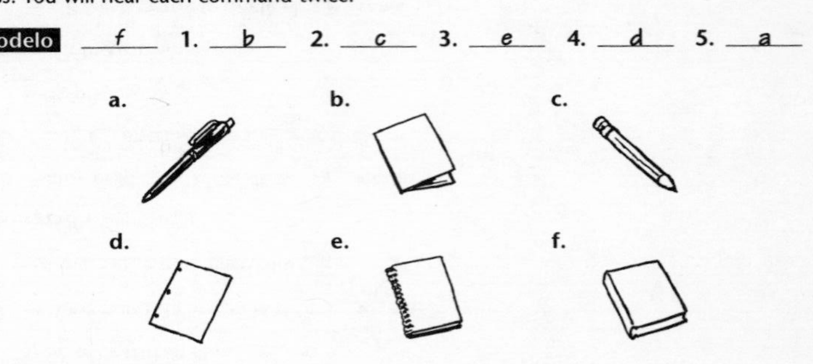

Actividad 4

Your teacher is using a map and an alphabet/number grid to plan a class trip to Spain. The five dots on the grid represent cities in Spain where your group will stop. Listen as you hear the first letter/number combination, as in the game of Bingo. Find that dot on the grid and label it "1." Next to it, write the name of the city. After you hear the second letter/number combination, find the second dot and label it "2," writing the name of the city next to it, and so on for the rest of the dots. Connect the dots to show the route of the class trip. You will hear each phrase twice.

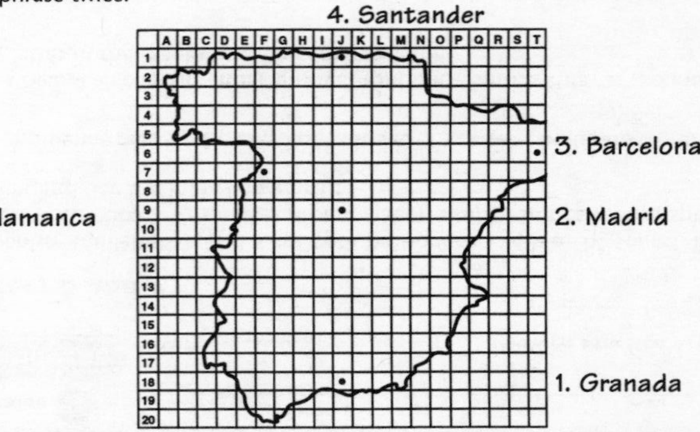

Realidades A — Nombre ____ Hora ____

Para empezar — Fecha ____ **AUDIO**

Actividad 5

While on vacation in Uruguay, your teacher visits an elementary school classroom. Each student in the class tells your teacher his or her birthday (**cumpleaños**) and what the weather is like at that time of the year in Uruguay. Remember, in South America the seasons are the reverse of those in the United States. In the first column write out each student's date of birth, and in the second column what season his or her birthday is in. You will hear each sentence twice.

	DATE OF BIRTH	SEASON
1. Juan	20 de julio	el invierno
2. María	11 de septiembre	el invierno
3. Miguel	7 de mayo	el otoño
4. Óscar	19 de diciembre	el verano
5. Carolina	15 de enero	el verano
6. Marta	16 de octubre	la primavera
7. Elena	31 de marzo	el otoño
8. Pedro	25 de junio	el invierno

Realidades A — Nombre ____ Hora ____

Para empezar — Fecha ____ **WRITING**

Actividad 6

Describe the monster below, telling how many of each body part he has (**El monstruo tiene ...**). Each blank corresponds to one letter. Each letter corresponds to a number, which appears underneath the blank. Use these numbers to figure out which sentence refers to which body part. The first one has been done for you.

Modelo El monstruo tiene D O S (9 15 20) C A B E Z A S (2 10 19 1 3 10 20).

1. El monstruo tiene O C H O (15 2 8 15) O J O S (15 17 15 20).
2. El monstruo tiene U N A (6 22 10) N A R I Z (22 10 4 5 3) en cada cabeza.
3. El monstruo tiene U N A (6 22 10) B O C A (19 15 2 10) en cada cabeza.
4. El monstruo tiene C U A T R O (2 6 10 11 4 15) B R A Z O S (19 4 10 3 15 20).
5. El monstruo tiene T R E S (11 4 1 20) D E D O S (9 1 9 15 20) en cada mano.
6. El monstruo tiene S E I S (20 1 5 20) P I E R N A S (16 5 1 4 22 10 20).

Realidades A — Nombre ______ Hora ______

Para empezar — Fecha ______ **WRITING**

Actividad 7

A. It is September and school is finally in session. You already have some important dates to mark on the calendar. To make sure you have the right day, write the day of the week that each date falls on.

SEPTIEMBRE						
lunes	**martes**	**miércoles**	**jueves**	**viernes**	**sábado**	**domingo**
		1	2	3	4	5
6	7	8	9	10	11	12
13	14	15	16	17	18	19
20	21	22	23	24	25	26
27	28	29	30			

1. el tres de septiembre — viernes
2. el veinte de septiembre — lunes
3. el primero de septiembre — miércoles
4. el veinticuatro de septiembre — viernes
5. el doce de septiembre — domingo
6. el dieciocho de septiembre — sábado
7. el siete de septiembre — martes

B. Now, write in what month the following holidays occur.

1. el Día de San Valentín — febrero
2. el Día de San Patricio — marzo
3. la Navidad — diciembre
4. el Año Nuevo — enero
5. el Día de la Independencia — julio

Realidades A — Nombre ______ Hora ______

Para empezar — Fecha ______ **WRITING**

Actividad 8

Answer the questions below according to the map.

1. ¿Qué tiempo hace en el norte de México?
   Hace calor.
2. ¿Hace buen tiempo en el sur?
   No, no hace buen tiempo en el sur (llueve).
3. ¿Qué tiempo hace en el centro de México?
   Llueve.
4. ¿Hace frío o calor en el oeste?
   Hace calor.
5. ¿Qué tiempo hace en el este?
   Está nublado.
6. ¿Qué estación es, probablemente?
   Answers will vary.

Table of Contents

Tema 1: Mis amigos y yo

Capítulo 1A: ¿Qué te gusta hacer?

Capítulo 1B: Y tú, ¿cómo eres?

Theme Project

Mis amigos y yo
Álbum de recuerdos

Overview:
You will create two pages for a scrapbook featuring photos of you and your friends with captions written underneath. Then you will give an oral presentation of your scrapbook, describing the people in the photos and telling what they like and don't like to do.

Materials:
Construction paper, photographs, magazines, colored pencils, markers, glue, scissors

Sequence:

STEP 1. Review the instructions with your teacher.

STEP 2. Submit a rough sketch of your scrapbook pages. Incorporate your teacher's suggestions into your draft. Work with a partner and present your drafts to each other.

STEP 3. Do a layout on construction paper.

STEP 4. Submit a draft of your captions.

STEP 5. Complete your scrapbook and present it to the class, describing the people in the photos and telling what they like and don't like to do.

Assessment:
Your teacher will use the rubric on the following page to assess this project.

Theme 1 Project: Álbum de recuerdos

RUBRIC	Score 1	Score 3	Score 5
Evidence of Planning	No written draft or page layouts provided.	Draft was written and layout created, but not corrected.	Evidence of corrected draft and layout.
Use of Illustrations	No photos/visuals included.	Photos/visuals were included, but the layout was unorganized.	Scrapbook was easy to read, complete, and accurate.
Presentation	Includes little of the required information for each photo.	Includes most of the required information for each photo.	Includes all of the required information for each photo.

School-to-Home Connection

Dear Parent or Guardian,

The theme for the chapter is *Mis amigos y yo* (My Friends and I) and this chapter is called *¿Qué te gusta hacer?* (What do you like to do?).

Upon completion of this chapter, your child will be able to:

- talk about activities he or she likes or doesn't like
- ask others what they like to do
- compare popular activities in the U.S. with those in some Spanish-speaking countries

Also, your child will explore:

- the correct pronunciation of the vowels *a, e,* and *i*
- how to recognize Spanish words based on their similarity to English words

Realidades helps with the development of reading, writing, and speaking skills through the use of strategies, process speaking, and process writing. In this chapter, students will:

- read e-mails from four students
- speak about their likes and dislikes

Remember that additional help is available online at www.realidades.com by using the Web Codes in the Student Edition or in the Leveled Vocabulary and Grammar Workbook.

Check it out! Have your child use the new vocabulary from this chapter to write five sentences about things he or she likes to do. Then have him or her explain the sentences to you in English.

Sincerely,

For: Tips to Parents
Visit: www.realidades.com
Web Code: jce-0010

Realidades A

Capítulo 1A Chapter Resource Checklist

Resources	CO†	APV	VH	MAN	LEC	CV	PO	MH	REP	PREP
Teacher										
Teacher's Resource Book										
Input Script										
Audio Script										
GramActiva BLM										
Communicative Activities BLM										
School-to-Home Connection BLM										
Clip Art										
Situation Cards BLM										
TPR Stories Book										
Fine Art Transparencies Teacher's Guide										
Pre-AP* Resource Book										
Student										
Leveled Vocabulary and Grammar Workbook										
Guided Practice										
Core Practice										
Communication Workbook with Test Preparation										
Writing										
Audio										
Video										
Test Preparation										
RPH Workbook										
Lecturas para hispanohablantes										
Grammar Study Guides										
Transparencies										
Answers on Transparencies										
Vocabulary and Grammar										
Fine Art										
Assessment										
Assessment Program										
Quizzes										
Chapter Test										
realidades.com										
ExamView Test Bank CD-ROM										
QuickTake on PresentationExpress										
MindPoint QuizShow CD-ROM										
Alternate Assessment Program										
Performance-Based Speaking										
Self-Test on realidades.com & CWS										
Assessment Program RPH										
Technology										
realidades.com										
myeBook										
TeacherExpress CD-ROM										
PresentationExpress DVD										
Video Program DVD										
Culture Video DVD										
Audio Program CD 2										
Assessment CD 20										
Song CD 22										
Canciones de hip hop on realidades.com & CWS										

† *See Abbreviation Key on page iv.*

Input Script

Presentation

Input Vocabulary: Place the overhead transparency on the screen. Point to each activity, model its pronunciation, and act it out. Then call out activities and have students act them out. Next, hand out copies of the Vocabulary Clip Art and have students tear them into individual images. Have them draw seven squares horizontally on a blank sheet of paper and write the days of the week above the squares. Tell students the day you like to do different activities and have them place the activities on the days you say. Or, to review time, have students draw a large clock on a sheet of paper and tell at what time you like to do the activities. Students will place the activities on the hour you say.

Input Dialogue 1: Role-play the first dialogue. Then ask for a student volunteer to play the role of the girl. Play the role of the boy in the dialogue. Point to one of the activities on the transparency. Have the student respond *"A mí también. Y también me gusta ___* (the activity you indicate)." Repeat with different student volunteers and different activities.

Input Dialogue 2: Role-play the second dialogue. Model *"¿Te gusta ___? / Sí, me gusta ___."* Then point to activities on the transparency and ask students *"¿Te gusta ___?"* Students will respond with *"Sí, me gusta ___"* and the activity. Next, model *"¿Qué te gusta hacer? / Me gusta ___."* Point to activities on the transparency and ask students *"¿Qué te gusta hacer?"* Students will respond with *"Me gusta ___"* and the activity. Then model *"Me gusta ___. ¿Y a ti? ¿Qué te gusta hacer?"* Students will respond with *"Me gusta ___"* and the activity of their choice. Finally, do a chain activity. Start with one student who says what he or she likes to do and then turns and asks another student what he or she likes to do *("Me gusta ___. ¿Y a ti? ¿Qué te gusta hacer?")*.

Input Dialogue 3: Model the third dialogue. Play the role of both people. Be sure to emphasize with body language the negative meaning of *"No me gusta nada"* and *"A mí tampoco."* Then point to activities on the transparency and model *"No me gusta nada __."* Have students respond *"A mí tampoco."* Then have students group their Clip Art images into these categories: ***Me gusta más, Me gusta mucho, Me gusta, No me gusta,*** and ***No me gusta nada.*** Have students tell the class one of the activities they placed in each category.

Input Dialogue 4: Model the fourth dialogue. Play the role of both people. Then point to activities on the transparency and model *"¿Qué te gusta más, ___ o ___?"* Emphasize the idea of two alternatives by holding out first your left hand, palm up, and then your right hand, palm up, as if weighing two choices. Point to activities on the transparency and ask students *"¿Qué te gusta más, ___ o ___?"* Next, model the phrase *"No me gusta ni ___ o ___."* Then tell students that when you say *"No me gusta ni ___ o ___. ¿Y a ti?"*, they should agree with you by saying *"A mí tampoco, no me gusta ni ___ o ___."*

Comprehension Check

- Talk about your own likes and dislikes. When students hear you say that you like an activity, have them hold up the Clip Art image of the activity and give you a "thumbs-up" sign. When students hear you say that you dislike an activity, have them hold up the image and give you a "thumbs-down" sign.
- Say that you are different famous people, either modern-day or historical, and then ask the class which activity they think you like more. Say, for example, *"Me llamo Picasso. ¿Qué me gusta más, escribir cuentos o dibujar?"* Students will hold up the Clip Art image of the activity they think the person would like more.

Audio Script

Audio CD, Capítulo 1A

Track 01: *A primera vista,* Student Book, p. 26 (2:16)

You will hear each word or phrase twice. After the first time there will be a pause so you can pronounce it, then you will hear the word or phrase a second time.

bailar	nadar
escuchar música	correr
practicar deportes	esquiar

Read along as you listen to the dialogues.

Male Teen 1: ¡Me gusta mucho bailar!

Female Teen 2: A mí también. Y también me gusta escuchar música.

Female Teen 1: ¡Hola, Beatriz! ¿Qué te gusta hacer? ¿Te gusta practicar deportes?

Female Teen 2: ¡Sí! Me gusta mucho practicar deportes. Me gusta correr, nadar y esquiar. ¿Y a ti? ¿Qué te gusta hacer?

Track 02: *A primera vista,* Student Book, p. 27 (2:11)

You will hear each word or phrase twice. After the first time there will be a pause so you can pronounce it, then you will hear the word or phrase a second time.

escribir cuentos	dibujar
montar en monopatín	cantar
ver la tele	montar en bicicleta
usar la computadora	jugar videojuegos

Read along as you listen to the dialogues.

Male Teen: A mí me gusta mucho escribir cuentos y dibujar. ¡No me gusta nada cantar!

Male Teen: ¡Uy! A mí tampoco.

Male Teen: ¿Qué te gusta más, ver la tele o montar en bicicleta?

Female Teen: Pues, no me gusta ni ver la tele ni montar en bicicleta. Me gusta usar la computadora y jugar videojuegos. Y a ti, ¿qué te gusta más?

Track 03: *A primera vista:* Act. 1, Student Book, p. 27 (1:21)

¿Te gusta o no te gusta?

You will hear Rosa say what she likes to do and doesn't like to do. Give a "thumbs-up" sign when you hear her say something she likes to do and a "thumbs-down" sign when she says something she doesn't like to do. You will hear each statement twice.

Female Teen: ¡Hola! Me llamo Rosa y me gusta mucho bailar.

También me gusta escuchar música y cantar.

No me gusta ver la tele ni jugar videojuegos.

Y tampoco me gusta nadar.

¡Uy! ¡Me gusta más bailar!

Track 04: *A primera vista:* Act. 2, Student Book, p. 27 (1:46)

Me gusta …

Listen to what some people like to do. Point to the picture of the activity each describes. You will hear each statement twice.

Male Teen 1: ¡Hola! Me llamo Sebastián y me gusta mucho montar en monopatín. También me gusta escribir cuentos y ver la tele.

Female Teen 1: Yo soy Valentina y a mí me gusta bailar, dibujar y montar en bicicleta.

Female Teen 2: Mi nombre es Carmen. Me gusta usar la computadora, escuchar música y esquiar.

Male Teen 2: Yo soy Daniel. A mí me gusta correr, practicar deportes y nadar.

Track 05: *A primera vista: Videohistoria,* Student Book, pp. 28–30 (1:37)

See Student Book pages 28–30 for script.

Track 06: *Pronunciación:* The vowels *a, e,* and *i,* Student Book, p. 35 (2:32)

The vowel sounds in Spanish are different from those in English. In Spanish, each vowel has just one sound. Spanish vowels are also quicker and shorter than those in English.

The letter *a* is similar to the sound in the English word *pop.* Listen to and say these words:

You will hear each word twice. After the word is pronounced the first time, there will be a pause so you can pronounce it. Then you will hear the word a second time.

andar	nadar
hablar	trabajar
cantar	pasar

The letter *e* is similar to the sound in the English word *met.* Listen to and say these words:

tele	Elena
me	deportes
es	

The letter *i* is similar to the sound in the English word *see.* As you have already seen, the letter *y* sometimes has the same sound as *i.* Listen to and say these words:

sí	lápiz
escribir	ti
patinar	mí

- Try it out! Listen to and say this rhyme.
  A E I El perro canta para ti.
  A E I El tigre baila para mí.

- Try it again, substituting *el gato* for *el perro* and *la cebra* for *el tigre.*

Track 07: Audio Act. 5, Writing, Audio & Video Workbook, p. 10 (2:48)

You can learn a lot about a person from what he or she likes to do. You will hear two people from each group of three describe themselves. Listen and match the descriptions to the appropriate pictures. Put an *A* underneath the first person described, and a *B* underneath the second person described. You will hear each set of statements twice.

1. **FEMALE TEEN 1:** ¡Hola! Me gusta hablar por teléfono.
   FEMALE TEEN 2: ¡Hola! Me gusta mucho nadar.
2. **MALE TEEN 1:** ¡Hola! Me gusta tocar la guitarra.
   MALE TEEN 2: ¡Hola! Me gusta montar en monopatín.
3. **FEMALE TEEN 3:** ¡Hola! Me gusta dibujar.
   FEMALE TEEN 4: ¡Hola! Me gusta bailar.
4. **MALE TEEN 3:** ¡Hola! Me gusta esquiar.
   MALE TEEN 4: ¡Hola! Me gusta leer revistas.
5. **FEMALE TEEN 5:** ¡Hola! Me gusta practicar deportes.
   FEMALE TEEN 6: ¡Hola! Me gusta usar la computadora.

Track 08: Audio Act. 6, Writing, Audio & Video Workbook, p. 11 (1:40)

A group of students from Peru will visit your school. Since your class will be hosting the students, your teacher is trying to match each of you with a visiting student who likes to do the same things as you do. Listen to the questions and write the students' answers in the blanks. Then write which of the activities you like better. Find out if the student has the same preference as you do. Follow the model. You will hear each conversation twice.

PROFESORA: ¿Te gusta más bailar o cantar?
GUILLERMO: Me gusta más cantar.

1. **PROFESORA:** ¿Te gusta más ver la tele o usar la computadora?
   PACO: Me gusta más usar la computadora.
2. **PROFESORA:** ¿Te gusta más jugar videojuegos o escuchar música?
   ANA MARÍA: Me gusta más escuchar música.
3. **PROFESORA:** ¿Te gusta más dibujar o leer?
   JOSÉ LUIS: Me gusta más dibujar.
4. **PROFESORA:** ¿Te gusta más escribir cuentos o practicar deportes?
   MARICARMEN: Me gusta más escribir cuentos.
5. **PROFESORA:** ¿Te gusta más pasar tiempo con amigos o hablar por teléfono?
   LUISA: Me gusta más pasar tiempo con amigos.

Track 09: *Manos a la obra:* Act. 13, Student Book, p. 37 (2:19)

Tres papeles
You will hear eight infinitives. After you hear the infinitive, hold up the piece of paper with the correct infinitive ending. You will hear each word twice.

1. patinar
2. correr
3. trabajar
4. escribir
5. leer
6. nadar
7. compartir
8. hacer

Track 10: *Manos a la obra:* Act. 18, Student Book, p. 38 (3:17)

Escucha y escribe
Write the numbers 1–7 on a sheet of paper. You will hear Raúl say seven things that he likes to do. Write them down as he says them. Spelling counts! You will hear each statement twice.

1. Me gusta tocar la guitarra.
2. Me gusta ver la tele.
3. También me gusta jugar videojuegos.
4. Me gusta ir a la escuela.
5. Me gusta patinar.
6. Me gusta usar la computadora.
7. ¡Y me gusta mucho escuchar música!

Track 11: *Manos a la obra:* Act. 20, Student Book, p. 41 (3:38)

El baile y la música del mundo hispano
Listen to each of the musical selections and make a list of instruments you hear in the different selections. You might need to listen to the music again.

Track 12: Song: *Castellana* (Traditional song from Spain) **(3:28)**

El flamenco es un baile típico de España. El instrumento más importante en el flamenco es la guitarra.

Track 13: Song: *La paloma* (0:26)

En Argentina, el tango es muy popular. Es un baile romántico.

Track 14: Song: *Merengue de la noche* (0:58)

En la República Dominicana, el baile tradicional es el merengue. El merengue tiene muchos ritmos africanos.

Track 15: Song: *Carnival salsa* (0:37)

En Puerto Rico, la salsa es el baile preferido. El ritmo de la salsa es popular en la música de Estados Unidos también.

Track 16: Song: *Cumbia sampuesana* (Traditional song from Colombia) **(0:44)**

La cumbia es el baile más famoso de Colombia.

Track 17: Audio Act. 7, Writing, Audio & Video Workbook, p. 12 (0:59)

As one of the judges at your school's fall carnival, your job is to mark on the master tic-tac-toe board the progress of a live tic-tac-toe competition between Team X and Team O.

As each contestant comes to the microphone, you will hear "*por X*" or "*por O*" to indicate for which team he or she is playing. The contestant has to answer a question about activities in order to claim the square. Listen for the activity mentioned in each question, and put either an *X* or an *O* in the box under the picture of that activity.

At the end of this game round, see which team won! You will hear each statement twice.

1. **Female Teen 1:** Por X … ¿Te gusta montar en bicicleta?
   Male Teen 1: Sí, me gusta montar en bicicleta.
2. **Female Teen 1:** Por O … ¿Te gusta usar la computadora?
   Female Teen 2: Sí, me gusta usar la computadora.
3. **Female Teen 1:** Por X … ¿Te gusta bailar?
   Male Teen 2: No, no me gusta bailar.
4. **Female Teen 1:** Por O … ¿Te gusta ver la tele?
   Male Teen 3: Sí, me gusta ver la tele.
5. **Female Teen 1:** Por X … ¿Te gusta correr?
   Male Teen 4: No, no me gusta correr.
6. **Female Teen 1:** Por O … ¿Te gusta dibujar?
   Female Teen 3: Sí, me gusta dibujar.
7. **Female Teen 1:** Por X … ¿Te gusta leer revistas?
   Female Teen 4: No, no me gusta leer revistas.

Track 18: Audio Act. 8, Writing, Audio & Video Workbook, p. 13 (0:38)

Luisa, the host of your school's radio station talk show, is interviewing four new students. As you listen to the interview, write down one thing that each student likes to do, and one thing that each student does not like to do. You will hear the entire question and answer session repeated. You will hear this conversation twice.

Adult Female: ¡Bienvenidos! Soy Luisa Luna. Quiero presentarles a cuatro estudiantes nuevos. Por favor, digan "hola."

Several Teens: ¡Hola!

Adult Female: Armando. ¿Te gusta practicar deportes?

Male Teen 1: No, no me gusta nada practicar deportes. Me gusta más jugar videojuegos.

Adult Female: Josefina. ¿Te gusta escuchar música?

Female Teen 1: No me gusta mucho escuchar música. Pero me gusta tocar la guitarra.

Adult Female: Carlos. ¿Te gusta nadar?

Male Teen 2: A mí no. No me gusta nadar en el verano. Hace mucho calor. Me gusta más leer.

Adult Female: Marta. ¿Qué te gusta hacer en el verano?

Female Teen 2: Pues… Me gusta nadar y montar en bicicleta. ¡A mí no me gusta hacer nada en el invierno! Ni esquiar, ni patinar.

Adult Female: Bueno. ¡Mucho gusto de hablar con Armando, Josefina, Carlos y Marta! Ahora, ¡hasta luego, les dice Luisa! Nos vemos en esta estación, KOTA, el miércoles a las siete de la noche! ¡Adiós!

You are going to hear this conversation again.

Track 19: Audio Act. 9, Writing, Audio & Video Workbook, p. 13 (3:36)

As you turn on the radio, you hear a Spanish radio D.J. talking about the "Top Ten Tips" for being happy during this school year. As you listen, match the suggestion to one of the pictures and number them in the order the suggestions were given on the air. Remember to listen for cognates!

Hola, muy buenos días. ¿Qué tal? Hoy es un día muy especial con una lista para ti… "Diez consejos para la escuela." Ahora…

Número diez… ¡Escribir cuentos!
Número nueve… ¡Montar en bibicleta!
Número ocho… ¡Leer un buen libro!
Número siete… ¡Escuchar a los amigos!
Número seis… ¡Hablar con amigos por teléfono!
Número cinco… ¡Cantar por la mañana!
Número cuatro… ¡Pasar más tiempo con amigos!
Número tres… ¡Bailar cuando llueve!
Número dos… ¡Tocar un instrumento musical!
Y número uno… ¡Preparar algo de chocolate!

You are going to hear this dialogue again.

Track 20: *La cultura en vivo*, Student Book, p. 48 (1:05)

¿Te gusta bailar?
First, listen to some mambo music. Then, read the directions and practice the dance steps.

Track 21: *Repaso*, Student Book, p. 52 (2:50)

Vocabulario y gramática
Listen to these words and expressions that you have learned in this chapter. You will hear each word or expression once.

Track 22: *Preparación para el examen*, Student Book, p. 52 (0:45)

Escuchar
Practice task.
Listen to a voice mail from a student looking for a "match-up" to the homecoming dance. a) What are two things this person likes doing? b) What is one thing this person dislikes doing?

Female Teen: "Pues … a mí me gusta practicar deportes y pasar tiempo con amigos. ¿Y bailar? No me gusta nada bailar. ¿Y a ti?"

Realidades A

Capítulo 1A

Video Script

A primera vista: ***Y tú, ¿cómo eres?*** **(3:56)**

Narrador: Bienvenidos al Capítulo 1A. Throughout the REALIDADES video program, teenagers from four countries will help you learn Spanish. Let's meet some of them now. First, let's go to Spain!

Ignacio: ¡Hola! ¿Qué tal? Me llamo Ignacio. Tengo 17 años.

Ana: Y yo me llamo Ana, y tengo 15 años. Ignacio, ¿qué te gusta hacer?

Ignacio: A mí me gusta tocar la guitarra. Me gusta la música.

Ana: Me gusta escuchar música también. Pero me gusta más hablar por teléfono.

Ignacio y Ana: ¡Hasta luego desde España!

Narrador: Now let's go to México.

Claudia: Hola. Me llamo Claudia y tengo 16 años.

Teresa: Y yo soy Teresa. Tengo 15 años.

Claudia: Me gusta usar la computadora. Y también pasar tiempo con mis amigos.

Teresa: A mí me gusta la computadora también, pero me gusta más jugar videojuegos.

Claudia y Teresa: Adiós desde México.

Narrador: Now let's visit San Antonio, Texas.

Esteban: Hola. Me llamo Esteban y tengo 15 años.

Angélica: Y yo me llamo Angélica, y tengo 16 años. Me gusta practicar deportes.

Esteban: ¿Te gusta correr?

Angélica: ¡Claro que sí! Y también me gusta montar en bicicleta.

Esteban: A mí no me gusta ni correr ni montar en bicicleta. A mí me gusta patinar.

Esteban y Angélica: Adiós desde San Antonio.

Narrador: Let's check in now on our friends in Costa Rica, the other country we'll visit.

Raúl: Hola. Me llamo Raúl y tengo 15 años.

Gloria: Y yo me llamo Gloria. Tengo 14 años. Raúl, ¿qué te gusta hacer?

Raúl: Me gusta leer. Me gusta leer libros y revistas.

Gloria: A mí me gusta ir a la escuela. Es importante estudiar.

Raúl: ¿Ir a la escuela?

Gloria: Sí. Y a ti, Raúl, ¿te gusta ir a la escuela?

Raúl: Pues … más o menos.

Gloria y Raúl: Adiós desde Costa Rica.

Narrador: Now you've met some of the teenagers who will be part of the REALIDADES video program. The episode for each chapter will help you learn the new vocabulary and grammar. ¡Buena suerte!

GramActiva Videos: infinitives; making negative statements **(4:37)**

Infinitives

Girl: We're going to jump in with both feet today and get going with the words that make it happen.

All: VERBS!

Hero: To infinitives and beyond!

Host: When you look for Spanish verbs in the dictionary, they are in the infinitive form. This is the most basic form. Infinitives always end in *-ar, -er,* or *-ir.*

Hero: And now, ten seconds of *-ar* verbs.

Host: *Jugar* is an *-ar* verb that means "to play," *usar* means "to use," *hablar* means "to talk," *escuchar* means "to listen," *tocar* means "to touch or play," *dibujar* means "to draw," *cantar* means "to sing," *bailar* means "to dance," *trabajar* means "to work," and *nadar* means "to swim."

Host: So do all verbs end in *-ar?* No. There are also verbs that end in *-er* like *correr,* which means "to run," and verbs that end in *-ir,* like *escribir,* which means "to write."

Hero: To infinitives and beyond!

Quiz

Host: It's a bird! It's a plane! It's a quiz?
The word that tells you what is happening in a sentence is called the verb.
Spanish verbs are found in the infinitive form.
The three types of infinitives are *-ar, -er,* and *-ir.*

Making Negative Statements

Host: We're not doing nothing today. We're all about negatives. In Spanish, to make a sentence negative, you simply add the word *no* before the verb or expression. So if someone said to you …

Hero: *Me gusta bailar.*

Host: You might say …

Old Man: Why is he running around in that costume?

Host: Uhmm. Or you might say …

Old Man: *No me gusta bailar.*

Host: See how simple that is?

Lesko: But wait, there's more. There's another word called *nada,* and when you use it together with *no,* it means *not at all.* Like this.

Old Man: *No me gusta nada la primavera.*

Host: In Spanish it tells us that you really don't like spring at all.

Lesko: Yeah, you tell 'em.

Host: And if you want to say you don't like either of two choices, use *ni … ni.*

Lesko: *¿Ni … ni?*

Girl: *Ni … ni.* The Spanish equivalents of "neither/nor." You can dislike all kinds of things. Put the word *no* before the verb, and *ni* before each of the things you don't like.

Old Man: *No me gusta ni bailar ni cantar.*

Girl: That's right.

Lesko: *No me gusta ni nadar ni esquiar.*

Girl: You got it.

Old Man: That's crazy, I don't like it.

Orange: Yeah, me neither.

Apple: You mean *a mí tampoco.*

Orange: What?

Apple: *A mí tampoco,* it means "me neither." *A mí tampoco.*

Orange: *¿A mí tampoco?*

Apple: *A mí tampoco.*

Host: So there you have it. *Adiós.*

Quiz

Host: How do you say you don't like to ski in Spanish?
No me gusta esquiar.
How do you say you don't like either to dance or swim?
No me gusta ni bailar ni nadar.
How do you say "me neither" in Spanish?
To say "me neither" in Spanish, you say *a mí tampoco.*

Nombre ______________________

Fecha ______________________

Communicative Activity **1A-1**

Estudiante **A**

You have been assigned to interview Verónica, an exchange student from Mexico, for Spanish class. Find out what Verónica likes and dislikes by asking your partner the following questions. Record his or her answers on the lines below.

1. ¿Te gusta bailar?

   ____

2. ¿Te gusta ir a la escuela?

   ____

3. ¿Te gusta nadar?

   ____

4. ¿Te gusta patinar?

   ____

5. ¿Te gusta ver la tele?

   ____

6. ¿Te gusta usar la computadora?

   ____

7. ¿Te gusta dibujar?

   ____

8. ¿Te gusta correr?

   ____

9. ¿Te gusta esquiar?

   ____

10. ¿Te gusta trabajar?

   ____

Now pretend that you are Manolo, an exchange student from Spain. Your partner has been assigned to interview you for the school newspaper. Answer your partner's questions according to the pictures.

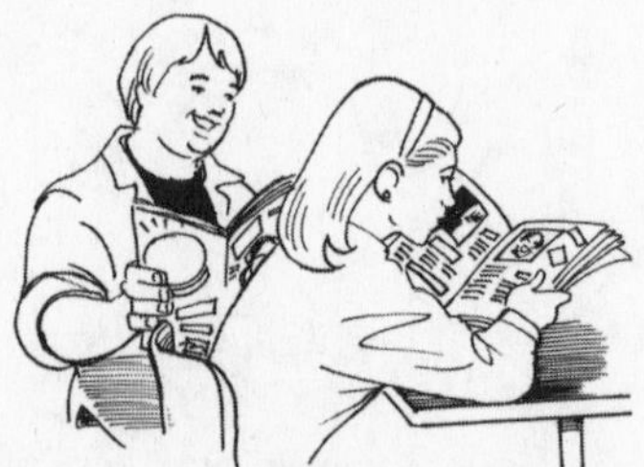

Nombre ______________________

Fecha ______________________

Pretend that you are Verónica, an exchange student from Mexico. Your partner has been assigned to interview you for Spanish class. Answer your partner's questions according to the pictures.

Now interview Manolo, an exchange student from Spain, for the school newspaper. Find out what Manolo likes and dislikes by asking your partner the following questions. Record his or her answers on the lines below.

1. ¿Te gusta tocar la guitarra?
   ____
2. ¿Te gusta cantar?
   ____
3. ¿Te gusta jugar videojuegos?
   ____
4. ¿Te gusta montar en bicicleta?
   ____
5. ¿Te gusta practicar deportes?
   ____
6. ¿Te gusta escuchar música?
   ____
7. ¿Te gusta hablar por teléfono?
   ____
8. ¿Te gusta escribir cuentos?
   ____
9. ¿Te gusta leer revistas?
   ____
10. ¿Te gusta pasar tiempo con amigos?
   ____

Realidades A Nombre ____________________

Capítulo 1A Fecha ____________________

Communicative Activity **1A-2**
Estudiante **A y B**

What do you like to do? From the list below, choose five activities that you like to do. Write them on the lines under *JUEGO UNO (Me gusta escuchar música.)*. Then, with a partner, take turns asking questions *(¿Te gusta nadar?)* to see who is the first to guess the other person's five characteristics. Respond to your partner's answers with the conversational responses below *(Reacciones)*. For *JUEGO DOS*, choose five characteristics that do not describe you *(No me gusta ver la tele.)*, and proceed as in *JUEGO UNO*. Use the columns marked 1 and 2 to record your partner's responses.

1	2	
______	______	bailar
______	______	cantar
______	______	correr
______	______	dibujar
______	______	escribir cuentos
______	______	escuchar música
______	______	esquiar
______	______	hablar por teléfono
______	______	ir a la escuela
______	______	jugar videojuegos
______	______	leer revistas
______	______	montar en bicicleta
______	______	nadar
______	______	pasar tiempo con amigos
______	______	patinar
______	______	practicar deportes
______	______	tocar la guitarra
______	______	trabajar
______	______	usar la computadora
______	______	ver la tele

JUEGO UNO

____

____

____

____

____

JUEGO DOS

____

____

____

____

____

REACCIONES

Yo no.

Yo sí.

Yo también.

Yo tampoco.

Realidades A Nombre ____________________

Capítulo 1A

Fecha ____________________

Communicative Activity 1A-3
Estudiante A

You have joined the Spanish Club and are getting to know other students in the club. Introduce yourself to your partner and ask him or her the questions below (you will have to fill in some information before you ask the questions). Use the responses provided to tell your partner if you like the same activities. Write your parner's answers on the lines next to the questions.

1. Hola. ¿Cómo te llamas? ____________________ .
2. Me llamo ____________________ . Mucho gusto ____________________ .
3. ¿Qué tal? ____________________ .
4. ¿Qué te gusta hacer? ____________________ . A mí también. / A mí tampoco.
5. ¿Qué te gusta más, ____________________ o ____________________ ?

   ____________________ . A mí también. / A mí tampoco.
6. ¿Te gusta ____________________ ? ____________________ . A mí también. / A mí tampoco.
7. ¡Hasta luego! ____________________

Realidades A Nombre ____________________

Capítulo 1A

Fecha ____________________

Communicative Activity 1A-3
Estudiante B

You have joined the Spanish Club and are getting to know other students in the club. Introduce yourself to your partner and ask him or her the questions below (you will have to fill in some information before you ask the questions). Use the responses provided to tell your partner if you like the same activities. Write your parner's answers on the lines next to the questions.

1. Buenos días. ¿Cómo estás? ____________________ .
2. Me llamo ____________________ . Y tú, ¿cómo te llamas? ____________________ .
3. Mucho gusto. ____________________ .
4. ¿Qué te gusta hacer? ____________________ . A mí también. / A mí tampoco.
5. ¿Qué te gusta más, ____________________ o ____________________ ?

   ____________________ . A mí también. / A mí tampoco.
6. ¿Te gusta ____________________ ? ____________________ . A mí también. / A mí tampoco.
7. ¡Hasta luego! ____________________

Situation Cards

Capítulo 1A **Realidades A** **1A**

Describing things you like to do

You are talking with a new student in your school.

— Greet the new student and then introduce yourself.

— Name an activity you really like to do. Ask the student if he or she enjoys it also.

— Respond to your classmate's question.

— Say good-bye to the student.

Capítulo 1A **Realidades A** **1B**

Describing things you like to do

You are talking with a student in your new school.

— Respond to your classmate with a greeting and your name.

— Answer the question positively. Ask the student what else he or she likes to do.

— Say good-bye to the student.

Capítulo 1A **Realidades A** **2A**

Describing things you don't like to do

You are talking with a friend about things you dislike doing.

— Greet your friend.

— Tell your friend one thing you don't like to do, and then ask if he or she dislikes doing it also.

— Respond to your friend's question.

— Say good-bye.

Capítulo 1A **Realidades A** **2B**

Describing things you don't like to do

You are talking with a friend about things you dislike doing.

— Greet your friend.

— Respond to your friend's question negatively, and then ask what else he or she doesn't like to do.

— Say good-bye.

Realidades A

Capítulo 1A

GramActiva

¿Qué te gusta hacer?

A mí me gusta mucho ..., p. 49

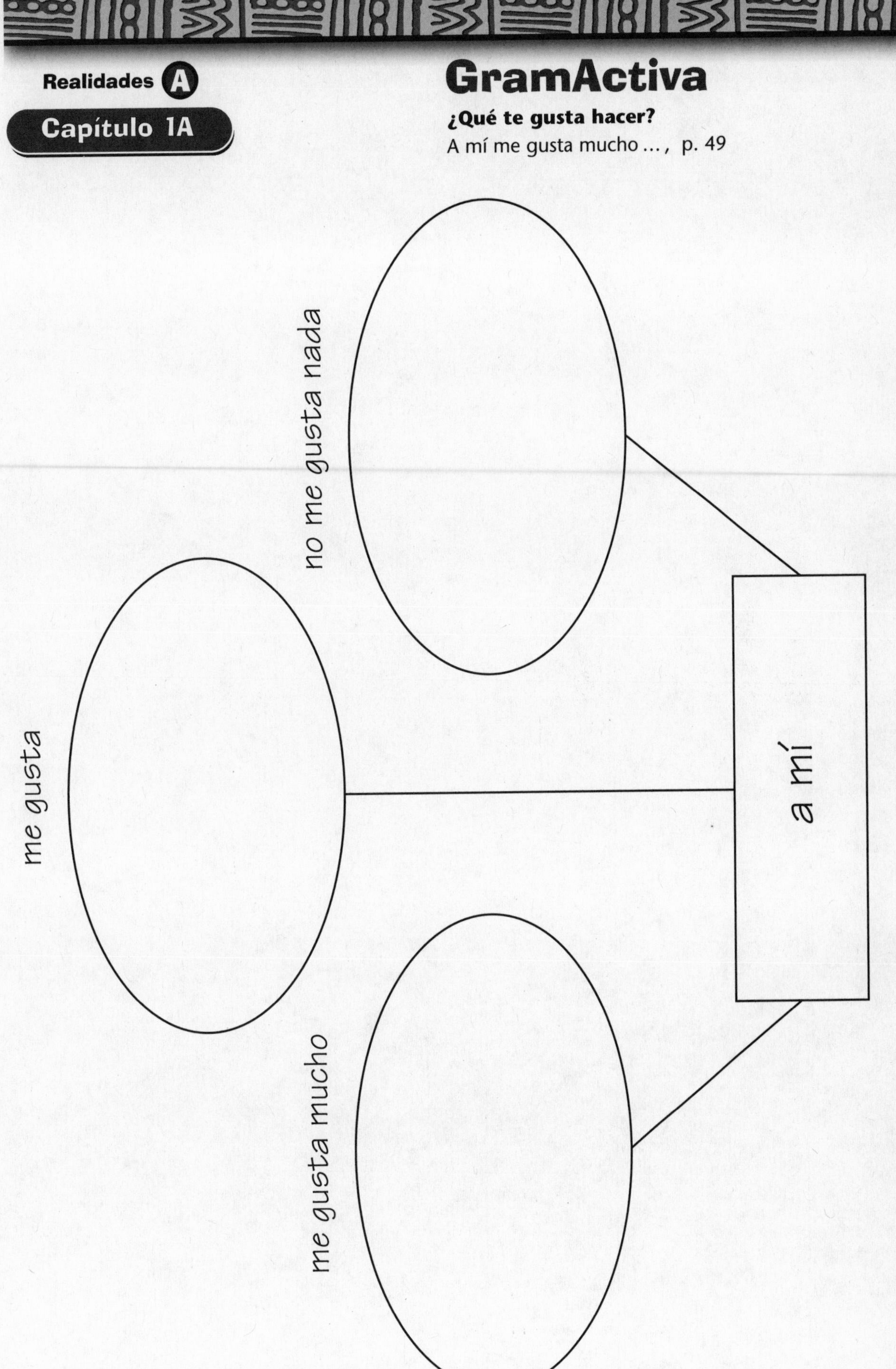

Realidades 

Capítulo 1A

Vocabulary Clip Art

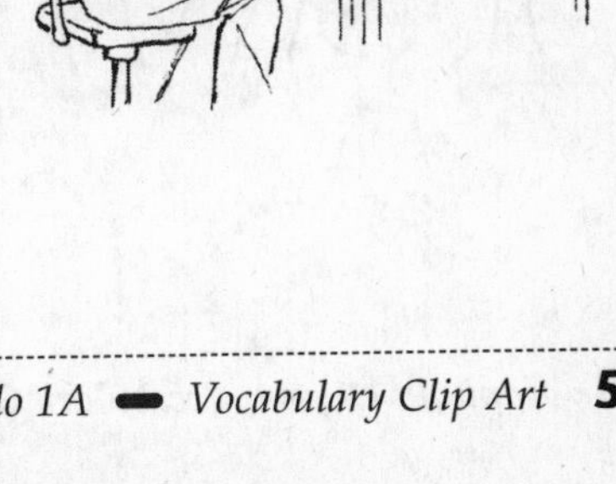

Vocabulary Clip Art

Realidades 

Capítulo 1A

Vocabulary Clip Art

Realidades A

Capítulo 1A

Core Practice Answers

1A-1
1. dibujar
2. cantar
3. bailar
4. montar en bicicleta
5. usar la computadora
6. esquiar
7. escuchar música
8. nadar
9. montar en monopatín
10. correr

1A-2
1. ENRIQUE: practicar deportes
   DOLORES: a mí también me gusta practicar deportes
2. PABLO: usar la computadora
   MARTA: no me gusta usar la computadora
3. JAIME: ver la tele
   JULIO: a mí tampoco me gusta (ver la tele)
4. MARÍA: nadar y correr
   JULIA: no me gusta ni nadar ni correr
5. CARMEN: escribir cuentos
   JOSEFINA: (amí) me gusta escribir cuentos
6. ROBERTO: montar en bicicleta
   PEDRO: también me gusta montar en bicicleta

1A-3
1. —leer
   —No, no me gusta nada.
2. —montar en bicicleta
   —Sí, me gusta mucho.
3. —ver la tele
   —Sí, me gusta mucho.
4. —bailar
   —No, no me gusta nada.
5. —jugar videojuegos
   —Sí, me gusta mucho.
6. —escuchar música
   —Sí, me gusta mucho.

1A-4
1. RITA: Me gusta / a ti
   MIGUEL: ir a la escuela / ni / ni
   RITA: A mí
2. JUAN: me gusta
   PAULA: A mí
   JUAN: Qué te gusta / hablar por teléfono
   PAULA: Me gusta más
   JUAN: también
3. AMELIA: me gusta
   CARLOS: pasar tiempo con mis amigos
   AMELIA: ____
   CARLOS: no me gusta trabajar
   AMELIA: A mí

1A-5
1. leer (col. 2)
2. esquiar (col. 1)
3. ir a la escuela (col. 3)
4. nadar (col. 1)
5. correr (col. 2)
6. hablar por teléfono (col. 1)
7. usar la computadora (col. 1)
8. ver la tele (col. 2)

1A-6
1. LOLA: ¿Te gusta ver la tele?
   CRISTINA: No, no me gusta nada ver la tele.
2. LOLA: ¿Te gusta ir a la escuela?
   CRISTINA: No, no me gusta nada ir a la escuela.
3. LOLA: ¿Te gusta cantar?
   CRISTINA: No, no me gusta nada cantar.
4. LOLA: ¿Te gusta trabajar?
   CRISTINA: No, no me gusta nada trabajar.
5. LOLA: ¿Te gusta nadar?
   CRISTINA: No, no me gusta nada nadar.

1A-7
GRACIELA: ____
SARA: Me gusta nadar.
GRACIELA: ____
SARA: me gusta ver la tele
GRACIELA: ____
SARA: te gusta
GRACIELA: Me gusta jugar videojuegos y usar la computadora.
SARA: ____
GRACIELA: Te gusta patinar
SARA: no me gusta
GRACIELA: ____
SARA: no me gusta ni bailar ni cantar
GRACIELA: te gusta hacer
SARA: Me gusta

Crucigrama (1A-8)
Across:
1. escribir
3. cantar
5. trabajar
6. leer
9. estudiar
10. bailar
13. practicar
14. patinar

Down:
2. correr
4. nadar
7. esquiar
8. usar
11. dibujar
12. hablar

Organizer (1A-9)
I. Vocabulary Answers will vary.
II. Grammar
1. to / -ar, -er, -ir
2. no
3. también / tampoco
4. ni, ni (ni)

Realidades A · Capítulo 1A

Nombre ____ Hora ____

Fecha ____

Vocabulary Flash Cards, Sheet 1

Write the Spanish vocabulary word below each picture. If there is a word or phrase, copy it in the space provided. Be sure to include the article for each noun.

Realidades A · Capítulo 1A

Nombre ____ Hora ____

Fecha ____

Vocabulary Flash Cards, Sheet 2

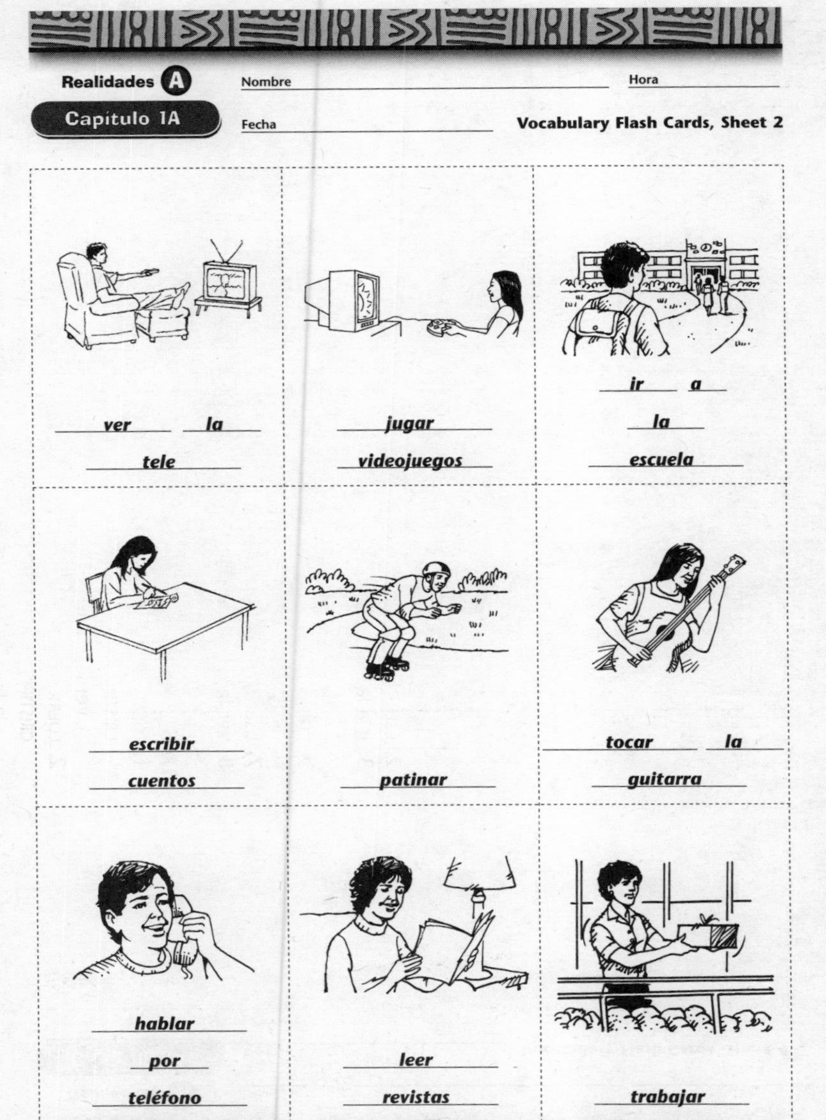

Realidades A — Capítulo 1A

Nombre ______ Hora ______

Fecha ______ **Vocabulary Flash Cards, Sheet 3**

pasar tiempo con amigos	*practicar deportes*	**sí** / *sí*
correr	**también** / *también*	**y** / *y*
pues... / *pues...*	**ni... ni** / *ni... ni*	**o** / *o*

Realidades A — Capítulo 1A

Nombre ______ Hora ______

Fecha ______ **Vocabulary Flash Cards, Sheet 4**

Realidades A | Nombre ______ | Hora ______

Capítulo 1A | Fecha ______ | **Vocabulary Check, Sheet 1**

Tear out this page. Write the English words on the lines. Fold the paper along the dotted line to see the correct answers so you can check your work.

bailar	***to dance***
cantar	***to sing***
correr	***to run***
dibujar	***to draw***
escribir cuentos	***to write stories***
escuchar música	***to listen to music***
esquiar	***to ski***
hablar por teléfono	***to talk on the phone***
ir a la escuela	***to go to school***
jugar videojuegos	***to play video games***
leer revistas	***to read magazines***
montar en bicicleta	***to ride a bicycle***
montar en monopatín	***to skateboard***

Fold In ←

Realidades A | Nombre ______ | Hora ______

Capítulo 1A | Fecha ______ | **Vocabulary Check, Sheet 2**

Tear out this page. Write the Spanish words on the lines. Fold the paper along the dotted line to see the correct answers so you can check your work.

to dance	***bailar***
to sing	***cantar***
to run	***correr***
to draw	***dibujar***
to write stories	***escribir cuentos***
to listen to music	***escuchar música***
to ski	***esquiar***
to talk on the phone	***hablar por teléfono***
to go to school	***ir a la escuela***
to play video games	***jugar videojuegos***
to read magazines	***leer revistas***
to ride a bicycle	***montar en bicicleta***
to skateboard	***montar en monopatín***

Fold In ←

Realidades A | Nombre ______ | Hora ______

Capítulo 1A | Fecha ______

Vocabulary Check, Sheet 3

Tear out this page. Write the English words on the lines. Fold the paper along the dotted line to see the correct answers so you can check your work.

nadar	***to swim***
pasar tiempo con amigos	***to spend time with friends***
patinar	***to skate***
practicar deportes	***to play sports***
tocar la guitarra	***to play the guitar***
trabajar	***to work***
usar la computadora	***to use the computer***
ver la tele	***to watch television***

Fold In ↓

Realidades A | Nombre ______ | Hora ______

Capítulo 1A | Fecha ______

Vocabulary Check, Sheet 4

Tear out this page. Write the Spanish words on the lines. Fold the paper along the dotted line to see the correct answers so you can check your work.

to swim	***nadar***
to spend time with friends	***pasar tiempo con amigos***
to skate	***patinar***
to play sports	***practicar deportes***
to play the guitar	***tocar la guitarra***
to work	***trabajar***
to use the computer	***usar la computadora***
to watch television	***ver la tele***

Fold In ↓

To hear a complete list of the vocabulary for this chapter, go to www.realidades.com and type in the Web Code jcd-0189. Then click on **Repaso del capítulo.**

Realidades A | Nombre ______ | Hora ______

Capítulo 1A | Fecha ______ | Guided Practice Activities 1A-1

Infinitives (p. 36)

- The most basic form of a verb is an *infinitive.*
- In English, infinitives have the word "to" in front of them such as *to walk* or *to swim.*
- In Spanish, infinitives end in **-ar (nadar)**, **-er (leer)**, or **-ir (escribir)**.

A. Look at each infinitive below and underline its ending. Follow the model.

Modelo patinar

1. escribir
2. nadar
3. correr
4. esquiar
5. usar
6. dibujar
7. leer
8. jugar
9. ver

B. Now, write the infinitive in the correct column of the chart. Is it an **-ar** verb, **-er** verb, or **-ir** verb? The first one has been done for you.

-ar verbs	*-er* verbs	*-ir* verbs
patinar	***correr***	***escribir***
nadar	***leer***	
esquiar	***ver***	
usar		
dibujar		
jugar		

C. Complete the sentences with infinitives from **part A** to express what you like and don't like to do. ***Answers will vary.***

1. Me gusta ______ y ______.
2. No me gusta ______.
3. Me gusta mucho ______.

realidades.com • Web Code: jcd-0103

Realidades A | Nombre ______ | Hora ______

Capítulo 1A | Fecha ______ | Guided Practice Activities 1A-2

Negatives (p. 42)

- To make an English sentence negative, you usually use the word "not": *I do **not** like to sing.*
- To make a Spanish sentence negative, you usually put **no** in front of the verb or expression: ***No* me gusta cantar.**
- To answer a Spanish question negatively, you often use **no** twice: **¿Te gusta bailar? *No, no* me gusta.**
- To say that you do not like something at all, you add the word **nada**: **No, no me gusta *nada*.**
- To say you don't like either of two choices, use **ni... ni: No me gusta *ni* correr *ni* practicar deportes.**

A. Look at the sentences and circle only the *negative* words you see. Some sentences do not have negative words. Follow the model. (*Hint:* There should be eight words circled.)

Modelo (No) me gusta cantar.

1. ¿Te gusta bailar?
2. (No), (no) me gusta bailar.
3. ¿Te gusta patinar?
4. (No), (no) me gusta (nada).
5. (No) me gusta (ni) bailar (ni) patinar.

B. You circled three different negative words in **part A** above. What are they? Write them on the lines.

no ______ ***nada*** ______ ***ni*** ______

C. Use the negative words **no, ni,** and **nada** to complete the following conversation.

ELENA: Enrique, ¿te gusta escuchar música?
ENRIQUE: No, ***no*** me gusta.
ELENA: ¿Te gusta bailar?
ENRIQUE: ***No***, no me gusta bailar.
ELENA: No te gusta ***ni*** escuchar música ***ni*** bailar. ¿Qué te gusta hacer?
ENRIQUE: ¡Me gusta ver la tele!
ELENA: ¡Uy, no me gusta ***nada***!

realidades.com • Web Code: jcd-0104

Realidades A | Nombre ______ | Hora ______

Capítulo 1A | Fecha ______ | Guided Practice Activities **1A-3**

Negatives *(continued)*

D. Complete the sentences with activities you don't like. You can use the drawings for ideas of activities. ***Answers will vary.***

1. No me gusta ______________.
2. No me gusta ______________.
3. No me gusta ni ____________ ni ____________.

E. Now answer the questions negatively. Follow the models.

Modelos ¿Te gusta esquiar?
No, no me gusta esquiar.
¿Te gusta correr y nadar?
No, no me gusta ni correr ni nadar.

1. ¿Te gusta dibujar?
   No, no me gusta dibujar.
2. ¿Te gusta cantar?
   No, no me gusta cantar.
3. ¿Te gusta escribir cuentos?
   No, no me gusta escribir cuentos.
4. ¿Te gusta esquiar y nadar?
   No, no me gusta ni esquiar ni nadar.
5. ¿Te gusta patinar y correr?
   No, no me gusta ni patinar ni correr.

realidades.com • Web Code: jcd-0104

Realidades A | Nombre ______ | Hora ______

Capítulo 1A | Fecha ______ | Guided Practice Activities **1A-4**

Expressing agreement or disagreement (p. 44)

- To agree with what another person likes, use **a mí también**:
  —Me gusta patinar.
  —**A mí también.**
- To agree with what another person dislikes, use **a mí tampoco**:
  —No me gusta cantar.
  —**A mí tampoco.**

A. The word web shows positive (agreement) words and negative (disagreement) words that you have learned. Look at the sample conversation, paying attention to the words **también** and **tampoco**. One of these two words is positive and one is negative. Write each word in the correct circle of the word web.

JUAN: A mí me gusta correr.
ANA: A mí **también**.
JUAN: No me gusta cantar.
ANA: A mí **tampoco**.

B. Now, complete the following exchanges with either **también** or **tampoco**.

1. JORGE: A mí me gusta mucho dibujar.
   SUSANA: A mí ***también***. +
2. LUIS: No me gusta nada hablar por teléfono.
   MARCOS: A mí ***tampoco***. –
3. OLIVIA: A mí no me gusta ni bailar ni correr.
   ALBERTO: A mí ***tampoco***. –
4. NATALIA: Me gusta esquiar. ¿Y a ti?
   JAVIER: A mí ***también***. +
5. SARA: A mí no me gusta trabajar.
   PABLO: A mí ***tampoco***. –
6. LORENA: Me gusta mucho montar en bicicleta. ¿Y a ti?
   MARTA: A mí ***también***. +

C. Look back at the exchanges in **part B** above. Put a plus (+) next to the exchange if it is positive. Put a minus (–) next to it if it is negative.

realidades.com • Web Code: jcd-0105

Lectura: ¿Qué te gusta hacer? (pp. 46–47)

A. The reading in your textbook contains four self-descriptions by students from various parts of the Spanish-speaking world. Read the following selection about Marisol. Then answer the questions that follow.

> *"¿Te gusta practicar deportes y escuchar música? ¡A mí me gusta mucho! También me gusta jugar al básquetbol. ¡Hasta luego!"*

1. Go back to the reading above and circle the sentence where Marisol is asking you a question.
2. Underline the words that tell you that Marisol is talking about things that she likes.
3. Now list the activities that Marisol likes to do in the spaces below:

   practicar deportes ***escuchar música*** ***jugar al básquetbol***

B. Read the following selection written by Pablo and answer the questions that follow.

> *"Me gusta mucho jugar al vóleibol y al tenis. Me gusta escribir cuentos y también me gusta organizar fiestas con amigos. No me gusta ni jugar videojuegos ni ver la tele. ¡Hasta pronto!"*

1. Underline the words that tell you that Pablo is talking about things that he likes.
2. Circle the things Pablo does not like.
3. Pablo is from «Guinea Ecuatorial». How would you write that in English?

   Equatorial Guinea

C. Some quotes from the reading are listed below. Identify the speaker of each by writing in their name and country of origin. Follow the model.

Modelo "Me gusta jugar al básquetbol." *Marisol* *Puerto Rico*

1. "Me gusta mucho ver la tele." ***Daniel*** ***Colombia***
2. "Me gusta escribir cuentos." ***Pablo*** ***Guinea Ecuatorial***
3. "Me gusta hablar por teléfono con amigos." ***Silvia*** ***España***
4. "Me gusta organizar fiestas con amigos." ***Pablo*** ***Guinea Ecuatorial***
5. "Me gusta tocar el piano." ***Daniel*** ***Colombia***

realidades.com
• Web Code: jcd-0106

Presentación oral (p. 49) ***Answers will vary.***

Task: Pretend that you are a new student at school. You have been asked to tell the class a little bit about your likes and dislikes.

A. Fill in each empty space in the diagram with at least two activities that represent you.

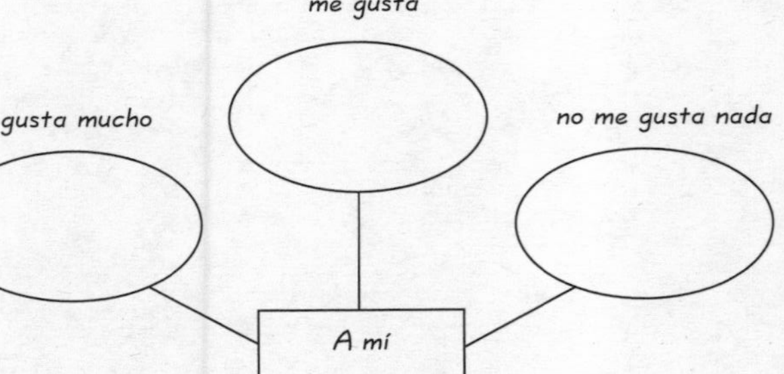

B. As part of your presentation, you will need to introduce yourself to everyone before you begin talking about your likes and dislikes. Think about how you would introduce yourself in Spanish to someone you don't know. Write one possibility below.

____

C. Now, add to your greeting by talking about what you like and dislike. Using your information from the diagram in **part A**, write three sentences describing what you like, what you like a lot, and what you do not like.

1. Me gusta ______________.
2. Me gusta mucho ______________.
3. No me gusta ______________.

D. Your teacher will always evaluate your presentations using a rubric, which is like a checklist of elements needed to perform your task. The fewer items completed, the lower the score. Some of the items for this presentation include:

- how much information you communicate
- how easy it is to understand you
- how clearly and neatly your visuals match what you are saying

Realidades A | Nombre ______ Hora ______

Capítulo 1A | Fecha ______ VIDEO

Introducción

Actividad 1

Do you like the video so far? Did you enjoy meeting the characters? Are you curious to find out more about their home cities? Look at the map below. Then, write the names of the video friends that live at each location. As you are doing this exercise, begin to familiarize yourself with the names of these locations: Madrid, España; Ciudad de México, México; San José, Costa Rica; San Antonio, Texas.

Esteban y Angélica	Ignacio y Ana	Claudia y Teresa	Raúl y Gloria

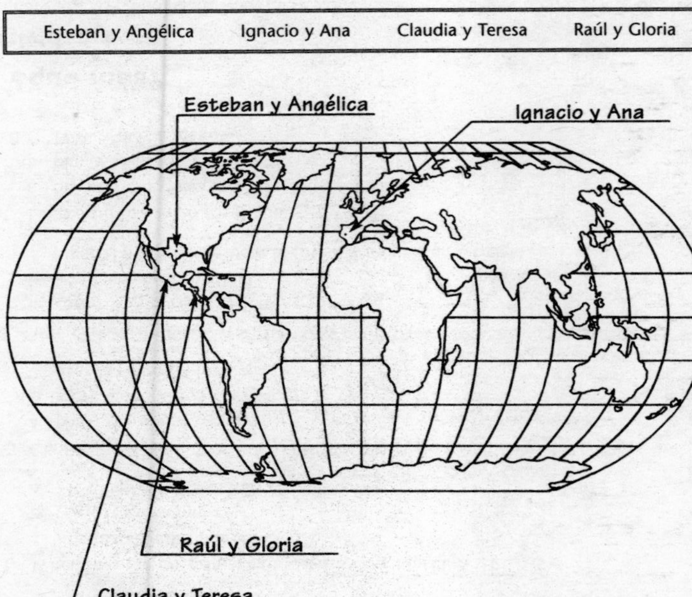

¿Comprendes?

Actividad 2

Match the characters with the activities they like to do or do not like to do.

1. Me llamo Ignacio y tengo 17 años. c
2. Yo me llamo Ana y tengo 15 años. a
3. Me llamo Claudia y tengo 16 años. b
4. Y yo soy Teresa. Tengo 15 años. g
5. Soy Esteban. Tengo 15 años. h
6. Yo me llamo Angélica y tengo 16 años. d
7. Soy Raúl y tengo 15 años. e
8. Me llamo Gloria y tengo 14 años. f

a. Me gusta escuchar música también. Pero me gusta más hablar por teléfono.
b. Me gusta usar la computadora.
c. A mí me gusta tocar la guitarra.
d. Me gusta practicar deportes, correr y montar en bicicleta.
e. Me gusta leer libros y revistas.
f. A mí me gusta ir a la escuela.
g. Me gusta más jugar videojuegos.
h. A mí no me gusta ni correr ni montar en bicicleta. A mí me gusta patinar.

Actividad 3

Decide whether response a, b, or c best describes the characters in each question.

1. When they are outside, what does Ana ask Ignacio? b
   a. ¿Te gusta hablar por teléfono?
   b. ¿Qué te gusta hacer?
   c. ¿Te gusta tocar la guitarra?
2. Claudia and Teresa live in Mexico. What do they both like to do? c
   a. pasar tiempo con amigos
   b. jugar videojuegos
   c. usar la computadora
3. What sports do Esteban and Angélica talk about? a
   a. correr, montar en bicicleta y patinar
   b. esquiar, correr y nadar
   c. jugar al básquetbol, jugar al fútbol y montar en bicicleta
4. Does Raúl like to go to school? c
   a. Sí. A Raúl le gusta mucho ir a la escuela.
   b. No. No le gusta nada.
   c. Pues… más o menos.

Y, ¿qué más?

Actividad 4

You have just seen and heard what these eight video friends like or do not like to do. Now fill in the blanks below to tell about things that you like to do and do not like to do.

1. Me gusta Answers will vary.
2. A mí me gusta más ____.
3. A mí no me gusta ____.
4. A mí no me gusta ni ____.

Realidades A Nombre ______ Hora ______

Capítulo 1A Fecha ______ AUDIO

Actividad 5

You can learn a lot about a person from what he or she likes to do. You will hear two people from each group of three describe themselves. Listen and match the descriptions to the appropriate pictures. Put an *A* underneath the first person described, and a *B* underneath the second person described. You will hear each set of statements twice.

1. Luisa ______	Marta A	Carmen B
2. Marco A	Javier ______	Alejandro B
3. Mercedes A	Ana B	María ______
4. Carlos ______	Jaime B	Luis A
5. Isabel B	Margarita A	Cristina ______

Realidades A Nombre ______ Hora ______

Capítulo 1A Fecha ______ AUDIO

Actividad 6

A group of students from Peru will visit your school. Since your class will be hosting the students, your teacher is trying to match each of you with a visiting student who likes to do the same things as you do. Listen to the questions and write the students' answers in the blanks. Then, write which of the activities you like better. Find out if the student has the same preferences as you do. Follow the model. You will hear each conversation twice.

Modelo Guillermo: *cantar*

A mí: *Me gusta más bailar*.

1. Paco: usar la computadora
   A mí: Answers will vary.
2. Ana María: escuchar música
   A mí: Answers will vary.
3. José Luis: dibujar
   A mí: Answers will vary.
4. Maricarmen: escribir cuentos
   A mí: Answers will vary.
5. Luisa: pasar tiempo con amigos
   A mí: Answers will vary.

Realidades A Nombre ______ Hora ______

Capítulo 1A Fecha ______ AUDIO

Actividad 7

As one of the judges at your school's fall carnival, your job is to mark on the master tic tac toe board the progress of a live tic-tac-toe competition between Team X and Team O.

As each contestant comes to the microphone, you will hear "por X" or "por O" to indicate for which team he or she is playing. The contestant has to answer a question about activities in order to claim the square. Listen for the activity mentioned in each question, and put either an *X* or an *O* in the box under the picture of that activity.

At the end of this game round, see which team won! You will hear each statement twice.

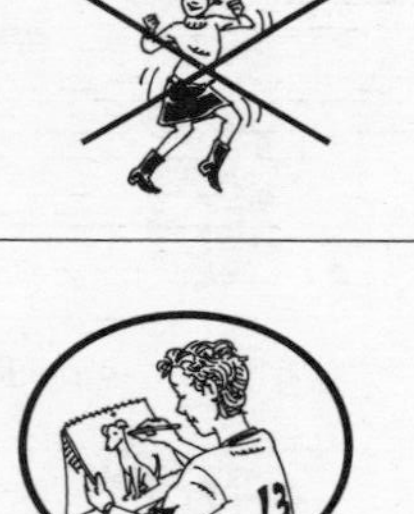

Who won the game? Team X

Realidades A Nombre ______ Hora ______

Capítulo 1A Fecha ______ AUDIO

Actividad 8

Luisa, the host of your school's radio station talk show, is interviewing four new students. As you listen to the interview, write down one thing that each student likes to do, and one thing that each student does not like to do. You will hear the entire question and answer session repeated. You will hear this conversation twice.

	Armando	Josefina	Carlos	Marta
Likes	jugar videojuegos	tocar la guitarra	leer	nadar y montar en bicicleta
Dislikes	practicar deportes	escuchar música	nadar en el verano	esquiar patinar

Actividad 9

As you turn on the radio, you hear a Spanish radio D.J. talking about the "Top Ten Tips" for being happy during this school year. As you listen, match the suggestion to one of the pictures and number them in the order the suggestions were given on the air. Remember to listen for cognates!

a. # 7	b. # 9	c. # 3	d. # 8	e. # 2
f. # 10	g. # 6	h. # 5	i. # 1	j. # 4

Actividad 10

Students like to do all sorts of activities during their free periods. Look at the picture below and write what each student is saying he or she likes to do. Then say whether or not you like to do those things. Follow the model.

Modelo EL PROFESOR: *A mí me gusta trabajar.*

TÚ: *A mí me gusta trabajar también.*

ESTUDIANTE #1: A mí me gusta tocar la guitarra.

TÚ: Answers will vary.

ESTUDIANTE #2: A mí me gusta leer revistas.

TÚ: Answers will vary.

ESTUDIANTE #3: A mí me gusta escuchar música.

TÚ: Answers will vary.

ESTUDIANTE #4: A mí me gusta jugar videojuegos.

TÚ: Answers will vary.

ESTUDIANTE #5: A mí me gusta hablar por teléfono.

TÚ: Answers will vary.

ESTUDIANTE #6: A mí me gusta dibujar.

TÚ: Answers will vary.

Actividad 11

It is your first day at your new school, and your new friend Elena is interviewing you for the school newspaper. In the spaces provided, write your answers to the questions that Elena asks you.

ELENA: —Buenos días. ¿Cómo estás?

TÚ: — Answers will vary.

ELENA: —¿Qué te gusta hacer?

TÚ: —

ELENA: —¿Te gusta ir a la escuela?

TÚ: —

ELENA: —¿Qué te gusta hacer en casa?

TÚ: —

ELENA: —¿Te gusta escribir o leer cuentos?

TÚ: —

ELENA: —¿Qué más te gusta hacer?

TÚ: —

ELENA: —Pues, muchas gracias por la entrevista. Buena suerte.

TÚ: —

Realidades A | Nombre ____ | Hora ____

Capítulo 1A | Fecha ____ | WRITING

Actividad 12

A. Your classmates have signed up for different clubs. Look at the flyers below to see who signed up for which club. Then, decide how each student might answer the questions below based on the club that each one signed up for.

El Club Educativo
El club ideal para estudiantes a quienes les gusta ir a la escuela.
Actividades:
- usar la computadora
- leer y escribir cuentos
- estudiar

Eduardo ____
Eugenia ____
Esteban ____

El Club Deportista
El club ideal para estudiantes a quienes les gusta practicar deportes.
Actividades:
- nadar
- correr
- practicar deportes

Diana ____
Dolores ____
Diego ____

EL CLUB MUSICAL
El club ideal para estudiantes a quienes les gusta la música.
ACTIVIDADES:
- TOCAR EL PIANO O LA GUITARRA
- CANTAR
- BAILAR

MARICARMEN ____
MANOLO ____
MÓNICA ____

Modelo Eduardo, ¿te gusta tocar la guitarra?

No, no me gusta tocar la guitarra. Me gusta estudiar. **Answers may vary.**

1. Diana, ¿te gusta leer o escribir cuentos?

   No, no me gusta ni leer ni escribir cuentos. Me gusta practicar deportes.

2. Manolo, ¿qué te gusta hacer?

   Me gusta tocar el piano y cantar.

3. Diego, ¿te gusta ir a la escuela para usar la computadora?

   No, no me gusta usar la computadora. Me gusta nadar y correr.

4. Mónica, ¿te gusta nadar o correr?

   No, me gusta ni nadar ni correr. Me gusta cantar y bailar.

5. Eugenia, ¿qué te gusta hacer?

   Me gusta leer y estudiar.

B. Now, pick which club you would join and say why. Follow the model.

Modelo *Prefiero el Club Educativo porque me gusta ir a la escuela.*

Prefiero el Club ____ porque ____

Answers will vary.

Realidades A | Nombre ____ | Hora ____

Capítulo 1A | Fecha ____ | WRITING

Actividad 13

A. Write two sentences about things that you like to do, and two sentences about things that you do not like to do. Follow the model.

Modelo *A mí me gusta leer.*

No me gusta correr.

1. **Answers will vary.**
2. ____
3. ____
4. ____

B. Now, use your sentences from Part A to write a letter to your new penpal that will tell her a little bit about you.

29/9/2003

Saludos,

Answers will vary, based on Part A.

También ____

Un abrazo,

____

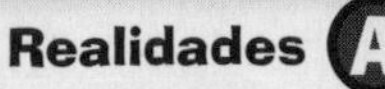

Test Preparation Answers

Reading Skills
p. 115 2. **c**
p. 116 2. **c**

Integrated Performance Assessment
p. 117
Answers will vary.

Practice Test: Friendship Among Latin Americans
p. 119

1. A
2. H
3. B
4. H
5. Answers will vary but may include: Advantages are learning to respect members of older and younger age groups, learning more about one's heritage and family traditions from older family members, learning to be more tolerant of those who are older and younger, learning to feel comfortable with diverse groups of people. Disadvantages may include that Latin Americans might not make a big effort to go beyond their circle of friends and family to meet new people. Also, the formality between young people and adults might be inhibiting to a close, personal relationship.

Realidades 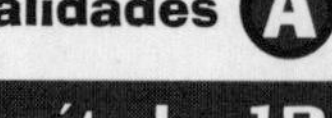

Capítulo 1B School-to-Home Connection

Dear Parent or Guardian,

The theme for the chapter is *Mis amigos y yo* (My Friends and I) and this chapter is called *Y tú, ¿cómo eres?* (What are you like?).

Upon completion of this chapter, your child will be able to:

- talk about personality traits
- ask and tell what people are like
- use adjectives to describe people
- understand cultural perspectives on what makes a good friend

Also, your child will explore:

- the correct pronunciation of the vowels *o* and *u*
- how to recognize words in Spanish that begin with *es-*

Realidades helps with the development of reading, writing, and speaking skills through the use of strategies, process speaking, and process writing. In this chapter, students will:

- read a personality self-quiz
- write a letter to a pen pal

Remember that additional help is available online at www.realidades.com by using the Web Codes in the Student Edition or in the Leveled Vocabulary and Grammar Workbook.

Check it out! Have your child write down the names of all the members of your family. Then have him or her write down an adjective from the chapter to describe each person.

Sincerely,

For: Tips to Parents
Visit: www.realidades.com
Web Code: jce-0010

Realidades **A**

Capítulo 1B Chapter Resource Checklist

Resources	CO†	APV	VH	MAN	LEC	PER	PE	MH	REP	PREP
Teacher										
Teacher's Resource Book										
Input Script										
Audio Script										
GramActiva BLM										
Communicative Activities BLM										
School-to-Home Connection BLM										
Clip Art										
Situation Cards BLM										
TPR Stories Book										
Fine Art Transparencies Teacher's Guide										
Pre-AP* Resource Book										
Student										
Leveled Vocabulary and Grammar Workbook										
Guided Practice										
Core Practice										
Communication Workbook with Test Preparation										
Writing										
Audio										
Video										
Test Preparation										
RPH Workbook										
Lecturas para hispanohablantes										
Grammar Study Guides										
Transparencies										
Answers on Transparencies										
Vocabulary and Grammar										
Fine Art										
Assessment										
Assessment Program										
Quizzes										
Chapter Test										
realidades.com										
ExamView Test Bank CD-ROM										
QuickTake on PresentationExpress										
MindPoint QuizShow CD-ROM										
Alternate Assessment Program										
Performance-Based Writing										
Self-Test on realidades.com & CWS										
Assessment Program RPH										
Technology										
realidades.com										
myeBook										
TeacherExpress CD-ROM										
PresentationExpress DVD										
Video Program DVD										
Culture Video DVD										
Audio Program CD 3										
Assessment CD 20										
Song CD 22										
Canciones de hip hop on realidades.com & CWS										

† *See Abbreviation Key on page iv.*

Input Script

Presentation

Input Vocabulary: Place the overhead transparency on the screen. Hand out copies of the Vocabulary Clip Art and have students tear the images into individual traits. Point to each trait and model its pronunciation as you act it out. Do the same for the traits in the box on page 51. Ask students about each trait: "*¿Es una característica positiva o negativa?*" Have them categorize the images into two piles: ***positiva*** and ***negativa***. Next, with an erasable marker, write on the transparency the name of a celebrity who clearly represents each trait and the name of a celebrity who clearly does not represent each trait. For example, by ***deportista*** write *Michael Jordan* on one side and *Michael Jackson* on the other side. Ask students if each one has that trait. Students will say "yes" by holding the Clip Art image of that trait right side up. Students will hold the image upside down to say "no."

Input Monologue 1: Model the first four sentences of the monologue. Then point to a male student and say "*¿El chico? Es mi amigo. ¿Cómo se llama? Se llama ___.*" Next, point to several male students and ask the class "*¿El chico, cómo se llama?*" Then point to female students and ask "*¿Y la chica? ¿Cómo se llama?*"

Then point to the first picture of Marcos and say "*¿Cómo es? Él es deportista. Le gusta mucho practicar deportes.*" Then approach pairs of male students. Ask one student "*¿Cómo es ___?*" Point to one of the positive traits on the transparency and nod your head to show that he should say that the other student has that trait. Then point to one of the negative traits and ask "*¿Pero a veces es un chico ___?*" and have the student agree with you. Get the rest of the class involved by asking "*¿Es la verdad?*" Students will hold up the Clip Art image of the trait only if they agree. Repeat with other students and traits.

Input Monologue 2: Model the first sentence. Then approach pairs of female students whom you know to be friends and ask each student "*¿Es ___ una buena amiga?*"

Next, point to the first picture of Sarita on the transparency and say "*Ella no es muy deportista pero es una chica artística.*" Then point to one of the female students and say "*___ no es muy deportista, pero es una chica ___.*" and point to one of the traits on the transparency. Have her friend agree with you by saying "*Sí, ___ no es muy deportista, pero es una chica ___.*" Involve the rest of the class by asking individual students and the whole class "*¿Es la verdad?*" Repeat with other students and traits.

Input Monologue 3: Model the third monologue. Emphasize "*¿Yo? ¿Cómo soy?*" by pointing to yourself dramatically. Point to each picture as you say and then act out the rest of the monologue. Then ask students "*¿Cómo eres?*" and point to a personality trait.

Comprehension Check

- Tell students that they are all twins who were separated at birth. Give each student a Clip Art image showing a personality trait. On the back of each image, write two activities from Chapter 1A. Hand out the Clip Art, making sure there are pairs of the Clip Art that are identical. Students will circulate around the room asking each other "*¿Cómo eres? ¿Qué te gusta hacer?*" to find their twin.
- Make statements about teachers at your school and have students give "thumbs-up" or "thumbs-down" signs to show they agree or disagree.

Realidades A

Capítulo 1B

Audio Script

Audio CD, Capítulo 1B

Track 01: *A primera vista,* Student Book, p. 56 (1:35)

Vocabulario y gramática en contexto

Read along as you listen to the dialogues.

Adult Female: La chica

Female Teen 1: ¿El chico? Es mi amigo. ¿Cómo se llama? Se llama Marcos. ¿Cómo es? Pues … él es deportista. Le gusta mucho practicar deportes. Pero a veces es impaciente, también es un chico desordenado.

Adult Female 2: El chico

Male Teen 1: Mi amiga Sarita es una buena amiga. Ella no es muy deportista … pero es una chica artística y muy ordenada. Es una chica muy inteligente.

Track 02: *A primera vista,* Student Book, p. 57 (1:59)

Female Teen 2: Hola, me llamo Luz. ¿Yo? ¿Cómo soy? Pues … soy estudiosa … y trabajadora y también graciosa pero según mi familia, ¡a veces soy perezosa! Y tú, ¿cómo eres?

Más vocabulario

You will hear each word twice. After the word is pronounced the first time there will be a pause so you can pronounce it, then you will hear the word a second time.

atrevido, atrevida
paciente
reservado, reservada
simpático, simpática
talentoso, talentosa

Track 03: *A primera vista,* Act. 1, Student Book, p. 57 (1:45)

¿Marcos o Sarita?

Look at the pictures of Marcos and Sarita. Listen to the descriptions. If a word describes Marcos, point to his picture. If a word describes Sarita, point to her picture. You will hear each word or phrase twice.

1. deportista
2. artística
3. inteligente
4. impaciente
5. ordenada
6. desordenado
7. el chico
8. buena amiga

Track 04: *A primera vista,* Act. 2, Student Book, p. 57 (1:31)

¿Cierto o falso?

You will hear some statements about Luz. Give a "thumbs-up" sign if the statement is true, or a "thumbs-down" sign if it is false. You will hear each statement twice.

¿Cómo es Luz?
Es estudiosa.
Es impaciente.
Es muy graciosa.
Es ordenada.
Es trabajadora.
Es talentosa.
Pero, según la familia, ¡a veces es perezosa!

Track 05: *A primera vista, Videohistoria,* Student Book, pp. 58–60 (2:30)

Amigos por Internet

Read along as you listen to the *Videohistoria.*

See Student Book pages 58–60 for script.

Track 06: Audio Act. 5, Writing Audio, & Video Workbook, p. 21 (4:34)

You are a volunteer for a service at your school that helps new students meet other new students in order to make the transition easier. People who are interested in participating in this program have left messages describing themselves. Listen as the students describe themselves, and put a check mark in at least two columns that match what each student says. Then write the names of the most well-matched students. You will hear each statement twice.

1. **Female Teen 1:** Hola. Me llamo Carmen. Soy estudiosa y me gusta ir a la escuela. Soy trabajadora y muy seria. A veces me gusta escribir cuentos también.
2. **Male Teen 1:** Hola. Me llamo Pablo. Soy deportista. Me gusta Arnold Schwarzenegger. Él es deportista también. Según mis amigos, soy gracioso y sociable.
3. **Female Teen 2:** Hola. Me llamo Ana. Me gusta leer novelas y revistas románticas. Según mis amigos, soy muy reservada. Me gusta dibujar y soy artística.
4. **Male Teen 2:** Hola. Me llamo Andrés. Me gusta pasar tiempo con mis amigos, pero soy muy reservado. Soy artístico, y me gusta mucho el arte moderno. Me gusta leer, dibujar y escuchar música.
5. **Female Teen 3:** Hola. Me llamo Raquel. Soy deportista y me gusta mucho jugar a los deportes. A veces soy atrevida. Según mis amigas, soy muy graciosa y sociable.
6. **Male Teen 3:** Hola. Me llamo Jorge. Me gusta ir a la escuela y soy estudioso. Soy bastante serio y muy trabajador, pero también me gusta escribir cuentos y tocar la guitarra.

Track 07: Audio Act. 6, Writing, Audio & Video Workbook, p. 22 (3:26)

What is your favorite season of the year? Your choice could say a lot about you. Listen as talk-show psychologist Doctor Armando describes people according to their preferred season *(estación preferida)* of the year. What characteristics go with each season? Listen and put a check mark in the appropriate boxes. By the way, is it true what he says about you and your favorite season? You will hear each statement twice.

Adult Male 1: Hola, ¿cómo estás? ¡Soy yo, el doctor Armando! ¡El tema para hoy es … ¡la conexión de las estaciones del año y las personalidades de las personas! ¿Cuál es tu estación favorita? ¿Cómo eres tú?

1. ¿Te gusta el verano? ¿Eres muy deportista, no? Según tu estación preferida, eres gracioso y atrevido. También te gusta nadar y bailar.
2. ¿Te gusta el invierno? No tienes personalidad de verano. Según tu estación preferida, eres muy talentoso. Eres muy serio y estudioso. También eres reservado y trabajador.
3. ¿Te gusta la primavera? Según tu estación preferida, eres impaciente, pero simpático. Eres una persona artística, ¿no? Probablemente te gusta dibujar o cantar.
4. Y finalmente … ¿te gusta el otoño? ¡A mí también! Yo soy muy sociable y paciente. ¿Y tú?

Track 08: Audio Act. 7, Writing, Audio & Video Workbook, p. 23 (2:33)

Your Spanish teacher encourages you to speak Spanish outside of class. As you walk down the hall, you hear parts of your classmates' conversations in Spanish. Listen to the conversations and decide whether they are talking about a boy, a girl, or if you can't tell by what is being said. Place a check mark in the appropriate box of the table. You will hear each statement twice.

1. **Male Teen 1:** Es una chica muy estudiosa.
2. **Male Teen 2:** Según mis amigos, es muy atrevida y graciosa.
3. **Female Teen 1:** Le gusta practicar deportes y es muy sociable.
4. **Female Teen 2:** Es un chico muy inteligente.
5. **Female Teen 3:** A veces es perezoso y *muy* desordenado.
6. **Male Teen 3:** Le gusta cantar y es muy talentosa.
7. **Male Teen 2:** ¿Cómo es? Según Carlos, es muy serio y trabajador.
8. **Female Teen 1:** Es sociable, y muy deportista también.

Track 09: *Manos a la obra,* Act. 19, Student Book, p. 70 (1:53)

¿El o la?

Write the word *el* in large letters on a sheet of paper or on an index card. Write *la* in large letters on another sheet. You will hear eight words you already know. When you hear a masculine word, hold up the paper with *el.* When you hear a feminine word, hold up the paper with the word *la* on it. You will hear each word twice.

1. libro	5. escuela
2. carpeta	6. chico
3. chica	7. sábado
4. profesor	8. amiga

Track 10: Audio Act. 8, Writing, Audio & Video Workbook, p. 23 (3:22)

Listen as Nacho describes his ex-girlfriend. How many things do they have in common? Put an X on the pictures that show ways in which they are very different and put a circle around the pictures that show ways they are very similar. You will hear each set of statements twice.

1. ¡No es una chica muy independiente! A mí me gusta pasar mucho tiempo con mis amigos. Pero a ella le gusta pasar tiempo conmigo: el lunes, el martes, el miércoles, el jueves, el viernes, el sábado y el domingo.
2. Es una chica muy estudiosa y le gusta ir a la escuela. A mí me gusta ir a la escuela también. Soy muy trabajador y ella también.
3. Ella es muy artística, pero yo no. Me gusta más montar en bicicleta o en monopatín.
4. Soy un chico impaciente. No me gusta hablar treinta minutos por teléfono. ¡Pero a ella le gusta hablar y hablar y hablar!
5. Soy un chico ordenado, pero ella es muy desordenada. Según mi familia, soy "Nacho el ordenado." Según la familia de ella, ella es "Dora la desordenada."

Track 11: Audio Act. 9, Writing, Audio & Video Workbook, p. 24 (3:25)

Some people say we are what we dream! Listen as Antonieta calls in and describes her dream *(sueño)* to Doctor Armando, the radio talk-show psychologist. Draw a circle around the pictures below that match what she dreams about herself.

After you hear Antonieta's call, tell a partner what kinds of things would be in a dream that reveals what you like to do and what kind of person you are. You might begin with, *"En mi sueño, me gusta …"* You will hear this dialogue twice.

Girl: Hola, Doctor Armando. Me llamo Antonieta. Pues … en mi sueño me gusta esquiar en las montañas de Colorado con mis amigos.

Doctor: Hmmm. Muy interesante. ¡Eres una chica muy atrevida! Y deportista también. ¿Qué más?

Girl: También me gusta bailar cuando nieva y me gusta cantar cuando llueve.

Doctor: ¿Bailar y cantar? Eres muy talentosa.

Girl: Pues … en mi sueño, hay un profesor con libros y mapas. Es el Sr. Cruz. En la clase me gusta hacer, hmmm …

Doctor: ¿Qué te gusta hacer, chica?

Girl: ¡Pues, en mi sueño me gusta ir a la escuela! Me gusta leer libros de México, Costa Rica, España, etcétera.

Doctor: ¡Ah! ¡Eres una chica inteligente y trabajadora! ¡Te gusta ver el mundo, niña! Hasta luego, Antonieta.

You are going to hear this conversation again.

Track 12: *Pronunciación,* The vowels *o* and *u,* Student Book, p. 71 (1:21)

In Spanish, the pronunciation of the letter *o* is similar to the vowel sound in the English word *boat* but is always cut very short. Say these words, concentrating on making a short *o* sound:

You will hear each word twice. After the word is pronounced the first time, there will be a pause so you can pronounce it. Then you will hear the word a second time.

bolígrafo	tampoco
teléfono	cómo
gracioso	otoño

In Spanish, the pronunciation of the letter *u* is similar to the vowel sound in the English word *zoo*. Say these words:

mucho	estudioso
octubre	usted
lunes	según

¡Ojo! Careful! Sometimes the words we mispronounce most are the ones that remind us of English words. Try it out! Pronounce these words, concentrating on the Spanish vowel sounds:

agosto	tropical
gusto	Uruguay
regular	música
universidad	Cuba

Track 13: *Manos a la obra,* Act. 24, Student Book, p. 73 (3:34)

You will hear a description of Arturo, Marta, and Belinda. Write what you hear. You will hear each sentence twice.

Arturo es un chico atrevido y serio. Le gusta mucho esquiar.
Marta es una chica inteligente, paciente y trabajadora.
Belinda es muy sociable. Le gusta hablar con los amigos.

Track 14: *Repaso del capítulo,* Student Book, p. 82 (3:27)

Listen to these words and expressions that you have learned in this chapter. You will hear each word or expression once.

See Student Book page 82 for vocabulary list.

Track 15: *Preparación para el examen,* Student Book, p. 83 (0:53)

Practice task.

Listen as a character in a Spanish soap opera describes his ex-girlfriend. What does he think her good qualities are? What does he think her shortcomings are? Can you understand why he broke up with her?

MALE TEEN 2: ¿Cómo es María Elena? Pues … es una chica inteligente y talentosa, pero es muuuy seria. Y no es sociable. Yo soy un chico gracioso y muy sociable. A mí me gustan más las chicas atrevidas.

Realidades A

Capítulo 1B

Video Script

A primera vista: ***Amigos por Internet*** **(6:36)**

Esteban: Hola desde San Antonio. Hola, Pedro. ¿Cómo estás?

Pedro: Regular, ¿y tú?

Esteban: Bien. Vamos a la computadora …

Pedro: Sí, vamos. Escucha.

Hola. ¿Cómo eres? ¿Qué te gusta hacer? ¡Escríbeme!

Chica sociable

Hola, *Chica sociable:*

Me llamo *Chico sociable.* ¡Qué coincidencia! Me gusta pasar tiempo con mis amigos...

Esteban: ¿ … bailar y cantar?

Pedro: Buena idea …

Esteban: Pero, eres reservado. No te gusta ni bailar ni cantar.

Pedro: No importa.

Me gusta escuchar música. Según mis amigos soy muy gracioso. No soy muy serio. Escríbeme.

Chico sociable

Pedro: ¿Está bien?

Esteban: Magnífico.

Pedro: ¡Ya!

Teresa: Claudia, ¡mira!

Claudia: ¡Es increíble!

Teresa: Hola, *Chica sociable:*

Claudia: ¡*Chica sociable!* ¡Qué nombre!

Teresa: Yo soy *Chica sociable.*

Claudia: ¡No! ¿Tú eres *Chica sociable?* Mi buena amiga, *Chica sociable.* ¡Ay no!

Teresa: ¡Sí!

Claudia: Muy bien, *Chica sociable.*

Me llamo *Chico sociable.* ¡Qué coincidencia! Me gusta pasar tiempo con mis amigos, bailar y cantar. Me gusta escuchar música. Según mis amigos, soy muy gracioso. No soy muy serio. Escríbeme.

Chico sociable

Claudia: A ver, vamos a contestar …

Teresa: ¿De veras?

Claudia: ¡Sí!

Hola, *Chico sociable:*

Te gusta bailar y cantar, ¿no? ¿Y no eres serio? Pues, yo tampoco. Soy muy desordenada. Me gusta hablar por teléfono. Y no me gusta ir a la escuela. Escríbeme.

Chica sociable

Teresa: Muy bien.

Claudia: Un mensaje más. De mí.

Teresa: ¿Sí? ¿Y cómo te llamas?

Claudia: Eh, *Chica misteriosa.*

Teresa: ¡Fabuloso!

Claudia: *Chico sociable:* Soy amiga de *Chica sociable.* Según mis amigas …

Pedro: … soy muy simpática. Y me gusta la escuela.

Claudia: Soy estudiosa y trabajadora. Me gustan los chicos inteligentes y ordenados…

Pedro: … No eres mi chico ideal. Pero, ¿tienes un amigo?

Claudia: *Chica misteriosa.*

Esteban: Pues, Pedro. ¿*Chica sociable* o *Chica misteriosa?*

Pedro: Uh … pues, *Chica misteriosa.* Me gusta la escuela y a ella le gusta la escuela también. Y me gusta una chica inteligente.

Esteban: Perfecto. Para mí, *Chica sociable* y para ti, *Chica misteriosa.*

Pedro: Sí... sí. Ahora. Ya voy. Esteban, tengo que ir. Adiós … y gracias. Hasta mañana.

Esteban: Bueno, hasta mañana.

Esteban: Hola, *Chica misteriosa.* Yo también soy muy estudioso. No soy perezoso. Me gusta la escuela …

GramActiva Videos: adjectives; definite and indefinite articles; word order; placement of adjectives **(6:56)**

Adjectives

Guy: Are you artistic, athletic, funny, smart, or talented? You should use some adjectives and let the world know! Here's how it works.

Host: Nouns are things. *Cat*'s a noun, *dog*'s a noun, *Arizona* is a noun, a *bus* is a noun, and the *Artist Formerly Known as Prince* is a noun. But let's face it, some nouns are boring on their own. That's why we created adjectives: to pick it up a notch. Bam! Adjectives describe nouns in more detail. So now we have big cats, mad dogs, and Arizona is really, really hot.

Host: In English, you usually place adjectives in front of the noun they describe like, she's a smart student. In Spanish, the adjectives usually come after the nouns.

Foreman: For example, if a female student is intelligent, you might say *una estudiante inteligente,* and a patient young man would be *un chico paciente.*

Girl: In Spanish, every noun has a gender. Your eyes, for example, are masculine but your head is feminine, and the telephone is masculine.

Host: When you use an adjective, you have to use the masculine form in Spanish with masculine nouns, and the feminine form with feminine nouns.

Song: You say *graciosa*, I say *gracioso.* You say *artística,* I say *artístico, ordenada, ordenado, talentosa,* …

Girl: *Nada talentoso.*

Host: All you have to do is to match them together.

chica atrevida

amigo reservado

Remember that in Spanish, the adjective usually goes after the noun. It's as simple as that.

Boy: You say *paciente,* I say *paciente.* You say *inteligente,* I say *inteligente, impaciente, impaciente.* I don't get it.

Host: Not all adjectives have masculine and feminine forms. Adjectives that end in *e* describe either gender.

Chico impaciente y chica impaciente.

Un chico inteligente y una chica inteligente.

Lesko: But wait, there's more! Some adjectives are convertible! If it ends in *or,* like *trabajador,* it is a masculine adjective! To make it feminine just add an *a* to the end! Like this!
Un chico trabajador y una chica trabajadora.

Quiz

Host: Let's review. Which of these words are masculine, which of these are feminine, and which ones do not indicate any gender?
Paciente, impaciente, artístico, graciosa, inteligente, atrevido, reservada, ordenado, desordenada, estudioso, talentosa, trabajadora, perezoso.

Host: Thanks for joining us.

Articles in Agreement

Host: We're here in the United States Library of Congress. We're going to look at a few of my favorite articles.

Host: In the English language there is only one definite article, *the. The* cat, *the* dog, *the* cats, *the* dogs. It's all the same to the word *the.* In Spanish, the articles change according to the gender and number of the noun. We're going to look at the two singular ones, *el* and *la.*

Dog: If you remember, in Spanish, all nouns have a gender. You use *el* or *la* depending on the gender of the noun they accompany. *El* is masculine; *la* is feminine. So we say things like:
el chico, la chica, el profesor, la profesora, etc. …

Host: Feminine nouns: *la carpeta, la profesora, la hoja de papel.* Masculine nouns: *el libro, el cuaderno, el pupitre, el bolígrafo.*

Host: That was just the definite articles. Definite articles talk about one noun in particular. There are also indefinite articles.

Host: So, for instance, if it was raining cats and dogs and the Queen said, "Get me *a* dog," any dog would do; that makes it indefinite. But if she said "Get me *the* cat," she's looking for one in particular; that makes it definite.

Host: The indefinite articles in English are *a/an. A* bug, *an* insect. In Spanish the singular indefinite articles are *un* and *una,* and guess what?

Host: *Un* is masculine, *una* is feminine. You use *un* with masculine nouns, and *una* with feminine nouns. So you would say *una carpeta, una profesora, una hoja de papel; un libro, un cuaderno, un pupitre, un bolígrafo.*

Host: It's as simple as that. Let's review.

Quiz

Host: Match the following English articles with their Spanish equivalents.
El libro.
La carpeta.

Host: *Un chico.*
Una profesora.

Nombre ______________________

Fecha ______________________

Get to know your partner better by asking the following questions. Write down your partner's answers. You don't need to write complete sentences every time. Respond to your partner's answers with the expressions below *(Reacciones)*.

1. ¿Eres más artístico o deportista?

   ____

2. ¿Eres más desordenado o reservado?

   ____

3. ¿Eres más serio o gracioso?

   ____

4. ¿Eres más perezoso o trabajador?

   ____

5. ¿Eres más inteligente o talentoso?

   ____

6. ¿Eres más paciente o impaciente?

   ____

7. ¿Eres más ordenado o desordenado?

   ____

8. ¿Eres más reservado o sociable?

   ____

REACCIONES

Yo también.

No soy ______________ tampoco.

Realidades A

Capítulo 1B

Nombre ______________________________

Fecha ______________________________

Communicative Activity **1B-1**

Estudiante **B**

Get to know your partner better by asking the following questions. Write down your partner's answers. You don't need to write complete sentences every time. Respond to your partner's answers with the expressions below *(Reacciones)*.

1. ¿Eres más atrevido o reservado?

   ____

2. ¿Eres más estudioso o perezoso?

   ____

3. ¿Eres más simpático o impaciente?

   ____

4. ¿Eres más perezoso o deportista?

   ____

5. ¿Eres más ordenado o desordenado?

   ____

6. ¿Eres más inteligente o estudioso?

   ____

7. ¿Eres más trabajador o perezoso?

   ____

8. ¿Eres más talentoso o artístico?

   ____

REACCIONES

Yo también.

No soy ____________________ tampoco.

Realidades A

Capítulo 1B

Nombre ______

Fecha ______

Communicative Activity **1B-2**

Estudiante **A**

You have just met Alicia and Iván, two new students at your school, and want to know more about them. Your partner will describe them to you by reading a list of characteristics. You have to decide whether each characteristic you hear describes Alicia or Iván. Write each characteristic in the column under the person it describes.

Hint: Listen carefully to the end of each adjective in order to decide if the adjective describes a girl, Alicia, or a boy, Iván.

Alicia	Iván

Now describe José and Ana, two exchange students from Costa Rica, to your partner by reading the list of characteristics below. Be careful not to say the name of the person each characteristic describes. Your partner will have to decide if the characteristics describe José or Ana.

1. Es artístico. (José)
2. Es graciosa. (Ana)
3. Es reservado. (José)
4. Es desordenado. (José)
5. Es simpática. (Ana)
6. Es atrevida. (Ana)
7. Es trabajadora. (Ana)
8. Es ordenada. (Ana)
9. Es serio. (José)
10. Es perezoso. (José)

Realidades A | Nombre

Capítulo 1B

Fecha

Communicative Activity **1B-2**
Estudiante **B**

Describe Alicia and Iván, two new students at your school, to your partner by reading the list of characteristics below. Be careful not to say the name of the person each characteristic describes. Your partner will have to decide if the characteristics describe Alicia or Iván.

1. Es talentosa. (Alicia)
2. Es ordenada. (Alicia)
3. Es trabajador. (Iván)
4. Es seria. (Alicia)
5. Él es deportista. (Iván)
6. Es estudiosa. (Alicia)
7. Es atrevido. (Iván)
8. Es graciosa. (Alicia)
9. Es desordenado. (Iván)
10. Es simpático. (Iván)

You have just met José and Ana, two exchange students from Costa Rica, and want to know more about them. Your partner will describe them to you by reading a list of characteristics. You have to decide whether each characteristic you hear describes Alicia or Iván. Write each characteristic in the column under the person it describes.

Hint: Listen carefully to the end of each adjective in order to decide if the adjective describes a girl, Ana, or a boy, José.

José	Ana

Situation Cards

Capítulo 1B **Realidades A** **1A**

Describing yourself and others

You and a new friend are talking about what you are like.

— Greet your new friend.

— Ask your friend what he or she is like.

— Respond to your friend's question and then ask what your friend's teacher is like.

— Respond to your friend's question.

— Say good-bye.

Capítulo 1B **Realidades A** **2A**

Talking about a friend

You and a friend are talking about what other people are like.

— Greet your friend.

— Ask your friend the name of a friend.

— Now ask what his or her friend is like.

— Finally ask what his or her friend likes or doesn't like.

Capítulo 1B **Realidades A** **1B**

Describing yourself and others

You and a new friend are talking about what you are like.

— Greet your new friend.

— Respond to your friend's question and then ask what he or she is like.

— Answer your friend's question. Ask what his or her teacher is like.

— Say good-bye.

Capítulo 1B **Realidades A** **2B**

Talking about a friend

You and a friend are talking about what other people are like.

— Greet your friend.

— Respond to your friend's questions.

GramActiva

Y tú, ¿cómo eres?
El poema "Soy Elena," p. 69

____

____

____

____

____

____

____

____

Vocabulary Clip Art

Vocabulary Clip Art

Realidades A

Capítulo 1B

Core Practice Answers

1B-1
1. deportista
2. graciosa
3. impaciente
4. desordenado
5. sociable
6. estudiosa
7. talentoso
8. artística

1B-2
1. artística
2. atrevido
3. desordenado
4. trabajadora
5. graciosa
6. perezosa
7. reservado
8. estudiosa

1B-3
1. soy talentoso
2. soy estudiosa
3. no soy desordenado (soy ordenado)
4. no soy deportista
5. soy sociable
6. no soy paciente (soy impaciente)
7. soy inteligente
8. no soy artística

1B-4
1. Esteban es talentoso.
2. Pedro es sociable.
3. Claudia es deportista.
4. Teresa es estudiosa (inteligente / trabajadora / seria).
5. Luz es perezosa.
6. Manuela es estudiosa (trabajadora / seria).
7. Carmen es sociable.
8. Lucía es artística.

1B-5
1. me gusta practicar deportes / soy deportista
2. me gusta dibujar / soy artística
3. me gusta estudiar / soy estudioso
4. me gusta trabajar / soy trabajadora
5. me gusta hablar por teléfono / soy sociable
6. me gusta montar en monopatín / soy atrevido

1B-6

A.
1. un libro
2. una carpeta
3. una computadora
4. un lápiz
5. un cuaderno
6. un bolígrafo

B.
1. El estudiante es ordenado.
2. El chico es artístico.
3. La chica es perezosa.
4. La familia es deportista.
5. La profesora es inteligente.
6. El profesor es desordenado.

1B-7

Answers will vary.

Crucigrama (1B-8)

Across:

4. seria
7. simpática
9. bueno
10. cómo
12. inteligente
14. estudiosa
17. ordenado
19. trabajador
20. artística

Down:

1. familia
2. impaciente
3. desordenado
5. deportista
6. gusta
8. atrevida
11. perezoso
13. reservado
15. talentosa
16. sociable
18. eres

Organizer (1B-9)

I. Vocabulary Answers will vary.

II. Grammar
1. -a / -o
2. -ista (deportista) / -e (inteligente)
3. el, la / un, una
4. after

Realidades A | Nombre _______ Hora _______

Capítulo 1B | Fecha _______

Vocabulary Flash Cards, Sheet 1

Write the Spanish vocabulary word below each picture. If there is a word or phrase, copy it in the space provided. Be sure to include the article for each noun.

artística	trabajadora	deportista
graciosa	perezosa	sociable
desordenado	estudiosa	inteligente

Realidades A | Nombre _______ Hora _______

Capítulo 1B | Fecha _______

Vocabulary Flash Cards, Sheet 2

serio	la chica	el chico
impaciente	ordenada	**bueno, buena** bueno, buena
atrevido, atrevida atrevido, atrevida	**paciente** paciente	**reservado, reservada** reservado, reservada

Realidades A | Nombre | Hora

Capítulo 1B | Fecha | **Vocabulary Flash Cards, Sheet 3**

simpático, simpática *simpático*, *simpática*	**talentoso, talentosa** *talentoso*, *talentosa*	**yo** *yo*
él *él*	**ella** *ella*	**la familia** *la* *familia*
el amigo *el* *amigo*	**la amiga** *la* *amiga*	**a veces** *a* *veces*

Realidades A | Nombre | Hora

Capítulo 1B | Fecha | **Vocabulary Flash Cards, Sheet 4**

muy *muy*	**pero** *pero*	**según** *según*
según mi familia *según* *mi* *familia*		

Realidades A

Nombre ____ Hora ____

Capítulo 1B

Fecha ____ **Vocabulary Check, Sheet 1**

Tear out this page. Write the English words on the lines. Fold the paper along the dotted line to see the correct answers so you can check your work.

artístico, artística	***artistic***
atrevido, atrevida	***daring***
bueno, buena	***good***
deportista	***sports-minded***
desordenado, desordenada	***messy***
estudioso, estudiosa	***studious***
gracioso, graciosa	***funny***
impaciente	***impatient***
inteligente	***intelligent***
ordenado, ordenada	***neat***
paciente	***patient***
perezoso, perezosa	***lazy***

Fold In

Realidades A

Nombre ____ Hora ____

Capítulo 1B

Fecha ____ **Vocabulary Check, Sheet 2**

Tear out this page. Write the Spanish words on the lines. Fold the paper along the dotted line to see the correct answers so you can check your work.

artistic	***artístico, artística***
daring	***atrevido, atrevida***
good	***bueno, buena***
sports-minded	***deportista***
messy	***desordenado, desordenada***
studious	***estudioso, estudiosa***
funny	***gracioso, graciosa***
impatient	***impaciente***
intelligent	***inteligente***
neat	***ordenado, ordenada***
patient	***paciente***
lazy	***perezoso, perezosa***

Fold In

Realidades A | Nombre ______ Hora ______

Capítulo 1B | Fecha ______ **Vocabulary Check, Sheet 3**

Tear out this page. Write the English words on the lines. Fold the paper along the dotted line to see the correct answers so you can check your work.

reservado, reservada	***reserved, shy***
serio, seria	***serious***
simpático, simpática	***nice, friendly***
sociable	***sociable***
talentoso, talentosa	***talented***
trabajador, trabajadora	***hardworking***
el chico	***boy***
la chica	***girl***
el amigo	***friend (male)***
la amiga	***friend (female)***
yo	***I***
él	***he***
ella	***she***
muy	***very***
según mi familia	***according to my family***

Fold In

Realidades A | Nombre ______ Hora ______

Capítulo 1B | Fecha ______ **Vocabulary Check, Sheet 4**

Tear out this page. Write the Spanish words on the lines. Fold the paper along the dotted line to see the correct answers so you can check your work.

reserved, shy	***reservado, reservada***
serious	***serio, seria***
nice, friendly	***simpático, simpática***
sociable	***sociable***
talented	***talentoso, talentosa***
hardworking	***trabajador, trabajadora***
boy	***el chico***
girl	***la chica***
friend (male)	***el amigo***
friend (female)	***la amiga***
I	***yo***
he	***él***
she	***ella***
very	***muy***
according to my family	***según mi familia***

To hear a complete list of the vocabulary for this chapter, go to www.realidades.com and type in the Web Code jcd-0199. Then click on **Repaso del capítulo.**

Fold In

Adjectives (p. 64)

- Words that describe people and things are called adjectives.
- Most Spanish adjectives have two forms: masculine (ends in **-o** like **simpático**) and feminine (ends in **-a** like **estudiosa**).
- Masculine adjectives are used with masculine nouns: **Tomás es simpático.**
- Feminine adjectives are used with feminine nouns: **Luisa es estudiosa.**
- Adjectives that end in **-e** and **-ista** may be used with either masculine or feminine nouns:
  - **Tomás es inteligente. Luisa es inteligente también.**
  - **Marcos es muy deportista. Ana es muy deportista también.**
- Adjectives with the masculine form **-dor** have **-dora** as the feminine form:
  - **Juan es trabajador. Susana es trabajadora también.**

A. Look at the adjectives below. Circle the ending of the adjective: **-o, -a, -or, -ora, -e,** or **-ista**.

1. trabajador
2. deportista
3. paciente
4. ordenada
5. inteligente
6. simpática
7. trabajadora
8. sociable
9. estudioso

B. Now, organize the adjectives from **part A** by writing them in the chart under the correct column heading. One has been done for you.

Masculine endings		Feminine endings		Masculine or feminine	
-o	*-or*	*-a*	*-ora*	*-e*	*-ista*
estudioso	*trabajador*	***ordenada***	***trabajadora***	***paciente***	***deportista***
		simpática		***inteligente***	
				sociable	

C. Now look at the following sentences. Write **M** next to the sentences where the adjective is masculine. Write **F** next to the sentences where the adjective is feminine. Write **E** next to the sentences where the adjective could be *either* masculine or feminine.

F 1. Yo soy muy simpática.
M 2. Tú eres muy estudioso.
M 3. Tú eres muy ordenado.
F 4. Yo soy muy trabajadora.
E 5. Yo soy muy inteligente.
M 6. Tú eres muy trabajador.
E 7. Yo soy muy paciente.
E 8. Yo soy muy deportista.
F 9. Tú eres muy reservada.
E 10. Tú eres muy impaciente.

Adjectives *(continued)*

D. Choose the correct adjective to complete each sentence and write it in the blank.

1. Raúl es (estudioso / estudiosa) ***estudioso***.
2. Rebeca es (artístico / artística) ***artística***.
3. Pedro es muy (ordenado / ordenada) ***ordenado***.
4. Paulina es muy (atrevido / atrevida) ***atrevida***.
5. Javier es (trabajador / trabajadora) ***trabajador***.
6. Elena es (perezoso / perezosa) ***perezosa***.

E. Now, choose the correct adjective in each sentence to describe yourself. Write the adjective in the blank. ***Answers will vary.***

1. Yo soy (**paciente / impaciente**) ________.
2. Soy (**simpático / simpática**) ________.
3. También soy (**trabajador / trabajadora**) ________.
4. No soy (**serio / seria**) ________.

Realidades A | Nombre ______ | Hora ______

Capítulo 1B | Fecha ______ | **Guided Practice Activities 1B-3**

Definite and indefinite articles (p. 70)

- **El** and **la** are the Spanish *definite articles*. They mean the same as "the" in English.
- You use **el** with masculine nouns: **el libro**. You use **la** with feminine nouns: **la carpeta**.
- **Un** and **una** are the Spanish *indefinite articles*. They mean the same as "a" and "an" in English.
- You use **un** with masculine nouns: **un libro**. You use **una** with feminine nouns: **una carpeta**.

A. Look at the ending of each noun in this group. Decide if the noun is masculine or feminine. Write **M** next to the masculine words and **F** next to the feminine words. Follow the model.

Modelo *F* computadora

1. *M* año
2. *F* semana
3. *M* libro
4. *F* hoja
5. *F* carpeta
6. *M* profesor

B. Now, look at the words from **part A** again and circle the definite article **el** for the masculine words and the definite article **la** for the feminine words.

1. ([el] / la) año
2. (el / [la]) semana
3. ([el] / la) libro
4. (el / [la]) hoja
5. (el / [la]) carpeta
6. ([el] / la) profesor

C. Look at the ending of each noun below. Decide if the word is masculine or feminine. Write **M** next to the masculine words and **F** next to the feminine words.

1. *M* cuaderno
2. *M* amigo
3. *F* revista
4. *F* familia
5. *F* bicicleta
6. *M* cuento

D. Now, look at the words from **part C** again and circle the indefinite article **un** for the masculine words and the indefinite article **una** for the feminine words.

1. ([un] / una) cuaderno
2. ([un] / una) amigo
3. (un / [una]) revista
4. (un / [una]) familia
5. (un / [una]) bicicleta
6. ([un] / una) cuento

E. Circle the correct definite or indefinite article to complete each sentence.

1. (El / [La]) estudiante es estudiosa.
2. (El / [La]) profesora es buena.
3. ([Un] / Una) amigo es simpático.
4. (Un / [Una]) estudiante es atrevida.
5. ([El] / La) profesor es trabajador.
6. ([Un] / Una) estudiante es artístico.
7. (El / [La]) amiga es inteligente.
8. (Un / [Una]) estudiante es reservada.

realidades.com • Web Code: jcd-0113

Realidades A | Nombre ______ | Hora ______

Capítulo 1B | Fecha ______ | **Guided Practice Activities 1B-4**

Word order: Placement of adjectives (p. 72)

- English adjectives usually come *before* the noun they describe.
- Spanish adjectives usually come *after* the noun they describe:
  Olga es una chica talentosa.
- Many Spanish sentences follow this pattern:
  subject noun (1) + verb (2) + indefinite article and noun (3) + adjective (4)
  Roberto (1) es (2) un estudiante (3) bueno (4). **Serena (1) es (2) una chica (3) inteligente (4).**

A. Look at the following groups of words. Write a number from **1** to **4** below each word according to what kind of word it is. Follow the model and use the examples above.

- Write **1** for subject nouns.
- Write **2** for verbs.
- Write **3** for indefinite articles and nouns.
- Write **4** for adjectives.

Modelo es / Diego / talentoso / un estudiante
2 1 4 3

1. seria / Olga / una estudiante / es
   4 1 3 2
2. un amigo / es / bueno / Guillermo
   3 2 4 1
3. Javier / un estudiante / es / trabajador
   1 3 2 4
4. es / Concha / simpática / una chica
   2 1 4 3
5. es / una estudiante / Ana / inteligente
   2 3 1 4
6. Manuel / es / atrevido / un chico
   1 2 4 3

B. Now, write the complete sentence for each example from **part A** by putting the words in order by the numbers you added, going from 1 to 4. Follow the model.

Modelo *Diego es un estudiante talentoso.*

1. ***Olga es una estudiante seria.***
2. ***Guillermo es un amigo bueno.***
3. ***Javier es un estudiante trabajador.***
4. ***Concha es una chica simpática.***
5. ***Ana es una estudiante inteligente.***
6. ***Manuel es un chico atrevido.***

realidades.com • Web Code: jcd-0115

Realidades A | Nombre ______ Hora ______

Capítulo 1B | Fecha ______ **Guided Practice Activities 1B-5**

Lectura: Un *self-quiz* (p. 76–77)

A. You have seen many cognates used in your textbook. Cognates are related words in different languages; for example, the word **profesor** in Spanish is a *professor* or *teacher* in English. Cognates occur in your vocabulary lists and in readings. Look at the cognates below and write the English word for each on the line provided. Follow the model.

Modelo bicicleta *bicycle*

1. computadora ***computer***
2. básquetbol ***basketball***
3. la tele ***T.V.***
4. los colores ***colors***
5. verbo ***verb***
6. usar ***to use***
7. organizar ***to organize***
8. estudiar ***to study***

B. Now, read the following section from your textbook. You will find even more cognates in this reading. Find the Spanish word that corresponds to each English word below. Write the Spanish word on the lines provided.

> *¡Los colores revelan tu personalidad!*
> *¿Eres una chica? ¿Te gusta el verde? Eres una chica natural.*
> *¿Eres una chica? ¿Te gusta el azul? Eres muy talentosa.*
> *¿Eres una chica? ¿Te gusta el violeta? Eres muy independiente.*

- personality ***personalidad***
- natural ***natural***
- talented ***talentosa***
- independent ***independiente***
- violet ***violeta***

C. The reading in your textbook is a self-quiz that tells you information about your personality based on the colors you like and whether you are a boy or a girl. Based on the information given below and what you learned from the reading, circle if you are a boy or a girl. Then, write what color you like. Follow the model.

Modelo Eres romántico. Eres (**un chico** [circled] / **una chica**). Te gusta *el violeta*.

1. Eres atrevido. Eres (**un chico** [circled] / **una chica**). Te gusta ***el rojo*** .
2. Eres muy talentosa. Eres (**un chico** / **una chica** [circled]). Te gusta ***el azul*** .
3. Eres artística. Eres (**un chico** / **una chica** [circled]). Te gusta ***el anaranjado*** .

realidades.com
• Web Code: jcd-0116

Realidades A | Nombre ______ Hora ______

Capítulo 1B | Fecha ______ **Guided Practice Activities 1B-6**

Presentación escrita (p. 79) *Answers will vary.*

Task: Write an e-mail in which you introduce yourself to a prospective pen pal.

1 Prewrite. In order to introduce yourself to a new friend, you need to first organize what you are going to include. Fill in the form below with your personal information.

Me llamo ______.

Soy (*use adjectives to describe yourself*) ______.

Me gusta ______.

No me gusta ______.

2 Draft. Read the following e-mail that another student has written. You should use this to guide you in drafting your own e-mail.

> *¡Hola! Me llamo Pilar. Soy una chica artística y muy independiente. Me gusta mucho dibujar y usar la computadora, pero me gusta más bailar. Me gusta la música salsa. No me gusta nada practicar deportes. ¿Cómo eres tú? Escríbeme pronto.*

Now, create an e-mail similar to the one above writing in your information from **part 1**.

¡Hola! Me llamo ______. Soy (**un chico** / **una chica**) ______ y ______. Me gusta mucho ______, pero me gusta más ______. Me gusta ______. No me gusta ______.

¿Cómo eres tú? Escríbeme pronto.

3 Revise. Exchange papers with another student in your class. Use the following checklist to review your partner's e-mail and also when you rewrite yours. If you need help figuring out what is correct, use the model from the **Prewrite** section above.

____ Is there enough information provided for each question in the prewrite stage?
- stated his/her name
- described himself/herself
- said what he/she likes to do
- said what he/she doesn't like to do

____ Is the spelling correct? (Use a dictionary if you are not sure.)

____ Are the adjectives in the correct form? (Think, is the student male or female?)

____ Is there an opening and a closing?

4 Publish. Write your revised e-mail on a separate sheet of paper. Your teacher may ask you to type the e-mail and send it to a prospective pen pal.

Antes de ver el video

Actividad 1

During the video, Teresa, Claudia, Pedro, and Esteban describe each other in e-mails. How would you describe yourself? Below is a list of descriptive words. Check off the words that describe you. **Answers will vary.**

Soy...

- ❑ artístico, -a
- ❑ atrevido, -a
- ❑ deportista
- ❑ desordenado, -a
- ❑ estudioso, -a
- ❑ gracioso, -a
- ❑ impaciente
- ❑ inteligente
- ❑ ordenado, -a
- ❑ paciente
- ❑ reservado, -a
- ❑ serio, -a
- ❑ simpático, -a
- ❑ sociable
- ❑ talentoso, -a
- ❑ trabajador, -ora

¿Comprendes?

Actividad 2

Fill in the blanks with the appropriate word or phrase from the bank. You may have to watch the video several times to remember each character well.

misteriosa	reservado	ordenados	inteligente
serio	trabajadora	sociable	
simpática	hablar por teléfono	buena	

1. A Pedro no le gusta ni bailar ni cantar. Es **reservado**.
Pero él escribe: "Soy muy gracioso. No soy muy **serio**."

2. Teresa, desde un cibercafé en la Ciudad de México, escribe: "Yo soy *Chica* **sociable**."
3. Ella es la **buena** amiga de Claudia.
4. Le gusta **hablar por teléfono**, pero no le gusta ir a la escuela.
5. En la computadora, Claudia se llama *Chica* **misteriosa**.
6. A ella le gusta la escuela; es muy **simpática**, estudiosa

y **trabajadora**.
7. También le gustan los chicos inteligentes y **ordenados**.
8. A Pedro le gusta *Chica misteriosa*. Ella también es una chica **inteligente**.

Realidades A — Nombre ______ Hora ______

Capítulo 1B — Fecha ______ VIDEO

Actividad 3

According to Esteban, Pedro is quiet and reserved. Yet, in his e-mail, he writes the opposite. Read what he writes about himself in his e-mail. Then, write what he is really like by filling in the blanks.

> Me llamo Chico sociable. ¡Qué coincidencia! Me gusta pasar tiempo con mis amigos... Me gusta escuchar música. Según mis amigos soy muy gracioso. No soy muy serio. Escríbeme.

1. *Chico sociable*, el ___amigo___ de Esteban, se llama ___Pedro___.
2. Según Esteban, él no es un chico ___sociable___. Él es ___reservado___.
3. A Pedro no le gusta ni ___bailar___ ni ___cantar___.
4. Pedro no es muy ___gracioso___. Él es muy ___serio___.

Y, ¿qué más?

Actividad 4

Describe people you know using each of the adjectives from the following list. Follow the model.

paciente	inteligente	sociable	impaciente	deportista

Modelo *La profesora de español es muy inteligente.*

Answers will vary.

Realidades A — Nombre ______ Hora ______

Capítulo 1B — Fecha ______ AUDIO

Actividad 5

You are a volunteer for a service at your school that helps new students meet other new students in order to make the transition easier. People who are interested in participating in this program have left messages describing themselves. Listen as the students describe themselves, and put a check mark in at least two columns that match what each student says. Then write the names of the most well-matched students. You will hear each statement twice.

BUENOS AMIGOS

	CARMEN	PABLO	ANA	ANDRÉS	RAQUEL	JORGE
serio(a)	✓					✓
reservado(a)			✓	✓		
deportista		✓			✓	
estudioso(a)	✓					✓
talentoso(a)						✓
gracioso(a)		✓			✓	
atrevido(a)					✓	
trabajador(a)	✓					✓
artístico(a)			✓	✓		✓
sociable		✓			✓	
romántico(a)			✓			

BUENOS AMIGOS:

1. ___Carmen___ y ___Jorge___
2. ___Ana___ y ___Andrés___
3. ___Raquel___ y ___Pablo___

Realidades A — Nombre ______ Hora ______

Capítulo 1B — Fecha ______ AUDIO

Actividad 6

What is your favorite season of the year? Your choice could say a lot about you. Listen as talk-show psychologist Doctor Armando describes people according to their preferred season (**estación preferida**) of the year. What characteristics go with each season? Listen and put a check mark in the appropriate boxes. By the way, is it true what he says about you and your favorite season? You will hear each statement twice.

	(summer)	(winter)	(spring)	(fall)
		✔		
			✔	
	✔			
				✔
		✔		
	✔			
		✔		
				✔
			✔	

Mi estación preferida es ______. Según el Dr. Armando, yo soy

Answers will vary.

Realidades A — Nombre ______ Hora ______

Capítulo 1B — Fecha ______ AUDIO

Actividad 7

Your Spanish teacher encourages you to speak Spanish outside of class. As you walk down the hall, you hear parts of your classmates' conversations in Spanish. Listen to the conversations and decide whether they are talking about a boy, a girl, or if you can't tell by what is being said. Place a check mark in the appropriate box of the table. You will hear each statement twice.

	#1	#2	#3	#4	#5	#6	#7	#8
(boy)				✔	✔		✔	
(girl)	✔	✔				✔		
?			✔					✔

Actividad 8

Listen as Nacho describes his ex-girlfriend. How many things do they have in common? Put an *X* on the pictures that show ways in which they are very different and put a circle around the pictures that show ways they are very similar. You will hear each set of statements twice.

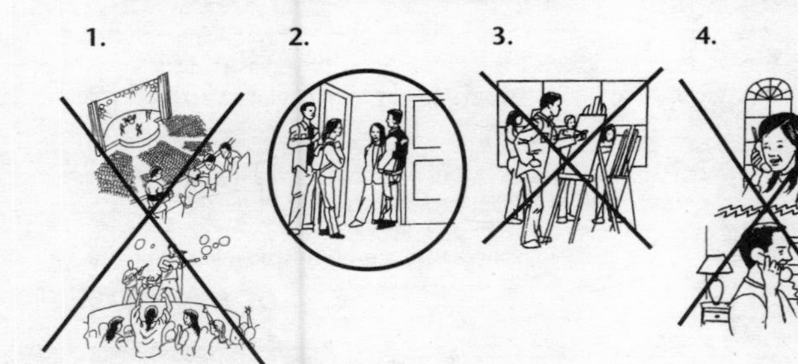

1. 2. 3. 4. 5.

Realidades A — Nombre ____ Hora ____

Capítulo 1B — Fecha ____ AUDIO

Actividad 9

Some people say we are what we dream! Listen as Antonieta calls in and describes her dream (**sueño**) to Doctor Armando, the radio talk show psychologist. Draw a circle around the pictures below that match what she dreams about herself.

After you hear Antonieta's call, tell a partner what kinds of things would be in a dream that reveals what you like to do and what kind of person you are. You might begin with "**En mi sueño, me gusta...**". You will hear this dialogue twice.

Realidades A — Nombre ____ Hora ____

Capítulo 1B — Fecha ____ WRITING

Actividad 10

A. Fill in the words using the art as clues.

1. Marta es una chica _trabajadora_.
2. Cristina es mi amiga _estudiosa_.
3. Alicia es muy _ordenada_.
4. Isa es una chica _artística_.
5. Alejandro es muy _deportista_.
6. Carlos es un chico _desordenado_.
7. Kiko es _sociable_.
8. Pepe es mi amigo _gracioso_.

B. Now, check your answers by finding them in the word search.

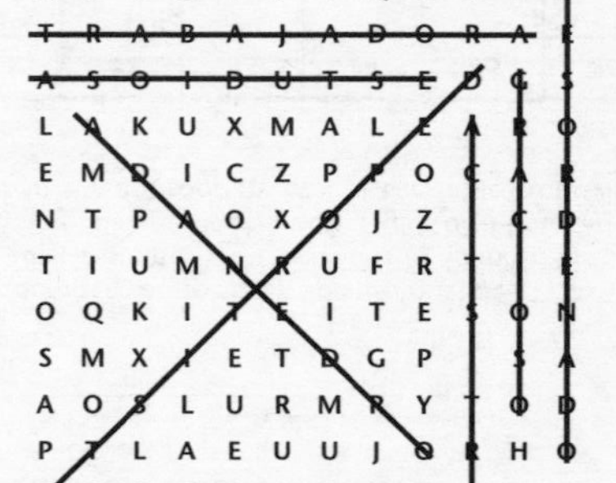

N	E	P	M	V	P	I	Q	U	U	T	D
T	R	A	B	A	J	A	D	O	R	A	E
A	S	O	I	D	U	T	S	E	D	G	S
L	A	K	U	X	M	A	L	E	A	R	O
E	M	D	I	C	Z	P	P	O	C	A	R
N	T	P	A	O	X	O	J	Z	I	C	D
T	I	U	M	N	R	U	F	R	T	I	E
O	Q	K	I	T	E	I	T	E	S	O	N
S	M	X	I	E	T	D	G	P	I	S	A
A	O	S	L	U	R	M	R	Y	T	O	D
P	T	L	A	E	U	U	J	O	R	H	O
A	S	O	C	I	A	B	L	E	A	E	T

Realidades A | Nombre ______ | Hora ______

Capítulo 1B | Fecha ______ | WRITING

Actividad 11

Frida and Diego, who are opposites, are talking on the phone. Frida, the sociable one, is doing all the talking. Using the pictures of the friends below, write what Frida might be saying about herself and about Diego. Follow the models.

Modelo *Yo soy deportista.*

1. Yo soy desordenada.
2. Yo soy sociable.
3. Yo soy atrevida.
4. Yo soy graciosa.
5. Yo soy trabajadora.

Modelo *Tú eres paciente.*

1. Tú eres ordenado.
2. Tú eres estudioso.
3. Tú eres artístico.
4. Tú eres trabajador.
5. Tú eres serio.

Realidades A | Nombre ______ | Hora ______

Capítulo 1B | Fecha ______ | WRITING

Actividad 12

Answer the following questions. Be sure to use the definite or indefinite article where appropriate. Follow the model.

Modelo ¿Cómo es tu mamá (*mother*)?

Ella es simpática y graciosa.

1. ¿Cómo eres tú?
   Answers will vary.
2. ¿Cómo es tu profesor(a) de español?
   Answers will vary.
3. ¿Cómo es tu mejor amigo(a)?
   Answers will vary.
4. ¿Cómo es el presidente?
   Answers will vary.
5. ¿Cómo es el director/la directora (*principal*) de tu escuela?
   Answers will vary.
6. ¿Qué te duele?
   Answers will vary.
7. ¿Cuál es la fecha de hoy?
   Answers will vary.
8. ¿Cuál es la fecha del Día de la Independencia?
   Es el cuarto de julio.
9. ¿Cuál es tu estación favorita?
   Answers will vary.
10. ¿Qué hora es?
    Answers will vary.

Realidades A | Nombre ______ Hora ______

Capítulo 1B | Fecha ______ **WRITING**

Actividad 13

A reporter for the school newspaper has asked you and several other students in your classroom to submit an article for the paper. The article is about personality traits and activities people like and dislike.

A. Think about your own personality traits. Write four adjectives that describe what you are like and four that describe what you are not like.

SOY	NO SOY
Answers will vary.	Answers will vary.

B. Now, write four things that you like to do and four things that you do not like to do.

ME GUSTA	NO ME GUSTA
Answers will vary.	Answers will vary.

C. Now, write your article using the information you have compiled about yourself.

Answers will vary.

Test Preparation Answers

Reading Skills

p. 121 2. **C**

p. 122 2. **D**

Integrated Performance Assessment

p. 123

Answers will vary.

Practice Test: ¡Hola! Me llamo Pedro

p. 125

1. B
2. H
3. B
4. H
5. Answers will vary but should follow the letter format used in the reading selection, including the date, addressee, salutation, body, complimentary close, and signature.

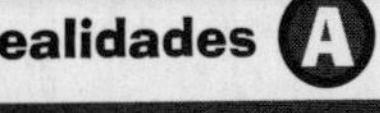

Tema 2

Table of Contents

Tema 2: La escuela

Capítulo 2A: Tu día en la escuela

Capítulo 2B: Tu sala de clases

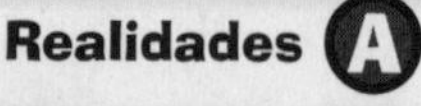

Theme Project

La escuela
Página Web

Overview:

You will create a Web page for your school featuring the name, address, and phone number of the school, and at least four symbols or photos that represent different classes. Under each symbol or photo, write a description of the class represented. Then you will present your Web page to the class, describing all the information featured on the page.

Materials:

Poster board, magazines, colored pencils, markers, glue, scissors, bilingual dictionary

Sequence:

STEP 1. Review the instructions with your teacher.

STEP 2. Submit a rough sketch of your Web page. Incorporate your teacher's suggestions into your draft. Work with a partner and present your drafts to each other.

STEP 3. Create layouts of your Web page on poster board.

STEP 4. Submit a draft of your descriptions for each class.

STEP 5. Complete your Web page and present it to the class, reading and/or describing all the information featured on the page.

Assessment:

Your teacher will use the rubric on the following page to assess this project.

Theme 2 Project: Página Web

RUBRIC	Score 1	Score 3	Score 5
Evidence of Planning	No written draft or page layout provided.	Draft was written and layout created, but not corrected.	Evidence of corrected draft and layout.
Use of Illustrations	No photos/visuals included.	Photos/visuals were included, but layout was unorganized.	Web page was easy to read, complete, and accurate.
Presentation	Includes little of the required information for the Web page.	Includes most of the required information for the Web page.	Includes all of the required information for the Web page.

Realidades A

Capítulo 2A

School-to-Home Connection

Dear Parent or Guardian,

The theme for the chapter is *La escuela* (School) and this chapter is called *Tu día en la escuela* (Your school day).

Upon completion of this chapter, your child will be able to:

- talk about school schedules and subjects
- discuss what students do during the day
- ask and tell who is performing an action
- compare his or her school with that of a student in a Spanish-speaking country

Also, your child will explore:

- the correct pronunciation of the letter *c*
- connections between Latin, English, and Spanish

Realidades helps with the development of reading, writing, and speaking skills through the use of strategies, process speaking, and process writing. In this chapter, students will:

- read about a language school in Costa Rica
- speak about their classes

Remember that additional help is available online at www.realidades.com by using the Web Codes in the Student Edition or in the Leveled Vocabulary anf Grammar Workbook.

Check it out! Have your child write out his or her class schedule using the appropriate Spanish terms from this chapter.

Sincerely,

For: Tips to Parents
Visit: www.realidades.com
Web Code: jce-0010

Realidades **A**

Capítulo 2A

Chapter Resource Checklist

Resources	CO†	APV	VH	MAN	LEC	CV	PO	MH	REP	PREP
Teacher										
Teacher's Resource Book										
Input Script		■								
Audio Script		■	■	■					■	■
GramActiva BLM				■						
Communicative Activities BLM				■						
School-to-Home Connection BLM	■									
Clip Art		■								■
Situation Cards BLM									■	
TPR Stories Book		■	■	■						
Fine Art Transparencies Teacher's Guide	■									
Pre-AP* Resource Book			■	■	■		■			
Student										
Leveled Vocabulary and Grammar Workbook										
Guided Practice		■	■	■	■		■		■	■
Core Practice		■	■	■					■	■
Communication Workbook with Test Preparation										
Writing				■						
Audio				■						
Video			■							
Test Preparation				■	■					■
RPH Workbook	■	■	■	■	■	■	■		■	
Lecturas para hispanohablantes					■					
Grammar Study Guides				■					■	■
Transparencies										
Answers on Transparencies		■	■	■	■					■
Vocabulary and Grammar	■	■	■	■						
Fine Art	■									
Assessment										
Assessment Program										
Quizzes			■	■						
Chapter Test										■
realidades.com			■	■						■
ExamView Test Bank CD-ROM										■
QuickTake on PresentationExpress		■	■	■						■
MindPoint QuizShow CD-ROM									■	
Alternate Assessment Program										■
Performance-Based Speaking							■			■
Self-Test on realidades.com & CWS										■
Assessment Program RPH			■	■						■
Technology										
realidades.com	■	■	■	■	■	■	■	■	■	■
myeBook	■	■	■	■	■	■	■	■	■	■
TeacherExpress CD-ROM	■	■	■	■	■	■	■	■	■	■
PresentationExpress DVD		■	■	■						■
Video Program DVD			■	■						
Culture Video DVD	■									
Audio Program CD 4		■	■	■						■
Assessment CD 20										■
Song CD 22		■								
Canciones de hip hop on realidades.com & CWS			■							■

† *See Abbreviation Key on page iv.*

Realidades A

Capítulo 2A

Input Script

Presentation

Input Vocabulary: Place the overhead transparency on the screen. Point to each school subject on Alicia's schedule. Say the subject and tell how much you like or dislike each one. Ask students about their likes and dislikes. Next, hand out scissors and copies of the Vocabulary Clip Art and have students cut the class hours, pictures of school subjects, and the names of school subjects into individual pieces. First practice the school hours by having the students scramble their pile of hours and then rearrange them back in order as you call out *"primera hora," "segunda hora,"* and so forth. Then call out a school schedule and have students place the pictures and names by the times you call out.

Input Monologue 1: Model the first two sentences of Alicia's monologue. Then ask students about the rest of Alicia's schedule by saying *"Soy Alicia. ¿Qué tengo en la segunda hora? ¿Y en la tercera?"* and so forth. Then with an erasable marker, draw four columns and write the headings ***Clase favorita, Interesante, Práctica,*** and ***Difícil*** above the columns. Model the rest of the monologue, using gestures to act out ***interesante*** and ***difícil.*** (You might bring a hammer and a funny-looking home decoration such as a lawn gnome to demonstrate ***práctica*** and ***no muy práctica.***) Then take a survey of how students feel about the school subjects. Make the statements *"___ es mi clase favorita / ___ es interesante / es práctica / es difícil"* about each school subject and have students hold up the Clip Art image of the subject when they agree with your statement. Write the results on the transparency.

Input Monologue 2: Model Alicia's statements *"Tengo mucha tarea en la clase de inglés."* and *"Estudio mucho en la clase de español."* Then point to other school subjects and say *"Tengo mucha tarea en la clase de ___. ¿Y tú?"* or *"Estudio mucho en la clase de ___. ¿Y tú?"* Have students hold the Clip Art image right side up if they also have a lot of homework or study a lot in that class and upside down if they do not. Next, model Alicia's sentence that begins *"Para mí ..."* Then write *___ es más interesante que la clase de español.* Ask a student volunteer to come up and point to a school subject. Act shocked and slightly offended and ask if the class agrees *("¿La clase de tecnología es más interesante que la clase de español? ¿Verdad? ¡Imposible!").* Then erase ***interesante*** and write ***práctica*** and repeat with another student volunteer. Finally, model Alicia's last statements, holding up the objects she mentions. Make logical and illogical statements about what you need for different classes. Have students nod their head "yes" when they hear a logical statement *("Para la clase de inglés, necesito un diccionario.")* and shake their head "no" when they hear an illogical statement *("Para la clase de educación física, necesito una calculadora.").*

Comprehension Check

- Borrow textbooks from other teachers that represent each school subject. Hold up the textbooks and have students name the school subject.
- Have students arrange their cut-up Vocabulary Clip Art to reflect their own school schedules. Ask *"¿Qué tienes primero, (segundo, etc.)?"* and have students tell you what they have first hour, second hour, and so forth.
- Make an enlarged copy of the Vocabulary Clip Art, and cut it into individual pieces. On the back side of the school subject pictures and school subject names, write the numbers 1–18. Tape the pieces on the chalkboard face down and have students play Concentration by calling out two numbers to try to match a school subject picture with its name.

Audio Script

Audio CD, Capítulo 2A

Track 01: *A primera vista,* Student Book, p. 86 (3:11)

Vocabulario y gramática en contexto
You will hear each word or phrase twice. After the first time there will be a pause so you can pronounce it, then you will hear the word or phrase a second time.

primera hora/tecnología
segunda hora/arte
tercera hora/ciencias sociales
cuarta hora/ciencias naturales
quinta hora/el almuerzo
sexta hora/español
séptima hora/matemáticas
octava hora/inglés
novena hora/educación física

Read along as you listen to the statements.

Me gusta mucho mi horario. En la primera hora, tengo la clase de tecnología ... ¡es mi clase favorita! Es interesante y práctica. Pero a veces es díficil.

Track 02: *A primera vista,* Student Book, p. 87 (1:10)

Vocabulario y gramática en contexto
Read along as you listen to the statements.

Tengo mucha tarea en la clase de inglés.
Estudio mucho en la clase de español. Para mí, la clase de español es más interesante que la clase de matemáticas.
Para la clase de español necesito un diccionario.
Para la clase de matemáticas necesito una calculadora y una carpeta de argollas.

Más vocabulario
You will hear each word twice. After the word is pronounced the first time there will be a pause so you can pronounce it, then you will hear the word a second time.

décimo, décima

Track 03: *A primera vista,* Act. 1, Student Book, p. 87 (1:45)

¿Sí o no?
You will hear Alicia make several statements about her school day and schedule. Give a "thumbs-up" sign if what she says is true or a "thumbs-down" sign if what she says is false. You will hear each statement twice.

1. Estudio mucho en la clase de español.
2. Mi clase favorita es la clase de tecnología.
3. La clase de tecnología es fácil.
4. Tengo mucha tarea en la clase de inglés.
5. Para la clase de español necesito una calculadora.
6. ¡No me gusta nada mi horario!

Track 04: *A primera vista,* Act. 2, Student Book, p. 87 (2:40)

El horario de Alicia

Listen to Alicia as she describes her class schedule. Touch the picture of each class as you hear it. You will hear each statement twice.

Tengo ocho clases.

1. Mi clase favorita, la clase de tecnología, está en la primera hora.
2. La clase de español está en la sexta hora.
3. La clase de educación física está en la novena hora.
4. La clase de matemáticas está en la séptima hora.
5. La clase de arte está en la segunda hora.
6. La clase de ciencias sociales está en la tercera hora.
7. La clase de inglés está en la octava hora.
8. La clase de ciencias naturales está en la cuarta hora.
9. En la quinta hora tengo el almuerzo.

Track 05: *A primera vista, Videohistoria,* Student Book, pp. 88–90 (2:02)

El primer día de clases
Es el primer día de clases en la Escuela Bilingüe en la Ciudad de México.
Read along as you listen to the *Videohistoria.*

See Student Book pages 88–90 for script.

Track 06: Audio Act. 5, Writing, Audio & Video Workbook, p. 31 (3:33)

You overhear several people in the hall trying to find out if they have classes together this year. As you listen to each conversation, write an X in the box under *Sí* if they have a class together, or under *No* if they do not. You will hear each conversation twice.

1. **Female Teen 1:** Oye, María. ¿Qué clase tienes en la primera hora?
   Female Teen 2: ¿En la primera hora? Un momento. Tengo la clase de música.
   Female Teen 1: Yo tengo la clase de inglés.
2. **Female Teen 3:** ¡Hola! Tienes la clase de ciencias en la tercera hora, ¿no?
   Male Teen 1: Sí, el profesor es muy bueno.
   Female Teen 3: Pues, ¡nos vemos en la tercera hora!
3. **Male Teen 2:** ¡Hola, Carlos!
   Male Teen 3: Hola, Miguel. Mira, ¿qué tienes en la segunda hora?
   Male Teen 2: Yo tengo clase de matemáticas. ¿Y tú?
   Male Teen 3: ¡Yo también!
4. **Female Teen 3:** ¡Hola! ¿Tienes un libro de español? ¿A qué hora tienes la clase?
   Male Teen 1: Sí, tengo un libro de español. Tengo la clase en la sexta hora.
   Female Teen 3: Yo tengo español en la quinta hora.
5. **Male Teen 4:** Oye, Antonio. ¿Tienes la clase de arte hoy?
   Male Teen 5: No, no me gusta el arte. Pero tengo la clase de música en la cuarta hora.

MALE TEEN 4: ¡Yo también! ¡Me gusta estar con mis amigos en clase!

Track 07: Audio Act. 6, Writing, Audio & Video Workbook, p. 31 (4:00)

As you stand outside the school counselor's office, you hear four students trying to talk to him. They are all requesting to get out of a certain class.

From the part of the conversation that you hear, write in the blank the class from which each student is requesting a transfer. You will hear each statement twice.

1. **MALE TEEN 1:** Por favor, Sr. Treviño. No soy deportista. No me gusta practicar deportes. Soy estudioso, pero necesito una clase diferente. Y ... y ... el Sr. Fernández no es buen profesor para mi personalidad. ¡Es muy impaciente!
2. **FEMALE TEEN 1:** Perdón, Sr. Treviño. No me gusta esta clase. No soy muy artística, y no me gusta dibujar tampoco. Soy trabajadora, pero me gusta más estudiar y leer libros. ¡Necesito dos clases de inglés!
3. **MALE TEEN 2:** Pues, tengo un problema, Sr. Treviño. Me gusta ver la tele y hablar por teléfono. Me gusta conversar y soy muy gracioso. No me gusta ni leer ni escribir. No me gusta nada la clase de la profesora Ochoa. Ella es muy seria. ¡Me gusta estar con mis amigos, no con una profesora seria!
4. **FEMALE TEEN 2:** Por favor, necesito una clase de tecnología. Es una clase muy importante para mí. ¡Los problemas de álgebra como "equis es cinco, i griega es seis" no son interesantes. Yo necesito una clase más práctica.

Track 08: *Manos a la obra,* Act. 16, Student Book, p. 100 (4:21)

¿Una mano o dos?

You will hear eight *-ar* verbs. If the ending tells you one person is performing the action, raise one hand. If the ending tells you more than one person is doing something, raise both hands. You will hear each word twice.

1. hablo
2. enseñan
3. dibujamos
4. trabaja
5. cantas
6. estudian
7. necesitan
8. practico

Track 09: *Manos a la obra,* Act. 21, Student Book, p. 103 (1:28)

Escucha y escribe

Listen to a student describe the picture on the right of himself and other students during their *recreo.* Write what you hear. You will hear each statement twice.

1. Dos amigos y yo hablamos de las clases.
2. Tomás estudia español.
3. Ana canta.
4. Y María escucha música.

Track 10: *Pronunciación,* The letter *c*, Student Book, p. 107 (2:30)

In Spanish the pronunciation of the letter *c* depends on the letter that follows it.

When the letter *c* comes before *a, o, u,* or another consonant, it is pronounced like the *c* in *cat.* Listen to and say these words:

You will hear each word twice. After the word is pronounced the first time, there will be a pause so you can pronounce it. Then you will hear the word a second time.

computadora
tampoco
correr
cantar
cómo
practicar
escuela
tocar
Carlos

When the letter *c* comes before *e* or *i,* most Spanish speakers pronounce it like the *s* in "Sally." Listen to and say these words:

veces
hacer
sociable
once
gracioso
doce
gracias
trece

Try it out! Listen to this rhyme. Listen particularly for the sound of the letter *c.* Then repeat the rhyme.

Cero más cuatro,
o cuatro más cero,
siempre son cuatro.
¿No es verdadero?

Say the rhyme again, first replacing *cuatro* with *doce,* then replacing *cuatro* with *trece.* Then say the rhyme quickly several times.

Track 11: Audio Act. 7, Writing, Audio & Video Workbook, p. 32 (3:14)

Emilio, a new student from Bolivia, is attending his first pep assembly! He is eager to make friends and begins talking to Diana, who is sitting next to him. Listen to their conversation. If they have something in common, place a check mark in the column labeled *Ellos.* If the statement only applies to Emilio, place a check mark in the column labeled *Él.* If the statement only applies to Diana, place a check mark in the column labeled *Ella.* Note: Be sure you have placed a check mark in ONLY one of the columns for each statement. You will hear the conversation twice.

EMILIO: Hola. Me llamo Emilio. ¿Cómo te llamas?
DIANA: Hola. Me llamo Diana.
EMILIO: Mucho gusto. Yo tengo la clase de español en la primera hora. ¿Y tú?

Diana: Yo tengo la clase de español en la segunda hora. La señora Santiago enseña la clase. Ella es muy simpática.
Emilio: La señora Mason enseña mi clase de español. Ella es muy graciosa. ¿Qué tienes en la quinta hora? Yo estudio arte en la quinta hora. Dibujo mucho.
Diana: A ver … Eres muy artístico. Yo, no. Yo soy más atlética. Tengo la clase de educación física en la quinta hora.
Emilio: ¡Yo soy atlético también! Practico muchos deportes. Es muy divertido.
Diana: Necesito estudiar mucho para mi clase de matemáticas. Es muy difícil para mí. No me gusta mucho, pero yo soy muy trabajadora.
Emilio: Yo también. Trabajo mucho en la clase de matemáticas.
Diana: ¿Tienes mucha tarea? Yo sí. Necesito estudiar en la cafetería. Tengo el almuerzo a las once y media.
Emilio: Siempre tengo mucha tarea. ¡Bueno! ¡Nos vemos en el almuerzo a las once y media para estudiar!

You are going to hear this conversation again.

Track 12: Audio Act. 8, Writing, Audio & Video Workbook, p. 33 (4:44)

Listen as four people talk about what they do during the day. There will be some things that all four people do and other things that not all of them do. Fill in the grid with a check mark if the person says he or she does a certain activity. Also fill in the *Yo* column with a check mark for the activities that you do every day. You will hear each set of statements twice.

1. **Female Teen 1:** Yo soy Eva. Me gusta mucho mi primera hora. Es la clase de tecnología. Estudio mucho y uso la computadora. Con mis amigos, escucho música y practico deportes.
2. **Male Teen 1:** Me llamo David. A ver … Uso la computadora para mi segunda y quinta hora. Estudio y trabajo mucho, pero veo la tele también. ¿Mi actividad favorita? ¡Practicar deportes!
3. **Female Teen 2:** Soy Raquel. Eva es mi amiga. Nosotras montamos en bicicleta y practicamos deportes. Yo uso la computadora para jugar videojuegos. También veo la tele con mi amigo David.
4. **Male Teen 2:** Soy muy perezoso. Me llamo José. ¡Uso mi computadora para jugar, no para estudiar! Veo la tele y escucho música con mis amigos. Es muy divertido ver la tele con Raquel y David.

Track 13: Audio Act. 9, Writing, Audio & Video Workbook, p. 34 (3:40)

You and your family are considering hosting a student from Costa Rica for a semester. Before you make the decision, you want to know a little about the student. Listen to part of a recording that the students from Costa Rica made for your class. Use the grid to keep track of what each of the students says. You will then use this information to decide which student would be the most compatible for you and your family. You will hear each set of statements twice.

1. **Male Teen 1:** Hola. Me llamo Jorge. Yo soy un chico deportista. Según mis amigos, soy gracioso también. Mis amigos y yo practicamos deportes y montamos en bicicleta. Mi clase favorita es educación física. Es una clase muy divertida. ¿Y tú? ¿Eres como yo?
2. **Female Teen 1:** Hola. Soy Luz. Según mis amigos, soy una chica talentosa. Canto y bailo. Me gusta mucho. En la escuela, mi profesor favorito es el Sr. Rivas. Él enseña música. Es mi clase favorita. Cantamos todos los días en esa clase. ¿Y a ti? ¿Te gusta cantar?
3. **Male Teen 2:** Hola. Soy Marco. ¿Estudias inglés y matemáticas? Yo sí. Mi clase favorita es matemáticas. Es una clase muy interesante y fácil para mí. Soy un chico estudioso. Yo toco la guitarra también con una banda musical. ¿Cómo eres tú?
4. **Female Teen 2:** Buenos días. Me llamo Cristina. Mis amigos me llaman Tina. Soy muy artística. Dibujo y escribo cuentos. Me gusta mucho el arte de Max Jiménez. Él es un artista muy famoso de Costa Rica. ¿Mi clase favorita? ¡La clase de arte! ¿Y tú? ¿Eres artístico también?

Now … look at your chart. Which person is most like you? Jorge? Luz? Marco? Cristina?

Track 14: *Repaso del capítulo*, Student Book, p. 114 (3:42)

Vocabulario y gramática
Listen to these words and expressions that you have learned in this chapter. You will hear each word or expression once.

See Student Book page 114 for vocabulary list.

Track 15: *Preparación para el examen*, Student Book, p. 115 (1:13)

Escuchar
Practice task.
Listen to two students who have just attended some of the classes on their new schedules. a) Which class does each one like? Why? b) Which class does each one dislike? Why?

Male Teen: Me gusta mucho la clase de arte. Me gusta dibujar. Es una clase fantástica. Pero la clase de matemáticas … ¡Uf! Es mucho más difícil que mi clase de arte. A veces hay mucha tarea.
Female Teen: ¡La clase de matemáticas no es difícil! La tarea es muy fácil. Me gusta mucho el profesor. Él es muy divertido. Pero no me gusta la clase de educación física. No soy atlética.

Realidades A

Capítulo 2A

Video Script

A primera vista: *Mis clases de matemáticas* (7:50)

Claudia: ¡Hola, chico…! Un momento, ¿cómo te llamas? Bueno, ¡qué día tan difícil! Hoy en la escuela …

Claudia: Teresa, ¿qué tienes en la primera hora?

Teresa: Pues, tengo la clase de inglés. El señor Marín enseña la clase. Es un profesor muy divertido. ¿Y tú?

Claudia: La clase de matemáticas. Para mí es muy fácil. ¿Y en la segunda? ¿Qué tienes en la segunda hora?

Teresa: La clase de educación física. Y después, en la tercera hora, tengo la clase de matemáticas. Es muy difícil. En la cuarta hora, tengo ciencias sociales. Tengo la clase de ciencias naturales en la quinta hora. Y en la sexta hora, español. Y tú, ¿qué tienes?

Claudia: En la segunda hora, tengo la clase de matemáticas.

Teresa: ¿Qué? No entiendo.

Claudia: Pues sí. Y también tengo la clase de matemáticas en la tercera, la cuarta, la quinta y la sexta hora. Hmm. Me gustan las matemáticas, pero seis clases en un día …

Teresa: ¿De veras? ¿Y el almuerzo? ¿Cuándo tienes el almuerzo?

Claudia: A las doce y diez.

Teresa: Yo también. ¡Qué bueno! ¿Por qué no hablas con el señor Treviño?

Claudia: ¿Quién?

Teresa: El señor Treviño. En la oficina.

Claudia: Buena idea.

Teresa: Bueno, tengo mi primera clase. ¡Hasta luego! ¡Adiós!

Claudia: Hmmm. Buenos días, Sr. Treviño. Hola, Marta. ¿Qué tal?

Sr. Treviño: Hola, Claudia. ¿Qué necesitas?

Claudia: Sr. Treviño, tengo un problema con mi horario. Tengo la clase de matemáticas …

Sr. Treviño: Sí, sí. Claudia, ahora no es posible. A ver … escribe tu nombre en la hoja de papel. Hablamos … mañana. Hasta luego.

Claudia: Mañana, mañana.

Profesora: Hola, estudiantes. Bienvenidos a la clase de matemáticas. Las matemáticas son muy interesantes y prácticas, ¿verdad?

Estudiantes: Sí, profesora.

Profesora: Es muy importante estudiar y trabajar mucho, ¿sí?

Estudiantes: ¡Sí!

Profesora: Ahora... Francisco Arias Romero …

Paco: Presente.

Profesora: Claudia Díaz Rodríguez …

Claudia: Presente.

Profesora: Guillermo López Alemán …

Teresa: ¿Y qué tal tu clase de matemáticas?

Claudia: Muy bien. ¿Y tu clase de inglés?

Teresa: ¡Fantástica!

Claudia: ¿Sí? ¿El Sr. Marín es un buen profesor?

Teresa: Sí, él es muy interesante. ¡Y muy simpático! Hasta luego.

Claudia: ¡Nos vemos!

Profesora: Hola, estudiantes … Claudia, ¿estás aquí otra vez?

Claudia: Sí, profesora. Tengo un problema con mi horario.

Profesora: Necesitas hablar con el señor Treviño, en la oficina.

Claudia: Sí, mañana.

Profesora: Muy bien. Bueno, ahora vamos a …

Profesora: Hola, estudiantes. Bienvenidos a la clase de matemáticas. Las matemáticas son muy interesantes, ¿verdad?

Estudiantes: ¡Sí, muy interesantes!

Profesora: ¿Claudia?

Claudia: Sí, profesora Santoro, ¡tengo seis clases de matemáticas hoy!

Profesora: Ven, ayúdame con los libros, por favor.

Claudia: Muy bien …

GramActiva Videos: subject pronouns; present tense of *-ar* verbs **(7:43)**

Subject pronouns

Host: Yo! Subject pronouns are words that substitute for the subject of a sentence. In English they are words like *I, you, he, she, we,* and *they.* You use them instead of someone's name.

Host: In Spanish the subject pronouns are *yo,* which means "I," *tú,* which means "you," *usted,* which is the word you use to say "you" to someone other than a close friend, *él,* which means "he," *ella,* which means "she," *nosotros* and *nosotras,* which are the masculine and feminine forms of "we," *vosotros, vosotras* used only in Spain and it means "two or more people you individually call *tú,*" *ustedes,* the plural form of "you," and *ellos* and *ellas,* the masculine and feminine forms of "they."

Boy: *Yo.*

Girl: *Tú.*

Boy: *Usted.*

Girl: *Él.*

Boy: *Ella.*

Girl: *Nosotros.*

Boy And Girl: *Ustedes*

Girl And Boy: *Ellos.*

Turtle: Whoooooo. Thaaaat waasss toooo faaasst. Hoowww aaaabooouuttt aaa slllooww mmoootionnnn reeeplaaay.

Boy: *Yo.*

Girl: *Tú.*

Boy: *Usted.*

Girl: *Él.*

Boy: *Ella.*

Girl: *Nosotros.*

Boy And Girl: *Ustedes*
Girl And Boy: *Ellos.*
Host: You may have noticed that for the use of *we, you,* and *they,* the masculine forms *nosotros, vosotros,* and *ellos* are used. That is because in both cases the group of people the pronoun was standing in for was mixed in gender. Any time the group is mixed you use the masculine form. Even if there are 100 girls and only one guy, you still would use the masculine form.
Host: *Ella.*
Ellos.
Ellos.
Ellas.
Él.

Quiz
Host: What Spanish subject pronouns would you use instead of the following names or English pronouns? Congratulations.

Present tense of *-ar* verbs
Lesko: Feel like these verbs are going to drive you crazy? Don't sweat it. I know a few secrets that are going to help you out.
Host: You've seen a few verbs used already, and even if you don't understand everything, there's some good news. Verbs come in groups, and all the verbs in a group work the same way, so once you learn how to use one, you can pretty much use them all just as easily. We're going to start by looking at regular verbs, and specifically a group of regular verbs that all end in *-ar.*
Hero: To infinitives and beyond!
Host: Verbs start out as infinitives. Every Spanish infinitive ends in *-ar, -er,* or *-ir.* A whole bunch end in *-ar.* When we use verbs, usually we conjugate them. We chop off the *-ar, -er,* or *-ir* ending, leaving the stem, then add new endings.
Host: The verb *hablar* means "to speak." When we use *hablar* we remove the *-ar* and add the endings. In the present tense they are *-o* for the *yo* form, *yo hablo; -as* for the *tú* form, *tú hablas; -a* for the *usted, él,* and *ella* forms, *él habla; -amos* for the *nosotros/nosotras* forms, *nosotras hablamos; -áis* for the *vosotros/vosotras* forms, *vosotros habláis;* and *-an* for the *ustedes, ellos* and *ellas, ellas hablan.*
Host: Think it's a lot to remember? Watch how easy *bailar* is.
Yo bailo.
Tú bailas.
Ud., él, ella baila.
Nosotros/nosotras bailamos.
Vosotros/vosotras bailáis.
Uds., ellos, ellas bailan.
That's more like it, isn't it?
Host: But that's just the beginning. Check out *cantar.*
Yo canto.
Tú cantas.
Ud., él, ella canta.
Nosotros, nosotras cantamos.
Vosotros, vosotras cantáis.
Uds., ellos, ellas cantan.
It's getting more fun now. *Trabajar.*
Yo trabajo.
Tú trabajas.
Ud., él, ella trabaja.
Nosotros, nosotras trabajamos.
Vosotros, vosotras trabajáis.
Uds., ellos, ellas trabajan.
Host: There it is. It works for any regular *-ar* verb in the present tense. Easy as pie.
Old Man: This is too much. I don't like it.
Host: Well there's more good news. In English, *I work, you work, we work, they work,* all are the same conjugation of the verb *to work.* But in Spanish, every form has its own distinct conjugation. Rarely two are alike. "How does that help?" You might ask.
Hero: In Spanish you don't even have to use the subject pronouns if you don't want to, because each subject has a specific ending, so you usually know who the subject is without having to use the pronoun.
Host: For example, you could say *hablo español* and know that it means "I speak Spanish." And *estudiamos ciencias* always means "we study science."

Quiz
Host: Match the following.
Yo hablo.
Tú trabajas.
Ud., él, ella canta.
Nosotros, nosotras cantamos.
Uds., ellas, ellos hablan.

Nombre ______________________

Fecha ______________________

A high school counselor has lost the schedule of Yolanda, a transfer student. The counselor phones the student to complete the missing information. Play the role of the counselor and ask your partner the following questions. Record the answers on the class schedule below.

1. ¿Qué clase tienes en la primera hora?
2. ¿En qué hora tienes español?
3. ¿En qué hora tienes educación física?
4. ¿Qué clase tienes en la tercera hora?
5. ¿En qué hora tienes almuerzo?
6. ¿En qué hora tienes ciencias sociales?
7. ¿Qué clase tienes en la sexta hora?
8. ¿Qué clase tienes en la segunda hora?

HORARIO DE CLASES

1ª	
2ª	
3ª	
4ª	
5ª	
6ª	
7ª	
8ª	

Now imagine that your partner is Miguel, a new student who has lost his schedule on the way to school. You have the same schedule as he does. Answer Miguel's questions about his schedule based on the information below.

HORARIO DE CLASES

1ª	arte
2ª	educación física
3ª	inglés
4ª	almuerzo
5ª	ciencias sociales
6ª	tecnología
7ª	español
8ª	matemáticas

Nombre ______________________

Fecha ______________________

Communicative Activity **2A-1**
Estudiante **B**

A high school counselor has lost the schedule of Yolanda, a transfer student. The counselor phones the student to complete the missing information. Play the role of the transfer student. Answer your partner's questions based on the information below.

HORARIO DE CLASES

1ª	tecnología
2ª	inglés
3ª	ciencias naturales
4ª	educación física
5ª	almuerzo
6ª	arte
7ª	español
8ª	ciencias sociales

Now play the role of Miguel, a new student. You have lost your schedule on the way to school. Ask your partner, who has the same schedule as you, what your classes are. Record the answers on the class schedule below.

1. ¿Qué clase tienes en la séptima hora?
2. ¿En qué hora tienes inglés?
3. ¿En qué hora tienes educación física?
4. ¿Qué clase tienes en la octava hora?
5. ¿En qué hora tienes tecnología?
6. ¿En qué hora tienes arte?
7. ¿Qué clase tienes en la cuarta hora?
8. ¿Qué clase tienes en la quinta hora?

HORARIO DE CLASES

1ª	
2ª	
3ª	
4ª	
5ª	
6ª	
7ª	
8ª	

Nombre ______________________

Fecha ______________________

In this activity, you and your partner take turns. You are **O** and he or she is **X.** Begin by having your partner choose a number from 1 to 9. Read the sentence in that box and wait for his or her answer. For each sentence, your partner must say the correct form of the verb. If your partner responds correctly, mark **X** in the box. If the response is incorrect, make no marks and do not tell the correct answer. Your partner may choose that number again later. During your turn, your partner will mark **O** in the appropriate box if your answer is correct. The first person to have three correct answers in a row is the winner!

La escuela

1 La profesora (hablar) en la clase de español. (habla)	**2** Tú (estudiar) inglés en la cuarta hora. (estudias)	**3** Los profesores (enseñar) clases interesantes. (enseñan)
4 Yo (usar) la computadora en la clase de tecnología. (uso)	**5** Nosotros (dibujar) mucho en la clase de arte. (dibujamos)	**6** Ud. (trabajar) en la escuela. (trabaja)
7 Pepita y yo (necesitar) calculadoras para la clase de matemáticas. (necesitamos)	**8** Sergio (practicar) deportes en la clase de educación física. (practica)	**9** Josefina y Mateo (escuchar) al profesor de ciencias sociales. (escuchan)

Realidades A

Capítulo 2A

Nombre ______________________

Fecha ______________________

Communicative Activity **2A-2**

Estudiante **B**

In this activity, you and your partner take turns. You are **X** and he or she is **O.** You begin by choosing a number from 1 to 9. Listen to the sentence in that box as your partner reads it, and say the correct form of the verb. If you respond correctly, your partner will mark an **X** in the box. If the response is incorrect, the box will be left with no marks. You may choose that number again later. During your partner's turn, you will read the sentence that he or she chooses and will mark **O** in the appropriate box if the answer is correct. The first person to have three correct answers in a row is the winner!

La escuela

1 Luisa y Carmen (estudiar) tecnología. (estudian)	**2** Nosotros (escuchar) música en la clase de inglés. (escuchamos)	**3** Tú (pasar) tiempo con amigos en el almuerzo. (pasas)
4 Maricarmen (hablar) mucho en la clase de arte. (habla)	**5** Marco y yo (bailar) en la clase de educación física. (bailamos)	**6** Yo (trabajar) mucho en la clase de ciencias naturales. (trabajo)
7 El profesor Rodríguez (enseñar) la clase de matemáticas. (enseña)	**8** Los profesores (usar) la computadora en las clases difíciles. (usan)	**9** Rita (necesitar) un diccionario para la clase de español. (necesita)

Situation Cards

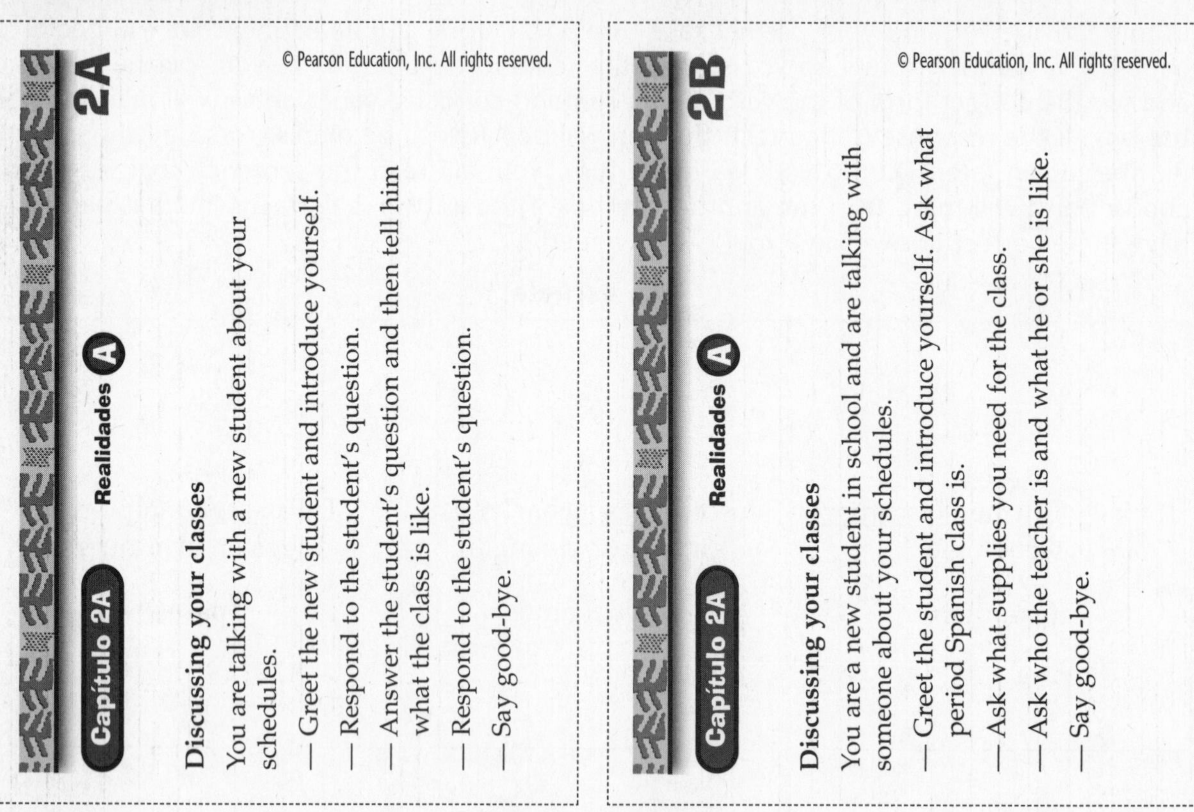

Realidades A — Capítulo 2A — **2A**

Discussing your classes

You are talking with a new student about your schedules.

— Greet the new student and introduce yourself.

— Respond to the student's question.

— Answer the student's question and then tell him what the class is like.

— Respond to the student's question.

— Say good-bye.

Realidades A — Capítulo 2A — **2B**

Discussing your classes

You are a new student in school and are talking with someone about your schedules.

— Greet the student and introduce yourself. Ask what period Spanish class is.

— Ask what supplies you need for the class.

— Ask who the teacher is and what he or she is like.

— Say good-bye.

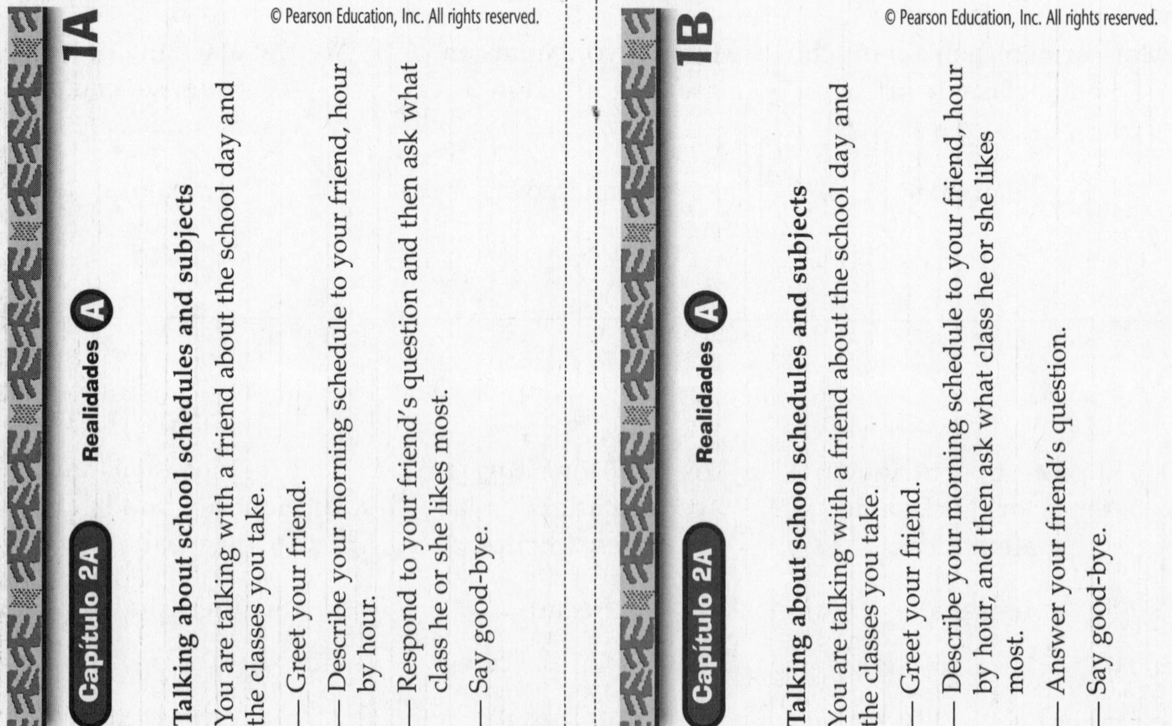

Realidades A — Capítulo 2A — **1A**

Talking about school schedules and subjects

You are talking with a friend about the school day and the classes you take.

— Greet your friend.

— Describe your morning schedule to your friend, hour by hour.

— Respond to your friend's question and then ask what class he or she likes most.

— Say good-bye.

Realidades A — Capítulo 2A — **1B**

Talking about school schedules and subjects

You are talking with a friend about the school day and the classes you take.

— Greet your friend.

— Describe your morning schedule to your friend, hour by hour, and then ask what class he or she likes most.

— Answer your friend's question.

— Say good-bye.

Realidades A

Capítulo 2A

GramActiva

Tu día en la escuela

Juego, p. 102

Vocabulary Clip Art

Horario

Hora	Clase
Primera hora	Inglés
Segundo hora	matemáticas
Tercera hora	arte
Cuarta hora	clenclas sociales
Quinta hora	el almuerzo
Sexta hora	tecnología
Séptima hora	español
Octova hora	educación física
Novena hora	ciencas ndturales

Vocabulary Clip Art

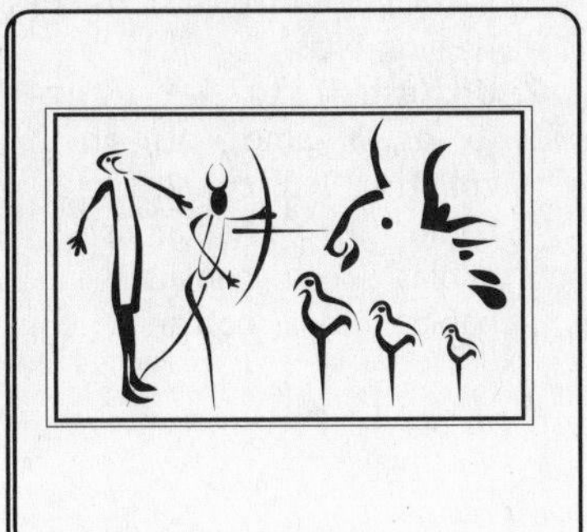

Core Practice Answers

2A-1

A.

1. un libro / la clase de español
2. una calculadora / la clase de matemáticas
3. un libro / la clase de inglés
4. una computadora / la clase de tecnología
5. un diccionario / la clase de español
6. una carpeta de argollas / la clase de ciencias sociales

B.

1. inglés
2. arte
3. diccionario
4. lápiz
5. calculadora
6. tecnología
7. libro
8. español
9. matemáticas
10. tarea

2A-2

Order of answers may vary.

1. Tengo la clase de matemáticas en la segunda hora.
2. Tengo la clase de arte en la tercera hora.
3. Tengo la clase de ciencias sociales en la cuarta hora.
4. Tengo el almuerzo en la quinta hora.
5. Tengo la clase de tecnología en la sexta hora.
6. Tengo la clase de español en la séptima hora.
7. Tengo la clase de educación física en la octava hora.
8. Tengo la clase de ciencias naturales en la novena hora.

2A-3

Answers will vary. All adjectives should be in feminine form.

1. es práctica
2. es fácil y muy divertida
3. es difícil
4. es interesante
5. es aburrida
6. no es fácil
7. no es muy difícil
8. es mi clase favorita

2A-4

1. tengo un libro
2. no necesito una calculadora
3. no tengo una carpeta de argollas para la clase de matemáticas
4. necesito un diccionario para la clase de español
5. no tengo el cuaderno para la clase de arte
6. tengo un lápiz
7. no necesito el horario
8. tengo un bolígrafo

2A-5

A.

1. él
2. ellas
3. nosotros (nosotras)
4. vosotros (vosotros) / Uds
5. él
6. ellos
7. ella
8. ellos
9. ellos

B.

1. usted (Ud.)
2. ustedes (Uds.)
3. Uds.
4. tú
5. Ud.
6. tú
7. Ud.

2A-6

A.

Row 1: ____ , hablas, habla, hablamos, ____ , ____

Row 2: estudio, estudias, estudia, ____ , ____ , estudian

Row 3: enseño, ____ , enseña, enseñamos, ____ , enseñan

Row 4: uso, usas, usa, usamos, ____ , usan

Row 5: necesito, necesitas, ____ , necesitamos, ____ , necesitan

B.

1. estudia
2. bailo
3. hablamos
4. usan
5. necesita
6. montas
7. dibujan
8. patinamos
9. enseña
10. necesitan
11. camina
12. bailamos
13. cantan

2A-7

A.

1. tú cantas
2. yo hablo por teléfono
3. él patina
4. Ud. dibuja
5. ella practica deportes

B.

1. nosotros (nosotras) cantamos
2. Uds. usan la computadora
3. ellos montan en bicicleta
4. nosotros (nosotras) hablamos por teléfono
5. ellos tocan la guitarra
6. ellos bailan

Crucigrama (2A-8)

Across:

2. fácil
4. clase
5. tarea
8. física
12. arte
14. aburrida
15. naturales
16. séptimo
17. inglés
18. enseña

Down:

1. computadora
3. ciencias
6. almuerzo
7. argollas
9. horario
10. quinta
11. matemáticas
13. tercero

Organizer (2A-9)

I. Vocabulary Answers will vary.

II Grammar

1. yo, tú, él, ella, usted, nosotros (-as), vosotros (-as), ustedes, ellos, ellas
2. Ud. (usted) / tú
3. -o, -as, -a, -amos, -áis, -an

col. 1.	col. 2.
hablo	hablamos
hablas	habláis
habla	hablan

Realidades A — Nombre ______ Hora ______

Capítulo 2A — Fecha ______

Vocabulary Flash Cards, Sheet 1

Write the Spanish vocabulary word below each picture. If there is a word or phrase, copy it in the space provided. Be sure to include the article for each noun.

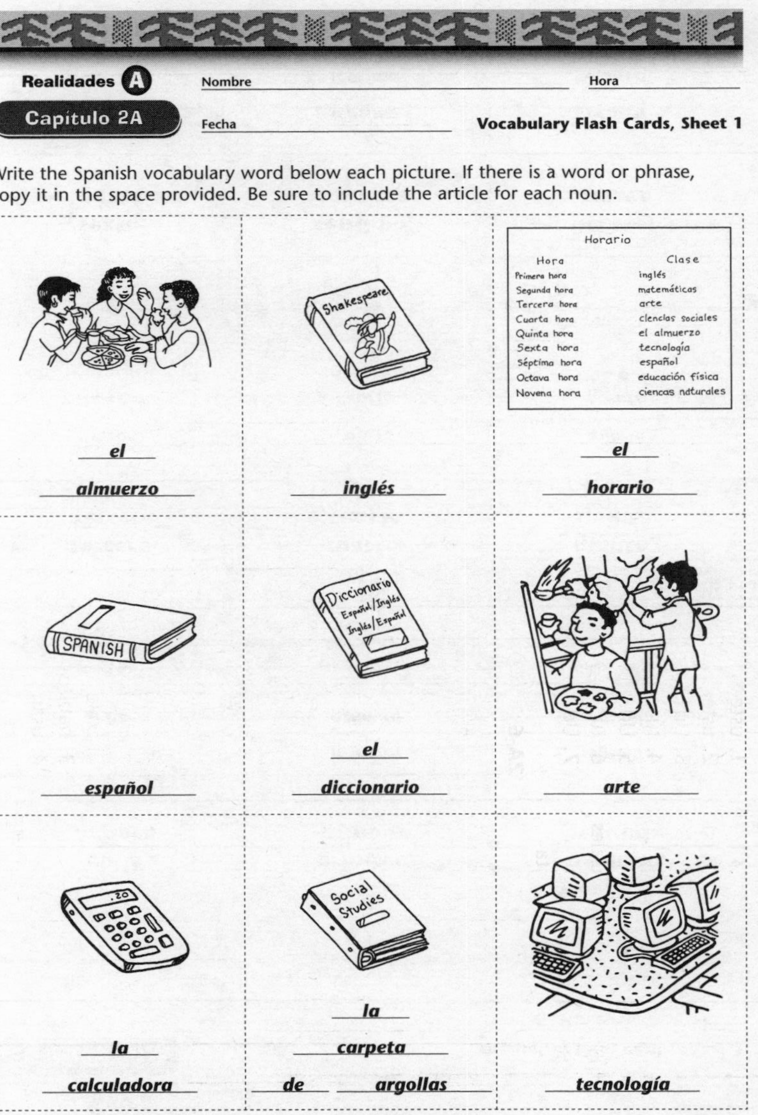

el almuerzo	***inglés***	***el horario***
español	***el diccionario***	***arte***
la calculadora	***la carpeta de argollas***	***tecnología***

Realidades A — Nombre ______ Hora ______

Capítulo 2A — Fecha ______

Vocabulary Flash Cards, Sheet 2

matemáticas	***ciencias sociales***	***educación física***
estudiar	***ciencias naturales***	***enseñar***
la clase — ***la clase***	**hablar** — ***hablar***	**necesito** — ***necesito***

Realidades A
Capítulo 2A

Nombre ______ Hora ______

Fecha ______

Vocabulary Flash Cards, Sheet 3

en la ... hora	**primero, primera**	**segundo, segunda**
en *la* / *... hora*	*primero*, / *primera*	*segundo*, / *segunda*
tercero, tercera	**cuarto, cuarta**	**quinto, quinta**
tercero, / *tercera*	*cuarto*, / *cuarta*	*quinto*, / *quinta*
sexto, sexta	**séptimo, séptima**	**octavo, octava**
sexto, / *sexta*	*séptimo*, / *séptima*	*octavo*, / *octava*

Realidades A
Capítulo 2A

Nombre ______ Hora ______

Fecha ______

Vocabulary Flash Cards, Sheet 4

noveno, novena	**décimo, décima**	**aburrido, aburrida**
noveno, / *novena*	*décimo*, / *décima*	*aburrido*, / *aburrida*
difícil	**divertido, divertida**	**fácil**
difícil	*divertido*, / *divertida*	*fácil*
favorito, favorita	**interesante**	**práctico, práctica**
favorito, / *favorita*	*interesante*	*práctico*, / *práctica*

Realidades A — Nombre ______ Hora ______

Capítulo 2A — Fecha ______

Vocabulary Flash Cards, Sheet 5

más... que *más...* *que*	**a ver...** *a* *ver...*	**¿Quién?** *¿Quién?*
para *para*	**mucho** *mucho*	**la tarea** *la* *tarea*
la clase de... *la* *clase de...*	**necesitas** *necesitas*	**(yo) tengo** *(yo)* *tengo*

Realidades A — Nombre ______ Hora ______

Capítulo 2A — Fecha ______

Vocabulary Flash Cards, Sheet 6

(tú) tienes *(tú)* *tienes*		

Realidades A | Nombre ______ | Hora ______

Capítulo 2A | Fecha ______ | **Vocabulary Check, Sheet 1**

Tear out this page. Write the English words on the lines. Fold the paper along the dotted line to see the correct answers so you can check your work.

el almuerzo	***lunch***
la clase	***class***
arte	***art***
español	***Spanish***
ciencias naturales	***science***
ciencias sociales	***social studies***
educación física	***physical education***
inglés	***English***
matemáticas	***mathematics***
tecnología	***technology/computers***
el horario	***schedule***
la tarea	***homework***
enseñar	***to teach***
estudiar	***to study***
hablar	***to talk***
primero, primera	***first***
segundo, segunda	***second***

Fold In ←

Realidades A | Nombre ______ | Hora ______

Capítulo 2A | Fecha ______ | **Vocabulary Check, Sheet 2**

Tear out this page. Write the Spanish words on the lines. Fold the paper along the dotted line to see the correct answers so you can check your work.

lunch	***el almuerzo***
class	***la clase***
art	***arte***
Spanish	***español***
science	***ciencias naturales***
social studies	***ciencias sociales***
physical education	***educación física***
English	***inglés***
mathematics	***matemáticas***
technology/ computers	***tecnología***
schedule	***el horario***
homework	***la tarea***
to teach	***enseñar***
to study	***estudiar***
to talk	***hablar***
first	***primero, primera***
second	***segundo, segunda***

Fold In ←

Realidades A Nombre ______ Hora ______

Capítulo 2A Fecha ______ **Vocabulary Check, Sheet 3**

Tear out this page. Write the English words on the lines. Fold the paper along the dotted line to see the correct answers so you can check your work.

tercero, tercera	***third***
cuarto, cuarta	***fourth***
quinto, quinta	***fifth***
sexto, sexta	***sixth***
séptimo, séptima	***seventh***
octavo, octava	***eighth***
noveno, novena	***ninth***
décimo, décima	***tenth***
la calculadora	***calculator***
la carpeta de argollas	***three-ring binder***
el diccionario	***dictionary***
aburrido, aburrida	***boring***
difícil	***difficult***
fácil	***easy***

Fold In ←

Realidades A Nombre ______ Hora ______

Capítulo 2A Fecha ______ **Vocabulary Check, Sheet 4**

Tear out this page. Write the Spanish words on the lines. Fold the paper along the dotted line to see the correct answers so you can check your work.

third	***tercero, tercera***
fourth	***cuarto, cuarta***
fifth	***quinto, quinta***
sixth	***sexto, sexta***
seventh	***séptimo, séptima***
eighth	***octavo, octava***
ninth	***noveno, novena***
tenth	***décimo, décima***
calculator	***la calculadora***
three-ring binder	***la carpeta de argollas***
dictionary	***el diccionario***
boring	***aburrido, aburrida***
difficult	***difícil***
easy	***fácil***

To hear a complete list of the vocabulary for this chapter, go to www.realidades.com and type in the Web Code jcd-0289. Then click on **Repaso del capítulo.**

Fold In ←

Realidades A | Nombre ______ | Hora ______

Capítulo 2A | Fecha ______ | **Guided Practice Activities 2A-1**

Subject pronouns (p. 98)

- The subject of the sentence tells who is doing the action. It is often a name: **Ana canta.**
- Subject pronouns replace people's names to say who is doing an action: **Ella canta. Tú bailas.**
- Here are the Spanish subject pronouns:

Singular	Plural
yo (I)	**nosotros** (we, *masculine or mixed*)
tú (you, *familiar*)	**nosotras** (we, *feminine*)
usted (you, *formal*)	**vosotros** (you, *familiar plural, masculine or mixed*)
él (he)	**vosotras** (you, *familiar plural, feminine*)
ella (she)	**ustedes** (you, *formal plural*)
	ellos (they, *masculine or mixed*)
	ellas (they, *feminine*)

- **Vosotros** and **vosotras** are primarily used in Spain.
- **Usted** and **ustedes** are formal forms that are used with people you address with a title, such as **señor** and **doctor**.
- In Latin America, **ustedes** is also used when addressing two or more people you call **tú** individually.

A. Write the twelve subject pronouns listed above in the correct category of the chart. Follow the model.

Singular			Plural		
Masculine only	Feminine only	Masculine or feminine	Masculine or mixed	Feminine only	Masculine or feminine
él	***ella***	***yo***	***ellos***	***ellas***	***ustedes***
		tú	***nosotros***	***nosotras***	
		usted	***vosotros***	***vosotras***	

B. Look at the English subject pronouns below. Use the list above to help you circle the Spanish subject pronoun that corresponds to the English pronoun.

1. *I* (**él** / **yo**)
2. *we* (**nosotros** / **vosotros**)
3. *you* (**ella** / **usted**)
4. *they* (**ellos** / **ustedes**)
5. *he* (**tú** / **él**)
6. *we* (**usted** / **nosotras**)
7. *you* (**nosotras** / **tú**)
8. *you* (**ellas** / **ustedes**)
9. *she* (**él** / **ella**)
10. *they* (**nosotras** / **ellas**)

realidades.com • Web Code: jcd-0203

Realidades A | Nombre ______ | Hora ______

Capítulo 2A | Fecha ______ | **Guided Practice Activities 2A-2**

Subject pronouns *(continued)*

C. Circle the subject pronoun that is best associated with each group of names.

1. Susana, Luisa, Marta: (**ellos** / **ellas**)
2. Pablo: (**él** / **ella**)
3. el señor Rivas: (**tú** / **usted**)
4. la señora Rivas: (**tú** / **usted**)
5. Alberto y tú: (**ustedes** / **nosotros**)
6. Sandra y ella: (**ellos** / **ellas**)
7. Marcos y María: (**ellos** / **ellas**)
8. el señor Rodríguez y la señora Rodríguez: (**ustedes** / **vosotros**)
9. Teresa: (**él** / **ella**)
10. Martín y Roberto: (**ellos** / **ellas**)

D. Look at the following drawings and answer the questions using subject pronouns. Follow the model.

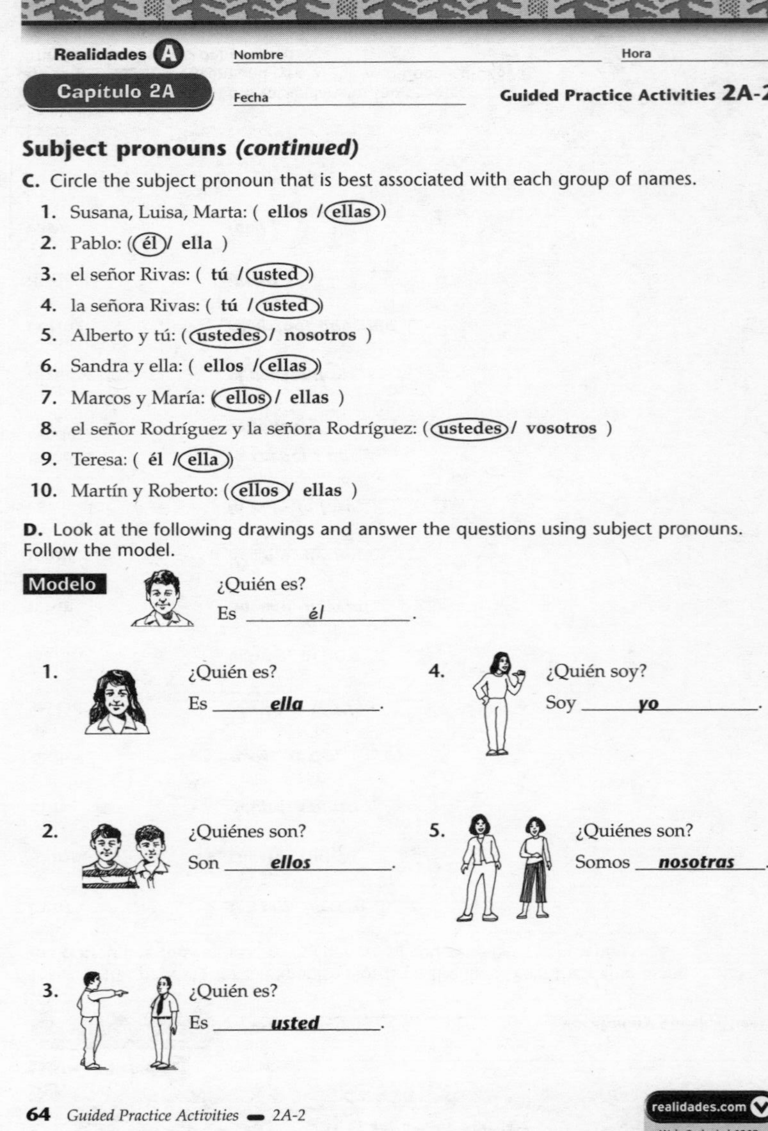

Modelo ¿Quién es? Es *él*.

1. ¿Quién es? Es ***ella***.
2. ¿Quiénes son? Son ***ellos***.
3. ¿Quién es? Es ***usted***.
4. ¿Quién soy? Soy ***yo***.
5. ¿Quiénes son? Somos ***nosotras***.

realidades.com • Web Code: jcd-0203

Realidades A Nombre ____ Hora ____

Capítulo 2A Fecha ____ Guided Practice Activities 2A-3

Present tense of *-ar* verbs (p. 100)

- An infinitive is the most basic form of a verb. In English, infinitives have the word "to" in front of them (to talk). In Spanish, infinitives end in **-ar**, **-er**, or **-ir**.
- The largest number of Spanish infinitives end in **-ar: hablar, cantar,** etc.
- To create the present tense of most of these verbs, drop the **-ar** from the stem: **habl-, cant-,** etc.
- Add the verb endings:

yo: add **-o: hablo**	nosotros/nosotras: add **-amos**: hablamos
tú: add **-as: hablas**	vosotros/vosotras: add **-áis**: habláis
usted/él/ella: add **-a: habla**	ustedes/ellos/ellas: add **-an**: hablan

A. Look at each verb form. Circle the ending. Follow the model.

Modelo estudi(a)

1. habl(as)
2. nad(o)
3. cant(a)
4. toc(amos)
5. trabaj(as)
6. patin(amos)
7. dibuj(an)
8. bail(o)
9. pas(an)
10. escuch(a)

B. Now, look at the same list of verb forms from **part A** and circle the subject pronoun that matches each verb.

1. (**usted** / **(tú)**) hablas
2. (**(yo)** / **ella**) nado
3. (**(usted)** / **yo**) canta
4. (**(nosotros)** / **vosotros**) tocamos
5. (**(tú)** / **usted**) trabajas
6. (**ellos** / **(nosotras)**) patinamos
7. (**(ustedes)** / **nosotros**) dibujan
8. (**(yo)** / **él**) bailo
9. (**(ellas)** / **usted**) pasan
10. (**(ella)** / **ustedes**) escucha

realidades.com • Web Code: jcd-0204

Realidades A Nombre ____ Hora ____

Capítulo 2A Fecha ____ Guided Practice Activities 2A-4

Present tense of *-ar* verbs *(continued)*

C. Complete each sentence by writing the correct **-ar** verb ending on the line provided. Follow the model.

Modelo Ellas mont*an* en bicicleta.

1. Marta trabaj***a***.
2. Yo cant***o***.
3. Tú esquí***as***.
4. Ellos patin***an***.
5. Nosotros bail***amos***.

D. Now, complete each sentence with the correct verb form of the infinitive in parentheses. Follow the model.

Modelo Tú (nadar) *nadas*.

1. Yo (bailar) ***bailo***.
2. Ella (cantar) ***canta***.
3. Nosotros (trabajar) ***trabajamos***.
4. Ustedes (patinar) ***patinan***.
5. Ellos (esquiar) ***esquían***.
6. Tú (nadar) ***nadas***.
7. Él (dibujar) ***dibuja***.
8. Ellas (usar) ***usan*** la computadora.

E. Create complete sentences using the subject pronoun provided. Follow the model.

Modelo tú / *Tú dibujas.*

1. él / 

Él patina.

2. nosotros /

Nosotros cantamos.

3. ellos / 

Ellos nadan.

4. yo / 

Yo dibujo.

realidades.com • Web Code: jcd-0204

Lectura: La Escuela Español Vivo (pp. 108–109)

A. The reading in your textbook is a brochure for a school called **Español Vivo**. The following is an excerpt from that reading. Read and answer the questions that follow.

> *Es verano, el mes de junio. Eres estudiante en (Santa Ana), un pueblo en las montañas de (Costa Rica).*

1. Underline the season and month in the paragraph above.
2. Circle the town and country where the school is located.
3. What does the word **montañas** mean? ***mountains***

B. Here is another excerpt from that same reading. Read and answer the questions below.

> *Hay cinco estudiantes en tu clase. Uds. (escuchan), (hablan) y (practican) el español todo el día. También (usan) la computadora.*

1. How many students are in the class? ***five***
2. Circle the four activities from the reading that students do in class (just circle the verbs).
3. How many of the verbs that you circled in number 2 go with the word **el español**?
   3 Which ones? ***escuchan, hablan, practican***

C. Look at the reading on the top of the second page in your textbook.

1. Circle the one activity listed below that is NOT something you can do on the weekends in Costa Rica.
   - **a.** visitar un volcán
   - **b.** visitar un parque nacional
   - (**c.** nadar en el mar Mediterráneo)
   - **d.** nadar en el océano Pacífico
2. There are many cognates in the four examples above. Write the Spanish word or words, choosing from examples **a** through **d**, that go with the English words below.
   - visit ***visitar***
   - volcano ***volcán***
   - national park ***parque nacional***
   - Mediterranean ***Mediterráneo***
   - Pacific Ocean ***océano Pacífico***

D. Look at the schedule for the school day in the **Español Vivo** school. Answer the questions that follow.

Hora	lunes a viernes
08:00–10:30	Clases de español
10:30–11:00	Recreo
11:00–13:00	Clases de español
13:00–14:00	Almuerzo
14:00–15:30	Conversaciones
15:30–16:30	Clase de música y baile

1. At what times do the students go to classes?
   at ***08:00***, ***11:00***, and ***15:30***
2. When do students have conversations? at ***14:00***
3. Since there is no A.M. or P.M., how do you know when the clock goes over to afternoon hours? ***The hour is more than 12:00.***

realidades.com
• Web Code: jcd-0205

Presentación oral (p. 111) *Answers will vary.*

Task: Imagine that a student from Costa Rica has just arrived at your school. Tell the student about some of your classes.

A. Fill in the chart below with information on three of your classes. Follow the model.

Hora	Clase	Comentarios	Profesor(a)
primera	*la clase de arte*	*me gusta dibujar*	*el Sr. Gómez*

B. Before writing up your own presentation, read the following sample. Read it out loud the second time through to get an idea of how long it will take you to do your presentation.

> *En la primera hora tengo la clase de arte. Me gusta dibujar. La clase es mi favorita. El Sr. Gómez es el profesor.*

When speaking, remember to do the following:

_____ speak clearly
_____ use complete sentences
_____ read all information

C. Now, fill in the paragraph below with information about one of your classes.

En la ____________ hora tengo la clase de ____________.
Me gusta ____________. La clase es ____________.
____________ es el (la) profesor(a).

D. When the teacher asks you to present your work, you will describe the one class as you see it in **part C.** Your teacher will be grading you on:

- how complete your preparation is
- how much information you communicate
- how easy it is to understand you.

Realidades A   Nombre ______ Hora ______

Capítulo 2A   Fecha ______   VIDEO

Antes de ver el video

Actividad 1

Think of two of your favorite and two of your least favorite classes. Write the name of each class, when you have it, and why it is your favorite or least favorite.

Clase	Hora	Comentarios
		Answers will vary.

¿Comprendes?

Actividad 2

Claudia had a bad day. Circle the correct answer to explain what happened to her.

1. Claudia tiene un día difícil en el colegio (*high school*). ¿Por qué?
   a. A Claudia no le gusta su colegio.
   b. Claudia no tiene amigos.
   c. Tiene problemas con el horario.
   d. A Claudia no le gustan las matemáticas.
2. ¿En qué hora tiene Claudia la clase de matemáticas?
   a. en la primera hora   c. en la quinta hora
   b. en la tercera hora   **d. todas las anteriores (*all of the above*)**
3. Claudia habla con la persona que hace el horario. ¿Cómo se llama?
   a. Sra. Santoro   b. Sr. López   c. Srta. García   **d. Sr. Treviño**
4. Para Teresa la clase de inglés es
   a. aburrida.   b. interesante.   **c. fantástica.**   d. difícil.
5. En la tercera hora Claudia piensa que las matemáticas son aburridas, porque
   a. es el primer día de clases.   **c. tiene seis clases de matemáticas hoy.**
   b. la profesora es muy divertida.   d. no entiende las matemáticas.

Realidades A | Nombre ____ | Hora ____

Capítulo 2A | Fecha ____ | VIDEO

Actividad 3

Write **cierto** (*true*) or **falso** (*false*) next to each statement.

1. La clase de matemáticas es muy fácil para Claudia. cierto
2. Teresa habla con el Sr. Treviño del problema con su horario. falso
3. Teresa y Claudia tienen el almuerzo a la misma hora. cierto
4. Teresa tiene la clase de ciencias sociales en la tercera hora. falso

Y, ¿qué más?

Actividad 4

Complete the paragraph with information about your teachers, classes, school, and friends.

Answers will vary.

El profesor / La profesora que más me gusta es el Sr. / la Sra. ____________.

Él / Ella enseña la clase de ____________ en la ____________ hora y su clase es muy ____________.

Después de la ____________ hora tengo el almuerzo. Me gusta mucho porque puedo estar con ____________ y ____________; ellos / ellas son mis amigos / amigas.

El director / La directora de mi colegio se llama ____________. Él / Ella es muy ____________ y ____________.

Realidades A | Nombre ____ | Hora ____

Capítulo 2A | Fecha ____ | AUDIO

Actividad 5

You overhear several people in the hall trying to find out if they have classes together this year. As you listen to each conversation, write an *X* in the box under ***SÍ*** if they have a class together, or under ***NO*** if they do not. You will hear each conversation twice.

	SÍ	NO
1.		X
2.	X	
3.	X	
4.		X
5.	X	

Actividad 6

As you stand outside the school counselor's office, you hear four students trying to talk to him. They are all requesting to get out of a certain class. From the part of the conversation that you hear, write in the blank the class from which each student is requesting a transfer. You will hear each statement twice.

CLASE	PROFESOR(A)
1. matemáticas	el profesor Pérez
2. arte	la profesora Muñoz
3. español	el profesor Cortez
4. ciencias sociales	la profesora Lenis
5. almuerzo	
6. ciencias	el profesor Gala
7. educación física	el profesor Fernández
8. inglés	la profesora Ochoa

1. La clase de educación física
2. La clase de arte
3. La clase de inglés
4. La clase de matemáticas

Realidades A | Nombre | Hora

Capítulo 2A | Fecha | AUDIO

Actividad 7

Emilio, a new student from Bolivia, is attending his first pep assembly! He is eager to make friends and begins talking to Diana, who is sitting next to him. Listen to their conversation. If they have something in common, place a check mark in the column labeled **Ellos**. If the statement only applies to Emilio, place a check mark in the column labeled **Él**. If the statement only applies to Diana, place a check mark in the column labeled **Ella**. **Note:** Be sure you have placed a check mark in ONLY one of the columns for each statement. You will hear the conversation twice.

INFORMACIÓN	ÉL	ELLA	ELLOS
Tiene la clase de español en la primera hora.	✔		
Tiene la clase de español en la segunda hora.		✔	
Tiene una profesora simpática.		✔	
Tiene una profesora graciosa.	✔		
Tiene una clase de arte en la quinta hora.	✔		
Tiene una clase de educación física en la quinta hora.		✔	
Practica deportes.	✔		
Estudia mucho en la clase de matemáticas.			✔
Es trabajador(a).			✔
Tiene mucha tarea.			✔
Tiene almuerzo a las once y media.			✔

Realidades A | Nombre | Hora

Capítulo 2A | Fecha | AUDIO

Actividad 8

Listen as four people talk about what they do during the day. There will be some things that all four people do and other things that not all of them do. Fill in the grid with a check mark if the person says he or she does a certain activity. Also, fill in the **Yo** column with a check mark for the activities that you do every day. You will hear each set of statements twice.

	EVA	DAVID	RAQUEL	JOSÉ	YO
	✔	✔			Answers will vary.
	✔	✔	✔	✔	
		✔	✔	✔	
			✔		
		✔			
	✔	✔	✔		
	✔			✔	

Nombre ______ Hora ______

Fecha ______ **AUDIO**

Actividad 9

You and your family are considering hosting a student from Costa Rica for a semester. Before you make the decision, you want to know a little about the student. Listen to part of a recording that the students from Costa Rica made for your class. Use the grid to keep track of what each of the students says. You will then use this information to decide which student would be the most compatible for you and your family. You will hear each set of statements twice.

Estudiante	Característica(s) de la personalidad	Clase favorita	Actividades favoritas
JORGE	deportista, gracioso	educación física	practicar deportes, montar en bicicleta
LUZ	talentosa	música	cantar, bailar
MARCO	estudioso	matemáticas	tocar la guitarra, estudiar matemáticas
CRISTINA	artística	arte	dibujar, escribir cuentos

Which student is most like you? Answers will vary.

Nombre ______ Hora ______

Fecha ______ **WRITING**

Actividad 10

Your classmates are curious about your schedule at school. Using complete sentences, tell them what classes you have during the day. Follow the model.

Modelo *Yo tengo la clase de inglés en la segunda hora.*

1. Answers will vary, but will look like model.
2. ______
3. ______
4. ______
5. ______
6. ______
7. ______

Actividad 11

Answer the following questions using the subject pronoun suggested by the pictures. Follow the model.

Modelo ¿Quiénes usan la computadora?
Ellos usan la computadora.

1. ¿Quién habla con Teresa?
Ella habla con Teresa.

2. ¿Quién habla con Paco?
Él habla con Paco.

Realidades A — Nombre ______ Hora ______

Capítulo 2A — Fecha ______ **WRITING**

3. ¿Quiénes hablan?

Ellas hablan.

4. ¿Cómo es el Sr. García?

Él es simpático. (adj. will vary) or Ud. es simpático.

5. Ana, ¿tienes la clase de arte en la primera hora?

Sí, **yo tengo la clase de arte en la primera hora.**

Ana

6. ¿Cristina y yo somos muy buenas amigas?

Sí, **nosotras somos muy buenas amigas.**

Cristina Yo

Realidades A — Nombre ______ Hora ______

Capítulo 2A — Fecha ______ **WRITING**

Actividad 12

A new student at your school has come to you for information about how things work at your school and what your day is like. Answer the student's questions truthfully in complete sentences. Follow the model.

Modelo ¿La secretaria habla mucho por teléfono?

Sí, ella habla mucho

1. ¿Estudias inglés en la primera hora?

   estudio

2. ¿Quién enseña la clase de matemáticas?

   enseña

3. ¿Necesito un diccionario para la clase de arte?

   necesitas

4. ¿Cantas en el coro (*choir*)?

   canto

5. ¿Pasas mucho tiempo en la cafetería?

   paso

6. ¿Uds. practican deportes en la clase de educación física?

   practicamos

7. ¿Los estudiantes usan las computadoras en la clase de ciencias naturales?

   usan

8. ¿Uds. bailan en la clase de español?

   bailamos

9. ¿Los profesores tocan el piano en la clase de música?

   tocan

10. ¿Los estudiantes hablan mucho en la clase de francés?

    hablan

WRITING

Actividad 13 Answers will vary.

A. List two classes that you have, when you have them, and who the teacher is.

	Clase	Hora	Profesor(a)
1.			
2.			

B. Now, write complete sentences about whether or not you like each class from Part A. Make sure to tell why you do or do not like each class.

Clase 1: Answers will vary.

Clase 2:

C. Now, using the information from Parts A and B, write a paragraph about one of the classes. Make sure to tell the name of the class, when you have it, and who the teacher is. You should also describe your teacher, tell what you do in class, and say whether or not you like the class.

Answers will vary.

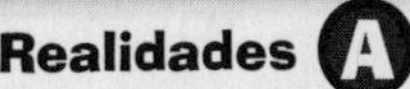

Realidades A

Capítulo 2A

Test Preparation Answers

Reading Skills
p. 127 2. **C**
p. 128 2. **B**

Integrated Performance Assessment
p. 129
Answers will vary.

Practice Test: The High-School Experience in Latin America
p. 131

1. A
2. H
3. B
4. G
5. Answers will vary but may include: Fluency in English is very important in today's competitive job market; students are interested in traveling to other parts of the world where English is the dominant language.

Realidades A

Capítulo 2B

School-to-Home Connection

Dear Parent or Guardian,

The theme for the chapter is *La escuela* (School) and this chapter is called *Tu sala de clases* (Your classroom).

Upon completion of this chapter, your child will be able to:

- describe a classroom
- indicate where things are located
- talk about more than one object or person
- understand cultural perspectives on school

Also, your child will explore:

- the correct pronunciation of the letter *g*
- nonverbal body language in the form of gestures

Realidades helps with the development of reading, writing, and speaking skills through the use of strategies, process speaking, and process writing. In this chapter, students will:

- read about UNICEF
- write about the classroom's layout

Remember that additional help is available online at www.realidades.com by using the Web Codes in the Student Edition or in the Leveled Vocabulary and Grammar Workbook.

Check it out! If you have a computer at home, have your child point to its different parts and name them in Spanish. If you do not have a computer, have your child draw a picture of one and label the parts in Spanish.

Sincerely,

For: Tips to Parents
Visit: www.realidades.com
Web Code: jce-0010

Realidades **A**

Capítulo 2B

Chapter Resource Checklist

Resources	CO†	APV	VH	MAN	LEC	PER	PE	MH	REP	PREP
Teacher										
Teacher's Resource Book										
Input Script		■								
Audio Script		■	■	■					■	■
GramActiva BLM				■						
Communicative Activities BLM				■						
School-to-Home Connection BLM	■									
Clip Art		■								■
Situation Cards BLM									■	
TPR Stories Book		■	■	■						
Fine Art Transparencies Teacher's Guide	■									
Pre-AP* Resource Book			■	■	■		■			
Student										
Leveled Vocabulary and Grammar Workbook										
Guided Practice		■	■	■	■		■		■	■
Core Practice		■	■	■					■	■
Communication Workbook with Test Preparation										
Writing				■						
Audio				■						
Video			■							
Test Preparation					■					■
RPH Workbook	■	■	■	■	■	■	■		■	
Lecturas para hispanohablantes					■					
Grammar Study Guides				■					■	■
Transparencies										
Answers on Transparencies		■	■	■	■					■
Vocabulary and Grammar	■	■	■	■						
Fine Art	■									
Assessment										
Assessment Program										
Quizzes			■	■						
Chapter Test										■
realidades.com			■	■						■
ExamView Test Bank CD-ROM										■
QuickTake on PresentationExpress		■	■	■						■
MindPoint QuizShow CD-ROM									■	
Alternate Assessment Program										■
Performance-Based Writing							■			■
Self-Test on realidades.com & CWS										■
Assessment Program RPH			■	■						■
Technology										
realidades.com	■	■	■	■	■	■	■	■	■	■
myeBook	■	■	■	■	■	■	■	■	■	■
TeacherExpress CD-ROM	■	■	■	■	■	■	■	■	■	■
PresentationExpress DVD		■	■	■						■
Video Program DVD			■	■						
Culture Video DVD	■									
Audio Program CD 5		■	■	■						■
Assessment CD 20										■
Song CD 22		■								
Canciones de hip hop on realidades.com & CWS			■							■

† *See Abbreviation Key on page iv.*

Input Script

Presentation

Input Vocabulary 1: Place the overhead transparency on the screen. Point to each classroom object and model its pronunciation. Hand out copies of the Vocabulary Clip Art and have students tear the images into individual classroom objects. Then take flashcards with the vocabulary words written on them and tape them to the different objects in the room, but tape them on all the wrong objects. As you tape them, say, for example, "*¡A ver, la bandera, aquí está!*" When you have finished and the students are looking at you quizzically, say "*¿No es correcto? ¿No es la bandera?*" Have students hold up the Clip Art image that matches the flashcard to tell you where to place the flashcard correctly. Remove the cards before doing the next activity.

Input Monologue: Model the first three sentences of Enrique's monologue. Then look around your classroom and declare "*¡Aquí está mi sala de clases!*" Then go to different classroom objects and say "*Y aquí está mi ... mi ...*" Act as if you cannot remember the word. Have students hold up the Clip Art image and call out the words for the objects. Then go to a student and pick up his or her dictionary and say "*¡Y aquí está mi diccionario!*" Encourage the student to say "*¡No, aquí está mi diccionario!*" Next, model the rest of Enrique's monologue. Look puzzled and say "*¡Uno, dos, tres, cuatro ... hay cuatro estudiantes! ¡Cuatro! ¡No hay muchos estudiantes en la clase de español de Enrique! Pero ...* (count your students quickly) *... ¡hay muchos estudiantes en mi clase de español!*" Then ask students "*¿Cuántos estudiantes hay en tu clase de ___?*" Ask about different classes. Have them give rough estimates.

Input Vocabulary 2: Model the pronunciation of the computer-related words. Hand out copies of the Vocabulary Clip Art showing parts of the computer and have students tear them into individual images. Say the words and have students arrange the images in the order you say them.

Input Location Expressions: Read the sentences that describe the location of objects in the visual. Make additional statements based on the visual *("La computadora está encima de la mesa.")* Then ask for a student volunteer. Hold a dictionary in different locations in relation to the student and make true and false location statements. Have students give a "thumbs-up" sign for true statements and a "thumbs-down" sign for false statements. Then give students directions and have them arrange the Clip Art images on their desks.

Input Dialogue: Model the pronunciation of the dialogue. Then have students trade binders (calculators, dictionaries) with other students. Ask students "*___, ¿es tu ___?*" and have them tell to whom the object belongs.

Comprehension Check

- Hide a ***tesoro*** (some small object) somewhere in the classroom. Also hide a series of clues. You will give students Clue #1 *("Está debajo de la papelera.")*, which will tell the location of Clue #2, *("Está detrás de la bandera.")*, which in turn will tell the location of Clue #3 *("Está al lado de la computadora.")*, which will tell the location of the ***tesoro.*** You might hide three or more ***tesoros*** with three sets of color-coded clues and have groups of students race to be the first ones to find their ***tesoro.***
- Tell students you are going to rearrange the classroom. Describe the new arrangement and have students draw the objects in their new locations.

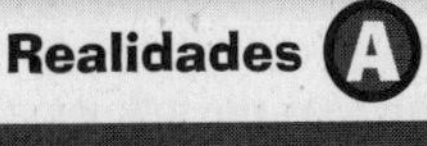

Audio Script

Audio CD, Capitulo 2B

Track 01: ***A primera vista,*** **Student Book, p. 118 (2:34)**

Vocabulario y gramática en contexto
You will hear each word or phrase twice. After the first time there will be a pause so you can pronounce it, then you will hear the word or phrase a second time.

la bandera
el reloj
el cartel
las ventanas
la computadora
la puerta
el escritorio
la papelera
el sacapuntas
la silla

Read along as you listen to the statements.

MALE TEEN: ¡Hola! Me llamo Enrique. Aquí está mi sala de clases. Son las nueve y los estudiantes están en la clase de español. Hay muchos estudiantes en mi clase. ¿Cuántos estudiantes hay en tu clase?

Track 02: ***A primera vista,*** **Student Book, p. 119 (1:52)**

Vocabulario y gramática en contexto
You will hear each word or phrase twice. After the first time there will be a pause so you can pronounce it, then you will hear the word or phrase a second time.

la pantalla
el disquete
el teclado
la mesa
el ratón

Read along as you listen to dialogue.

MALE TEEN: Elena, ¿es tu disquete?
FEMALE TEEN: No, es el disquete de David.

Read along as you listen to each statement.

El cuaderno está debajo de la calculadora.
La calculadora está encima del cuaderno.
Los bolígrafos están al lado del diccionario.
La bandera está detrás de la computadora.
La silla está delante de la mesa.

Track 03: ***A primera vista,*** **Act. 1, Student Book, p. 119 (2:02)**

¿Qué hay en la sala de clases?
Look at Enrique's classroom. You will be asked if certain things are there. If you see the item mentioned, raise your hand and give a "thumbs-up" sign. If you don't see it, give a "thumbs-down" sign. You will hear each question twice.

1. ¿Hay una computadora en la sala de clases?
2. ¿Hay un teclado?
3. ¿Hay una tele?
4. ¿Hay un sacapuntas?
5. ¿Hay una mochila?
6. ¿Hay una ventana?
7. ¿Hay un cartel?
8. ¿Hay una puerta?
9. ¿Hay una guitarra?
10. ¿Hay un reloj?

Track 04: ***A primera vista,*** **Act. 2, Student Book, p. 119 (1:53)**

En la sala de clases
Look at the picture of Enrique's classroom again. Listen to where several items are located. If the description is correct, raise one hand, but if the description is not correct, raise both hands.

1. La computadora está debajo del profesor.
2. La silla está delante del escritorio.
3. La bandera está detrás de la computadora.
4. La papelera está al lado del escritorio del profesor.
5. El cartel está en la pared.
6. El reloj está al lado del sacapuntas.

Track 05: ***A primera vista, Videohistoria,*** **Student Book, pp. 120–122 (1:55)**

Un ratón en la sala de clases
¿Qué pasa en la clase de estudios sociales? Lee la historia.

Read along as you listen to the *Videohistoria.*

See Student Book pages 120–122 for script.

Track 06: ***Manos a la obra,*** **Act. 16, Student Book, p. 130 (3:57)**

¿Cierto o falso?
Write the numbers 1 to 6 on a sheet of paper. Listen to the statements about Javier's Spanish Club photo and write *cierto* or *falso* based on the information provided as you view the photograph from *your* perspective. You will hear each statement twice.

1. Yo estoy detrás de Sara.
2. El señor Salas está debajo del escritorio.
3. Julián y Mateo están delante de Rosa.
4. Sara y yo estamos al lado del escritorio.
5. José y Lucita están encima del escritorio.
6. Benito está delante del señor Salas.

Track 07: Audio Act. 5, Writing, Audio & Video Workbook, p. 41 (4:12)

As you look at the picture, decide whether the statements you hear are *ciertos* or *falsos.* You will hear each statement twice.

1. El chico es muy ordenado.
2. Ellos están en la sala de clases durante el almuerzo.
3. La profesora es una persona muy desordenada.
4. Hay una mochila al lado de la puerta.
5. Encima de la mochila hay disquetes.
6. Estamos en el mes de diciembre.

7. Según el reloj, son las doce de la tarde.
8. Hay una bandera de México en la sala de clases.
9. Hay un cartel de Disneyland en la pared.
10. El ratón está encima de la silla.
11. Hay una papelera delante de la silla.
12. Hay una carpeta de argollas en la mochila.
13. Hay disquetes encima de la computadora de la profesora.
14. La puerta está al lado del escritorio de la profesora.
15. El chico necesita una calculadora para la tarea.

Track 08: Audio Act. 6, Writing, Audio & Video Workbook, p. 42 (2:03)

Tomás suddenly realizes in the middle of his science class that the diskette with his entire class project on it is missing! He asks several people if they know where it is. Listen as different people tell Tomás where they think his diskette is. In the timeline, write what classroom he goes to and where in the classroom he looks, in the order in which you hear them. You will hear this conversation twice.

TOMÁS: ¡Ay! ¿Dónde está mi disquete? ¡Necesito mi disquete para el proyecto! Susana… ¿Dónde está mi disquete?

SUSANA: ¿Tu disquete? Está en la clase de inglés encima de la mesa.

TOMÁS: Gracias, Susana. ¡Ay! No está aquí! Antonio, ¿sabes dónde está mi disquete?

ANTONIO: Está allí, en la sala de la clase de español, al lado de la ventana.

TOMÁS: Gracias…¡Ay! No está aquí tampoco. Oye, Noé. ¿Sabes dónde está mi disquete?

NOÉ: Hmmm. Está debajo del teclado de la computadora en la clase de tecnología.

TOMÁS: Gracias, Noé. ¡Hola, Sr. Akins! ¿Está mi disquete aquí en la sala de clase? ¿Debajo del teclado?

SR. AKINS: No, Tomás. No está ni debajo del teclado ni al lado de la computadora. Está en tu mochila.

TOMÁS: ¿En mi mochila? ¡Aquí está! ¡En mi mochila!

You are going to hear this conversation again.

Track 09: *Manos a la obra,* Act. 22, Student Book, p. 132 (3:47)

Más palabras plurales

You will hear eight words. Say the plural form of each word as you hear it.

1. la mesa
2. la ventana
3. el escritorio
4. la mochila
5. el teclado
6. el reloj
7. la bandera
8. el disquete

Track 10: *Pronunciación,* The letter *g*, Student Book, p. 137 (1:39)

In Spanish, the letter *g* sounds like *g* in *go* when it is followed by *a, o,* or *u,* although it often has a slightly softer sound than in English. Listen to and say the following words and sentences:

You will hear each word twice. After the word is pronounced the first time, there will be a pause so you can pronounce it. Then you will hear the word a second time.

Gustavo
agosto
amigo
domingo
pregunta
argollas
tengo
luego
gato

In Spanish, the letter *g* sounds like the letter *h* in *hot* when it is followed by *e* or *i*. Listen to and say the following words. Some of these words you have not yet heard or seen. Can you guess the meanings of the cognates?

inteligente
gimnasio
generoso
tecnología
general
biología

Try it out! See if you can guess how to pronounce the following Spanish first names. Keep in mind the pronunciation rules for the *g* sound.

Gabriela
Gilberto
Olga
Ángela
Gustavo
Rogelio
Gerardo
Rodrigo
Gregorio

Track 11: Audio Act. 7, Writing, Audio & Video Workbook, p. 42 (3:20)

It's time to take the Spanish Club picture for the yearbook, but there are several people who have still not arrived. Andrés, the president, decides to use his cell phone to find out where people are. As you listen to the first part of each conversation, complete the sentences below with the information he finds out. For example, you might write: *Beto está en el gimnasio.* You will hear each dialogue twice.

1. **ANDRÉS:** ¿Sr. Salas? Habla Andrés. ¿Dónde está usted? ¿Está con el Sr. Martín?
   SR. SALAS: El Sr. Martín y yo estamos aquí en la oficina.
2. **ANDRÉS:** ¿Javier? ¿Dónde estás?
   JAVIER: Estoy en la clase de tecnología. Necesito usar la computadora.
3. **ANDRÉS:** ¿Alejandra? ¿Estás con Sara? ¿Todo está bien?
   ALEJANDRA: Sí, nosotras estamos en la cafetería. Y estamos bien.

4. **Andrés:** ¿Mateo? Habla Andrés. ¿Dónde estás?
   Mateo: Estoy en casa porque estoy enfermo.
5. **Andrés:** Hola, José. Soy Andrés. ¿Dónde están ustedes dos?
   José: Antonieta y yo estamos en el gimnasio. ¿Por qué? ¿Necesitas algo?

Track 12: Audio Act. 8, Writing, Audio & Video Workbook, p. 43 (3:37)

One of your classmates from Spanish class is working in a store that sells school supplies. She overhears a customer speaking Spanish to his father and decides to try out her Spanish. As she asks him what he wants to buy, she discovers that he never wants just one of anything. As the customer tells your classmate what he wants, write the items on the sales receipt below. Use the pictures below to calculate the price of his purchases. You will hear each conversation twice.

1. **Female Teen:** ¿Necesitas unos disquetes?
   Male Teen: Sí, necesito cinco. Me gusta usar la computadora.
2. **Female Teen:** ¿Necesitas un cartel?
   Male Teen: No, necesito cuatro. Me encantan los carteles de los jugadores de básquetbol, como uno de Shaquille O'Neal.
3. **Female Teen:** ¿Necesitas un ratón?
   Male Teen: Sí, pero necesito siete. Son para la escuela.
4. **Female Teen:** ¿Necesitas una mochila?
   Male Teen: No, necesito dos. Tengo muchos libros.
5. **Female Teen:** ¿Necesitas un diccionario?
   Male Teen: Sí, pero necesito dos. Un diccionario de inglés y un diccionario de español.
6. **Female Teen:** ¿Necesitas unas carpetas?
   Male Teen: Sí, necesito nueve. Tengo seis clases y necesito tres para la profesora de ciencias.

Track 13: Audio Act. 9, Writing, Audio & Video Workbook, p. 44 (3:56)

Listen to two friends talking outside the door of the Spanish Club meeting. They want to go to the meeting, but they are afraid they won't remember everyone's names. Look at the drawing. In the grid, write in the name of the person who is being described. You will hear each dialogue twice.

1. **Male Teen 1:** ¿Quién es la chica reservada? Ella está al lado de la ventana.
   Male Teen 2: Se llama Inés. Sí, es reservada. Es talentosa también.
2. **Male Teen 1:** ¿Quién es ella, la chica que está debajo del reloj?
   Male Teen 2: Se llama Tina. Es una estudiante muy inteligente.
3. **Male Teen 1:** ¿Quién es el chico que está al lado de la puerta?
   Male Teen 2: ¿Con el cartel? Es Antonio. Es el presidente del club.
4. **Male Teen 2:** ¿Quién es la chica al lado de la computadora de la profesora?
   Male Teen 1: Es Elena. Es muy trabajadora. Hay algo muy interesante en la pantalla, ¿no?
5. **Male Teen 1:** ¿Quién es el chico encima de los pupitres?
   Male Teen 2: ¿Con la mochila? Es Juan. Es muy gracioso.
6. **Male Teen 2:** ¿Quién es la chica al lado de Elena? Está allá, enfrente de la papelera.
   Male Teen 1: Es Claudia. Es una amiga de Elena. Bueno. Vamos. ¿Estás listo?
   Male Teen 2: Sí, claro.

Track 14: *Repaso del capítulo*, Student Book, p. 144 (2:30)

Vocabulario y gramática

Listen to these words and expressions that you have learned in this chapter. You will hear each word or expression once.

See Student Book page 144 for vocabulary list.

Track 15: *Preparación para el examen*, Student Book, p. 145 (1:18)

Escuchar

Practice task.

Listen as a student frantically asks some of his friends where he left his homework. Can you identify all of the classrooms and places they suggest that he look?

Juan: ¡Ay! Mi tarea … ¿Dónde está? Necesito mi tarea para la clase de matemáticas. Ana, ¿dónde está mi tarea?

Ana: ¿Tu tarea? Está en la clase de ciencias sociales, en el escritorio del profesor.

Juan: Gracias, Ana. ¡Ay! No está aquí. Daniel, ¿dónde está mi tarea de matemáticas?

Daniel: Está en la clase de tecnología … al lado de la computadora.

Juan: Gracias.

Realidades A

Capítulo 2B

Video Script

A primera vista: *¿Un ratón en la sala de clases?* (5:20)

PROFESORA: ¡Buenos días, estudiantes! Atención. ¡Muy bien! La tarea, por favor.

CLAUDIA: ¿Qué es?

TERESA: Es mi hámster. Es para la clase de ciencias, en la quinta hora.

CLAUDIA: Y ¿cómo se llama?

TERESA: Paquito. Se llama Paquito.

CLAUDIA: ¡Qué divertido!

MANOLO: Carlos, no tengo mi tarea.

CARLOS: ¿Qué? ¿De veras?

MANOLO: Shh … Tengo una idea …

PROFESORA: Silencio, Claudia y Teresa. Manolo, ¿qué pasa? ¿No tienes tu tarea?

MANOLO: Bueno, eh, profesora, eh …

CLAUDIA: ¡Teresa! ¿Dónde está Paquito?

TERESA: ¿Qué dices? ¿Paquito? ¿Dónde está mi hámster? ¡Ay, no!

CARLOS: ¡Un ratón! Profesora, hay un ratón debajo de su silla. ¡Un ratón! ¡Hay un ratón en el salón de clases!

PROFESORA: ¿De verás? ¡Un ratón! ¿Un ratón en la clase de ciencias sociales? Imposible. ¿Dónde está, dónde?

CARLOS: Sí, profesora. Es posible. ¡Ojo! Ahora está debajo de su escritorio.

MANOLO: Y ahora está al lado de la puerta. Es un ratón muy impaciente.

PROFESORA: Manolo, por favor.

TERESA: ¡No es un ratón! Es mi hámster, y se llama Paquito.

CLAUDIA: Está allí, delante de la mesa. Veo su cabeza y su nariz. Es muy atrevido.

TERESA: ¡Ay, mi Paquito!

PROFESORA: ¡Cálmense, por favor! Y ahora, ¿dónde está … Paquito?

MANOLO: Pues ahora está detrás de la computadora, encima de los disquetes. Es muy inteligente.

PROFESORA: ¿Dónde?

TERESA: ¡Manolo! Es el ratón de la computadora. No es Paquito.

PROFESORA: Manolo, necesitas …

MANOLO: Lo siento.

ESTUDIANTE: No está detrás de la papelera. No está debajo de la mesa. Tampoco está al lado de la bandera.

PROFESORA: ¡Atención! Cálmense, por favor.

DIRECTOR: Profesora López. ¿Qué es esto? ¿Qué pasa?

PROFESORA: Pues, hay un ratón en el salón de clases.

DIRECTOR: ¡Imposible!

TERESA: No es un ratón. Es mi hámster.

DIRECTOR: Señorita, ¿tiene un hámster en la escuela? ¿Por qué?

TERESA: Es para la clase de ciencias.

DIRECTOR: Señorita, necesito hablar con usted más tarde.

CARLOS: ¡Aquí está! Está en mi mochila, con mis libros, mi calculadora, mi regla. Necesito mi calculadora. Por favor …

DIRECTOR: ¡Silencio, por favor!

TERESA: Paquito, mi precioso. Ven aquí. ¿Estás bien?

PROFESORA: Teresa. En la jaula. Ahora.

DIRECTOR: Teresa, hablamos en mi oficina.

TERESA: Sí, señor.

DIRECTOR: Hasta luego, estudiantes, Profesora López.

PROFESORA: Sí, señor. ¿Y ahora? ¡Ah, sí! Manolo, ¿tu tarea?

MANOLO: Pues, Profesora …

GramActiva Videos: the verb *estar;* plurals of nouns and articles **(7:16)**

The verb *estar*

HOST: *Estar* is not like other verbs that end in *-ar.* It's an irregular verb. *Estar* means "to be." It is used when describing emotions, feelings, conditions, and even locations.

HYPNOTIST: We're going back, into the past. We're looking at *-ar* verbs again. Tell me what conjugations you see.

PATIENT: I see *hablar.* Delete subject pronouns here. *hablo, hablas, habla, hablamos, habláis, hablan.* It conjugates the same as other *-ar* verbs.

HOST: *Estar* means "to be." But *estar* is an irregular verb. It is similar to the others, but in the *yo* form it ends in *oy, estoy,* instead of just *-o.*

HOST: The other forms follow the rules of *-ar* verbs. But you also need to add an accent mark to all forms except *yo* and *nosotros, nosotras.*
Yo estoy.
Tú estás.
Usted, él, ella está.
Nosotros, nosotras estamos.
Vosotros, vosotras estáis.
Ustedes, ellos, ellas están.

HOST: *El sacapuntas está debajo del reloj.*
Tú estás encima de la silla.
Yo estoy delante de la mesa.
Nosotros estamos delante del cartel.
Los ratones están debajo de la silla.

HOST: You can make a sentence with *estar* negative just like any other sentence. Insert the word *no* before the verb.

OLD MAN: *No estoy en mi escritorio.*
No estás en mi escritorio.
No estamos en mi escritorio.

Quiz

HOST: Fill in the blank with the correct form of *estar.*

está
estoy
está
estamos
están

Plurals of nouns and articles

Host: So far we've dealt primarily with the loneliest number—one. One pencil, one book, one chapter. But in real life, there is more.

Man: *Ojo* means "eye," but I have two, not just one. Since *ojo* ends in a vowel, to make it plural just add an *-s*. This works for any noun that ends with a vowel.
Now I have *dos ojos.*
I also have not *una pierna,* but *dos piernas.*
And not *un dedo del pie,* but *diez dedos del pie.*

Host: Not all nouns end in a vowel; a few of them end in *z,* like *lápiz,* or *nariz.* To make them plural, drop the *-z,* and add *-ces. Un lápiz, dos lápices, una nariz, dos narices.*

Host: And then there is the whole world of nouns that don't end in *-z,* or a vowel. Everything else gets *-es.*
Un ratón, dos ratones.
Un reloj, dos relojes.
Un cartel, dos carteles.

Twins: Well, that was easy enough.

Cowboy: Hold it right there, *chicos.* You seem to forget we got a way of agreeing on things around here.

Host: He's right, you know. Articles, words like *the, a,* and *an,* whether they are definite or indefinite, have to always agree with the noun in gender and number in Spanish. That means more rules for plurals.

Host: *El* or *la* is equivalent to the word *the* in English; they are definite articles. English has no plural form for *the. The* hand, *the* hands, *the* foot, *the* feet, it's all the same.

Lesko: But in Spanish *los* and *las* are the plural definite articles. *El disquete … los disquetes. La computadora, las computadoras.*

Host: The indefinite articles in Spanish work the same way. *Un* and *una* mean "a" or "an." The plural forms are *unos* and *unas* and they mean "some" or "a few"! *Un disquete, unos disquetes. Una computadora, unas computadoras.*
Let's review.

Cowboy: Alright, partners, here's the quiz.

Quiz

Host: What are the plurals of these words?

la pierna
el reloj
el dedo
una nariz
un teclado
una mochila

Nombre ____________________

Fecha ____________________

You are helping your computer teacher prepare her classroom by making sure that she has all the necessary materials. Pretend you are not in the classroom but that your partner just came out of the classroom and can tell you what is there. Ask your partner the following questions and circle his or her answers.

1.	¿Hay una silla?	Sí	No
2.	¿Hay una pantalla?	Sí	No
3.	¿Hay una mochila?	Sí	No
4.	¿Hay un disquete?	Sí	No
5.	¿Hay un teclado?	Sí	No
6.	¿Hay una mesa?	Sí	No
7.	¿Hay un ratón?	Sí	No
8.	¿Hay un pupitre?	Sí	No
9.	¿Hay un lápiz?	Sí	No
10.	¿Hay una ventana?	Sí	No

Now, imagine that you just walked out of a Spanish classroom. Your partner has not been in the classroom but needs to tell his or her teacher whether the classroom has the necessary materials. Use the picture below to answer your partner's questions.

Realidades A

Capítulo 2B

Nombre ______________________

Fecha ______________________

Communicative Activity **2B-1**

Estudiante **B**

Imagine that you just walked out of a computer classroom. Your partner has not been in the classroom but needs to tell his or her teacher whether the classroom has the necessary materials. Use the picture below to answer your partner's questions.

Now, you are helping your Spanish teacher prepare his or her classroom by making sure that all the necessary materials are there. Pretend you are not in the classroom but that your partner just came out of the classroom and can tell you what is there. Ask your partner the following questions and circle his or her answers.

1.	¿Hay un escritorio?	Sí	No
2.	¿Hay una papelera?	Sí	No
3.	¿Hay un cuaderno?	Sí	No
4.	¿Hay un sacapuntas?	Sí	No
5.	¿Hay un diccionario?	Sí	No
6.	¿Hay un cartel?	Sí	No
7.	¿Hay un reloj?	Sí	No
8.	¿Hay tarea?	Sí	No
9.	¿Hay un libro de español?	Sí	No
10.	¿Hay una bandera?	Sí	No

Realidades A

Nombre ______________________

Capítulo 2B

Communicative Activity **2B-2**

Fecha ______________________

Estudiante **A**

Your Spanish class just had a party and now the classroom is a mess. You and your partner are going to help put everything back in order, but you are not sure where everything is. Ask your partner where the following items are in the classroom *(¿Dónde está(n)?)*. Record the answers on the lines provided.

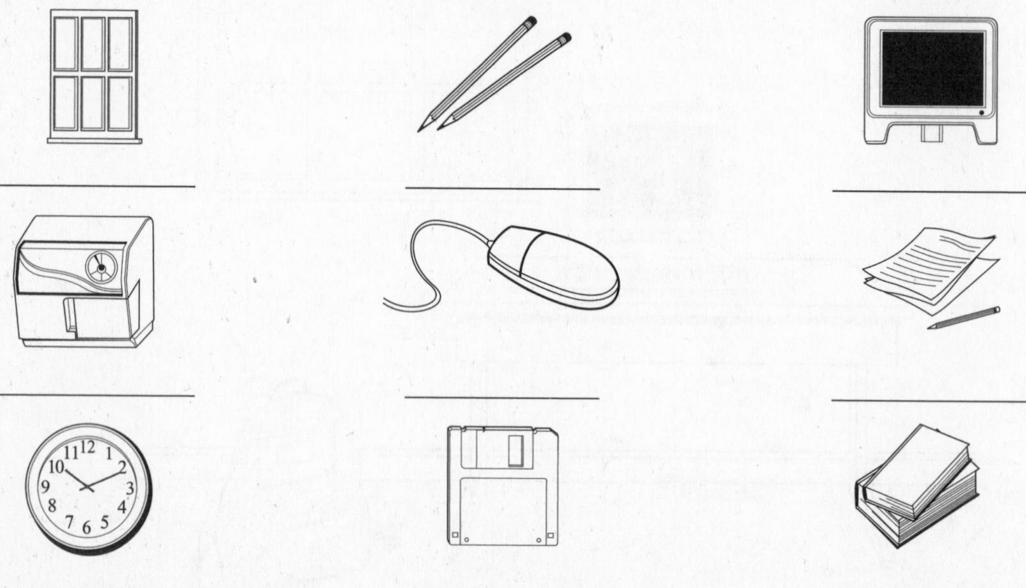

Now imagine that your partner is trying to move certain classroom items to another classroom but he or she cannot find the things to move. Answer your partner's questions about where certain items are located by saying if they are behind, in front of, to the side of, underneath, or over other items in the classroom.

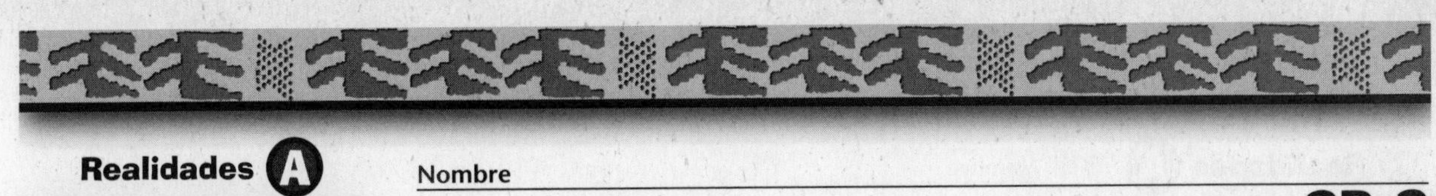

Realidades A

Capítulo 2B

Nombre ______________________

Fecha ______________________

Communicative Activity **2B-2**

Estudiante **B**

Your Spanish class just had a party and now the classroom is a mess. Your partner needs to know where everything is located so that he or she can put everything back in order. Answer your partner's questions about where certain items are located by saying if they are behind, in front of, to the side of, underneath, or over other items in the classroom.

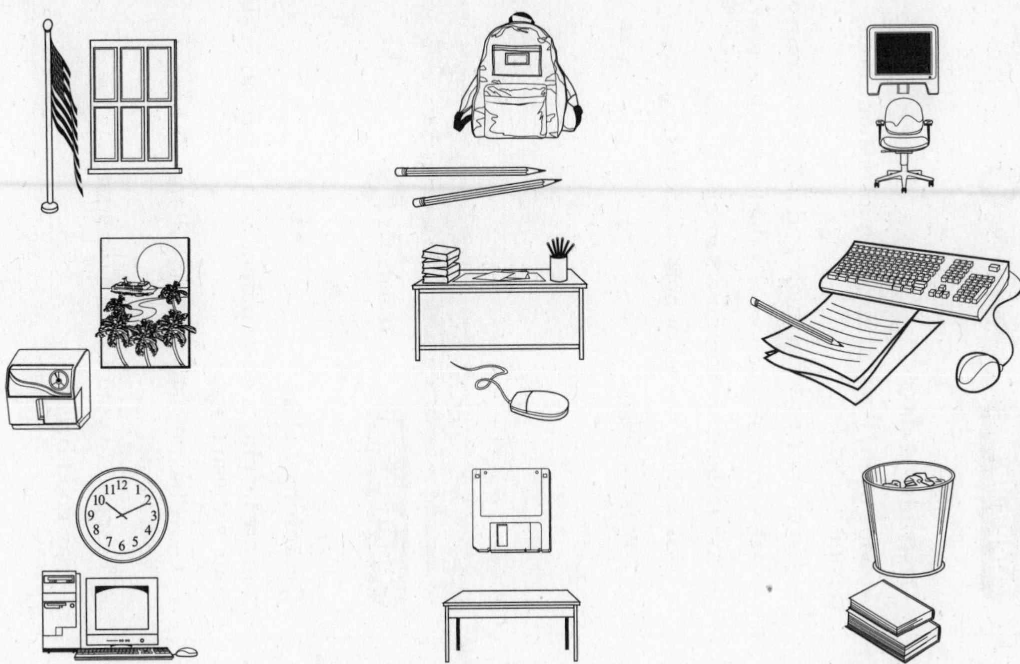

Now imagine that you need to find certain items in a classroom to move them into another classroom, but you cannot find what you need to move. Ask your partner where the following items are in the classroom *(¿Dónde está(n)?)*. Record the answers on the lines provided.

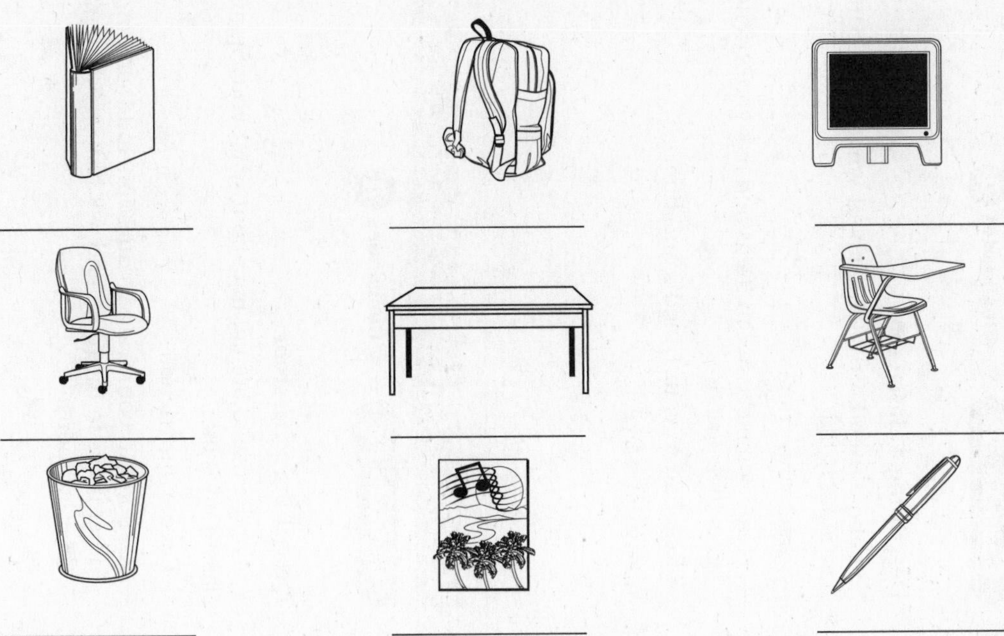

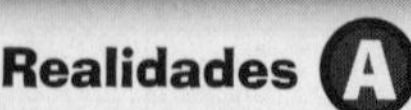

Situation Cards

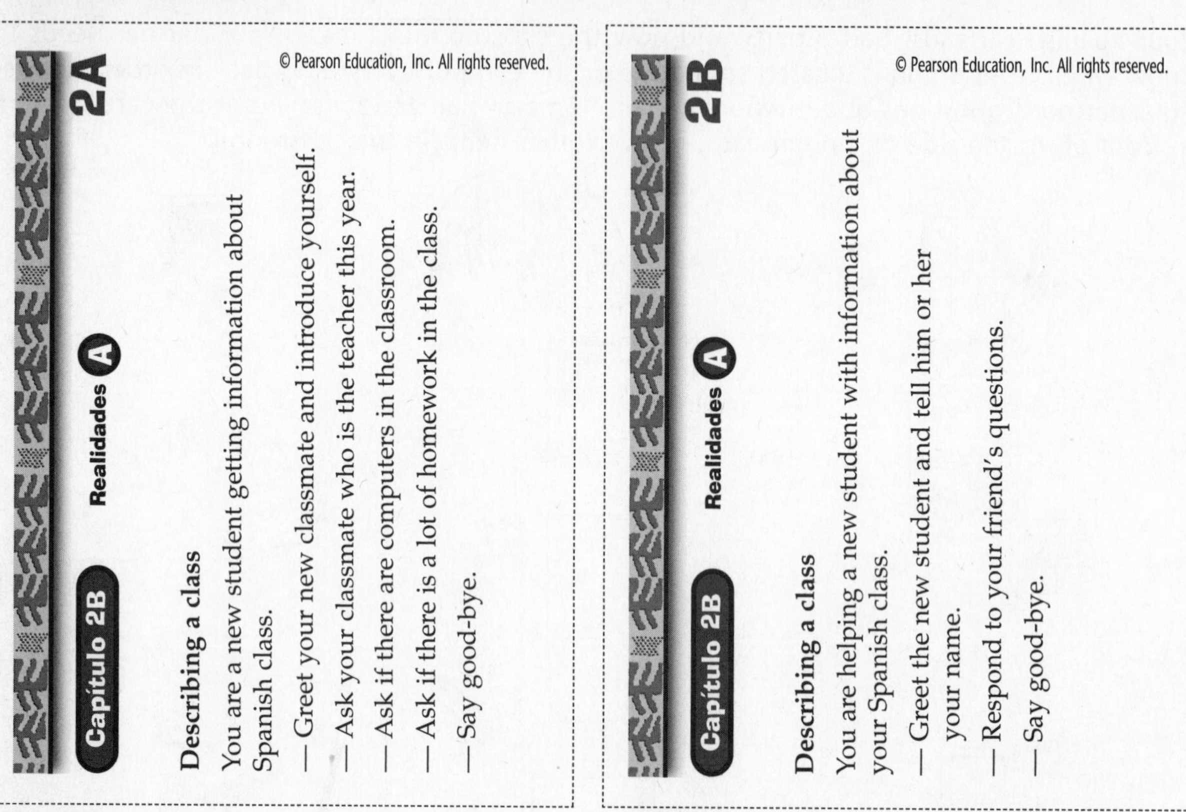

Capítulo 2B Realidades A **2A**

Describing a class

You are a new student getting information about Spanish class.

— Greet your new classmate and introduce yourself.
— Ask your classmate who is the teacher this year.
— Ask if there are computers in the classroom.
— Ask if there is a lot of homework in the class.
— Say good-bye.

Capítulo 2B Realidades A **2B**

Describing a class

You are helping a new student with information about your Spanish class.

— Greet the new student and tell him or her your name.
— Respond to your friend's questions.
— Say good-bye.

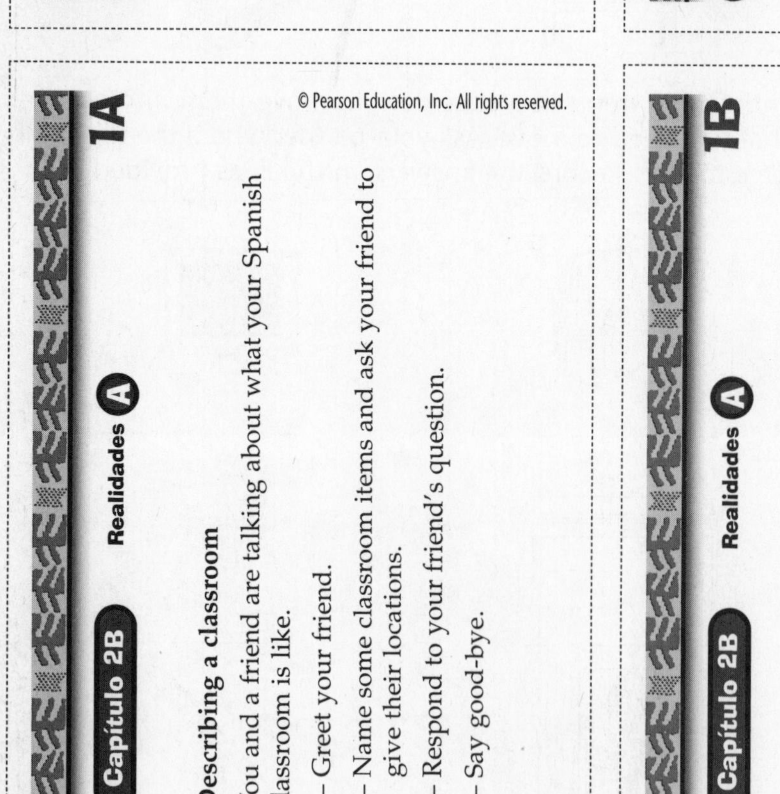

Capítulo 2B Realidades A **1A**

Describing a classroom

You and a friend are talking about what your Spanish classroom is like.

— Greet your friend.
— Name some classroom items and ask your friend to give their locations.
— Respond to your friend's question.
— Say good-bye.

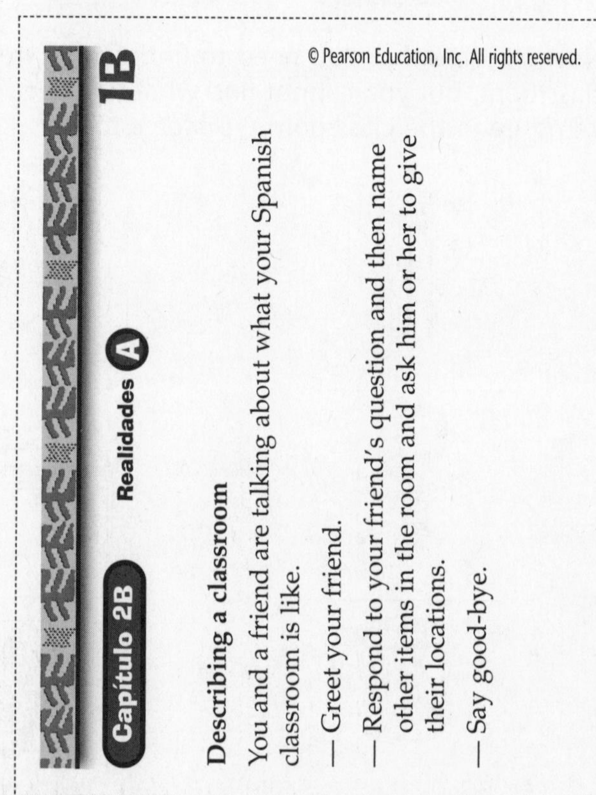

Capítulo 2B Realidades A **1B**

Describing a classroom

You and a friend are talking about what your Spanish classroom is like.

— Greet your friend.
— Respond to your friend's question and then name other items in the room and ask him or her to give their locations.
— Say good-bye.

Realidades 

Capítulo 2B

GramActiva

Tu sala de clases

Juego, p. 126

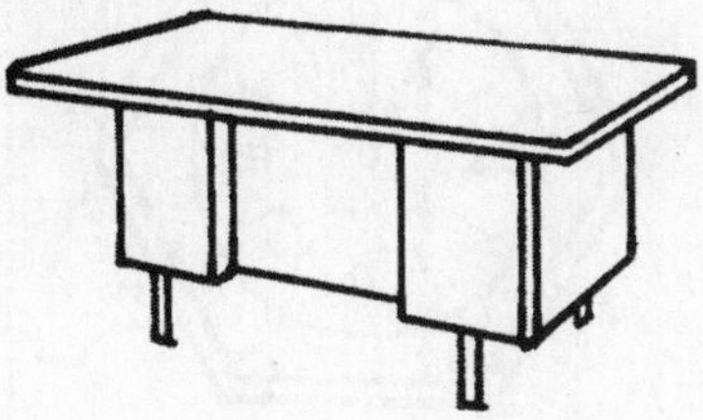

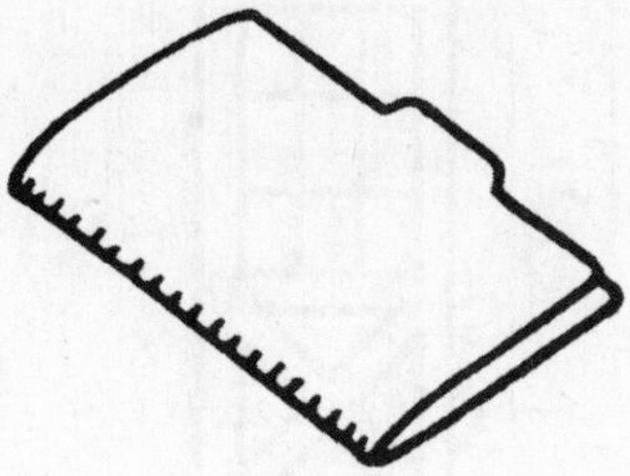

Vocabulary Clip Art

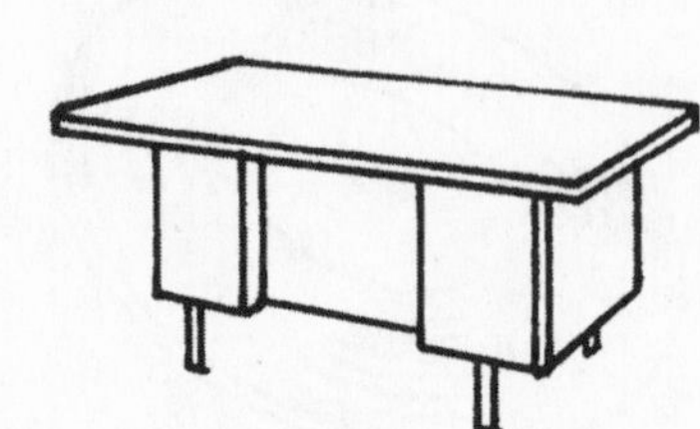

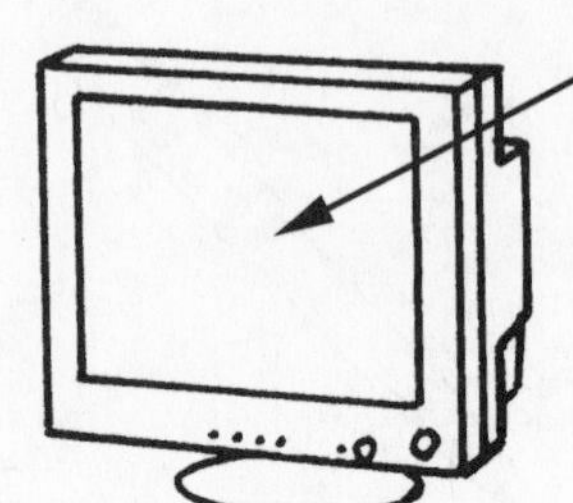

Realidades 

Capítulo 2B

Vocabulary Clip Art

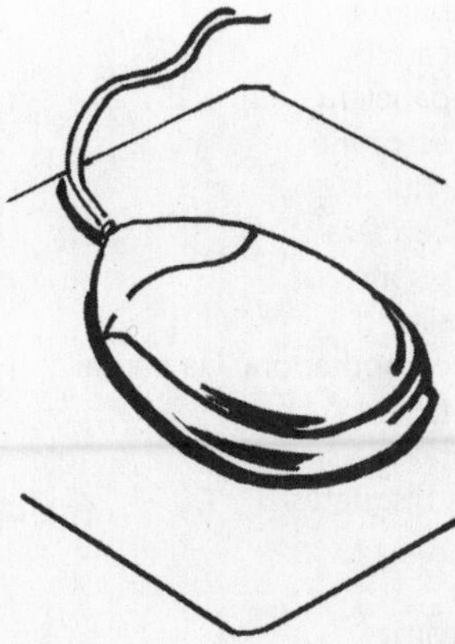

Core Practice Answers

2B-1
1. la ventana
2. la puerta
3. el cartel
4. la papelera
5. el escritorio
6. el reloj
7. la bandera
8. el pupitre
9. la silla
10. la computadora / la pantalla
11. el teclado
12. el ratón
13. los disquetes

2B-2
1. encima
2. debajo
3. delante
4. delante
5. encima
6. debajo
7. al lado
8. encima
9. al lado

2B-3
Answers may vary.
1. al lado de la puerta
2. encima del escritorio
3. al lado del escritorio
4. encima del escritorio /al lado de la computadora
5. al lado de la ventana
6. delante del escritorio
7. debajo de la ventana
8. debajo del escritorio

2B-4
Answers may vary.
1. A: Cuántos
   B: Hay
2. A: Qué es esto
   B: ____
3. A: Dónde
   B: ____
4. A: Hay
   B: ____
5. A: ____
   B: están en
6. A: ____
   B: de
7. A: ____
   B: Allí (Aquí)
8. A: en
   B: ____

2B-5
1. —está
   —Estoy
2. —está / está
   —está
3. —están
   —están
4. —están
   —están / está
5. —está
   —está
6. —están
   —está / están
7. —estamos / están

2B-6
A.
Row 1: ____
Row 2: el cuaderno, los cuadernos, ____ , unos cuadernos
Row 3: el disquete, los disquetes, un disquete, ____
Row 4: la computadora, ____ , una computadora, unas computadoras
Row 5: ____ , las mochilas, una mochila, unas mochilas
Row 6: el reloj, los relojes, un reloj, ____
Row 7: la bandera, las banderas, ____ , unas banderas
Row 8: ____ , las profesoras, una profesora, unas profesoras

B.
1. la bandera
2. un reloj
3. una computadora
4. La profesora
5. una mochila

2B-7
Answers will vary. Must use *está* and location words.

Crucigrama (2B-8)
Across:
2. teclado
5. sala
9. bandera
12. escritorio
14. mochila
15. silla
16. mesa
17. ventana
19. disquete
20. cartel

Down:
1. sacapuntas
3. debajo
4. pantalla
6. reloj
7. lado
8. detrás
10. puerta
11. papelera
13. ratón
18. allí

Organizer (2B-9)
I. Vocabulary Answers will vary.
II. Grammar
1.

col. 1.	**col. 2.**
estoy	estamos
estás	estáis
está	están

2. El / la / los / las
3. un / una / unos / unas

Realidades A — Capítulo 2B

Nombre ______ Hora ______

Fecha ______ **Vocabulary Flash Cards, Sheet 1**

Write the Spanish vocabulary word below each picture. If there is a word or phrase, copy it in the space provided. Be sure to include the article for each noun.

Realidades A — Capítulo 2B

Nombre ______ Hora ______

Fecha ______ **Vocabulary Flash Cards, Sheet 2**

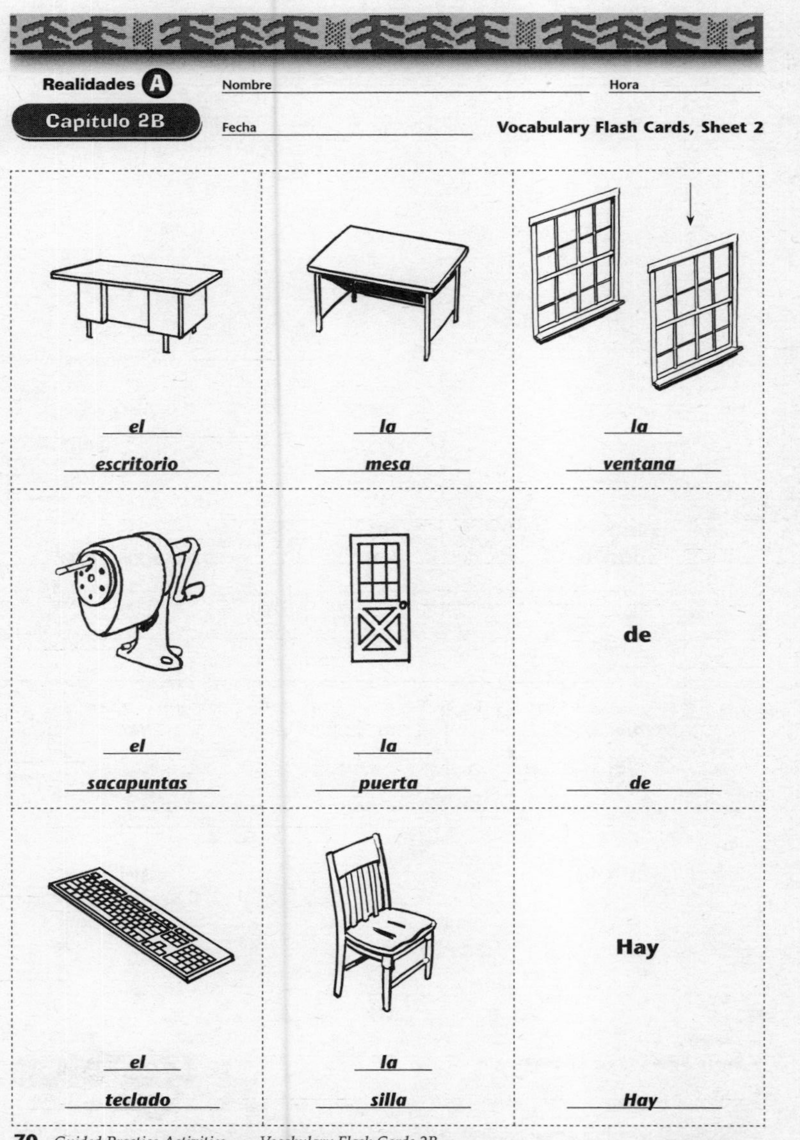

Nombre ______ Hora ______

Fecha ______

Vocabulary Flash Cards, Sheet 3

al lado de	**detrás de**	**allí**
al *lado* *de*	*detrás* *de*	*allí*
debajo de	**encima de**	**aquí**
debajo *de*	*encima* *de*	*aquí*
delante de	**en**	**¿Dónde?**
delante *de*	*en*	*¿Dónde?*

Nombre ______ Hora ______

Fecha ______

Vocabulary Flash Cards, Sheet 4

mi	**tu**	**Es un(a)...**
mi	*tu*	*Es* *un(a)...*
¿Qué es esto?	**los, las**	**unos, unas**
¿Qué *es* *esto?*	*los*, *las*	*unos*, *unas*

Realidades A — Capítulo 2B

Nombre ______ Hora ______

Fecha ______

Vocabulary Check, Sheet 1

Tear out this page. Write the English words on the lines. Fold the paper along the dotted line to see the correct answers so you can check your work.

la bandera	***flag***
el cartel	***poster***
la computadora	***computer***
el disquete	***diskette***
la mochila	***bookbag, backpack***
la pantalla	***(computer) screen***
la papelera	***wastepaper basket***
el ratón	***(computer) mouse***
el reloj	***clock***
el sacapuntas	***pencil sharpener***
el teclado	***(computer) keyboard***
el escritorio	***desk***
la mesa	***table***
la silla	***chair***
la puerta	***door***

Fold In ←

Realidades A — Capítulo 2B

Nombre ______ Hora ______

Fecha ______

Vocabulary Check, Sheet 2

Tear out this page. Write the Spanish words on the lines. Fold the paper along the dotted line to see the correct answers so you can check your work.

flag	***la bandera***
poster	***el cartel***
computer	***la computadora***
diskette	***el disquete***
bookbag, backpack	***la mochila***
(computer) screen	***la pantalla***
wastepaper basket	***la papelera***
(computer) mouse	***el ratón***
clock	***el reloj***
pencil sharpener	***el sacapuntas***
(computer) keyboard	***el teclado***
desk	***el escritorio***
table	***la mesa***
chair	***la silla***
door	***la puerta***

Fold In ←

Realidades A | Nombre | Hora

Capítulo 2B | Fecha | **Vocabulary Check, Sheet 3**

Tear out this page. Write the English words on the lines. Fold the paper along the dotted line to see the correct answers so you can check your work.

la ventana	***window***
al lado de	***next to***
allí	***there***
aquí	***here***
debajo de	***underneath***
delante de	***in front of***
detrás de	***behind***
¿Dónde?	***Where?***
en	***in, on***
encima de	***on top of***
Hay	***There is, There are***

Fold In

Realidades A | Nombre | Hora

Capítulo 2B | Fecha | **Vocabulary Check, Sheet 4**

Tear out this page. Write the Spanish words on the lines. Fold the paper along the dotted line to see the correct answers so you can check your work.

window	***la ventana***
next to	***al lado de***
there	***allí***
here	***aquí***
underneath	***debajo de***
in front of	***delante de***
behind	***detrás de***
Where?	***¿Dónde?***
in, on	***en***
on top of	***encima de***
There is, There are	***Hay***

To hear a complete list of the vocabulary for this chapter, go to www.realidades.com and type in the Web Code jcd-0299. Then click on **Repaso del capítulo.**

Fold In

The verb *estar* (p. 128)

- Irregular verbs do not follow the same pattern as regular verbs.
- **Estar** (*to be*) is irregular. Its **yo** form (**estoy**) is different from the regular **-ar yo** form. Its **tú, usted/él/ella,** and **ustedes/ellos/ellas** forms are different because they have an accent on the **a: estás, está, están.**
- Here are the forms of **estar**:

yo	estoy	nosotros/nosotras	estamos
tú	estás	vosotros/vosotras	estáis
usted/él/ella	está	ustedes/ellos/ellas	están

- **Estar** is used to tell how someone feels or to give a location.

A. Circle the ending of each form of **estar**.

1. yo est(oy)
2. tú est(ás)
3. Ud. est(á)
4. nosotras est(amos)
5. ellos est(án)

B. Now, complete each sentence by writing in the correct ending for the correct form of **estar**.

1. Tú est***ás*** en la clase de arte.
2. Ellos est***án*** en la clase de ciencias.
3. Nosotros est***amos*** en la clase de español.
4. Yo est***oy*** en la clase de matemáticas.
5. Él est***á*** en la clase de literatura.
6. Usted est***á*** en la oficina.
7. Ustedes est***án*** en la sala de clase.
8. Nosotras est***amos*** en la clase de tecnología.

C. Complete each sentence with the correct form of **estar**.

1. Yo ***estoy*** bien.
2. Tú ***estás*** muy bien.
3. Ella ***está*** regular.
4. Nosotras ***estamos*** bien.
5. Usted ***está*** regular.
6. Ellos ***están*** bien.
7. Él ***está*** regular.
8. Ustedes ***están*** bien.

The verb *estar* (continued)

D. Complete the conversation with correct forms of **estar**.

LUISA: ¡Buenos días! ¿Cómo ***están*** ustedes?

ANA E INÉS: Nosotras ***estamos*** bien. ¿Y tú? ¿Cómo ***estás***?

LUISA: Yo ***estoy*** muy bien. ¿Dónde ***están*** Marcos y Marta?

ANA: Marcos ***está*** en la clase de español. Marta ***está*** en la clase de matemáticas.

E. Create complete sentences with **estar**. Follow the model.

Modelo usted / estar / en la clase de matemáticas
Usted está en la clase de matemáticas.

1. tú / estar / en la clase de español
Tú estás en la clase de español.
2. ellas / estar / en la clase de arte
Ellas están en la clase de arte.
3. nosotros / estar / en la clase de inglés
Nosotros estamos en la clase de inglés.
4. usted / estar / en la clase de matemáticas
Usted está en la clase de matemáticas.
5. yo / estar / en la clase de tecnología
Yo estoy en la clase de tecnología.
6. él / estar / en la clase de ciencias sociales
Él está en la clase de ciencias sociales.

Realidades **A** Nombre ____ Hora ____

Capítulo 2B Fecha ____ **Guided Practice Activities 2B-3**

The plurals of nouns and articles (p. 132)

Plural of nouns		Plural definite articles		Plural indefinite articles	
Ends in vowel	Ends in consonant	Masculine	Feminine	Masculine	Feminine
add -s: **libros, sillas**	add -es: **relojes, carteles**	**los** (*the*) **los libros**	**las** (*the*) **las sillas**	**unos** (*some, a few*) **unos libros**	**unas** (*some, a few*) **unas sillas**

- Nouns that end in **-z** change the **z** to **c** in the plural: **lápiz** → **lápices.**

A. Circle the ending of each noun. Is it a vowel or a consonant? Write **V** for vowel or **C** for consonant next to each word.

1. ***C*** carte(l)
2. ***V*** teclad(o)
3. ***V*** mochil(a)
4. ***C*** me(s)
5. ***V*** bander(a)
6. ***C*** relo(j)
7. ***V*** disquet(e)
8. ***C*** profeso(r)

B. Now, look at the same words from **part A** and add the endings to make them plural.

1. cartel***es***
2. teclado***s***
3. mochila***s***
4. mes***es***
5. bandera***s***
6. reloj***es***
7. disquete***s***
8. profesor***es***

C. Now, write the *complete* plural form of each word from **part B.**

1. cartel ***carteles***
2. teclado ***teclados***
3. mochila ***mochilas***
4. mes ***meses***
5. bandera ***banderas***
6. reloj ***relojes***
7. disquete ***disquetes***
8. profesor ***profesores***

realidades.com • Web Code: jcd-0213

Realidades **A** Nombre ____ Hora ____

Capítulo 2B Fecha ____ **Guided Practice Activities 2B-4**

The plurals of nouns and articles (*continued*)

D. Identify whether each of the words from **part C** are masculine or feminine. Write **M** for masculine or **F** for feminine next to each word.

1. ***M*** cartel
2. ***M*** teclado
3. ***F*** mochila
4. ***M*** mes
5. ***F*** bandera
6. ***M*** reloj
7. ***M*** disquete
8. ***M*** profesor

E. Now, look at the words from **part D** in the plural. Circle the correct definite article, masculine or feminine.

1. (**(los)** / **las**) carteles
2. (**(los)** / **las**) teclados
3. (**los** / **(las)**) mochilas
4. (**(los)** / **las**) meses
5. (**los** / **(las)**) banderas
6. (**(los)** / **las**) relojes
7. (**(los)** / **las**) disquetes
8. (**(los)** / **las**) profesores

F. Look at each noun below and write **los** or **las**, depending on whether the word is masculine or feminine.

1. ***las*** puertas
2. ***las*** ventanas
3. ***los*** horarios
4. ***los*** lápices
5. ***los*** ratones
6. ***las*** pantallas

G. Look at the words from **part E** again. This time, circle the correct indefinite article, masculine or feminine.

1. (**(unos)** / **unas**) carteles
2. (**(unos)** / **unas**) teclados
3. (**unos** / **(unas)**) mochilas
4. (**(unos)** / **unas**) meses
5. (**unos** / **(unas)**) banderas
6. (**(unos)** / **unas**) relojes
7. (**(unos)** / **unas**) disquetes
8. (**(unos)** / **unas**) profesores

H. Look at the nouns from **part F** again. Now, write **unos** or **unas**, depending on whether the word is masculine or feminine.

1. ***unas*** puertas
2. ***unas*** ventanas
3. ***unos*** horarios
4. ***unos*** lápices
5. ***unos*** ratones
6. ***unas*** pantallas

realidades.com • Web Code: jcd-0213

Realidades A | Nombre ______ | Hora ______

Capítulo 2B | Fecha ______ | **Guided Practice Activities 2B-5**

Lectura: El UNICEF y una convención para los niños (pp. 138–139)

A. The reading in your textbook talks about the organization UNICEF (United Nations International Children's Emergency Fund). You will see many cognates in the reading. Look through the reading and find the Spanish words that most closely resemble the ones below. Write the words in the spaces provided.

1. convention ***convención***
2. dignity ***dignidad***
3. nations ***naciones***
4. protection ***protección***
5. special ***especial***
6. diet ***dieta***
7. opinions ***opiniones***
8. community ***comunidad***
9. violence ***violencia***
10. privilege ***privilegio***

B. Look at the first paragraph from the reading in your textbook. Write down three things that are said to be privileges for children.

1. ***being in school***
2. ***having a backpack***
3. ***a good teacher***

Other possible answers:
books, pencils, paper, a calculator

C. Read the following excerpt from your textbook and answer the questions that follow.

> *UNICEF...tiene siete oficinas regionales en diversas naciones y un Centro de Investigaciones en Italia.*

1. Where does UNICEF have seven regional offices?
   in various nations
2. Where is there a Center of Investigation for UNICEF?
   in Italy

D. Look again at the bulleted list in your textbook and list five things in the spaces below that the convention said that all children need.

1. ***Possible answers: dignity, a house, protection, a good diet,***
2. ***practicing sports, special attention to children with***
3. ***physical problems, love and understanding of a family,***
4. ***expressing their opinions, a community without violence,***
5. ***to go to school***

realidades.com
• Web Code: jcd-0215

Realidades A | Nombre ______ | Hora ______

Capítulo 2B | Fecha ______ | **Guided Practice Activities 2B-6**

Presentación escrita (p. 141) *Answers will vary.*

Task: Pretend you have a pen pal from Mexico who is coming to visit your school next semester. Write your pen pal a note describing your Spanish classroom.

1 Prewrite.

A. On a separate sheet of paper draw a sketch of your Spanish classroom. You will use this as a reference when writing your note. Try to include four or five different items.

B. Label the items in your sketch using words from your vocabulary.

2 Draft.

A. Read the sample note written by another student. Use this to guide your own writing.

> *En mi sala de clases hay cinco ventanas. Mi pupitre está al lado del escritorio del profesor. La puerta está detrás de mi pupitre. Hay una bandera encima de la mesa de computadoras.*

B. Look at the sample note again and list, in the spaces below, all of the classroom objects mentioned.

______ ______ ______
______ ______ ______

C. Compare the list of words in **part B** with the words you labeled in your sketch. This will help you get an idea of how similar your draft will be to the model. Create three sentences below filling in what items are in your classroom and where they are located.

1. Hay ______.
2. ______ está ______.
3. ______ está ______.

3 Revise. Read through your draft to see if it makes sense to you. Share your work with a partner who should check the following:

______ Are the sentences easy to understand?
______ Did you leave out anything from your drawing?
______ Are there any spelling or grammar errors?
______ If there are any problems with your draft, make a revised draft.

Antes de ver el video

Actividad 1

Look around your classroom and make a list of five items that you see. Then, describe their location. Follow the model.

	COSA	DÓNDE ESTÁ
Modelo	*la papelera*	*debajo del reloj*
1.	Answers will vary.	
2.		
3.		
4.		
5.		

¿Comprendes?

Actividad 2

Using the screen grabs as clues, answer the following questions with the correct information from the video.

1. ¿Quién es Paquito? **Paquito es el hámster.**
2. ¿Qué le pasa a Manolo? Él no tiene **su tarea**.
3. ¿Quién tiene el hámster? **Teresa tiene el hámster.**

4. Los estudiantes están en ___la clase de ciencias sociales___.
5. ¿Para qué es el hámster? Es para ___la clase de ciencias (naturales)___.

Actividad 3

Next to each phrase, write the name of the character who said it in the video.

1. "¿Un ratón en la clase de ciencias sociales? ¡Imposible!" ___la profesora___
2. "¡No es un ratón! Es mi hámster." ___Teresa___
3. "Señorita, necesito hablar con usted más tarde." ___el Sr. Treviño___
4. "Carlos, no tengo mi tarea." ___Manolo___
5. "¡Aquí está! Está en mi mochila." ___Carlos___
6. "Paquito, mi precioso. Ven aquí. ¿Estás bien?" ___Teresa___

Y, ¿qué más?

Actividad 4

Imagine that Paquito is running around in your classroom. Using the prepositions that you have just learned, indicate four places where he might be. Follow the example below.

Modelo *Paquito está encima de la mochila.*

1. Answers will vary.
2. ______
3. ______
4. ______

Actividad 5

As you look at the picture, decide whether the statements you hear are **ciertos** or **falsos**. You will hear each statement twice.

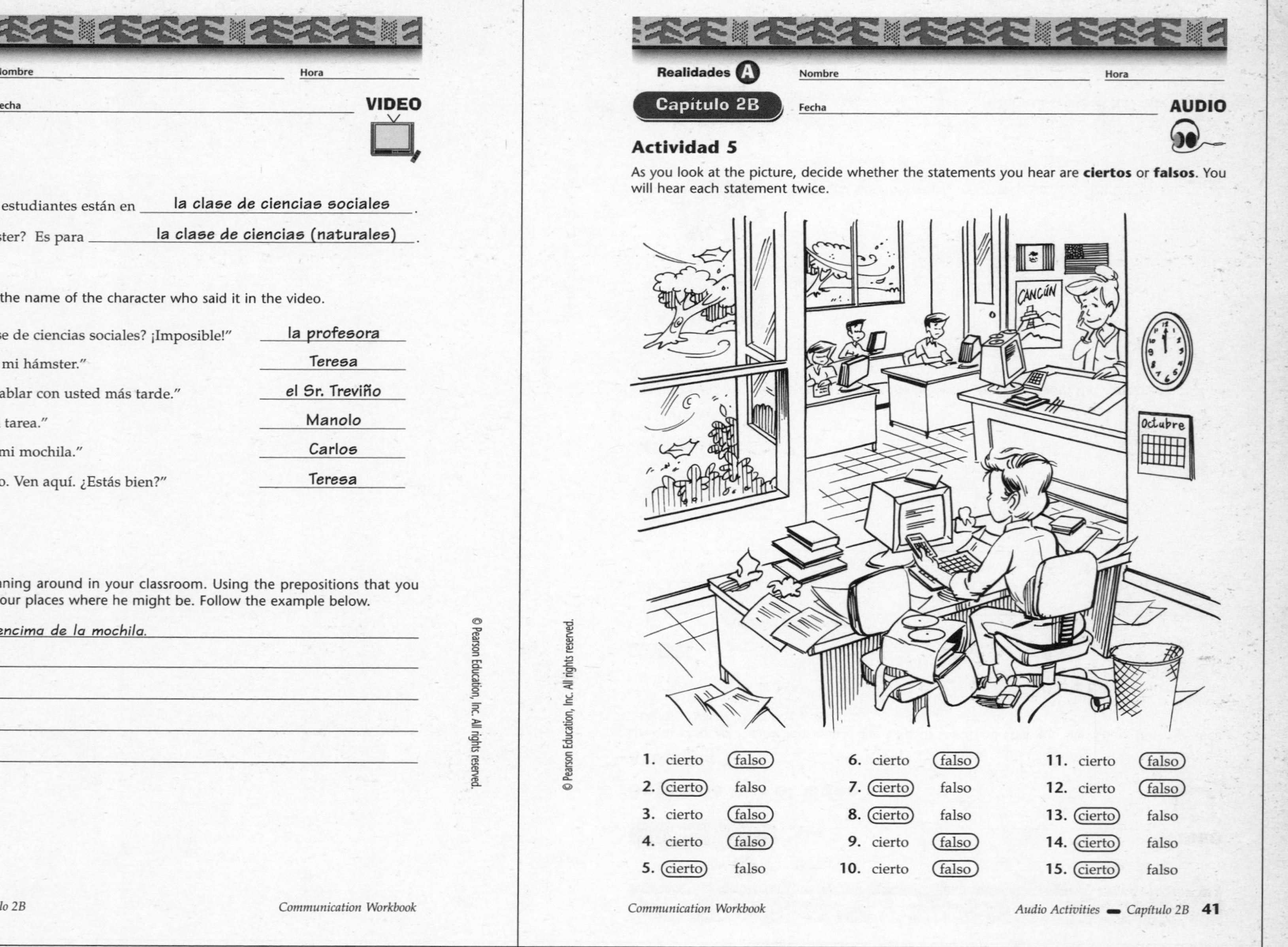

1.	cierto	**falso**	6.	cierto	**falso**	11.	cierto	**falso**
2.	**cierto**	falso	7.	**cierto**	falso	12.	cierto	**falso**
3.	cierto	**falso**	8.	**cierto**	falso	13.	**cierto**	falso
4.	cierto	**falso**	9.	cierto	**falso**	14.	**cierto**	falso
5.	**cierto**	falso	10.	cierto	**falso**	15.	**cierto**	falso

Realidades A — Nombre ______ Hora ______

Capítulo 2B — Fecha ______ AUDIO

Actividad 6

Tomás suddenly realizes in the middle of his science class that the diskette with his entire class project on it is missing! He asks several people if they know where it is. Listen as different people tell Tomás where they think his diskette is. In the timeline, write what classroom he goes to and where in the classroom he looks, in the order in which you hear them. You will hear this conversation twice.

	Susana	Antonio	Noé	Sr. Atkins
Classroom	la clase de inglés	la clase de español	la clase de tecnología	la clase de tecnología
Location in room	encima de la mesa	al lado de la ventana	debajo del teclado de la computadora	en la mochila de Tomás

Where did Tomás eventually find his diskette? in his bag, while in technology class (en su mochila, en la clase de tecnología)

Actividad 7

It's time to take the Spanish Club picture for the yearbook, but there are several people who have still not arrived. Andrés, the president, decides to use his cell phone to find out where people are. As you listen to the first part of each conversation, complete the sentences below with the information he finds out. For example, you might write:

Beto está en el gimnasio.

You will hear each dialogue twice.

1. Los dos profesores de español están en la oficina.
2. Javier está en la clase de tecnología.
3. Alejandra y Sara están en la cafetería.
4. Mateo está en casa.
5. José y Antonieta están en el gimnasio.

Realidades A — Nombre ______ Hora ______

Capítulo 2B — Fecha ______ AUDIO

Actividad 8

One of your classmates from Spanish class is working in a store that sells school supplies. She overhears a customer speaking Spanish to his father, and decides to try out her Spanish. As she asks him what he wants to buy, she discovers that he never wants just one of anything. As the customer tells your classmate what he wants, write the items on the sales receipt below. Use the pictures below to calculate the price of his purchases. You will hear each conversation twice.

$2.00 · $1.25 · $7.50 · $8.00 · $12.00 · DICTIONARY $4.00 · $1.00

	¿QUÉ NECESITA COMPRAR?	PRECIO
Modelo	*Tres bolígrafos*	*$6.00*
1.	Cinco disquetes	$6.25
2.	Cuatro carteles	$30.00
3.	Siete ratones	$56.00
4.	Dos mochilas	$24.00
5.	Dos diccionarios	$8.00
6.	Nueve carpetas	$9.00

Actividad 9

Listen to two friends talking outside the door of the Spanish Club meeting. They want to go to the meeting, but they are afraid they won't remember everyone's names. Look at the drawing. In the grid, write in the name of the person who is being described. You will hear each dialogue twice.

(A) Antonio	(B) Elena	(C) Inés
(D) Tina	(E) Claudia	(F) Juan

Actividad 10

After your first day of school, you are describing your classroom to your parents. Using the picture below, tell them how many of each object there are in the room. Follow the model.

Modelo *Hay un escritorio en la sala de clases.*

1. Hay cuatro computadoras en la sala de clases.
2. Hay tres banderas...
3. Hay dos carteles...
4. Hay doce pupitres...
5. Hay un sacapuntas...
6. Hay tres sillas...
7. Hay un ratón...

Actividad 11

You are describing your classroom to your Spanish-speaking pen pal. Using complete sentences and the verb **estar**, tell what is in your room and where each item is located. Follow the model.

Modelo *Hay una mesa en la clase. Está al lado de la puerta.*

1. Answers will vary.
2.
3.
4.
5.
6.
7.
8.

Actividad 12

Answer the following questions about things you have for school. Use the pictures as a guide. Follow the model.

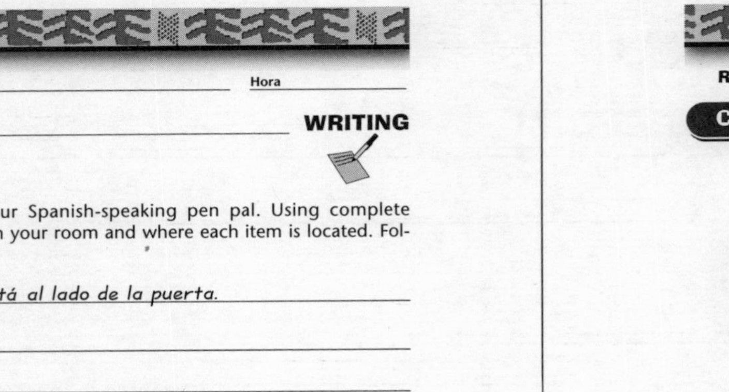

Modelo ¿Qué hay en la mochila?

En la mochila hay unos lápices y bolígrafos. También hay una calculadora y dos libros: el libro de matemáticas y el libro de inglés.

Answers will vary.

1. ¿Qué hay en la clase de ciencias sociales?

En la clase de ciencias sociales hay cuatro computadoras y unos libros encima de la mesa. Hay dos ventanas al lado de tres mapas. También hay un escritorio y unos diez pupitres.

2. ¿Qué hay encima del escritorio? ¿Y al lado? ¿Y detrás?

Encima del escritorio hay tres libros, dos son diccionarios, cuatro cuadernos y más hojas de papel. Al lado del escritorio hay dos papeleras. También una mochila está encima de una papelera. Detrás del escritorio hay una puerta, un sacapuntas, un cartel y un reloj.

Realidades A Nombre ______ Hora ______

Capítulo 2B Fecha ______ WRITING

Actividad 13

The two rooms pictured below were once identical, but Sala 2 has been rearranged. Look at each picture carefully. Circle seven items in Sala 2 that are different from Sala 1. Then, write sentences about how Sala 2 is different. Follow the model.

Sala 1

Sala 2

Modelo *En la sala 2 no hay libros encima del escritorio.*

1. Wording on answers will vary. Differences in rooms will be: 1) what is on the desk, 2) what is on the table, 3) location of the trash,
2. 4) location of pencil sharpener, 5) location of window, 6) location of clock, 7) existence of flag, 8) existence of posters
3. ______
4. ______
5. ______
6. ______
7. ______

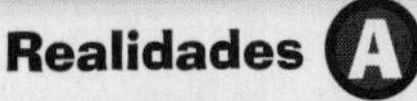

Realidades A

Capítulo 2B

Test Preparation Answers

Reading Skills
p. 133 2. **C**
p. 134 2. **D**

Integrated Performance Assessment
p. 135
Answers will vary.

Practice Test: Mi día escolar
p. 137

1. A
2. H
3. D
4. F
5. Answers will vary but may include: Carmen is influenced by the quality of instruction, how interesting the class is, whether the teacher seems to enjoy teaching, and whether she is successful in the class.

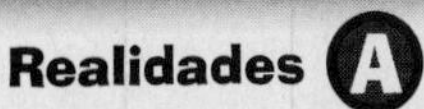

Table of Contents

Tema 3: La comida

Capítulo 3A: ¿Desayuno o almuerzo?

Capítulo 3B: Para mantener la salud

Theme Project

La Comida

Vacaciones para la salud

Overview:

You will create a brochure describing a typical day at a health resort. The brochure will include a schedule of the day's activities and descriptions of breakfast, lunch, and dinner. Photos or drawings will accompany each meal and one of the activities listed. Then you will present the brochures to the class as if you were a sales representative from the resort.

Materials:

Construction paper, magazines, scissors, glue, colored pencils and markers

Sequence:

STEP 1. Review the instructions with your teacher.

STEP 2. Submit a rough sketch of your brochure. Incorporate your teacher's suggestions into your sketch. Work with a partner and present your sketches to each other.

STEP 3. Do a layout on construction paper.

STEP 4. Submit a draft of your meal descriptions and schedule.

STEP 5. Complete your brochure and present it to the class, trying to "sell" your health package to classmates.

Assessment:

Your teacher will use the rubric on the following page to assess this project.

Theme 3 Project: Vacaciones para la salud

RUBRIC	Score 1	Score 3	Score 5
Evidence of Planning	No written draft or page layout provided.	Draft was written and layout created, but not corrected.	Evidence of corrected draft and layout.
Use of Illustrations	No photos/visuals included.	Photos/visuals were included, but layout was unorganized.	Brochure was easy to read, complete, and accurate.
Presentation	Includes little of the required information for the brochure. Student makes no attempt to "sell" the product.	Includes most of the required information for the brochure. Student makes some attempt to "sell" the product.	Includes all of the required information for the brochure. Student tries to "sell" the product.

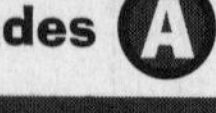

Realidades A

Capítulo 3A

School-to-Home Connection

Dear Parent or Guardian,

The theme for the chapter is *La comida* (Food) and this chapter is called *¿Desayuno o almuerzo?* (Breakfast or lunch?).

Upon completion of this chapter, your child will be able to:

- talk about foods and beverages for breakfast and lunch
- talk about likes and dislikes
- express how often something is done
- understand cultural perspectives on meals

Also, your child will explore:

- the correct pronunciation of the letters *h* and *j*
- how to use a noun to modify another noun

Realidades helps with the development of reading, writing, and speaking skills through the use of strategies, process speaking, and process writing. In this chapter, students will:

- read about fruits that are native to the Americas; a recipe
- speak about what a friend likes to study, his or her favorite activities, and what he or she likes to eat and drink for breakfast.

Remember that additional help is available online at www.realidades.com by using the Web Codes in the Student Edition or in the Leveled Vocabulary and Grammar Workbook.

Check it out! Have your child find five different foods and beverages in your kitchen. Ask him or her to name each item in Spanish and identify whether it is for breakfast or for lunch.

Sincerely,

For: Tips to Parents
Visit: www.realidades.com
Web Code: jce-0010

Capítulo 3A

Chapter Resource Checklist

Resources	CO†	APV	VH	MAN	LEC	CV	PO	MH	REP	PREP
Teacher										
Teacher's Resource Book										
Input Script										
Audio Script										
GramActiva BLM										
Communicative Activities BLM										
School-to-Home Connection BLM										
Clip Art										
Situation Cards BLM										
TPR Stories Book										
Fine Art Transparencies Teacher's Guide										
Pre-AP* Resource Book										
Student										
Leveled Vocabulary and Grammar Workbook										
Guided Practice										
Core Practice										
Communication Workbook with Test Preparation										
Writing										
Audio										
Video										
Test Preparation										
RPH Workbook										
Lecturas para hispanohablantes										
Grammar Study Guides										
Transparencies										
Answers on Transparencies										
Vocabulary and Grammar										
Fine Art										
Assessment										
Assessment Program										
Quizzes										
Chapter Test										
realidades.com										
ExamView Test Bank CD-ROM										
QuickTake on PresentationExpress										
MindPoint QuizShow CD-ROM										
Alternate Assessment Program										
Performance-Based Speaking										
Self-Test on realidades.com & CWS										
Assessment Program RPH										
Technology										
realidades.com										
myeBook										
TeacherExpress CD-ROM										
PresentationExpress DVD										
Video Program DVD										
Culture Video DVD										
Audio Program CD 6										
Assessment CD 20										
Song CD 22										
Canciones de hip hop on realidades.com & CWS										

† *See Abbreviation Key on page iv.*

Realidades A

Capítulo 3A

Input Script

Presentation

Input Vocabulary 1: Place the overhead transparency on the screen. As you point to each item, review the ***gustar*** expressions from Chapter 1A *("¿Qué te gusta más, el tocino o el jamón?")*. Then hand out copies of the Vocabulary Clip Art and have students tear them into individual images. Review the location expressions from Chapter 2B by describing the location of items on the transparency and having students guess the items *("Esto está debajo del yogur de fresa y encima del pan.")*. Then describe the layout of a new ad and have students arrange their Clip Art images according to your description.

Input Monologue 1: Model the first two sentences. Then call out good and bad food combinations. Students will rub their stomachs and nod their heads when they hear a good combination *("En el desayuno yo como huevos y tocino.")* and put both hands on their stomachs and shake their heads when they hear a bad one *("En el desayuno yo como cereal con huevos.")*. Mime pouring cereal into a bowl and cracking an egg on top of it.

Model the next two sentences. Point to all the days in a week on a calendar as you say *"Todos los días bebo jugo de naranja."* Cross out each day of the week with your finger and say *"Pero nunca bebo la limonada."* Then humorously try to trick students by asking *"¿Qué bebo el lunes?"* (point to the orange juice) *"¿Y el martes?"* (point to the lemonade and see if any students say ***la limonada*** instead of ***el jugo de naranja***). Next, say *"Nunca bebo té sin leche,"* and pretend to drink a cup of tea. Act as if it tastes bad and explain *"Necesito leche. Nunca bebo té sin leche."* Then substitute ***como*** for ***bebo*** and create new sentences. Have students raise their hand when a statement is true for them. Finally, point to food items and lead pairs of students through the short dialogue *"—En el desayuno, yo como ___. Y tú, ¿qué comes? —Yo como ___."*

Input Vocabulary 2: Model the pronunciation of the words on the menu. Hand out copies of the Vocabulary Clip Art showing the menu items. Then call out the names of restaurants in your area and a menu item. Have students hold the Clip Art image of the item right side up if that item can be ordered at that restaurant. Have them hold the item upside down if the item cannot be ordered there.

Input Monologue 2: Read the first two sentences. Then use restaurants from the previous activity to teach ***me encanta.*** Use varying degrees of enthusiasm as you say, for example, *"Me gusta George's Pizza House, pero me encanta Rosie's Diner. ¿Y a ti?"* Read the next sentence of the monologue. Then make statements and have students raise their hand when they hear an illogical statement *("En el almuerzo como huevos con tocino.")*. Finally, read the last two sentences. Substitute ***todos los días*** to convey the meaning of ***siempre.*** Then create different sentences that begin *"Es importante ..."* and have students give a "thumbs-up" sign if they agree or a "thumbs-down" sign if they disagree.

Comprehension Check

- Give students a copy of the transparency showing a grocery store ad. Tell them you're the store manager and you're marking down the prices. Give the new prices and have students write the prices by the correct food items.
- Hand out copies of the Vocabulary Clip Art. Have students cut out any nine of the items and arrange them in three rows of three items. Then call out items at random. When students hear one of the items they have on their desk, they will turn that picture over. The first student to turn over three items in a row wins.

Audio Script

Audio CD, Capítulo 3A

Track 01: *A primera vista,* Student Book, p. 148 (4:09)

¿Desayuno o almuerzo?

You will hear each word or phrase twice. After the first time there will be a pause so you can pronounce it, then you will hear the word or phrase a second time.

El supermercado de la Plaza
¡Abierto las 24 horas!
¡Ofertas de hoy!
¡Toda la comida que necesitas!

las salchichas
el tocino
el jamón
el cereal
el queso
el yogur de fresa
los huevos
los plátanos
el jugo de manzana
el jugo de naranja
la limonada
la leche
el té
el pan
las galletas
el agua

Read along as you listen to the statement.

FEMALE TEEN: El desayuno es mi comida favorita. En el desayuno, yo como cereal con leche, tocino y pan tostado. Todos los días bebo jugo de naranja. Nunca bebo té sin leche. Y tú, ¿qué comes en el desayuno?

Track 02: *A primera vista,* Student Book, p. 149 (2:46)

You will hear each word or phrase twice. After the first time there will be a pause so you can pronounce it, then you will hear the word or phrase a second time.

El Restaurante de la Plaza
¡Para un almuerzo rápido!

la ensalada de frutas
el sándwich de jamón y queso
la hamburguesa
el perrito caliente
las papas fritas
la sopa de verduras
la pizza
el café
los refrescos
los jugos
el té helado

Read along as you listen to the statement.

FEMALE TEEN: Me encanta el Restaurante de la Plaza. La comida es muy buena. En el almuerzo, como una ensalada de frutas o un sándwich de jamón y queso. Siempre bebo agua. Es importante beber mucha agua, ¿verdad?

Track 03: *A primera vista,* Act. 1, Student Book, p. 149 (1:55)

¿Beber o comer?

Listen to the names of ten foods and beverages. If an item is a food, pantomime eating. If it's a beverage, pantomime drinking. You will hear each word twice.

1. la pizza
2. el perrito caliente
3. el agua
4. el jamón
5. el té
6. el pan
7. el queso
8. la limonada
9. la leche
10. el cereal

Track 04: *A primera vista,* Act. 2, Student Book, p. 149 (1:55)

¿El desayuno o el almuerzo?

Listen as different people tell what they are eating. Hold up one hand if the meal is *el desayuno* and hold up both hands if it is *el almuerzo.* You will hear each statement twice.

1. Como un sándwich de jamón y queso.
2. Yo como el pan tostado y jugo de naranja.
3. Y yo como los huevos con tocino. ¡Mmmm!
4. Me gusta comer las hamburguesas.
5. Yo como la ensalada de frutas y pan.
6. Y yo siempre como el cereal con leche y salchichas.

Track 05: *A primera vista, Videohistoria,* Student Book, pp. 150–152 (2:15)

El desayuno

Tomás es americano. Está en Costa Rica para estudiar. ¿Qué come el primer día? Lee la historia.

Read along as you listen to the *Videohistoria.*
See Student Book pages 150–152 for script.

Track 06: *Manos a la obra,* Act. 8, Student Book, p. 155 (2:35)

¿Dónde están?

Vas a escuchar ocho descripciones sobre el dibujo de esta página. Escribe los números del 1 al 8 en una hoja de papel y escribe C si la descripción es cierta y *F* si es falsa.

1. Los huevos están al lado de la ensalada.
2. El queso está al lado del jamón.
3. La hamburguesa está al lado de las papas fritas.
4. Las manzanas están detrás de los plátanos.
5. El sándwich está detrás del perrito caliente.
6. Las salchichas y el tocino están debajo de los huevos y la ensalada.
7. El pan tostado está delante del cereal.
8. El yogur está al lado del jamón.

Track 07: Audio Act. 5, Writing, Audio & Video Workbook, p. 51 (4:26)

You are helping out a friend at the counter of Restaurante El Gaucho in Argentina. Listen to the orders and record the quantity of each item ordered by each customer in the appropriate box of the chart. You will hear each conversation twice.

Cliente 1:

MALE 1: Buenas tardes. Bienvenido al restaurante El Gaucho. ¿Qué desea comer usted?

MALE 2: Necesito dos sándwiches de jamón y queso y una hamburguesa con papas fritas.

MALE 1: Muy bien, ¿y para beber?

MALE 2: Tres refrescos.

Cliente 2:

MALE 1: Buenas tardes. Bienvenido al Gaucho. ¿Qué desea comer usted?

MALE 3: Una ensalada, por favor.

MALE 1: ¿Algo más?

MALE 3: Una pizza y una hamburguesa.

MALE 1: ¿Y algo para beber?

MALE 3: Sí. Un té helado y dos refrescos. Y dos galletas también.

MALE 1: Gracias.

Cliente 3:

MALE 1: ¡Bienvenida al Gaucho, el restaurante NÚMERO UNO!

FEMALE 1: Hola. Necesito un perrito caliente con papas fritas y una hamburguesa con queso y papas fritas.

MALE 1: ¿Es todo? ¿Algo para beber? ¿Un té helado o un refresco?

FEMALE 1: Ah, sí. Tres refrescos de cola.

Cliente 4:

MALE 1: Buenas tardes. Bienvenidos al Gaucho. ¿Qué desean comer ustedes?

MALE 4: Dos ensaladas y … un momento … ¿Una pizza para compartir? Bueno. Y una pizza. También una hamburguesa con queso.

MALE 1: ¿Algo más?

MALE 4: Sí. Cuatro galletas, dos refrescos de cola y un té helado.

MALE 1: Gracias.

Track 08: Audio Act. 6, Writing, Audio & Video Workbook, p. 52 (3:53)

While working at the Hotel Buena Vista, you need to record breakfast orders for room service. Use the grid to make your report. First, listen carefully for the room number and write it in the appropriate box. Then write in the time requested. Finally, put a check mark next to each item ordered by the person in that room. You will hear each set of statements twice.

1. Buenas noches. Es para la habitación cuarenta y ocho. A las seis y media de la mañana me gusta jugo de naranja, pan tostado, salchichas y café. Gracias.
2. Hola. Mi habitación es la cuarenta y uno. Mañana a las ocho me gusta cereal y huevos con jamón. Y también té. Gracias.
3. Hola. Es para la habitación veinticuatro. A las diez de la mañana me gusta un yogur de fresas, huevos, tocino y pan tostado. Y un café con leche también. Gracias.
4. Buenas noches. Es para la habitación número doce. A las nueve de la mañana un jugo de naranja, huevos con salchichas y café con leche. Gracias.
5. Es para la habitación treinta y cinco. A las siete y media de la mañana me gusta cereal, jugo de manzana, un yogur de fresas y té. Gracias.

Track 09: *Manos a la obra,* Act. 23, Student Book, p. 164 (4:16)

¿Gusta o gustan?

You will hear eight food items. Indicate whether you like each item by holding up one, two, or all three pieces of paper. Remember to use *me gustan* when the item you hear is plural! You will hear each word twice.

1. la sopa
2. las hamburguesas
3. el tocino
4. las fresas
5. el pan
6. el yogur
7. las galletas
8. los huevos

Track 10: *Pronunciación:* The letters *h* and *j,* Student Book, p. 167 (1:46)

In Spanish, the letter *h* is never pronounced. Listen to and say these words:

You will hear each word twice. After the word is pronounced the first time, there will be a pause so you can pronounce it. Then you will hear the word a second time.

hora	hasta
hoy	hacer
hablar	hola
hace	hotel

The letter *j* is pronounced like the letter *h* in *hat* but with more of a breathy sound. It is made far back in the mouth—almost in the throat. Listen to and say these words:

trabajar	jugar
hoja	junio
dibujar	videojuegos
jueves	julio

Try it out! Find and say five examples of foods or beverages from this chapter that have *h* or *j* in their spelling.

Try it out! Say this *trabalenguas* three times as fast as you can. Debajo del puente de Guadalajara había un conejo debajo del agua.

Track 11: Audio Act. 7, Writing, Audio & Video Workbook, p. 53 (5:33)

You are waiting in line at a restaurant counter. You hear people behind you talking about your friends. Listen carefully so you can figure out whom they're talking about. Pay close attention to verb and adjective endings. Put a check mark in the column after each conversation.

You will hear each set of statements twice.

1. **Male 1:** Es muy gracioso. Siempre come pizza en el desayuno y cereal en el almuerzo. ¡Qué asco! No me gusta comer pizza ni cereal. En realidad, nunca como desayuno.
2. **Female 1:** ¡Ah, son muy simpáticas! Compartimos todos los problemas con ellas, y comprenden muy bien.
3. **Male 2:** Es muy popular y le gusta hablar con sus amigos. ¡Todos los días, come su almuerzo en cinco minutos! Es muy impaciente y atrevido también.
4. **Female 2:** Son mis amigos, pero son MUY perezosos. Siempre beben refrescos y comen pizza enfrente de la tele. Nunca estudian.
5. **Male 3:** Son talentosas también. Escriben cuentos y me gustan mucho.
6. **Female 3:** Es muy deportista. Le gustan todos los deportes … el tenis, el fútbol, el básquetbol. Le encanta la música de México también. Es muy trabajadora.
7. **Male 4:** Son muy artísticos. Dibujan y cantan muy bien. Les encantan la guitarra y el piano. Escriben la música para una banda musical.

Track 12: Audio Act. 8, Writing, Audio & Video Workbook, p. 53 (3:12)

Listen as actors from a popular Spanish soap opera are interviewed on the radio program called *Las dietas de los famosos*. As you listen, write *sí* if the person mentions that he or she eats or drinks something most days. Write *no* if the person says that he or she never eats or drinks the item. You will hear this conversation twice.

Elvira: Hola. Soy Elvira … desde Miami. Bienvenidos al programa de radio *Las dietas de los famosos*. Están con nosotros los actores del popular programa "Con todo mi amor." Primero … mi buena amiga, ¡Lana Lote! ¡Hola, Lana!

Lana Lote: Hola, Elvira. Fantástico estar aquí hoy.

Elvira: Gracias, Lana. Hoy hablamos de tu dieta.

Lana Lote: ¿Mi dieta? Pues… nunca como papas fritas ni hamburguesas. No me gustan. Todos los días como una ensalada y un yogur. Por supuesto, siempre bebo mucha, mucha agua.

Elvira: Gracias, Lana. Y ahora, Óscar Oso. ¿Cómo estás, Óscar?

Óscar Oso: Hola, Elvira … y … ¡hola a tu público también!

Elvira: Óscar … ¿Cómo es tu dieta?

Óscar Oso: Me encanta la comida. Todos los días como hamburguesas y galletas. Yo nunca como ensaladas ni fresas. ¡Qué asco!

Elvira: Y ahora, Pepe Pluma. ¿Cómo estás, Pepe?

Pepe Pluma: Hola, Elvira. Hablamos de dieta, ¿no? Todos los días como huevos y salchichas. Me encantan, y son deliciosos en el desayuno. Nunca bebo café ni té.

Elvira: Gracias, Pepe. Y aquí con nosotros, Tita Trompo. Tita, ¿Cómo es tu dieta?

Tita Trompo: ¡Fruta, fruta, fruta! Todos los días como plátanos y fresas. Me encanta la fruta. Nunca como perritos calientes, ni tocino, ni salchichas.

Elvira: Gracias a todos. Elvira les dice ¡Hasta luego desde Miami! ¡Adiós!

You are going to hear this conversation again.

Track 13: Audio Act. 9, Writing, Audio & Video Workbook, p. 55 (2:59)

Listen as the woman at the table next to you tries to help a child order from the menu. As you listen, check off the items on the menu that the child says he likes and those he dislikes. Then in the space provided, write what you think would be an "acceptable" lunch for him. You will hear this conversation twice.

Lorena: ¿Beto, qué te gusta comer en el almuerzo? ¿Un sándwich de jamón y queso?

Beto: ¡Qué asco! No me gustan nada los sándwiches. Me encantan las galletas.

Lorena: No comemos galletas en el almuerzo. Compartimos una galleta por la noche. Ahora es el almuerzo. ¿Te gustan los perritos calientes?

Beto: No, no me gustan los perritos calientes ni los sándwiches. ¡Papas fritas! Me gustan las papas fritas

Lorena: Papas fritas yyyyyyy?

Beto: ¡Papas fritas y una galleta!

Lorena: Beto, ¿papas fritas y una hamburguesa? ¿Papas fritas y una ensalada? ¿Papas fritas y qué?

Beto: No me gustan las ensaladas ni las hamburguesas. Me gusta un yogur de fresas para comer y leche para beber.

Lorena: Bueno. Un yogur de fresas, papas fritas y leche. Para mí, una hamburguesa con papas fritas.

You are going to hear this conversation again.

Track 14: *Repaso del capítulo*, Student Book, p. 174 (3:38)

Vocabulario y gramática
Listen to these words and expressions that you have learned in this chapter. You will hear each word or expression once.

See Student Book page 174 for vocabulary list.

Track 15: *Preparación para el examen*, Student Book, p. 175 (1:10)

Escuchar
Practice task.
Listen as three students describe what they typically eat and drink for lunch. Which is most like the kind of lunch you eat? Did they mention anything you could not buy in your school cafeteria?

Marco: Siempre como una hamburguesa y papas fritas en el almuerzo. Por supuesto, necesito comer frutas y verduras, pero no me gustan.

Elena: ¡Qué asco! ¡Una hamburguesa y papas fritas! Nunca como papas fritas. Todos los días como una ensalada de frutas o sopa de verduras, ¡con una galleta, claro!

Tomás: ¿Cuál es mi comida favorita? Pues, no como mucho en el almuerzo. Como pizza o un perrito caliente y bebo un refresco.

Video Script

A primera vista: *¡Me encanta el desayuno!* (5:47)

Gloria: Buenos días, papá.

Papá: Buenos días.

Gloria: Buenos días, mamá.

Mamá: Buenos días.

Rosa: ¡Raúl! ¡Tomás! Ya son las ocho. El desayuno está preparado. ¡Rápido!

Raúl: Sí mamá. Un momento …

Raúl: Ah, de Claudia …

Claudia: ¿Cómo estás, Raúl? ¿Y Tómás? ¿Cómo es? ¿Es simpático? …

Tomás: ¿Quién es Claudia?

Raúl: Claudia es mi amiga por internet. Es de México. Le encantan las computadoras.

Rosa: Chicos, ahora. ¡El desayuno!

Raul: Si, mamá, un momento.

Lorenzo: Rosa, ¿qué es esto? ¿Es mucha comida, no? Cereal, huevos, jugo de naranja, leche, yogur …

Gloria: ¡Ay! Sí, es mucha comida.

Rosa: Es para Tomás.

Lorenzo: ¿Y qué preparas?

Rosa: Huevos, salchichas y tocino.

Lorenzo: Pero, nosotros nunca comemos mucho en el desayuno. ¡Y tú no comes nada!

Rosa: En los Estados Unidos, todos comen mucho en el desayuno. Tomás necesita mucha comida.

Lorenzo: ¿De veras?

Rosa: Por supuesto. ¿Más café?

Lorenzo: Sí. Muchas gracias.

Rosa: ¿Pan dulce?

Raúl: ¿Y qué comes en el desayuno? ¿Te gustan los huevos?

Tomás: ¡Qué asco! No me gustan nada los huevos.

Raúl: A mí tampoco.

Tomás: Normalmente como pan tostado y bebo jugo de naranja. Y tú, ¿qué comes?

Raúl: Aquí no comemos mucho. Un pan dulce, café, jugo de naranja. Y a veces, yogur. Vamos.

Raúl: Buenos días, mamá.

Raúl: Hola, papá. Hola, Gloria.

Lorenzo: Buenos días, hijo. Buenos días, Tomás. ¿Qué tal?

Tomás: Muy bien, gracias, tío Lorenzo. Buenos días, tía Rosa.

Rosa: Buenos días, Tomás.

Tomás: Hola, Gloria.

Rosa: ¡Tu primer día en Costa Rica!

Tomás: Estoy muy contento de estar aquí, tía.

Rosa: Muy bien. ¡A comer! Te gusta el desayuno, ¿no?

Tomás: Por supuesto. Me encanta el desayuno, tía.

Rosa: Muy bien. Tengo toda la comida favorita de los norteamericanos … huevos, salchichas, tocino, cereal, jugo de naranja, yogur y leche.

Gloria: Y también bananos.

Raúl: Mamá, es mucha comida.

Rosa: Pero, es la comida típica de los Estados Unidos. Uds. comen esta comida, ¿verdad, Tomás?

Tomás: Eh, pues, más o menos. Muchas gracias, tía. Raúl, ¿por qué no compartes los huevos, las salchichas, el tocino y el cereal conmigo?

Raúl: Por supuesto. Para beber, ¿quieres jugo de naranja o leche?

Tomás: Pues, ¿por qué no bebemos los dos, el jugo de naranja y la leche?

Raúl: Papá, ¿quieres huevos?

Lorenzo: No, muchas gracias. Toda la comida es para Uds. ¡Buen provecho!

Raúl: ¿Gloria?

Gloria: Gracias, pero no.

Rosa: Y para el almuerzo, ¡hamburguesas, pizza y ensalada!

GramActiva Videos: *-er* **and** *-ir* **verbs;** *me gusta(n), me encanta(n)* **(6:53)**

***-Er* and *-ir* verbs**

Host: By now you may have heard that there are things called regular verbs. These common verbs in Spanish come in three flavors: verbs that end in *-ar, -er,* and *-ir.* We already studied verbs that end in *-ar,* now let's take a bite out of verbs that end in *-er.*

Host: *Comer* will serve as a fine example for *-er* verbs. The endings for *-er* verbs are *-o* for the *yo* form, *-es* for the *tú* form, *-e* for the *usted/ él/ ella* forms, *-emos* for the *nosotros* and *nosotras* forms, *-éis* for the *vosotros* and *vosotras* forms, and *-en* for the *ustedes/ellos/ellas* forms.

Host: You can see that the endings of the present-tense conjugation for *-er* verbs are the same as those of the conjugation for verbs ending in *-ar*, with the letter *a* changed to *e.* In the *tú* form *hablas* ends in *-as*, and *comes* ends in *-es.* In the *usted, él,* and *ella* forms, *habla* ends in *-a* and *come* ends in *-e.*

Old Man: What about *-ir* verbs!? Let's go already! Get a move on.

Host: Calm down. *-Ir* verbs are almost the exact same as *-er* verbs. The *yo* form ends in *-o*, the *tú* form ends in *-es*, the *usted, él,* and *ella* forms end in *-e*, the *nosotros, nosotras* forms end in *imos*, the *vosotros, vosotras* forms end in *-ís*, and the *ustedes, ellos,* and *ellas* forms end in *-en.*

Looking at *correr,* "to run," and *compartir,* "to share," side by side, we see that they conjugate using the same endings in every way except for *nosotros* and *vosotros.* *-Er* verbs end in *-emos* in the *nosotros* form, whereas *-ir* verbs end in *-imos. -Er* verbs end in *-éis* in the *vosotros* form and *-ir* verbs end in *-ís.*

Quiz

Host: Complete the sentences with the correct verb form.

(comer) Yo _____.

Yo como.

(escribir) Tú _____.

Tú escribes.

(correr) Ud. _____.

Ud. corre.

(compartir) Nosotros _____.

Nosotros compartimos.

(escribir) Ellas _____.

Ellas escriben.

Me Gusta, Me Encanta

Host: To say that you like something in Spanish is a little different from the way you would say it in English. We'll cover the topic in detail later, but for now we're going to show you the basics enough to get started.

Host: *Me gusta el libro* means "I like the book"; but literally translated it means "the book pleases me." You might notice that the word *yo* is not in *Me gusta el libro,* just like the word *I* is not in the sentence "The book pleases me." Don't use it; you'll mess up the whole thing.

Old Man: But I don't like the book.

Host: Then all you have to do is add *no* to the beginning.

No me gusta el libro.

Old Man: *¿No me gusta el libro?*

Host: *No me gusta el libro.*

Lesko: But wait! There's more! If you order now you'll get two of everything! Double the fun!

Host: If you have a couple of things you like, use the word *gustan,* instead of *gusta. Me gustan los libros.*

Old Man: *No me gustan los libros.*

Host: Or of course if there are a few things you don't like, use *gustan* and add *no* to the beginning.

Goya: *Me gusta el plátano.*

Me gustan las fresas.

Me gustan las uvas.

No me gusta la lechuga.

No me gusta la cebolla.

No me gustan las zanahorias.

Host: It's pretty simple, really. So simple, we're going to give you another choice. If you're absolutely delighted by something, you can use the words *encanta* or *encantan* instead of the words *gusta* or *gustan.*

Goya: *Me encanta el plátano. Me encantan las fresas.*

Me encantan las uvas.

Old Man: *¡No me encanta el libro!*

Host: Well, not quite. If you really don't like something you don't use *encantar;* use *gusta* plus *nada,* like you would for any other negative sentence. *No me gusta nada el libro.*

Old Man: *¿No me gusta nada el libro?*

Host: Or *No me gustan nada los libros.*

Sounds like a lot, but it's really pretty simple.

Quiz

Host: How simple is it? You tell us! Fill in the blanks with the correct form of *gustar* or *encantar.*

How will these be read? You need to read the question on the screen for accessibility issues.

Me _____ la bandera.

Me gusta la bandera.

Me _____ el libro.

Me encanta el libro.

No me _____ el cartel.

No me gusta el cartel.

Me _____ las judías verdes.

Me encantan las judías verdes.

Nombre ______________________

Fecha ______________________

Communicative Activity **3A-1**

Estudiante **A**

Soledad, a new exchange student, will be staying with you and your family for a month. You want to know what she likes to eat for breakfast so that your family can make her feel comfortable. Your partner will play the role of Soledad. Ask him or her what he or she likes to eat for breakfast. (Example: *¿Te gustan los huevos?*)

Now, imagine that you are David, and that you are in Puerto Rico staying with a friend for a few weeks. Your partner will ask you what you like to eat so that the family can prepare your lunch. Respond based on the information below. The pictures that are crossed out are foods that you do not like.

Realidades A

Capítulo 3A

Nombre ____________________

Fecha ____________________

Communicative Activity **3A-1**

Estudiante **B**

Imagine that you are Soledad, a new exchange student staying with a family in the United States for a month. Your partner will ask you what you like to eat so that your host family can prepare your breakfast. Respond based on the information below. The pictures that are crossed out are foods that you do not like.

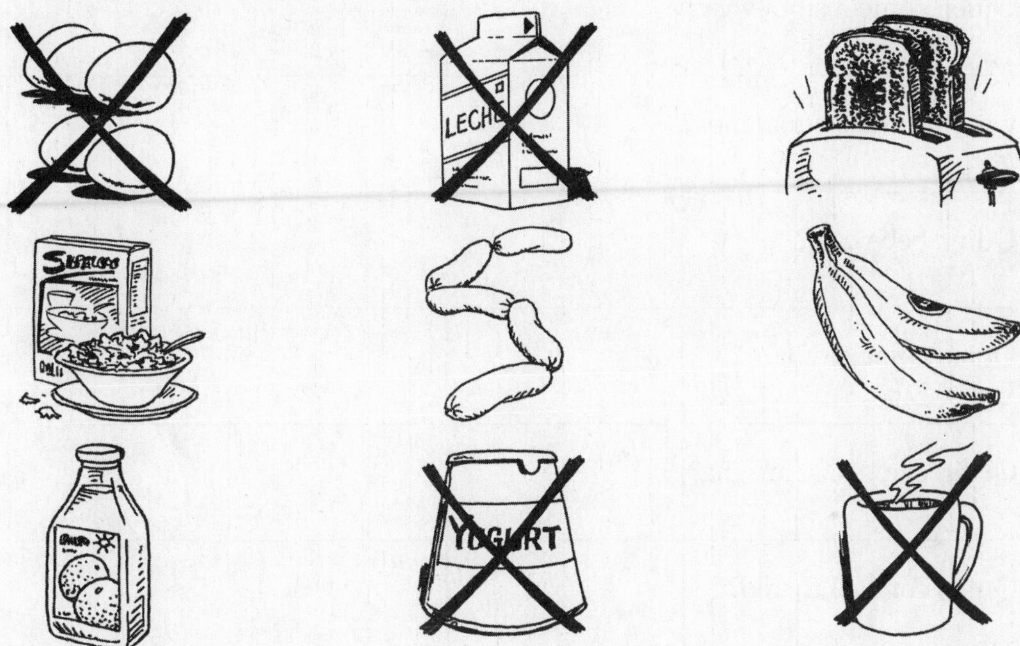

Now, pretend that you live in Puerto Rico and that David, your friend from Atlanta, is staying with your family for a few weeks. You want to know what David likes to eat for lunch so that your family can make him feel comfortable. Your partner will play the role of David. Ask him or her what he or she likes to eat for lunch. (Example: *¿Te gusta la ensalada?*)

Nombre ______________________

Communicative Activity **3A-2**

Fecha ______________________

Estudiante **A**

You and some friends are invited to breakfast at your partner's house this weekend. Each person's breakfast will be a little different. Ask your partner what you and your friends will eat and drink. Record your partner's answers on the lines provided.

1. ¿Quién come los huevos?

   ____

2. ¿Quién come los plátanos?

   ____

3. ¿Quién bebe café?

   ____

4. ¿Quién come el yogur?

   ____

5. ¿Quién come la salchicha?

   ____

6. ¿Quién come el tocino?

   ____

7. ¿Quién bebe el jugo de naranja?

   ____

8. ¿Quién come el pan tostado?

   ____

Now pretend that you and some friends are having a Spanish club meeting during lunch and your teacher asked you to order food for everybody. Each person's lunch will be a little different. Answer your partner's questions about what your friends will eat and drink with the information below. Some food and beverages will be served to more than one person.

	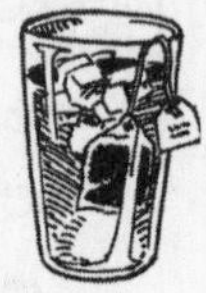	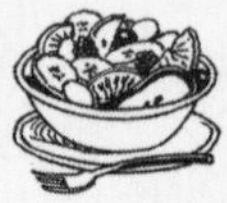	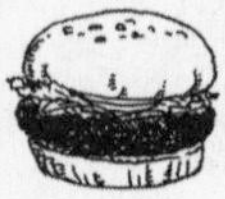	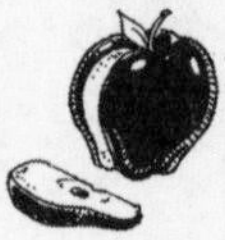	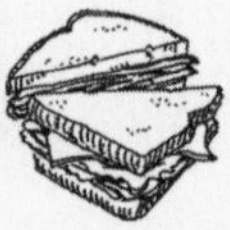	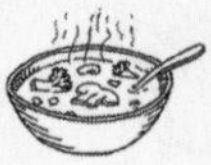	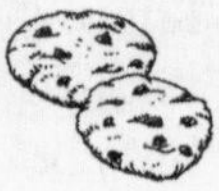	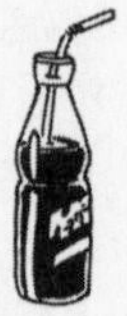
Raúl	X	X		X	X		X	
Isabel	X	X	X			X		
tu compañero(a)		X			X	X	X	X

Nombre ______________________

Fecha ______________________

You have invited some friends to your house for breakfast this weekend. Each person's breakfast will be a little different. Answer your partner's questions about what your friends will eat and drink with the information below. Some food and beverages will be served to more than one person.

	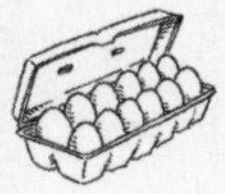	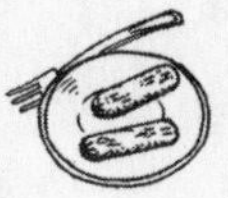	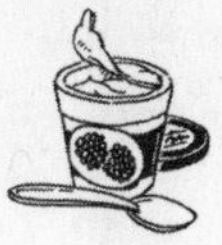	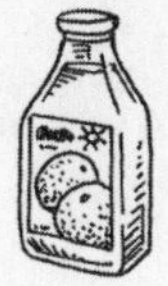	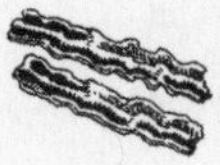	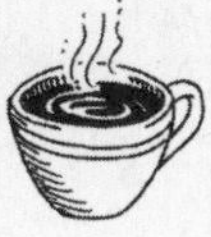	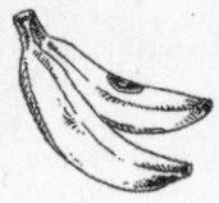	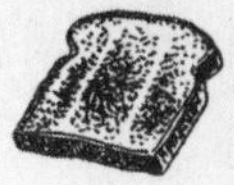
Óscar	X	X		X	X			
Gloria	X		X		X	X		
tu compañero(a)						X	X	X

Now pretend that you and some friends are having a Spanish club meeting during lunch and your teacher asked your partner to order food for everybody. Each person's lunch will be a little different. Ask your partner what you and your friends will eat and drink. Record your partner's answers on the lines provided.

1. ¿Quién come la hamburguesa?

____

2. ¿Quién come la ensalada de frutas?

____

3. ¿Quién bebe el refresco?

____

4. ¿Quién come las galletas?

____

5. ¿Quién come la sopa de verduras?

____

6. ¿Quién come el sándwich de jamón y queso?

____

7. ¿Quién bebe el té helado?

____

8. ¿Quién come la manzana?

____

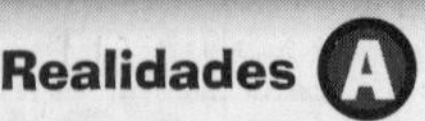

Capítulo 3A

Situation Cards

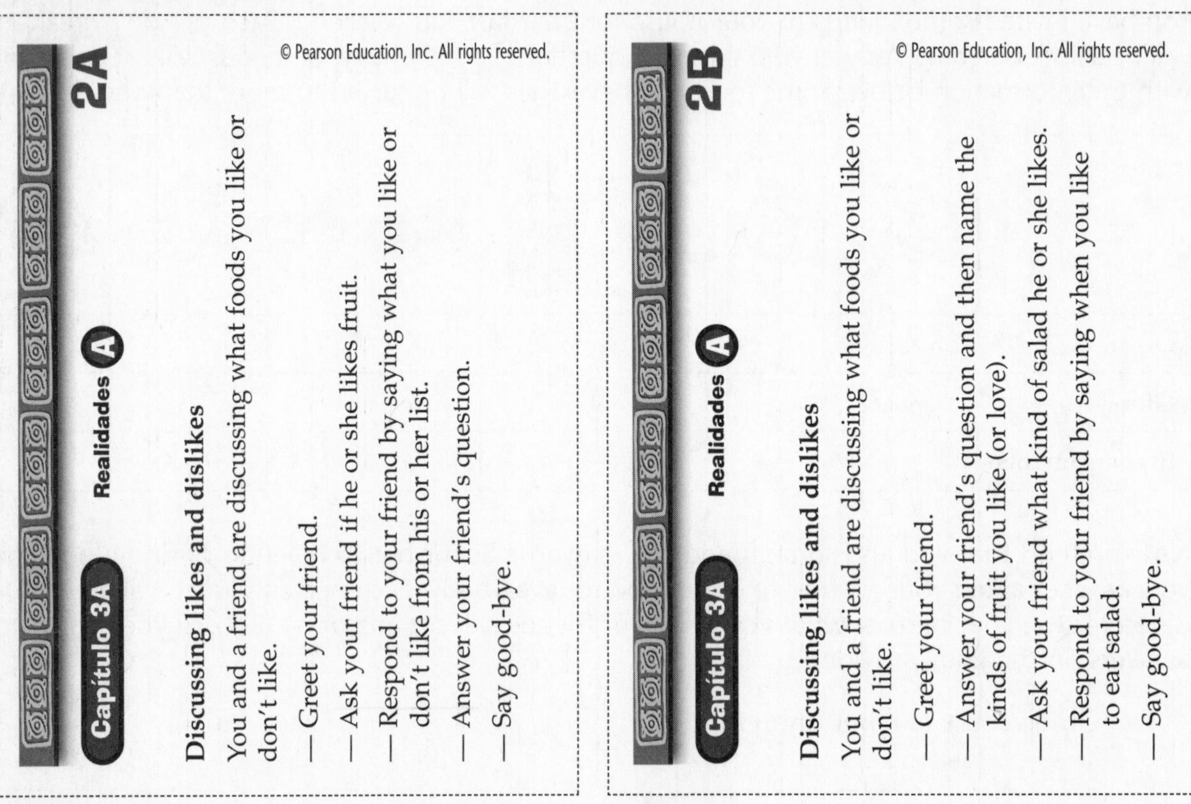

Capítulo 3A Realidades A **2A**

Discussing likes and dislikes

You and a friend are discussing what foods you like or don't like.

— Greet your friend.

— Ask your friend if he or she likes fruit.

— Respond to your friend by saying what you like or don't like from his or her list.

— Answer your friend's question.

— Say good-bye.

Capítulo 3A Realidades A **2B**

Discussing likes and dislikes

You and a friend are discussing what foods you like or don't like.

— Greet your friend.

— Answer your friend's question and then name the kinds of fruit you like (or love).

— Ask your friend what kind of salad he or she likes.

— Respond to your friend by saying when you like to eat salad.

— Say good-bye.

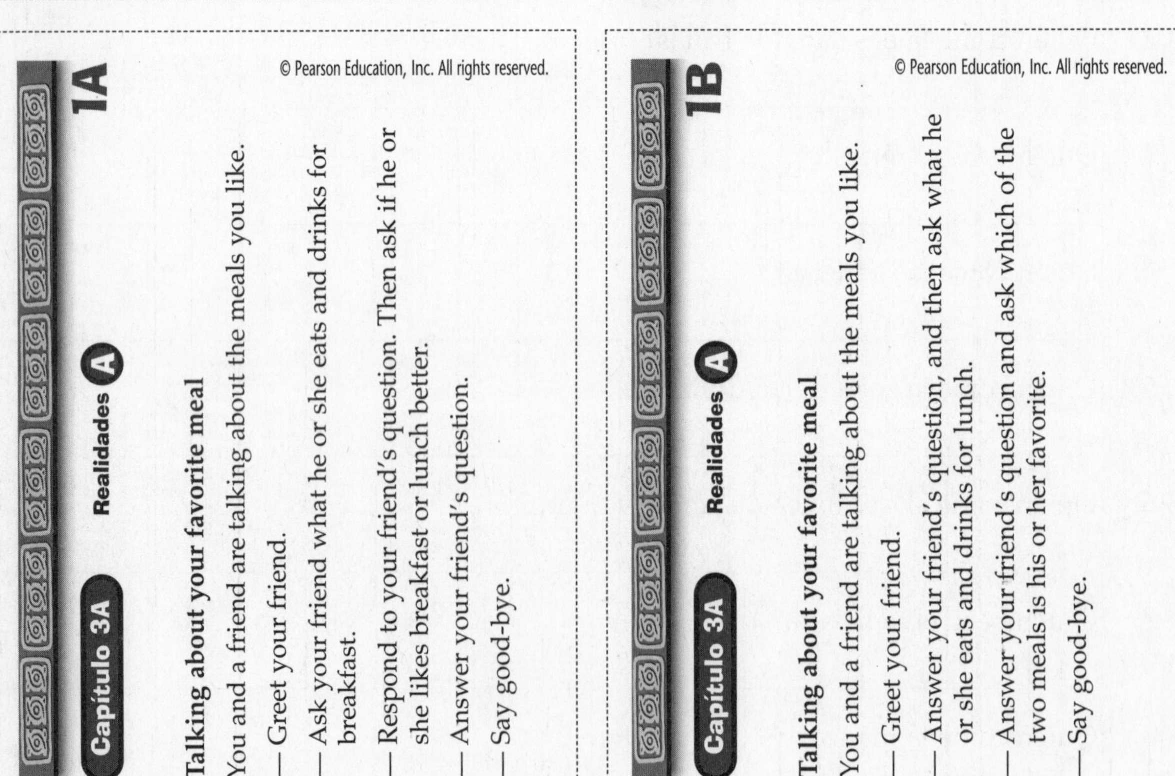

Capítulo 3A Realidades A **1A**

Talking about your favorite meal

You and a friend are talking about the meals you like.

— Greet your friend.

— Ask your friend what he or she eats and drinks for breakfast.

— Respond to your friend's question. Then ask if he or she likes breakfast or lunch better.

— Answer your friend's question.

— Say good-bye.

Capítulo 3A Realidades A **1B**

Talking about your favorite meal

You and a friend are talking about the meals you like.

— Greet your friend.

— Answer your friend's question, and then ask what he or she eats and drinks for lunch.

— Answer your friend's question and ask which of the two meals is his or her favorite.

— Say good-bye.

GramActiva

¿Desayuno o almuerzo?

Los sábados y la comida, p. 162

	el desayuno	el almuerzo
¿Qué bebes?		
¿Qué comes?		

Vocabulary Clip Art

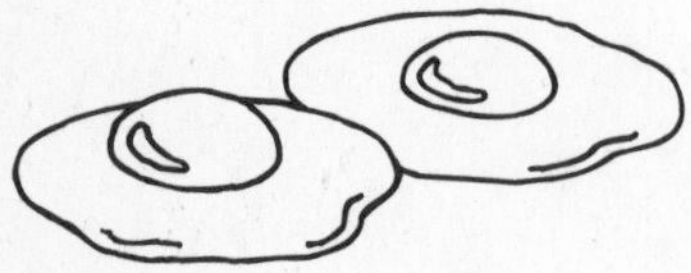

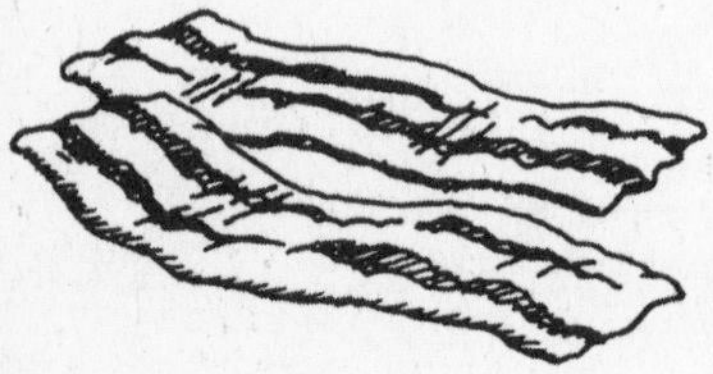

Vocabulary Clip Art

Vocabulary Clip Art

	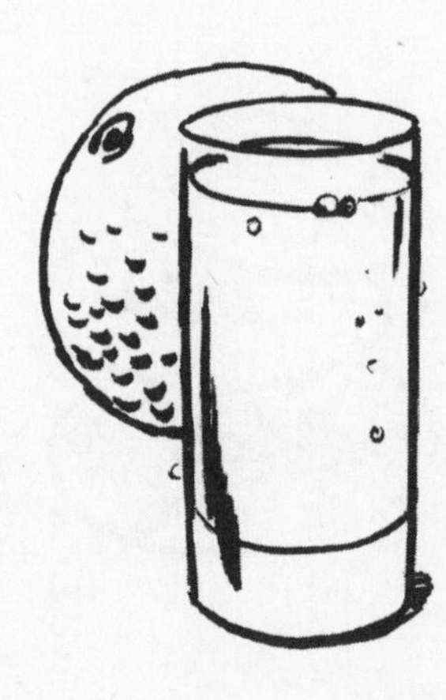	

Realidades A

Capítulo 3A

Core Practice Answers

3A-1

1. a
2. b
3. a
4. b
5. a
6. a
7. b
8. b
9. b
10. a

3A-2

Answers will vary. Under **El desayuno, comer** should be breakfast foods; under **desayuno, beber** should be drinks usually had at breakfast; under **El almuerzo, comer** should be lunch foods; under **almuerzo, beber** should be drinks usually had at lunch.

3A-3

1. Yo como tocino
2. el té / el café
   Me gusta más
3. Yo bebo mucha leche
4. Yo como mucha pizza
5. Yo bebo limonada
6. Yo comparto el almuerzo con amigos

3A-4

Answers will vary.

3A-5

A.

Row 1: como, comes, ____ , comemos, ____ , comen
Row 2: bebo, ____ , bebe, bebemos, ____ , beben,
Row 3: ____ , comprendes, comprende, comprendemos, ____ , comprenden
Row 4: escribo, escribes, escribe, ____ , ____ , escriben
Row 5: comparto, compartes, comparte, compartimos, ____ , ____

B.

1. comparte
2. comen
3. como
4. bebemos
5. comprende (escribe)
6. escribes
7. comparto
8. bebe
9. escribimos
10. comprenden (escriben)
11. Bebes
12. comparten

3A-6

A.
Answers will vary.

B.
Answers will vary.

C.

1. (No) Me gustan los plátanos.
2. (No) Me encanta la pizza.
3. (No) Me encantan las papas.
4. (No) Me gusta el pan.

3A-7

Some answers may vary.

1. compartimos
2. Corres
3. Comes plátanos
4. ¿Comprenden Uds. la lección?
5. ¿Cuál es tu jugo favorito?
6. ¿Te gusta el sándwich de jamón y queso?
7. ¿Te gusta el cereal en el desayuno?

Crucigrama (3A-8)

Across:

1. siempre
3. galletas
6. pan
9. queso
10. salchicha
12. jamón
13. desayuno
15. compartir
18. ensalada
21. fresas
22. huevos
23. café
24. caliente

Down:

2. menos
4. asco
5. tocino
6. plátano
7. helado
8. papas
11. comida
14. agua
16. manzana
17. verduras
19. almuerzo
20. jugo

Organizer (3A-9)

I. Vocabulary Answers will vary.

II. Grammar

1. **col. 1.** / **col. 2.**

col. 1.	col. 2.
-o	-emos
-es	-éis
-e	-en
col. 1.	**col. 2.**
bebo	bebemos
bebes	bebéis
bebe	beben

2. **col. 1.** / **col. 2.**

col. 1.	col. 2.
–o	-imos
-es	-ís
-e	-en
col. 1.	**col. 2.**
comparto	compartimos
compartes	compartís
comparte	comparten

3. -n

Realidades A | Nombre | Hora

Capítulo 3A | Fecha | **Vocabulary Flash Cards, Sheet 1**

Write the Spanish vocabulary word below each picture. If there is a word or phrase, copy it in the space provided. Be sure to include the article for each noun.

el agua	el tocino	la galleta
el café	la ensalada de frutas	la hamburguesa
el cereal	el yogur	los huevos

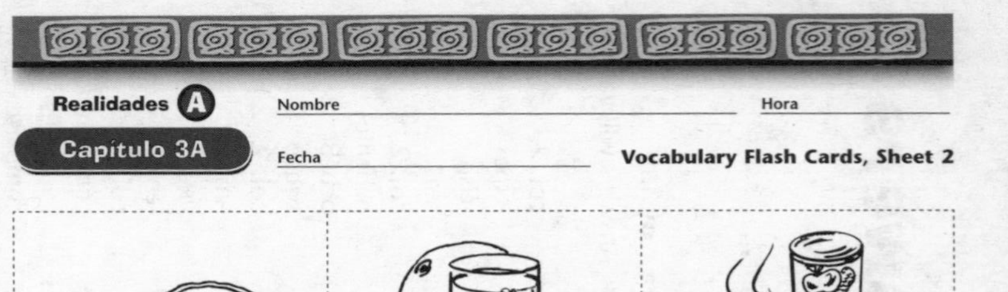

Realidades A | Nombre | Hora

Capítulo 3A | Fecha | **Vocabulary Flash Cards, Sheet 2**

el jamón	el jugo de naranja	la sopa de verduras
la leche	el té	el jugo de manzana
la limonada	el té helado	el pan

Realidades A — Capítulo 3A

Nombre ______ Hora ______

Fecha ______ **Vocabulary Flash Cards, Sheet 3**

la *pizza*	*el* *refresco*	*las* *papas* *fritas*
el *plátano*	*la* *salchicha*	*el* *perrito* *caliente*
el *queso*	*el* *sándwich* *de* *jamón* *y* *queso*	

Realidades A — Capítulo 3A

Nombre ______ Hora ______

Fecha ______ **Vocabulary Flash Cards, Sheet 4**

la manzana *la* *manzana*	**la ensalada** *la* *ensalada*	**en el almuerzo** *en* *el* *almuerzo*
la naranja *la* *naranja*	**las fresas** *las* *fresas*	**en el desayuno** *en* *el* *desayuno*
el pan tostado *el* *pan* *tostado*	**el desayuno** *el* *desayuno*	**la comida** *la* *comida*

Realidades A Nombre ____ Hora ____

Capítulo 3A Fecha ____ **Vocabulary Flash Cards, Sheet 5**

beber *beber*	**comer** *comer*	**compartir** *compartir*
nunca *nunca*	**siempre** *siempre*	**todos los días** *todos* *los* *días*
por supuesto *por* *supuesto*	**¡Qué asco!** *¡Qué* *asco!*	**¿Verdad?** *¿Verdad?*

Realidades A Nombre ____ Hora ____

Capítulo 3A Fecha ____ **Vocabulary Flash Cards, Sheet 6**

comprender *comprender*	**con** *con*	**¿Cuál?** *¿Cuál?*
más o menos *más* *o* *menos*	**sin** *sin*	**Me encanta(n). . .** *Me* *encanta(n)...*
Te encanta(n). . . *Te* *encanta(n)...*	**Me gusta(n). . .** *Me* *gusta(n)...*	**Te gusta(n). . .** *Te* *gusta(n)...*

Realidades A Nombre ______ Hora ______

Capítulo 3A Fecha ______ **Vocabulary Check, Sheet 1**

Tear out this page. Write the English words on the lines. Fold the paper along the dotted line to see the correct answers so you can check your work.

en el desayuno	***for breakfast***
los huevos	***eggs***
el pan	***bread***
el pan tostado	***toast***
el plátano	***banana***
la salchicha	***sausage***
el tocino	***bacon***
el yogur	***yogurt***
en el almuerzo	***for lunch***
la ensalada de frutas	***fruit salad***
las fresas	***strawberries***
la galleta	***cookie***
la hamburguesa	***hamburger***
el jamón	***ham***
las papas fritas	***French fries***
el perrito caliente	***hot dog***
la pizza	***pizza***

Fold In

Realidades A Nombre ______ Hora ______

Capítulo 3A Fecha ______ **Vocabulary Check, Sheet 2**

Tear out this page. Write the Spanish words on the lines. Fold the paper along the dotted line to see the correct answers so you can check your work.

for breakfast	***en el desayuno***
eggs	***los huevos***
bread	***el pan***
toast	***el pan tostado***
banana	***el plátano***
sausage	***la salchicha***
bacon	***el tocino***
yogurt	***el yogur***
for lunch	***en el almuerzo***
fruit salad	***la ensalada de frutas***
strawberries	***las fresas***
cookie	***la galleta***
hamburger	***la hamburguesa***
ham	***el jamón***
French fries	***las papas fritas***
hot dog	***el perrito caliente***
pizza	***la pizza***

Fold In

Realidades A　Nombre ______ Hora ______

Capítulo 3A　Fecha ______

Vocabulary Check, Sheet 3

Tear out this page. Write the English words on the lines. Fold the paper along the dotted line to see the correct answers so you can check your work.

el sándwich de jamón y queso	***ham and cheese sandwich***
la sopa de verduras	***vegetable soup***
el agua	***water***
el café	***coffee***
el jugo de manzana	***apple juice***
el jugo de naranja	***orange juice***
la leche	***milk***
la limonada	***lemonade***
el refresco	***soft drink***
el té helado	***iced tea***
beber	***to drink***
comer	***to eat***
la comida	***food, meal***
compartir	***to share***
nunca	***never***
siempre	***always***
todos los días	***every day***

Fold In ←

Realidades A　Nombre ______ Hora ______

Capítulo 3A　Fecha ______

Vocabulary Check, Sheet 4

Tear out this page. Write the Spanish words on the lines. Fold the paper along the dotted line to see the correct answers so you can check your work.

ham and cheese sandwich	***el sándwich de jamón y queso***
vegetable soup	***la sopa de verduras***
water	***el agua***
coffee	***el café***
apple juice	***el jugo de manzana***
orange juice	***el jugo de naranja***
milk	***la leche***
lemonade	***la limonada***
soft drink	***el refresco***
iced tea	***el té helado***
to drink	***beber***
to eat	***comer***
food, meal	***la comida***
to share	***compartir***
never	***nunca***
always	***siempre***
every day	***todos los días***

To hear a complete list of the vocabulary for this chapter, go to www.realidades.com and type in the Web Code jcd-0389. Then click on **Repaso del capítulo.**

Fold In ←

Realidades A | Nombre ______ | Hora ______

Capítulo 3A | Fecha ______ | Guided Practice Activities **3A-1**

Present tense of *-er* and *-ir* verbs (p. 160)

- Like the **-ar** verbs you learned previously, regular **-er** and **-ir** verbs follow a similar pattern in the present tense.
- For **-er** and **-ir** verbs, drop the **-er** or **-ir** from the infinitive (**comer, escribir**, etc.) and add the appropriate endings. The endings are the same for **-er** and **-ir** verbs except for in the **nosotros** and **vosotros** forms.

Present tense of *-er* verbs: *comer*	
yo: add **-o: como**	nosotros/nosotras: add **-emos: comemos**
tú: add **-es: comes**	vosotros/vosotras: add **-éis: coméis**
usted/él/ella: add **-e: come**	ustedes/ellos/ellas: add **-en: comen**

Present tense of *-ir* verbs: *escribir*	
yo: add **-o: escribo**	nosotros/nosotras: add **-imos: escribimos**
tú: add **-es: escribes**	vosotros/vosotras: add **-ís: escribís**
usted/él/ella: add **-e: escribe**	ustedes/ellos/ellas: add **-en: escriben**

A. Circle the ending in each verb form below.

1. escrib(imos)
2. compart(en)
3. beb(es)
4. corr(e)
5. v(en)
6. le(o)
7. escrib(es)
8. comprend(emos)
9. compart(o)
10. v(e)

B. Now, look at the list of verbs in **part A**. Circle the correct subject pronoun for each verb.

1. (**ustedes** / (**nosotros**)) escribimos
2. ((**ustedes**) / **ella**) comparten
3. (**nosotros** / (**tú**)) bebes
4. (**yo** / (**ella**)) corre
5. ((**ellos**) / **nosotros**) ven
6. ((**yo**) / **él**) leo
7. (**usted** / (**tú**)) escribes
8. ((**nosotras**) / **ellos**) comprendemos
9. (**usted** / (**yo**)) comparto
10. ((**usted**) / **ustedes**) ve

realidades.com
• Web Code: jcd-0303

Realidades A | Nombre ______ | Hora ______

Capítulo 3A | Fecha ______ | Guided Practice Activities **3A-2**

Present tense of *-er* and *-ir* verbs *(continued)*

C. Complete each sentence by writing the correct **-er** verb ending for each word.

1. Yo beb***o*** agua.
2. Nosotras corr***emos***.
3. Ella comprend***e*** todo.
4. Tú le***es*** una revista.
5. Ustedes com***en***.
6. Nosotros le***emos*** unos libros.

D. Now, complete each sentence by writing the correct **-ir** verb ending.

1. Tú escrib***es*** una carta.
2. Él compart***e*** la comida.
3. Ellas escrib***en*** cuentos.
4. Nosotros escrib***imos*** poemas.
5. Yo compart***o***.
6. Nosotras compart***imos***.

E. Complete each sentence with the correct verb form of the infinitive in parentheses. Follow the models.

Modelo Tú (escribir) *escribes*.
Ella (comer) *come*.

1. Yo (leer) ***leo***.
2. Ella (escribir) ***escribe***.
3. Nosotros (ver) ***vemos***.
4. Tú (compartir) ***compartes***.
5. Nosotros (escribir) ***escribimos***.
6. Ellos (beber) ***beben***.
7. Usted (compartir) ***comparte***.
8. Ellas (leer) ***leen***.

F. Now, write complete sentences using the words provided. Follow the model.

Modelo tú / ver / la / tele
Tú ves la tele.

1. yo / leer / una / revista
Yo leo una revista.
2. tú / compartir / el / cuarto
Tú compartes el cuarto.
3. ellos / beber / té / helado
Ellos beben té helado.
4. nosotros / comer / papas fritas
Nosotros comemos papas fritas.
5. ella / escribir / una / carta
Ella escribe una carta.
6. nosotros / compartir / la / comida
Nosotros compartimos la comida.
7. usted / correr / 10 kilómetros
Usted corre 10 kilómetros.
8. ustedes / escribir / cuentos
Ustedes escriben cuentos.

realidades.com
• Web Code: jcd-0303

Realidades A | Nombre ______ | Hora ______

Capítulo 3A | Fecha ______ | **Guided Practice Activities 3A-3**

Me gustan, me encantan (p. 164)

- To say you like one thing, use **me gusta** (*I like*) or **me encanta** (*I love*).
- To say you like more than one thing, use **me gustan** or **me encantan**.
- Put **no** in front of **me gusta** or **me gustan** to say you don't like one or more things:
  No me gusta el café. No me gustan los huevos.

One thing (singular)	More than one thing (plural)
Me **gusta** la leche.	Me **gustan** las manzanas.
Me **encanta** el té.	Me **encantan** los jugos.

A. Look at each noun. Write **S** if the noun is singular. Write **P** if it is plural.

1. ***S*** el cereal
2. ***S*** el tocino
3. ***P*** los huevos
4. ***P*** las manzanas
5. ***P*** las salchichas
6. ***P*** las papas
7. ***S*** el pan
8. ***S*** la pizza

B. Now, look at sentences using the same nouns from **part A.** Complete the verbs by writing **a** for the singular nouns and **an** for the plural nouns. Follow the models.

Modelos Me encant *a* el café.
Me encant *an* las fresas.

1. Me gust ***a*** el cereal.
2. Me gust***a*** el tocino.
3. Me encant***an*** los huevos.
4. Me gust***an*** las manzanas.
5. Me encant***an*** las salchichas.
6. Me gust***an*** las papas.
7. Me encant***a*** el pan.
8. Me gust***a*** la pizza.

C. Complete the following exchanges by circling the correct word in parenthesis.

1. ELENA: ¿Te (**(gusta)** / **gustan**) el helado?
   ENRIQUE: ¡Sí! Me (**(encanta)** / **encantan**) el helado.
2. BERTA: No me (**gusta** / **(gustan)**) las fresas.
   ANA: ¿No? ¡Me (**encanta** / **(encantan)**) las fresas!
3. JOSÉ: Me (**(encanta)** / **encantan**) la pizza.
   LUIS: ¿Sí? A mí no. ¡Pero me (**encanta** / **(encantan)**) las hamburguesas!

Realidades A | Nombre ______ | Hora ______

Capítulo 3A | Fecha ______ | **Guided Practice Activities 3A-4**

Me gustan, me encantan (continued)

D. Complete the following sentences by writing **encanta** or **encantan**.

1. Me ***encanta*** el queso.
2. Me ***encantan*** los plátanos.
3. Me ***encantan*** los jugos.
4. Me ***encanta*** el pan.
5. Me ***encanta*** el yogur.
6. Me ***encantan*** las galletas.

E. Complete the following sentences by writing **gusta** or **gustan**.

1. ¿Te ***gustan*** las sopas?
2. No me ***gusta*** el queso.
3. No me ***gusta*** la leche.
4. No me ***gusta*** el tocino.
5. ¿Te ***gustan*** las naranjas?
6. ¿Te ***gustan*** las papas fritas?

F. Choose words from the list to complete each sentence about what you like or don't like.

el cereal	**el desayuno**	**los huevos**	**las salchichas**	**el yogur**
las hamburguesas	**el jamón**	**el queso**	**el café**	**el té**
los perritos calientes	**la sopa de verduras**	**la pizza**	**las galletas**	**el jamón**

1. Me gusta ***Answers will vary.*** ______.
2. No me gusta ______.
3. Me gustan ______.
4. No me gustan ______.
5. ¡Me encanta ______!
6. ¡Me encantan ______!

G. Look at each drawing. Then write a sentence to say whether you like it or not. Follow the models.

Modelos *Me gustan los huevos*. OR *No me gustan los huevos*.
Me gusta la pizza. OR *No me gusta la pizza*.

1. ***Me gusta la leche. (No me gusta la leche.)***
2. ***Me gusta la limonada. (No me gusta la limonada.)***
3.  ***Me gustan las manzanas. (No me gustan las manzanas.)***
4.  ***Me gustan las salchichas. (No me gustan las salchichas.)***

realidades.com
• Web Code: jcd-0304

Lectura: Frutas y verduras de las Américas (pp. 168–169)

A. As you can see by its title, the reading in your textbook is about fruits and vegetables. Think about some fruits and vegetables that you eat. Write the names (in English) of three fruits and three vegetables in the spaces below. ***Answers will vary.***

FRUITS	VEGETABLES
______	______
______	______
______	______

B. Below are some Spanish words from the reading, categorized by whether they are a fruit or a vegetable. Choose the English word from the bank that you think is the best meaning for each example and write it in the blank.

potato beans corn pineapple avocado papaya

Frutas:

1. papaya ***papaya***
2. piña ***pineapple***
3. aguacate ***avocado***

Verduras:

4. papa ***potato***
5. frijoles ***beans***
6. maíz ***corn***

C. On the first page of the reading you see pictures of an avocado, a mango, and a papaya. Read the information below about each fruit and answer the questions that follow.

Aguacate:
- La pulpa es fuente de energía y proteínas.
- Tiene vitaminas A y B.

Mango:
- Es originalmente de Asia.
- Tiene calcio y vitaminas A y C.

Papaya:
- Contiene mucha agua.
- Tiene más vitamina C que la naranja.

1. Which fruits have vitamin A? ***aguacate*** ***mango***
2. Which fruits have vitamin C? ***mango*** ***papaya***
3. Which fruit is not originally from the Americas? ***mango***

D. Look at the recipe for a **Licuado de plátano** on the second page of the reading in your textbook. If the following statements are true, circle **C** for **cierto** (*true*); if they are false, circle **F** for **falso** (*false*).

1. C (F) The **licuado** is a hot beverage.
2. (C) F A **plátano** is a banana.
3. (C) F Milk is used in the recipe.
4. (C) F The blender is called a **licuadora**.
5. C (F) You should blend the ingredients for 2 minutes.

realidades.com
• Web Code: jcd-0305

Presentación oral (p. 171) *Answers will vary.*

Task: You and a partner will role-play a telephone conversation in Spanish between an American exchange student and a host student in Uruguay. You will each take one of the two roles and gather information about the other person.

A. You will role-play this conversation with a partner. Your role will be that of the host student. Here's how to prepare:

On a separate sheet of paper, make a list of two questions in Spanish that you might ask the exchange student. Find out:

(a) what his or her favorite activities are
(b) what he or she likes to eat and drink for breakfast (or lunch)

B. Revise your work.

1. Work with your partner to coordinate answers and to come up with a greeting and a farewell for your conversation. Here is a way to begin:

HOST STUDENT: ¡Hola, Pablo! Soy Rosa.
EXCHANGE STUDENT: ¡Hola, Rosa! ¿Cómo estás?
HOST STUDENT: Bien, gracias.

2. Now, work on completing the conversation. Use filler words that you have learned and the information you have collected from **part A**. See below for a model.

HOST STUDENT: Pues Pablo, ¿te gusta ir a la escuela?
EXCHANGE STUDENT: Sí, me gusta mucho. Me gusta dibujar y escribir cuentos. ¿Y tú? ¿Qué te gusta hacer en la escuela?
HOST STUDENT: A mí también me gusta ir a la escuela. Me gusta mucho correr y practicar deportes, pero no me gusta estudiar mucho. Me gusta más la hora de almuerzo. ¿Qué te gusta comer en el almuerzo?
EXCHANGE STUDENT: Yo como un sándwich de jamón y queso o una hamburguesa. ¿Y tú?
HOST STUDENT: A mí me encantan las ensaladas. No me gusta nada la carne. ¿Qué te gusta beber?
EXCHANGE STUDENT: Yo bebo los refrescos todos los días. ¿Qué bebes tú?
HOST STUDENT: A mí me gustan los jugos de frutas o bebo agua.

3. Finally, work on your ending. Look again at the **Para empezar** chapter in your textbook to get ideas for how to say good-bye. Below is a sample of how to end the conversation modeled above.

EXCHANGE STUDENT: Bien, pues, ¡Hasta luego!
HOST STUDENT: ¡Nos vemos!

C. You will be asked to present your conversation with your partner. The host student will go first. Listen to what your partner says and continue the conversation appropriately.

Nombre ____ Hora ____

Fecha ____ VIDEO

Antes de ver el video

Actividad 1

What do you like to eat for breakfast and lunch? Fill in the chart with that information.

Desayuno	Almuerzo
Answers will vary.	Answers will vary.

¿Comprendes?

Actividad 2

Think about the foods Rosa believes people in the United States eat for breakfast. What do Tomás and Raúl really eat?

1. ¿Qué come Tomás para el desayuno?

Tomás bebe jugo de naranja y come pan tostado para el desayuno.

2. Y, ¿qué come Raúl?

Raúl bebe jugo de naranja y café, come pan dulce, y a veces también come un yogur.

Actividad 3

Although Rosa makes a big breakfast for Tomás that day, the family does not eat very much regularly. Answer the questions below.

1. ¿Quién prepara el desayuno? *Rosa prepara el desayuno.*

2. Lorenzo: "Es mucha comida, ¿no? *cereal*, *huevos*, *jugo de naranja*, *leche*, *yogur* ..." Rosa: "En los Estados Unidos, todos comen mucho en el desayuno."

3. Lorenzo: "Nosotros nunca comemos mucho en el desayuno, Rosa. Mira, yo sólo bebo un *café* y a veces como un *pan dulce*."

4. Según Rosa, en los Estados Unidos comemos huevos, salchichas, tocino y pan tostado en el desayuno y *pizza, hamburguesas y ensalada* en el almuerzo.

Y, ¿qué más?

Actividad 4

Do you recall what you wrote in **Actividad** 1 about foods that you like to eat? Now that you have heard people in Costa Rica talk about what they eat, write down three questions of your own to ask a classmate about food. With a partner, ask your questions and compare answers.

¿ *Answers/Questions will vary.* ?

¿ ?

¿ ?

Actividad 5

You are helping out a friend at the counter of Restaurante El Gaucho in Argentina. Listen to the orders and record the quantity of each item ordered by each customer in the appropriate box of the chart. You will hear each conversation twice.

RESTAURANTE EL GAUCHO

El almuerzo	Cliente 1	Cliente 2	Cliente 3	Cliente 4
Ensalada		1		2
Hamburguesa	1	1		
Hamburguesa con queso			1	1
Sándwich de jamón y queso	2			
Perro caliente			1	
Pizza		1		1
Papas fritas	1		2	
Refresco	3	2	3	2
Té helado		1		1
Galletas		2		4

Realidades A — Nombre ______ Hora ______

Capítulo 3A — Fecha ______ **AUDIO**

Actividad 6

While working at the Hotel Buena Vista, you need to record breakfast orders for room service. Use the grid to make your report. First, listen carefully for the room number and write it in the appropriate box. Then write in the time requested. Finally, put a check mark next to each item ordered by the person in that room. You will hear each set of statements twice.

HOTEL BUENA VISTA

Número de habitación (*room number*)	48	41	24	12	35
Hora de servicio	6:30 A.M.	8:00 A.M.	10:00 A.M.	9:00 A.M.	7:30 A.M.
Jugo de naranja	✓			✓	
Jugo de manzana					✓
Cereal		✓			✓
Pan tostado	✓		✓		
Huevos		✓	✓	✓	
Jamón		✓			
Tocino			✓		
Salchichas	✓			✓	
Yogur de fresas			✓		✓
Café	✓				
Café con leche			✓	✓	
Té		✓			✓

Realidades A — Nombre ______ Hora ______

Capítulo 3A — Fecha ______ **AUDIO**

Actividad 7

You are waiting in line at a restaurant counter. You hear people behind you talking about your friends. Listen carefully so you can figure out whom they're talking about. Pay close attention to verb and adjective endings. Put a check mark in the column after each conversation. You will hear each set of statements twice.

	Carlos	Gabriela	Carlos y sus amigos	Gabriela y sus amigas
1.	✓			
2.				✓
3.	✓			
4.			✓	
5.				✓
6.		✓		
7.			✓	

Actividad 8

Listen as actors from a popular Spanish soap opera are interviewed on the radio program called **"Las dietas de los famosos"** (*Diets of the Famous*). As you listen, write **sí** if the person mentions that he or she eats or drinks something most days. Write **no** if the person says that he or she never eats or drinks the item. You will hear this conversation twice.

	Lana Lote	Óscar Oso	Pepe Pluma	Tita Trompo
			sí	
	sí			
			sí	no
				no

Realidades A | Nombre ____________ | Hora ____________

Capítulo 3A | Fecha ____________ | AUDIO

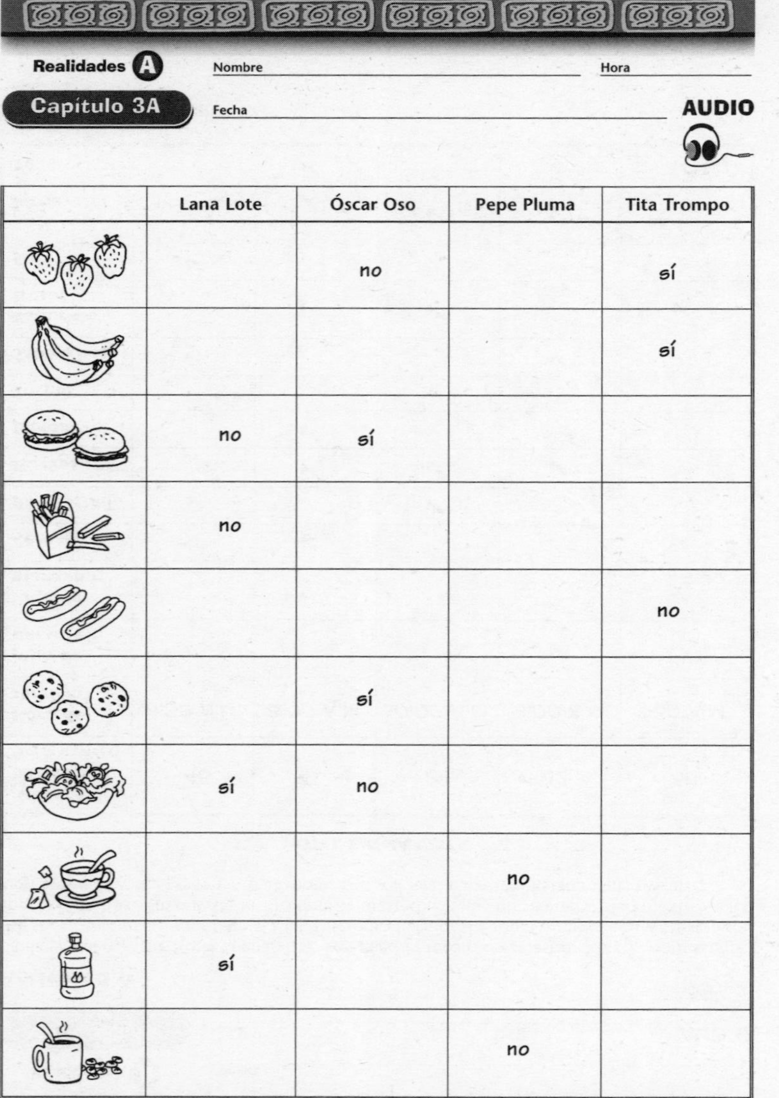

	Lana Lote	Óscar Oso	Pepe Pluma	Tita Trompo
(strawberries)		no		sí
(bananas)				sí
(hamburgers)	no	sí		
(french fries)	no			
(hot dogs)				no
(cookies)		sí		
(salad)	sí	no		
(tea)			no	
(bottle)	sí			
(coffee)			no	

Realidades A | Nombre ____________ | Hora ____________

Capítulo 3A | Fecha ____________ | AUDIO

Actividad 9

Listen as the woman at the table next to you tries to help a child order from the menu. As you listen, check off the items on the menu that the child says he likes and those he dislikes. Then in the space provided, write what you think would be an "acceptable" lunch for him. You will hear this conversation twice.

	(hamburgers)	(french fries)	(salad)	(hot dogs)	(sandwich)	(cookies)	(milk)	(yogurt)
le gusta		✔				✔	✔	✔
no le gusta	✔		✔	✔	✔			

Un almuerzo bueno para Beto es **Answers will vary.**

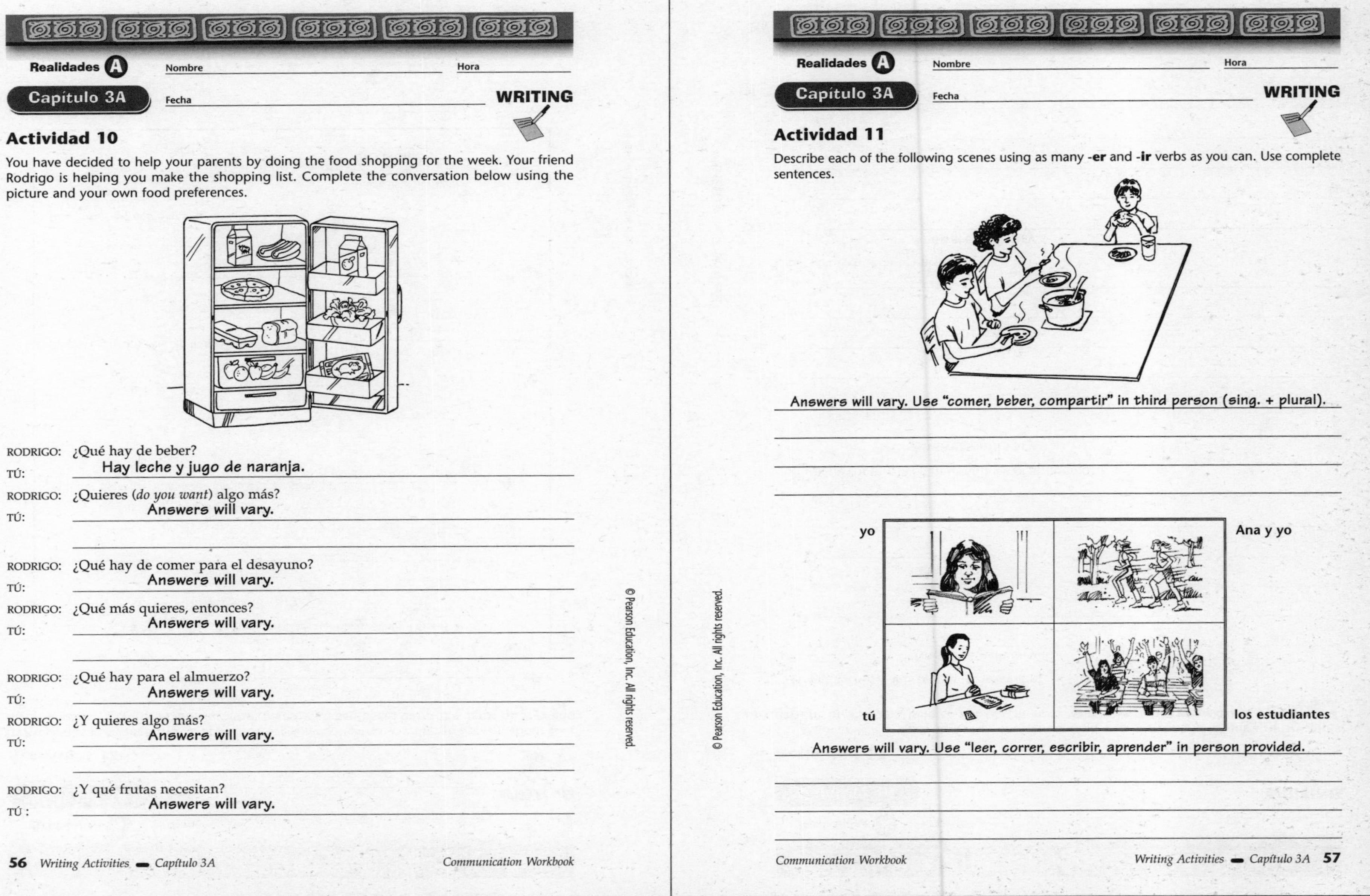

Realidades A — Nombre ____ Hora ____

Capítulo 3A — Fecha ____ **WRITING**

Actividad 10

You have decided to help your parents by doing the food shopping for the week. Your friend Rodrigo is helping you make the shopping list. Complete the conversation below using the picture and your own food preferences.

RODRIGO: ¿Qué hay de beber?
TÚ: Hay leche y jugo de naranja.

RODRIGO: ¿Quieres (*do you want*) algo más?
TÚ: Answers will vary.

RODRIGO: ¿Qué hay de comer para el desayuno?
TÚ: Answers will vary.

RODRIGO: ¿Qué más quieres, entonces?
TÚ: Answers will vary.

RODRIGO: ¿Qué hay para el almuerzo?
TÚ: Answers will vary.

RODRIGO: ¿Y quieres algo más?
TÚ: Answers will vary.

RODRIGO: ¿Y qué frutas necesitan?
TÚ : Answers will vary.

Realidades A — Nombre ____ Hora ____

Capítulo 3A — Fecha ____ **WRITING**

Actividad 11

Describe each of the following scenes using as many **-er** and **-ir** verbs as you can. Use complete sentences.

Answers will vary. Use "comer, beber, compartir" in third person (sing. + plural).

yo — Ana y yo

tú — los estudiantes

Answers will vary. Use "leer, correr, escribir, aprender" in person provided.

Realidades A — Nombre ______ Hora ______

Capítulo 3A — Fecha ______ **WRITING**

Actividad 12

In anticipation of your arrival in Spain next week, your host sister writes to ask you about your favorite foods. Complete your response below with sentences using the verbs **gustar** and **encantar**.

Estimada Margarita:

Gracias por su carta. Hay muchas comidas que me gustan. Para el desayuno,

Answers will vary. ______. También

______. Pero no

______.

Pero me encanta más el almuerzo. Por ejemplo, ______

______. También

______. Pero no ______

______.

¿Y a ti? ¿Te gustan las hamburguesas? ¿ ______

______? ¿ ______

______? ¿ ______

______?

Nos vemos en una semana.

Un fuerte abrazo,

Melinda

© Pearson Education, Inc. All rights reserved.

Realidades A — Nombre ______ Hora ______

Capítulo 3A — Fecha ______ **WRITING**

Actividad 13

The school nurse is teaching a class on nutrition and asks everyone to fill out a survey about what he or she eats. Using complete sentences, write your responses below.

1. ¿Qué comes y bebes en el desayuno?

   Answers will vary.

2. ¿Qué come y bebe tu familia en el almuerzo?

   Answers will vary.

3. ¿Qué comida te encanta?

   Answers will vary.

Test Preparation Answers

Reading Skills
p. 139 2. **C**
p. 140 2. **A**

Integrated Performance Assessment
p. 141
Answers will vary.

Practice Test: The Hidden Corn: A Mayan Legend
p. 143

1. B
2. H
3. D
4. F
5. Answers will vary but may include: Paragraph 2: "Finally, when the sun was almost gone and there was just a thin glow of gold left on the horizon, . . ." This quote paints a picture of what the sky looks like when the sun has almost disappeared from the sky. Paragraph 5: "In an instant, Yaluk tossed down a great lightning bolt [. . .]. The rock burst open, and thousands of golden ears of corn poured out." This quote creates a visual image of the lightning bolt striking and the ears of corn pouring out.

Realidades A

Capítulo 3B

School-to-Home Connection

Dear Parent or Guardian,

The theme for the chapter is *La comida* (Food) and this chapter is called *Para mantener la salud* (To maintain one's health).

Upon completion of this chapter, your child will be able to:

- talk about foods and beverages for dinner
- describe what people or things are like
- discuss food, health, and exercise choices
- understand cultural perspectives on diet and health

Also, your child will explore:

- the correct pronunciation of the letters *l* and *ll*
- the origins of some Spanish names for foods

Realidades helps with the development of reading, writing, and speaking skills through the use of strategies, process speaking, and process writing. In this chapter, students will:

- read about what athletes eat
- speak about what a friend likes to study, his or her favorite activities, and what he or she likes to eat and drink for breakfast

Remember that additional help is available online at www.realidades.com by using the Web Codes in the Student Edition or in the Leveled Vocabulary and Grammar Workbook.

Check it out! Have your child name one food in Spanish from each of the following food groups: bread, cereal, rice, and pasta; fruits; vegetables; milk, yogurt, and cheese; meat, poultry, fish, dry beans, eggs, and nuts.

Sincerely,

For: Tips to Parents
Visit: www.realidades.com
Web Code: jce-0010

Capítulo 3B Chapter Resource Checklist

Resources	CO†	APV	VH	MAN	LEC	PER	PE	MH	REP	PREP
Teacher										
Teacher's Resource Book										
Input Script										
Audio Script										
GramActiva BLM										
Communicative Activities BLM										
School-to-Home Connection BLM										
Clip Art										
Situation Cards BLM										
TPR Stories Book										
Fine Art Transparencies Teacher's Guide										
Pre-AP* Resource Book										
Student										
Leveled Vocabulary and Grammar Workbook										
Guided Practice										
Core Practice										
Communication Workbook with Test Preparation										
Writing										
Audio										
Video										
Test Preparation										
RPH Workbook										
Lecturas para hispanohablantes										
Grammar Study Guides										
Transparencies										
Answers on Transparencies										
Vocabulary and Grammar										
Fine Art										
Assessment										
Assessment Program										
Quizzes										
Chapter Test										
realidades.com										
Exam View Test Bank CD-ROM										
QuickTake on PresentationExpress										
MindPoint QuizShow CD-ROM										
Alternate Assessment Program										
Performance-Based Writing										
Self-Test on realidades.com & CWS										
Assessment Program: RPH										
Technology										
realidades.com										
myeBook										
TeacherExpress CD-ROM										
PresentationExpress DVD										
Video Program DVD										
Culture Video DVD										
Audio Program CD 7										
Assessment CD 20										
Song CD 22										
Canciones de hip hop on realidades.com & CWS										

† *See Abbreviation Key on page iv.*

Input Script

Presentation

Input Vocabulary: Bring three stuffed animals to class: a dog, a cat, and a rabbit (or use drawings or photos). Place the overhead transparency on the screen. Hand out copies of the Vocabulary Clip Art and have students tear the images into individual food items. Use the animals and the transparency to present the food vocabulary. Say *"Éste es mi perro Rico (mi gato Raúl, mi conejo Jorge). Le encanta la carne. Le gusta el pollo, el bistec y el pescado. Pero no le gustan las verduras."* Then have students draw three large food bowls and label them ***Rico, Raúl,*** and ***Jorge.*** Make true and false statements about what they like to eat. Students will place the food item in that pet's bowl only if it is true *("A Raúl le gusta el pescado.").*

Input Monologue 1: Read the entire monologue aloud. Then by each vegetable on the transparency, write E: ___ G: ___ (for ***me encantan*** and ***me gustan***). Take a survey of the class. Ask students *"¿Les encantan las cebollas?"* Have students who love onions raise their hand. Write down the number by E: ___. Then ask *"¿Les gustan las cebollas?"* Have students who merely like onions raise their hand and record that number by G: ___.

Input Monologue 2: Read the entire monologue. Then use other pairs of foods, either healthy and unhealthy, in the sentence *"Come muchos pasteles y helado."* Have students say *"¡Son horribles!"* when they hear unhealthy foods. Have students place their Clip Art images into two piles: ***buena para la salud*** and ***no buena para la salud.***

Input Dialogue 1: Act out the first dialogue, playing both roles or using one of the stuffed animals from the Input Vocabulary activity as an acting partner. Then substitute both physical activities ***(nadar, esquiar, bailar)*** and nonphysical activities ***(ver la tele, usar la computadora, jugar videojuegos)*** from Chapter 1A. Have students flex their arm muscles to show that an activity is good for maintaining one's health. Have them slump over and act out of shape to show that an activity is not very good for one's health.

Input Dialogue 2: Act out the second dialogue, playing using one of the stuffed animals again. You might bring graham crackers or other healthful snacks for your students to help teach ***Tengo hambre.*** Say to a student *"¡Tengo hambre! Y tú, ¿tienes hambre?"* Encourage the student to say *"Sí, ¡tengo hambre!"* and give him or her a cracker. Then point to different food items on the transparency and say *"¿Por qué no comemos ... ?"* Students will say, for example, *"¿Los espaguetis? ¡Por supuesto! Son muy sabrosos."*

Comprehension Check

- Draw a large food pyramid on the chalkboard and write the food groups in the appropriate places. Call out food items and have students tape the Clip Art image of the item in the right food group on the pyramid.
- Divide students into teams. Have a member of each team come to the front of the class. Draw a Clip Art food item from a bag. Show it to those students only. Have them return to their desks and when you say *"¡Adelante!"* they will draw the food item for their group to guess. First team to guess wins a point.
- Have students stand at their desks and say *"¿Simón, por qué no comemos el pollo (el bistec, el pescado)?"* If you say *"Simón"* in the sentence, students should cluck like a chicken, moo like a cow, or imitate a fish. If you don't say *"Simón,"* they must remain absolutely still and quiet. Students who make the sound or action when you don't say *"Simón"* must sit down.

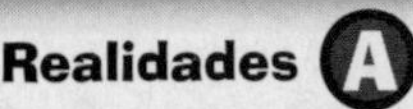

Realidades A

Capítulo 3B

Audio Script

Audio CD, Capítulo 3B

Track 01: *A primera vista,* Student Book, p. 178 (4:30)

Para mantener la salud

Read along as you listen to the statements.

MALE TEEN: La pirámide nutritiva es la forma más práctica de indicar la comida que debes comer cada día. Para mantener la salud, es importante comer de todos los grupos.

You will hear each word or phrase twice. After the first time there will be a pause so you can pronounce it, then you will hear the word or phrase a second time.

las grasas
la mantequilla
la carne
el pollo
el bistec
el pescado
la leche
las verduras
la cebolla
los guisantes
las papas
las frutas
las uvas
el pan y los cereales
los espaguetis
el arroz
la lechuga
los tomates
las zanahorias
las judías verdes
los pasteles
el helado

Read along as you listen to the dialogue.

MALE TEEN: ¡Me encantan las verduras! Como muchas ensaladas con lechuga y tomates. También me gustan las zanahorias y las judías verdes.

FEMALE TEEN: ¡Mi amiga Claudia no come comida buena para la salud! Come muchos pasteles y helado. Son horribles.

Track 02: *A primera vista,* Student Book, p. 179 (1:18)

You will hear each word or phrase twice. After the first time there will be a pause so you can pronounce it, then you will hear the word or phrase a second time.

caminar
levantar pesas

Read along as you listen to the dialogue.

FEMALE TEEN 1: ¿Qué haces para mantener la salud?

MALE TEEN: Pues, cada día hago ejercicio. Camino, monto en bicicleta y practico deportes.

FEMALE TEEN 2: ¡Uf! Tengo hambre. ¿Por qué no comemos algo en el restaurante "A tu salud"? Los sándwiches son muy sabrosos.

FEMALE TEEN 3: ¡Por supuesto!

Track 03: *A primera vista,* Act.1, Student Book, p. 179 (2:20)

¿Qué debes comer?

Your teacher is giving a lecture on foods that you should eat from the Food Guide Pyramid. Touch each item as it is mentioned. Listen carefully for the names of the foods. You will hear each statement twice.

1. Necesitas beber leche o comer queso.
2. El pescado y el pollo son buenos para la salud.
3. Las judías verdes y las zanahorias son verduras importantes.
4. No debes comer mucho helado.
5. Las papas son buenas para la salud.
6. El arroz es bueno para la salud.
7. No es bueno comer muchos pasteles.
8. Debes comer uvas u otra fruta cada día.

Track 04: *A primera vista,* Act. 2, Student Book, p. 179 (2:06)

Para mantener la salud

Listen to students talk about things they do. Give a "thumbs-up" sign if they are describing things that are healthy and a "thumbs-down" sign if they are unhealthy.

1. Me gusta mucho correr.
2. Nunca hago ejercicio.
3. Practico deportes.
4. Como pasteles cada día.
5. Mis amigos y yo levantamos pesas.
6. Bebo agua cada día.
7. Nunca como verduras. ¡Son horribles!
8. Me gustan los espaguetis con tomate.

Track 05: *A primera vista, Videohistoria,* Student Book, pp. 180–182 (1:57)

Para mantener la salud

¿Qué hacen Raúl, Tomás y Gloria para mantener la salud? Lee la historia.

Read along as you listen to the *Videohistoria*.

See Student Book pages 180–182 for script.

Track 06: Audio Act. 5, Writing, Audio & Video Workbook, p. 63 (5:35)

Listen to a radio announcer as he interviews people at the mall about their lifestyles. Pay close attention to the things that they say they do and eat. What in their lifestyles is good or bad for their health? Match what they say to the pictures below. Then write the corresponding letter in the appropriate column. You will hear this conversation twice.

Antonio: Hola. Soy Antonio, de la estación de radio ... ¡Zzzzz ETA! Estoy aquí en el centro comercial para hablar de la salud con nuestros participantes. Primero, hablo con Mariana y Jorge. Bueno. Mariana, ¿qué haces para mantener tu salud?

Mariana: Pues ... cada día camino por treinta minutos. También monto en bicicleta. Siempre como muchas verduras—judías verdes o zanahorias. Pero en realidad, como muuuucho helado. No es bueno, ¿verdad?

Antonio: Y tú, Jorge. ¿Qué haces?

Jorge: Mariana es muy deportista, pero yo no. Cada día juego videojuegos y veo la tele. ¡Soy muy perezoso! No me gusta hacer ejercicio. Cuando tengo hambre, como galletas y un pastel. Me gusta comer pescado. Creo que el pescado es bueno para la salud, ¿no?

Antonio: Creo que sí. Y ahora ... Luz. ¿Cómo estás?

Luz: Bien. Creo que soy una persona de muy buena salud. Nado por cuarenta y cinco minutos y levanto pesas en el gimnasio todos los días. Prefiero comer verduras, pescado y ensaladas. Nunca como pasteles.

Antonio: Gracias, Luz. Estoy de acuerdo. Tú eres una persona de buena salud. Y finalmente, Nacho.

Nacho: Hola, Antonio. Debo hacer algo, pero prefiero no hacer nada. El ejercicio que hago es muy fácil. ¡Levanto la pizza y me la llevo a la boca! Pero, en serio ... no hago mucho para mantener la salud. Veo la tele y hablo por teléfono con mis amigos. Prefiero comer pasteles en el almuerzo. No me gustan las ensaladas ni las frutas.

Antonio: ¡Gracias a todos! Hasta la próxima vez de ... tu estación favorita .... La ZETA!

You are going to hear this conversation again.

Track 07: Audio Act. 6, Writing, Audio & Video Workbook, p. 64 (3:37)

Listen as students in a health class in Costa Rica present a list of the "dos and don'ts" of staying healthy. Which are *consejos lógicos* and which are *consejos ridículos?* Place a check mark in the appropriate box of the chart. You will hear each set of statements twice.

1. Debes hacer ejercicio cinco minutos, todos los días. ¡Nada más!
2. Para mantener la salud, debes caminar con tus amigos.
3. Debes bailar más. Es muy divertido y es buen ejercicio cardiovascular.
4. No es bueno comer frutas, cereales ni verduras todos los días.
5. Debes ver la tele más de dos horas por día.
6. Debes comer pasteles en el almuerzo. Son muy malos.
7. Necesitas beber mucha agua todos los días.
8. Debes hacer ejercicio con tus amigos. Es muy divertido.
9. Debes usar la computadora para jugar videojuegos durante tres o cuatro horas por la noche.
10. Debes comer zanahorias cuando tienes hambre.

Track 08: *Pronunciación,* The letters *l* and *ll*, Student Book, p. 191 (2:34)

In Spanish, the letter *l* is pronounced much like the letter *l* in the English word *leaf*. Listen to and say these words: You will hear each word twice. After the word is pronounced the first time, there will be a pause so you can pronounce it. Then you will hear the word a second time.

lechuga
almuerzo
lunes
sol
pasteles
abril
helado
difícil

For most Spanish speakers, the letter combination *ll* is similar to the sound of the letter *y* in *yes*. Listen to and say these words:

llamo
cebolla
silla
pollo
allí
ella
llueve
mantequilla

Track 09: *Pronunciación,* Student Book, p. 191 (2:16)

Try it out! Listen to this song and then say it.

Canta el gallo, canta el gallo
con el kiri, kiri, kiri, kiri, kiri;
La gallina, la gallina
con el cara, cara, cara, cara, cara;
Los polluelos, los polluelos
con el pío, pío, pío, pío, pío, pí.

Track 10: Audio Act. 7, Writing, Audio & Video Workbook, p. 64 (2:46)

A Spanish-speaking telemarketer calls your home to interview you about the food preferences of teens. He must have gotten your name from your Spanish teacher! He asks you to tell him whether you think certain food items are *malo* or *sabroso*. Be sure to listen carefully so that you will be able to use the correct form of the adjective for each item. Write what you would say in the spaces below. You will hear each question twice.

1. ¿Cómo es la ensalada de lechuga y tomates?
2. ¿Cómo es el arroz con pollo?
3. ¿Cómo son las pizzas con cebollas y verduras?
4. ¿Cómo son los jugos de frutas—de manzana, de naranja ...?
5. ¿Cómo es el helado de fresa?
6. ¿Cómo son los espaguetis con salsa de tomate?
7. ¿Cómo son las papas con mantequilla y queso?
8. ¿Cómo son los pasteles de chocolate?
9. ¿Cómo son las bebidas de cola?
10. ¿Cómo es el pescado?

Track 11: *Manos a la obra,* Act. 21, Student Book, p. 193 (1:39)

Escucha y escribe
You will hear comments from five customers about the food being sold in a market. On a piece of paper, write the numbers 1 to 5. As you listen, write the comments next to the numbers. You will hear each statement twice.

1. Las zanahorias son muy buenas.
2. La papa es sabrosa.
3. Las cebollas son malas.
4. Señor, los guisantes son horribles.
5. El pescado no es bueno.

Track 12: Audio Act. 8, Writing, Audio & Video Workbook, p. 65 (5:06)

In an effort to improve food in the school cafeteria, students are asked to anonymously call in their opinions about school food. You are asked to chart the responses of the Spanish-speaking students. As you listen to their opinions, fill in the grid. If they say something "positive" about a particular menu item, put a plus sign in the appropriate column; if they say something "negative," put a minus sign in the column. You will hear each set of statements twice.

1. **Female Teen 1:** Soy estudiosa y me gusta mucho la escuela, pero no me gusta nada la comida de la cafetería. Creo que las ensaladas son malas y el pollo es horrible. Me gusta el helado, pero los pasteles no son buenos.
2. **Male Teen 1:** Siempre tengo hambre porque hago mucho ejercicio. Soy muy deportista. Creo que la comida en la cafetería es buena para la salud. Los espaguetis y el pescado son muy sabrosos. El pan no es bueno. Es muy difícil comer.
3. **Female Teen 2:** Me gusta ir a la escuela para pasar tiempo con amigos, no para comer comida buena. En realidad, el bistec y el pollo son horribles. Yo prefiero comer las ensaladas. Las ensaladas de frutas son saludables. Mis amigos y yo somos vegetarianos.
4. **Male Teen 2:** Para mantener la salud, prefiero comer comida saludable. Bebo mucha agua todos los días. En la cafetería como guisantes, judías verdes, zanahorias y tomates. Me gustan los platos de verduras con una papa. Son muy sabrosos y buenos para la salud.
5. **Female Teen 3:** ¿Por qué como yo en la cafetería? Por los pasteles y el helado. Son fantásticos. Los pasteles de fresas, de chocolate, de manzanas … me encantan todos. Me gusta mucho el helado de fresas. Es mi favorito. Es muy bueno para la salud. Hay leche y fruta en el helado, ¿no estás de acuerdo?

Track 13: Audio Act. 9, Writing, Audio & Video Workbook, p. 65 (4:58)

Listen as people call in to ask Dr. Armando their health questions on his radio program *Pregunte al doctor Armando.* While you listen to their questions and Doctor Armando's advice, fill in the chart below. Do you agree with his advice? You will hear this conversation twice.

Doctor: Beatriz, bienvenida al programa, *Pregunte al doctor Armando.*

Beatriz: Buenas tardes, doctor Armando. ¿Por cuántos minutos debo hacer ejercicio todos los días?

Doctor: Depende del ejercicio. Generalmente, debes hacer treinta minutos de ejercicio todos los días para mantener la salud. Gracias por tu pregunta. Mauricio, bienvenido a *Pregunte al doctor Armando.*

Mauricio: Hola, doctor Armando. ¿Cree usted que nunca debo comer pasteles? Me encantan los pasteles.

Doctor: Los pasteles no son malos para la salud, pero debes comer verduras, pescado, frutas y pan también. Gracias por tu pregunta. Loli, bienvenida a *Pregunte al doctor Armando.*

Loli: Buenas tardes, doctor Armando. Yo camino una hora en el centro comercial. Creo que es bueno para la salud. ¿Qué cree usted?

Doctor: Hmmm. No estoy de acuerdo. El centro comercial no es un gimnasio. ¿Prefieres ir de compras o caminar en serio? Debes ir a un gimnasio. Gracias por tu pregunta. Luis, bienvenido a *Pregunte al doctor Armando.*

Luis: Hola, doctor. Tengo un problema. Nunca tengo hambre. Debo comer más, pero no me gusta comer mucho.

Doctor: Debes hacer ejercicio: caminar, levantar pesas, correr. Tienes más hambre cuando haces ejercicio. Gracias por tu pregunta. Hasta luego …

You are going to hear this conversation again.

Track 14: *Repaso del capítulo,* Student Book, p. 204 (3:56)

Vocabulario y gramática
Listen to these words and expressions that you have learned in this chapter. You will hear each word or expression once.

See Student Book page 204 for vocabulary list.

Track 15: *Preparación para el examen,* Student Book, p. 205 (0:59)

Escuchar
Practice task.
Listen as two people are interviewed about their habits. See if you can tell which one is an Olympic skier and which one is a drummer. Be prepared to explain your "educated guesses."

Male 1: Cada día, a las cinco y media de la mañana, levanto pesas por treinta minutos y camino por una hora. Nunca como pasteles ni papas fritas porque son malos para la salud.

Male 2: Nunca como el desayuno porque no tengo tiempo para comer. Para el almuerzo prefiero la comida rápida: una hamburguesa con un refresco.

Video Script

A primera vista: *¡Qué sabroso!* (4:53)

TOMÁS: Tengo sed …

RAÚL: Yo también. ¿Te gusta el café? El café de aquí es muy bueno.

GLORIA: Sí, el café de Costa Rica es muy famoso.

TOMÁS: Sí, pero … el café, ¿no es malo para la salud?

GLORIA: ¿Tú crees? Pero el café es muy importante para nosotros.

RAÚL: ¡Vamos!

RAÚL: ¿Aquí está bien? Vamos.

RAÚL: Pues, ¿qué bebida prefieres?

TOMÁS: Prefiero un jugo de fruta.

RAÚL: ¡Ah! De acuerdo, un refresco.

TOMÁS: No, no; un refresco no; un jugo de fruta.

GLORIA: No, Tomás. En Costa Rica, un refresco es un jugo de fruta.

RAÚL: Dos refrescos de banano con leche …

GLORIA: Y un refresco de piña con agua, por favor.

CAMARERO: Son 1,050 colones.

RAÚL: Aquí está. Gracias.

TOMÁS: Hmmm … muy sabroso.

RAÚL: Estoy de acuerdo. Todos los refrescos de aquí son buenos …

TOMÁS: Y, son muy buenos para la salud.

GLORIA: Sí … es importante mantener la salud, ¿verdad?

TOMÁS: Creo que sí. Yo hago mucho ejercicio …

RAÚL: ¿Qué ejercicio haces?

TOMÁS: Cada día, levanto pesas, camino … ¿Y tú?

RAÚL: Aquí en San José, todos caminamos mucho.

GLORIA: También practicamos deportes. Montamos en bicicleta …

RAÚL: Bueno, Tomás, ¿quieres comer algo?

TOMÁS: Sí, ahora tengo hambre.

RAÚL: ¡Ah! Entonces, debemos comer en una soda.

TOMÁS: ¿Por qué? Ahora no tengo sed; tengo hambre. ¡Ahhh!

GLORIA: No, Tomás, aquí una soda no es una bebida; es un restaurante.

RAÚL: Carnes, pescado, ensaladas …

TOMÁS: Ah, está bien. Vamos a entrar.

RAÚL: Entonces, ¿te gusta la comida de Costa Rica?

TOMÁS: Sí, mucho. Me encanta el gallo pinto.

GLORIA: ¿Quieres comer algo más?

TOMÁS: No, no tengo hambre ahora. No puedo comer nada más. ¡Vamos a casa!

ROSA: Hola a todos. ¿Qué tal, Tomás? Mira, hamburguesa, pizza, ensalada y jugo de manzana… ¡Qué rico! ¿Verdad? ¡Vamos a comer la cena ahora!

GramActiva Videos: the plural of adjectives; the verb *ser* **(7:16)**

The Plural of Adjectives

HYPNOTIST: Looking back, we talked about how to make nouns plural. A little while before that we introduced adjectives, and how they match nouns. But how do you match adjectives to the noun, if the noun is plural? Let's start by reviewing the rules for making a noun plural in Spanish.

PATIENT: If the noun ends in a vowel, add an *-s*.
If the noun ends in *z*, drop the *z* and add *-ces*.
If the noun ends in anything else, add an *-es* to the end.

HOST: Whenever you use a plural noun in Spanish, any adjective you use must match the noun. Usually you just add an -s to make an adjective plural. But we may be getting ahead of ourselves. Let's go back to the very beginning.

FOREMAN: All nouns have gender and number. They are either masculine or feminine, and either singular or plural. When you use an adjective to describe a noun, the adjective has to match with the noun in both gender and number. So. If we were going to use the adjective *sabroso* to say that something was tasty, we would begin by looking at the noun. If the noun is masculine, like *un plátano*, you would use the masculine form of the adjective, *sabroso*, and say *un plátano sabroso*. If the noun was feminine, like *una hamburguesa*, you would use the feminine form of the adjective, *sabrosa*, and say *una hamburguesa sabrosa*.

HOST: After you choose the proper gender of the adjective, then you move on to whether it is singular or plural. If you had more than one hamburger, you would use the form of *sabroso* that is both feminine and plural, *sabrosas, unas hamburguesas sabrosas*. Or if you had more than one banana you would use the form of *sabroso* that is both masculine and plural, *sabrosos, unos plátanos sabrosos*.

SCARECROW: What if I have tasty burgers and bananas?

HOST: Good question. Whenever you have nouns of mixed genders, use the masculine form of the adjective. So you would say *las hamburguesas y los plátanos son sabrosos*.

Quiz

HOST: What other kind of things are tasty?
How about …
Unos plátanos sabrosos.
Una pizza sabrosa.
Un sándwich sabroso.
Unas judías verdes sabrosas.

The verb *ser*

HOST: Sometimes it seems like we're making these rules just so we can break them. This episode is no exception; we're going to look at an irregular *-er* verb, *ser*, which conjugates to the beat of its own drummer.

HOST: *Ser* means "to be," as in to be good for you. Its conjugation is so irregular that you've been using it all along and probably just never recognized it.

Host: Here is the conjugation for the verb *ser.*

soy
eres
es
somos
sois
son

Host: You can see *ser* doesn't have a lot in common with other *-er* verbs.

Hamburger: *Yo soy, yo soy, yo soy muy sabrosa.*
Tú eres, tú eres, tú eres el favorito.
Nosotros somos, nosotros somos, nosotros somos buenos amigos, ¿no?
Ustedes son, ustedes son, ustedes son, ¡Ay!, desordenados.

Host: We're going to take a quick look at another irregular verb that ends in *-er, hacer. Hacer* means "to make" or "to do." *Hacer* is not nearly as irregular as *ser. Hacer* is regular in every conjugation except for *yo.*

Host: In the *yo* form, *hacer* becomes *hago.* However, in the rest of the forms, it behaves just like any other *-er* verb.

Yo hago la tarea.
Tú haces pizzas sabrosas.
Ella hace el trabajo.
Nosotros no hacemos café.
Vosotros hacéis ejercicio.
Ustedes hacen el desayuno.

Quiz

Host: Fill in the blanks with the correct forms of *ser.*

Ella _____ trabajadora.
Ella es trabajadora.
Yo _____ estudiante.
Yo soy estudiante.
Nosotros _____ atrevidos.
Nosotros somos atrevidos.

Fill in the blanks with the correct forms of *hacer.*

Ellos _____ el té.
Ellos hacen el té.
Yo _____ la tarea.
Yo hago la tarea.
Tú _____ el almuerzo.
Tú haces el almuerzo.

Nombre ____________________

Fecha ____________________

Communicative Activity **3B-1**
Estudiante **A**

What do you like to eat? What does your partner prefer? Write your answers on line A. Then ask your partner the same questions and write his or her answers on line B.

1. ¿Qué prefieres comer, bistec, pollo o pescado?

   A. ____________________

   B. ____________________

2. ¿Qué prefieres beber, café, té o jugo de naranja?

   A. ____________________

   B. ____________________

3. ¿Qué te gusta más, el desayuno, el almuerzo o la cena?

   A. ____________________

   B. ____________________

4. ¿Qué prefieres, pan, arroz o papas?

   A. ____________________

   B. ____________________

5. ¿Qué prefieres, los plátanos, las uvas o las manzanas?

   A. ____________________

   B. ____________________

6. ¿Qué te gustan más, los guisantes, las judías verdes o las zanahorias?

   A. ____________________

   B. ____________________

7. ¿Qué te gustan más, las verduras, las frutas o los sándwiches?

   A. ____________________

   B. ____________________

8. ¿Qué te gusta más en el desayuno, los huevos, la leche o el cereal?

   A. ____________________

   B. ____________________

Nombre ______

Fecha ______

Communicative Activity **3B-1**

Estudiante **B**

What do you like to eat? What does your partner prefer? Write your answers on line A. Then ask your partner the same questions and write his or her answers on line B.

1. ¿Qué prefieres, la sopa de verduras, la sopa de pollo o la sopa de tomate?

   A. ______

   B. ______

2. ¿Qué prefieres beber, agua, limonada o un refresco?

   A. ______

   B. ______

3. ¿Qué te gusta más en el desayuno, cereal, pan tostado o plátanos?

   A. ______

   B. ______

4. ¿Qué prefieres beber, té helado, leche o jugo de manzana?

   A. ______

   B. ______

5. ¿Qué te gustan más, las hamburguesas, los sándwiches de jamón o los sándwiches de queso?

   A. ______

   B. ______

6. ¿Qué te gustan más, el helado, los pasteles o el café?

   A. ______

   B. ______

7. ¿Qué te gustan más, los tomates, las cebollas o las papas?

   A. ______

   B. ______

8. ¿Qué te gusta más en el almuerzo, las sopas, las ensaladas o los sándwiches?

   A. ______

   B. ______

Realidades A

Capítulo 3B

Nombre ____________________

Fecha ____________________

Communicative Activity **3B-2**

Estudiante **A**

First, express your opinions about food by completing the following sentences. Then read each sentence to your partner and listen to his or her response. Finally, check the *Sí* box if your partner agrees with you and the *No* box if your partner does not agree with you.

OPINIONES . . .	**Sí**	**No**
1. En el desayuno, prefiero comer ______________ .	☐	☐
2. ______________ es sabroso.	☐	☐
3. ______________ son buenas para la salud.	☐	☐
4. Siempre bebo ______________ en el almuerzo.	☐	☐
5. Nunca bebo ______________ .	☐	☐
6. ______________ es buena para la salud.	☐	☐
7. ______________ son buenas para la salud.	☐	☐
8. Me gusta ______________ .	☐	☐
9. ______________ son horribles.	☐	☐
10. ______________ es malo.	☐	☐
11. ______________ son malos.	☐	☐
12. No me gusta ______________ .	☐	☐

REACCIONES

A mí me gusta mucho.	Yo sí.
A mí no me gusta mucho.	Yo no.
A mí también.	Yo también.
A mí tampoco.	Yo tampoco.

Nombre ______________________

Fecha ______________________

First, express your opinions about food by completing the following sentences. Then read each sentence to your partner and listen to his or her response. Finally, check the *Sí* box if your partner agrees with you and the *No* box if your partner does not agree with you.

OPINIONES . . .	**Sí**	**No**
1. En la cena, prefiero comer ______________ .	☐	☐
2. ______________ es sabrosa.	☐	☐
3. ______________ son buenos para la salud.	☐	☐
4. Bebo ______________ en el desayuno.	☐	☐
5. Como ______________ en el almuerzo.	☐	☐
6. Me gusta comer ______________ .	☐	☐
7. ______________ es mala.	☐	☐
8. Me encanta ______________ .	☐	☐
9. No me gusta nada ______________ .	☐	☐
10. ______________ son sabrosas.	☐	☐
11. ______________ es horrible.	☐	☐
12. ______________ es bueno para la salud.	☐	☐

REACCIONES

A mí me gusta mucho.	Yo sí.
A mí no me gusta mucho.	Yo no.
A mí también.	Yo también.
A mí tampoco.	Yo tampoco.

Situation Cards

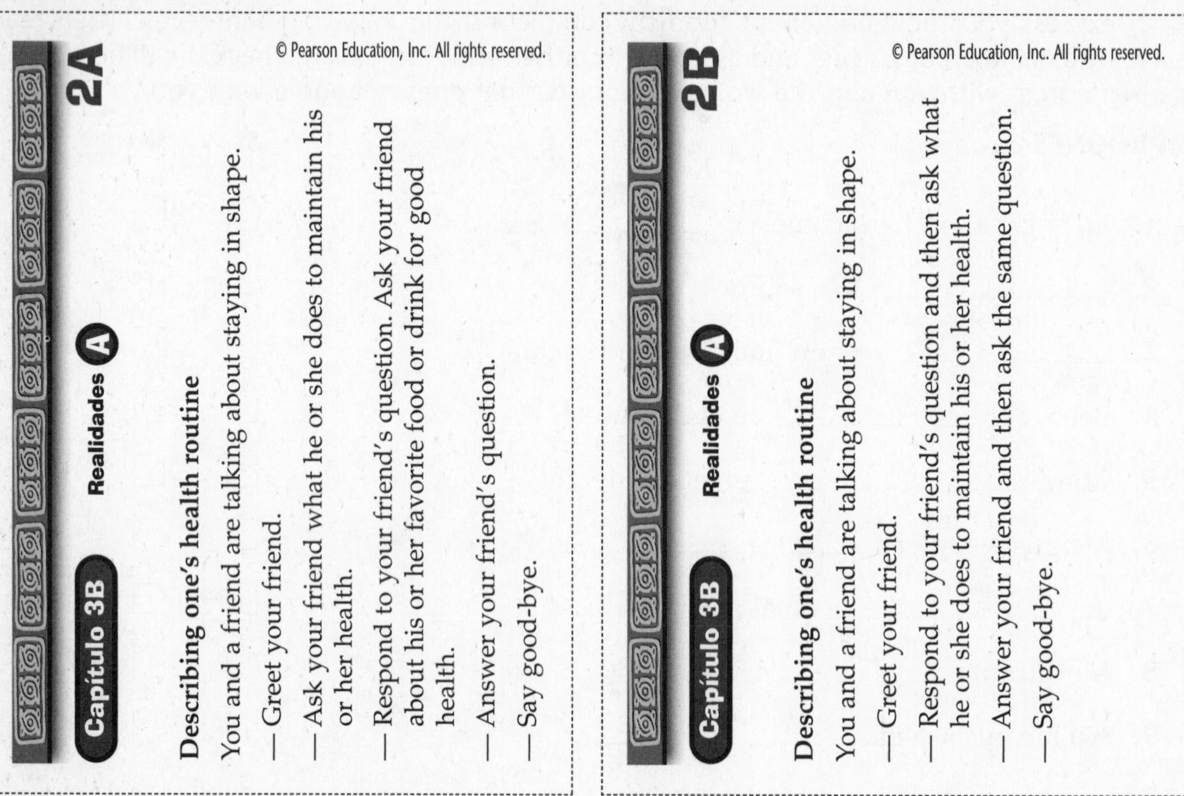

Capítulo 3B Realidades A **2A**

Describing one's health routine

You and a friend are talking about staying in shape.

— Greet your friend.

— Ask your friend what he or she does to maintain his or her health.

— Respond to your friend's question. Ask your friend about his or her favorite food or drink for good health.

— Answer your friend's question.

— Say good-bye.

Capítulo 3B Realidades A **2B**

Describing one's health routine

You and a friend are talking about staying in shape.

— Greet your friend.

— Respond to your friend's question and then ask what he or she does to maintain his or her health.

— Answer your friend and then ask the same question.

— Say good-bye.

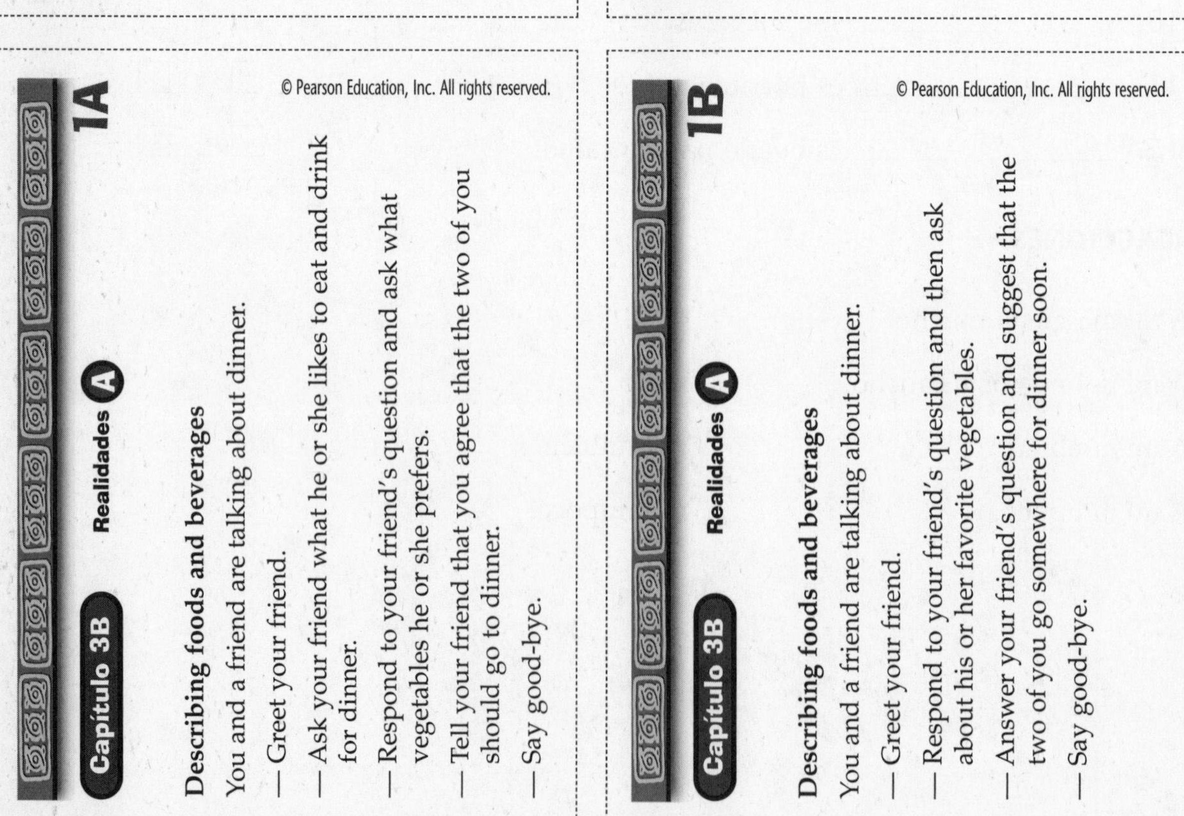

Capítulo 3B Realidades A **1A**

Describing foods and beverages

You and a friend are talking about dinner.

— Greet your friend.

— Ask your friend what he or she likes to eat and drink for dinner.

— Respond to your friend's question and ask what vegetables he or she prefers.

— Tell your friend that you agree that the two of you should go to dinner.

— Say good-bye.

Capítulo 3B Realidades A **1B**

Describing foods and beverages

You and a friend are talking about dinner.

— Greet your friend.

— Respond to your friend's question and then ask about his or her favorite vegetables.

— Answer your friend's question and suggest that the two of you go somewhere for dinner soon.

— Say good-bye.

GramActiva

Para mantener la salud

¿Sabroso o sabrosa?, p. 190

buen	-as
sabros	-os
mal	-a
	-o

Vocabulary Clip Art

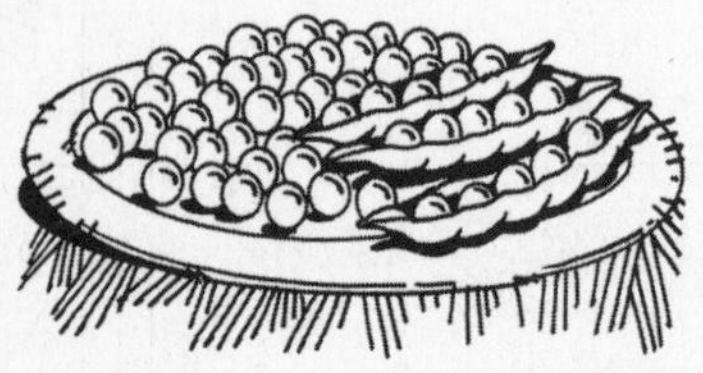

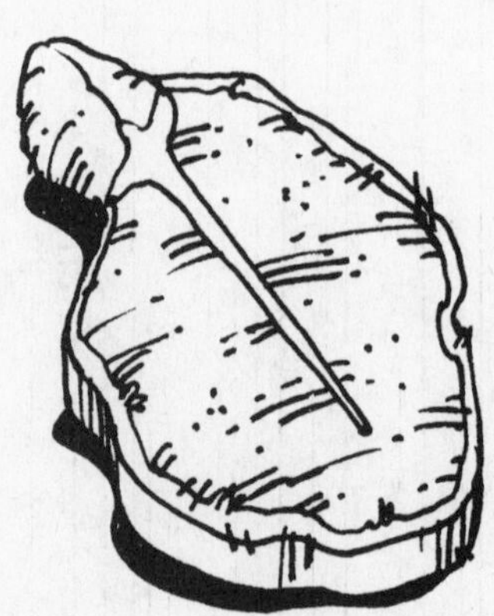

Vocabulary Clip Art

Vocabulary Clip Art

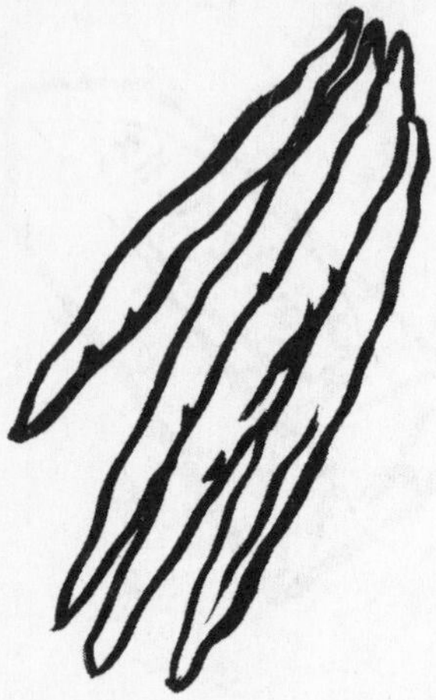

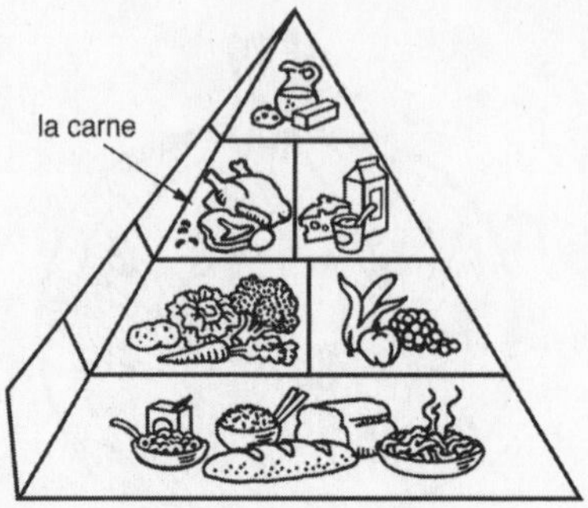

la carne

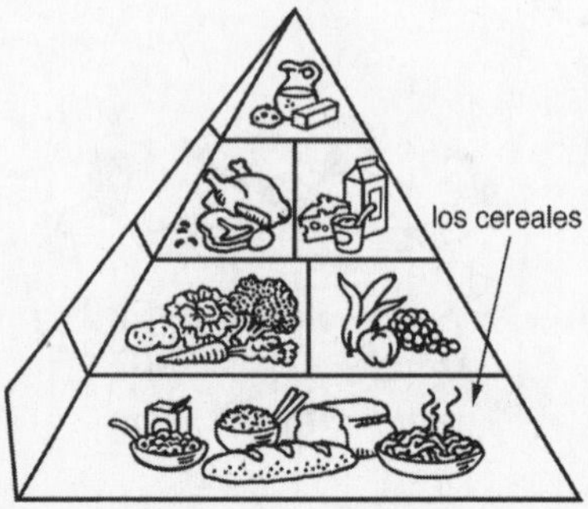

los cereales

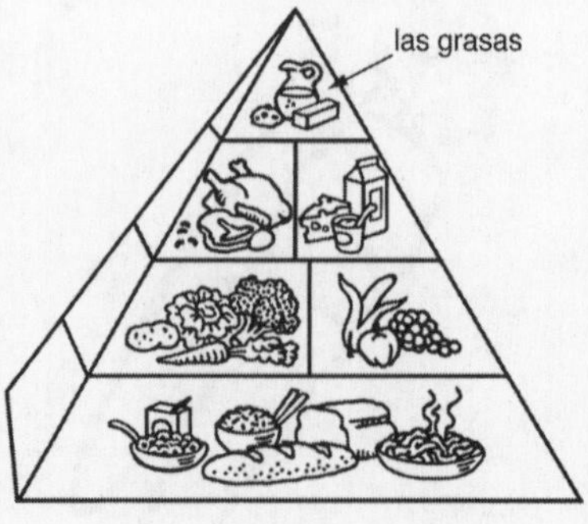

las grasas

Realidades A

Capítulo 3B

Core Practice Answers

3B-1

A.

Answers will vary.

La ensalada de frutas: list of fruits
La carne: list of meats
Las verduras: list of vegetables
Bebemos: list of beverages

B.

Answers will vary.

3B-2

A.

1. la carne
2. las verduras
3. las frutas
4. las grasas

B.

Answers may vary.

1. Debemos comer las uvas para mantener la salud.
2. La ensalada de frutas con plátanos es sabrosa.
3. Comemos la mantequilla con el pan tostado.
4. Bebemos el agua para mantener la salud.

C.

Answers will vary.

3B-3

Answers will vary. Possible answers include:

1. Sí, el tomate es bueno para la salud.
2. Camino todos los días para mantener la salud.
3. No, la mantequilla no es buena para la salud.
4. Estoy de acuerdo.
5. Debo caminar todos los días para mantener la salud.
6. Prefiero levantar pesas.
7. No estoy de acuerdo.

3B-4

1. —los guisantes
   —no me gustan los guisantes
2. —el arroz / pollo
   —Prefiero el arroz con pollo
3. —los espaguetis
   —me gustan los espaguetis
4. —el helado
   —Prefiero el helado
5. —el pescado
   —como el pescado
6. —pasteles
   —no como pasteles en el almuerzo
7. —bistec / papas
   —me gusta el bistec con papas

3B-5

A.

Row 1: ____ , sabrosos, sabrosa, sabrosas
Row 2: práctico, ____ , práctica, prácticas
Row 3: fácil, fáciles, ____ , fáciles
Row 4: aburrido, ____ , aburrida, aburridas
Row 5: difícil, difíciles, difícil, ____
Row 6: ——— , divertidos, divertida, divertidas
Row 7: artístico, artísticos, ____ , artísticas
Row 8: bueno, buenos, buena, ____
Row 9: ____ , trabajadores, trabajadora, trabajadoras

B.

Answers may vary. Any adjective given should agree in gender and number with answers given below.

1. buena
2. fáciles
3. difícil
4. prácticas
5. sabroso
6. artísticos
7. trabajadores
8. divertidas

3B-6

1. es / Es artístico
2. es / Es perezosa
3. son / Son estudiosas
4. son / Son sociables
5. somos / Somos (son) trabajadoras
6. soy / Soy (eres) deportista

3B-7

1. Para mantener la salud, Eva come muchas verduras y frutas cada día.
2. Sí, ella hace ejercicio.
3. Sí, a ella le gustan las frutas.
4. Eva prefiere levantar pesas para mantener la salud.
5. El agua es la bebida favorita de Eva.
6. No debemos comer pasteles porque son malos para la salud.

Crucigrama (3B-8)

Across:

3. ejercicio
5. pescado
6. lechuga
8. pollo
10. salud
12. bebidas
13. arroz
16. algo
18. hambre
20. acuerdo
22. pasteles
24. debes

Down:

1. carne
2. tomate
4. judías
7. espaguetis
9. mantener
11. uvas
14. zanahorias
15. sabrosa
17. helado
19. cebolla
21. cena
23. todos

Organizer (3B-9)

I. Vocabulary Answers will vary.

II. Grammar

1. singular / plural
2. -s, -es
3. **col. 1.** / **col. 2.**

col. 1.	col. 2.
soy	somos
eres	sois
es	son

Realidades A · Capítulo 3B

Nombre ______ Hora ______

Fecha ______

Vocabulary Practice, Sheet 1

Write the Spanish vocabulary word below each picture. If there is a word or phrase, copy it in the space provided. Be sure to include the article for each noun.

el arroz	*las bebidas*	la carne — *la carne*
el bistec	*los espaguetis*	los cereales — *los cereales*
la cebolla	*los guisantes*	las grasas — *las grasas*

Realidades A · Capítulo 3B

Nombre ______ Hora ______

Fecha ______

Vocabulary Practice, Sheet 2

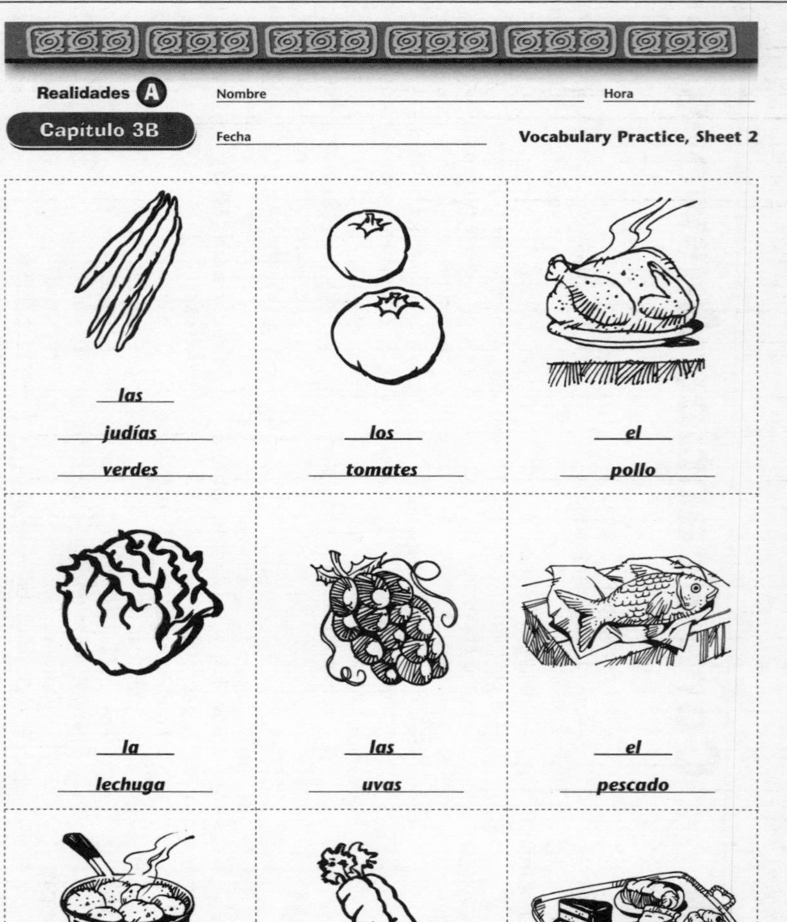

las judías verdes	*los tomates*	*el pollo*
la lechuga	*las uvas*	*el pescado*
las papas	*las zanahorias*	*los pasteles*

Realidades A | Nombre ____ Hora ____

Capítulo 3B | Fecha ____ **Vocabulary Practice, Sheet 3**

la *cena*	*Tengo* *sed.*	**levantar pesas** *levantar* *pesas*
el *helado*	**Tengo hambre.** *Tengo* *hambre.*	**hacer ejercicio** *hacer* *ejercicio*
la *mantequilla*	**caminar** *caminar*	**para la salud** *para* *la* *salud*

Realidades A | Nombre ____ Hora ____

Capítulo 3B | Fecha ____ **Vocabulary Practice, Sheet 4**

para mantener la salud *para* *mantener* *la* *salud*	**Creo que...** *Creo* *que...*	**Estoy de acuerdo.** *Estoy* *de* *acuerdo.*
prefiero *prefiero*	**Creo que sí.** *Creo* *que* *sí.*	**No estoy de acuerdo.** *No* *estoy* *de* *acuerdo.*
deber *deber*	**Creo que no.** *Creo* *que* *no.*	**cada día** *cada* *día*

Realidades A Nombre ____ Hora ____

Capítulo 3B Fecha ____ **Vocabulary Practice, Sheet 5**

¿Por qué?	muchos, muchas	malo, mala
¿Por qué?	*muchos, muchas*	*malo, mala*
porque	todos, todas	sabroso, sabrosa
porque	*todos, todas*	*sabroso, sabrosa*
algo	horrible	prefieres
algo	*horrible*	*prefieres*

Realidades A Nombre ____ Hora ____

Capítulo 3B Fecha ____ **Vocabulary Practice, Sheet 6**

hago	creer	ser
hago	*creer*	*ser*
haces	*cada día*	
haces	*cada día*	

Realidades A — Nombre ____ Hora ____

Capítulo 3B — Fecha ____

Vocabulary Check, Sheet 1

Tear out this page. Write the English words on the lines. Fold the paper along the dotted line to see the correct answers so you can check your work.

la cena	***dinner***
el bistec	***beefsteak***
la carne	***meat***
el pescado	***fish***
el pollo	***chicken***
la cebolla	***onion***
los guisantes	***peas***
las judías verdes	***green beans***
la lechuga	***lettuce***
las papas	***potatoes***
los tomates	***tomatoes***
las uvas	***grapes***
las zanahorias	***carrots***
el arroz	***rice***
los cereales	***grains***
los espaguetis	***spaghetti***
las grasas	***fats***
la mantequilla	***butter***
el helado	***ice cream***

Fold In ←

Realidades A — Nombre ____ Hora ____

Capítulo 3B — Fecha ____

Vocabulary Check, Sheet 2

Tear out this page. Write the Spanish words on the lines. Fold the paper along the dotted line to see the correct answers so you can check your work.

dinner	***la cena***
beefsteak	***el bistec***
meat	***la carne***
fish	***el pescado***
chicken	***el pollo***
onion	***la cebolla***
peas	***los guisantes***
green beans	***las judías verdes***
lettuce	***la lechuga***
potatoes	***las papas***
tomatoes	***los tomates***
grapes	***las uvas***
carrots	***las zanahorias***
rice	***el arroz***
grains	***los cereales***
spaghetti	***los espaguetis***
fats	***las grasas***
butter	***la mantequilla***
ice cream	***el helado***

Fold In ←

Nombre ____ Hora ____

Fecha ____

Vocabulary Check, Sheet 3

Tear out this page. Write the English words on the lines. Fold the paper along the dotted line to see the correct answers so you can check your work.

los pasteles	***pastries***
las bebidas	***beverages***
caminar	***to walk***
hacer ejercicio	***to exercise***
levantar pesas	***to lift weights***
para mantener la salud	***to maintain one's health***
algo	***something***
muchos, muchas	***many***
malo, mala	***bad***
sabroso, sabrosa	***tasty, flavorful***
todos, todas	***all***

Fold In ←

Nombre ____ Hora ____

Fecha ____

Vocabulary Check, Sheet 4

Tear out this page. Write the Spanish words on the lines. Fold the paper along the dotted line to see the correct answers so you can check your work.

pastries	***los pasteles***
beverages	***las bebidas***
to walk	***caminar***
to exercise	***hacer ejercicio***
to lift weights	***levantar pesas***
to maintain one's health	***para mantener la salud***
something	***algo***
many	***muchos, muchas***
bad	***malo, mala***
tasty, flavorful	***sabroso, sabrosa***
all	***todos, todas***

To hear a complete list of the vocabulary for this chapter, go to www.realidades.com and type in the Web Code jcd-0399. Then click on **Repaso del capítulo.**

Fold In ←

Realidades A | Nombre | Hora

Capítulo 3B | Fecha | **Guided Practice Activities 3B-1**

The plurals of adjectives (p. 190)

- Adjectives, just like definite articles, must match the noun they accompany. Singular adjectives go with singular nouns, and plural adjectives go with plural nouns.
- Adjectives that end in **-o** or **-a** must also match the noun. Masculine (**-o**) adjectives go with masculine nouns and feminine (**-a**) adjectives go with feminine nouns.
- Adjectives that end in **-e** do not change to match masculine or feminine nouns. They still change to match singular and plural nouns: **el libro interesante, las clases interesantes.**

	Definite article	Noun	Adjective
masculine singular	el	pan	sabroso
feminine singular	la	sopa	sabrosa
masculine plural	los	jamones	sabrosos
feminine plural	las	galletas	sabrosas

A. Look at each noun. Write **M** if it is masculine or **F** if it is feminine.

1. ***M, S*** pan
2. ***F, P*** sopas
3. ***M, S*** yogur
4. ***F, P*** salchichas
5. ***F, S*** pizza
6. ***M, S*** jamón
7. ***M, P*** huevos
8. ***M, P*** quesos
9. ***F, P*** galletas
10. ***F, S*** hamburguesa

B. Now, go back to **part A.** Next to the **M** or **F** you wrote next to each noun, write **S** if the noun is singular and **P** if it is plural.

C. Here are the nouns from **part A.** Now there are adjectives with them. Circle the correct adjective form for each noun.

1. pan (sabroso / sabrosos)
2. sopas (sabrosos / sabrosas)
3. yogur (sabrosos / sabroso)
4. salchichas (sabrosas / sabrosa)
5. pizza (sabrosos / sabrosa)
6. jamón (sabroso / sabrosa)
7. huevos (sabrosa / sabrosos)
8. quesos (sabrosos / sabrosas)
9. galletas (sabrosa / sabrosas)
10. hamburguesas (sabrosos / sabrosas)

realidades.com • Web Code: jcd-0313

Realidades A | Nombre | Hora

Capítulo 3B | Fecha | **Guided Practice Activities 3B-2**

The plurals of adjectives (*continued*)

D. Fill in the missing singular or plural form of each masculine adjective in the chart.

Masculine	
singular	plural
divertido	***divertidos***
simpático	***simpáticos***
atrevido	atrevidos
serio	serios
artístico	***artísticos***

E. Now, fill in the missing singular or plural form of each feminine adjective in the chart.

Feminine	
singular	plural
divertida	divertidas
simpática	***simpáticas***
atrevida	atrevidas
seria	***serias***
artística	artísticas

F. Choose an adjective from the group of words. Write its correct form in the space provided.

serio	seria	serios	serias
atrevido	atrevida	atrevidos	atrevidas
artístico	artística	artísticos	artísticas

1. Laura y Elena estudian mucho. Son ***serias***.
2. Sandra monta en monopatín. Es ***atrevida***.
3. Mario dibuja. Es ***artístico***.
4. Tomás y Beatriz trabajan mucho. Son ***serios***.
5. Lorenzo y Fernando esquían. Son ***atrevidos***.

The verb *ser* (p. 192)

- You have already learned and used some forms of the verb **ser**, which means *to be*:
  Yo soy serio. Tú eres simpática. Ella es artística.
- **Ser** is an irregular verb. You will need to memorize its forms.

yo	soy	nosotros/nosotras	somos
tú	eres	vosotros/vosotras	sois
usted/él/ella	es	ustedes/ellos/ellas	son

A. Choose the correct subject pronoun for each form of **ser** and circle it.

1. (yo / **(él)**) es
2. (**(ustedes)** / ella) son
3. (**(tú)** / ella) eres
4. (**(ella)** / yo) es
5. (**(usted)** / tú) es
6. (nosotros / **(ellas)**) son
7. (ellos / **(nosotros)**) somos
8. (**(yo)** / él) soy

B. Now, write the correct form of **ser** next to each subject pronoun.

1. tú ***eres***
2. usted ***es***
3. ellos ***son***
4. él ***es***
5. ellas ***son***
6. nosotras ***somos***
7. yo ***soy***
8. ustedes ***son***

C. Complete the exchanges by writing in the correct form of **ser**.

1. VERA: Yo ***soy*** estudiante. ¿Y tú?
   GONZALO: Yo ***soy*** estudiante también.
2. PABLO: Tú ***eres*** muy deportista, ¿no?
   ENRIQUE: Sí, pero yo también ***soy*** muy estudioso.
3. INÉS: Susana y Olivia ***son*** muy divertidas.
   MARCOS: Sí. Olivia ***es*** muy simpática también.
4. PACO Y LUIS: Nosotros ***somos*** perezosos. No estudiamos mucho.
   ANA: Bueno, yo ***soy*** muy trabajadora. Me gusta estudiar.

realidades.com
• Web Code: jcd-0314

The verb *ser* (*continued*)

D. Look at each drawing. Complete the question with a form of **ser**. Follow the model.

Modelo ¿Cómo ***es*** él?

1. ¿Cómo ***es*** él?
2. ¿Cómo ***eres*** tú?
3. ¿Cómo ***son*** ellas?
4. ¿Cómo ***somos*** nosotras?
5. ¿Cómo ***soy*** yo?

E. Now, complete each sentence with the correct form of **ser** and the correct adjective ending. Refer back to the art in **part D**. Follow the model.

Modelo Él ***es*** simpátic***o***.

1. Él ***es*** artístic***o***.
2. Tú ***eres*** perezos***o***.
3. Ellas ***son*** estudios***as***.
4. Nosotras ***somos*** inteligente***s***.
5. Yo ***soy*** atrevid***o***.

realidades.com
• Web Code: jcd-0314

Realidades A | Nombre ______ | Hora ______

Capítulo 3B | Fecha ______ | **Guided Practice Activities 3B-5**

Lectura: La comida de los atletas (pp. 198–199)

> **Skimming is a useful technique to help you get through a reading. You think of general information that you are looking for. Then you quickly read the words to find it.**

A. List three things you would expect to find in an article about an athlete's eating habits.

1. ***Answers will vary.***
2. ______
3. ______

B. Skim the article and check off the things in your list from **part A** that you find.

C. Note that the pie chart in your textbook shows how much of an athlete's diet can be divided into three categories. Next to each category below, write the English translation of the word. Then fill in the percentage number according to the pie chart.

	English	Number
1. carbohidratos	***carbohydrates***	***70*** %
2. proteínas	***proteins***	***17*** %
3. grasas	***fats***	***13*** %

D. The reading in your textbook gives a picture and a short description of what foods are good for each big meal of the day. Next to each food given below circle whether the reading says it is best for **D (desayuno), A (almuerzo),** or **C (cena).**

1. (D) A C pan con mantequilla
2. D (A) C pasta
3. (D) A C yogur
4. D A (C) papas
5. (D) A C jalea

E. Read the selection below and answer the questions that follow.

> *La noche antes del partido, el jugador bebe un litro de (jugo de naranja), y durante el partido bebe hasta dos litros de (agua) y (bebidas deportivas).*

1. Circle the three kinds of drinks mentioned in the reading.
2. What is a *litro* in English? ***liter***
3. When does the player drink a *litro* of orange juice? ***night before the game***

realidades.com
• Web Code: jcd-0315

Realidades A | Nombre ______ | Hora ______

Capítulo 3B | Fecha ______ | **Guided Practice Activities 3B-6**

Presentación escrita (p. 201) *Answers will vary.*

Task: You will make a poster in Spanish with three suggestions for better health. You will need to research what are proven good eating and exercise habits.

❶ Prewrite. Talk to classmates, teachers, the school nurse, or your parents about good eating and exercise habits, especially for teens. Then list their ideas under the following headings to help you organize your information:

- Debes comer ______.
- No debes comer mucho(a) ______.
- Debes beber ______.
- No debes beber mucho(a) ______.
- Debes ______ para mantener la salud.

❷ Draft. Create your first draft on a separate sheet of paper. (You do not need to use posterboard for this draft.) List your ideas from the prewrite stage. Organize them in a neat or artistic way. Sketch out the visuals you want to include on the poster.

❸ Revise.

A. Someone else will check your work for the following:

______ Have you communicated the three suggestions well?
______ Do the visuals help with the meaning?
______ Will the visuals make the poster attractive?
______ Are all words spelled correctly?
______ Are grammar and vocabulary used correctly?

B. Rewrite your poster using the person's suggestions.

❹ Publish. Your final draft will be on some sort of posterboard. You will want to carefully add any illustrations and designs you had sketched out in an earlier stage.

❺ Evaluate. Your teacher will tell you how your poster will be graded. Your teacher will check:

- your completion of the task
- the accuracy of your vocabulary and grammar
- your effective use of visuals

Realidades A | Nombre | Hora

Capítulo 3B | Fecha | VIDEO

Antes de ver el video

Actividad 1

Think about the typical diet of a teenager. Which foods are healthy choices and which ones are not? Make a list of five foods in each category.

Comida buena para la salud ☺	Comida mala para la salud ☹
Answers will vary.	Answers will vary.

¿Comprendes?

Actividad 2

Write the name of the person from the video who made each statement.

1. "El café de aquí es muy bueno." Raúl
2. "No, no; un refresco no; un jugo de fruta." Tomás
3. "En Costa Rica, un refresco es un jugo de fruta." Gloria
4. "Yo hago mucho ejercicio..." Tomás
5. "Aquí en San José, todos caminamos mucho." Raúl
6. "... aquí una soda no es una bebida; es un restaurante." Gloria
7. "Me encanta el gallo pinto." Tomás

Realidades A | Nombre | Hora

Capítulo 3B | Fecha | VIDEO

Actividad 3

Answer the questions.

1. ¿Qué es muy importante para Costa Rica?
   El café es muy importante para Costa Rica.
2. Según Raúl, ¿qué es bueno de Costa Rica?
   Según Raúl todos los refrescos de Costa Rica son buenos.
3. Según Tomás, ¿qué es bueno para la salud?
   Según Tomás los refrescos son buenos para la salud.
4. ¿Qué hacen todos en San José?
   Todos caminan en San José.
5. ¿Qué más hacen en San José?
   También montan en bicicleta.
6. ¿Qué es una *soda* en Costa Rica?
   Una soda es un restaurante con carnes, pescado y ensaladas.

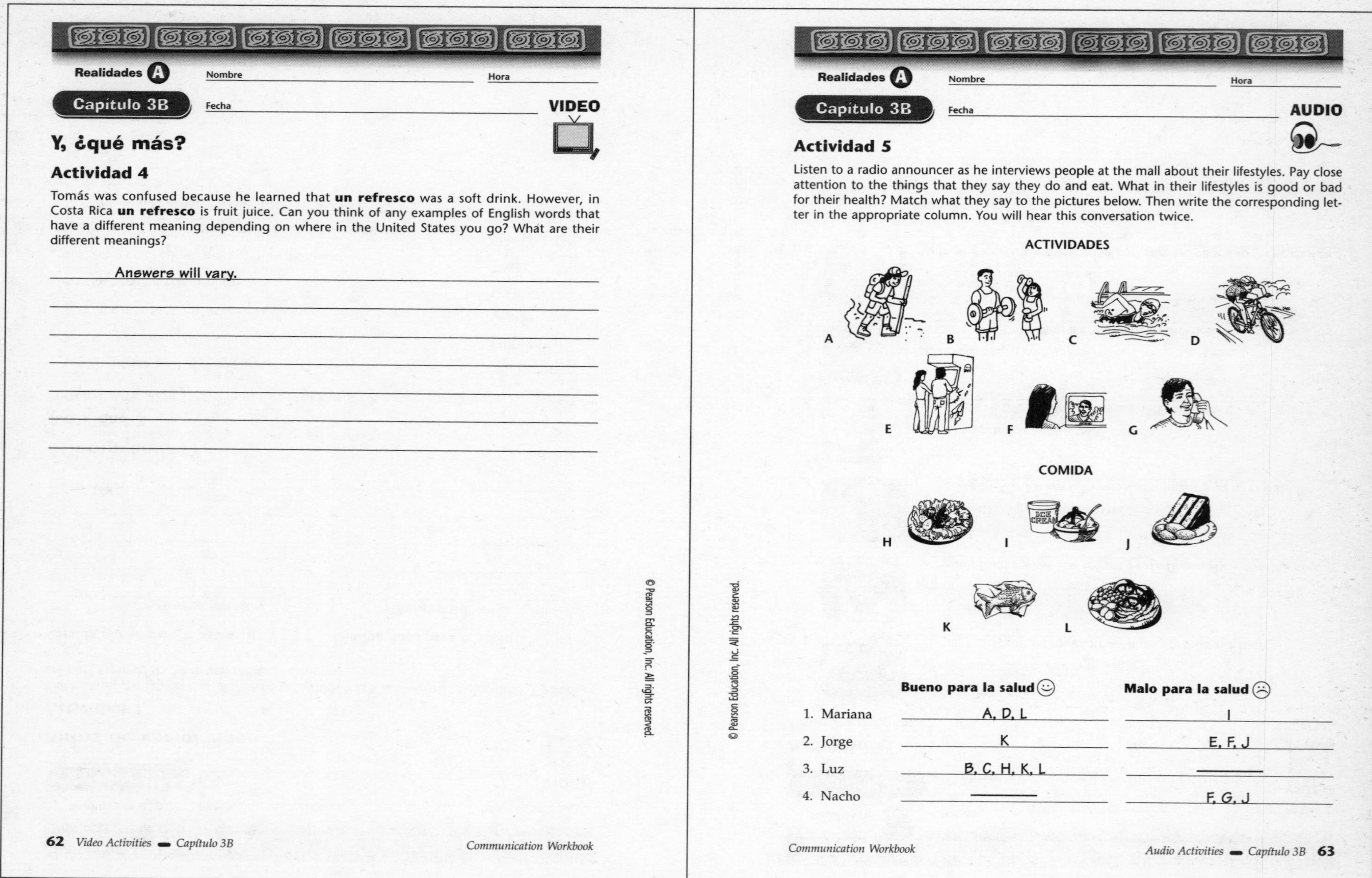

Realidades A | Nombre ______ Hora ______

Capítulo 3B | Fecha ______ VIDEO

Y, ¿qué más?

Actividad 4

Tomás was confused because he learned that **un refresco** was a soft drink. However, in Costa Rica **un refresco** is fruit juice. Can you think of any examples of English words that have a different meaning depending on where in the United States you go? What are their different meanings?

Answers will vary.

Realidades A | Nombre ______ Hora ______

Capítulo 3B | Fecha ______ AUDIO

Actividad 5

Listen to a radio announcer as he interviews people at the mall about their lifestyles. Pay close attention to the things that they say they do and eat. What in their lifestyles is good or bad for their health? Match what they say to the pictures below. Then write the corresponding letter in the appropriate column. You will hear this conversation twice.

ACTIVIDADES

A B C D

E F G

COMIDA

H I J

K L

	Bueno para la salud ☺	Malo para la salud ☹
1. Mariana	A, D, L	I
2. Jorge	K	E, F, J
3. Luz	B, C, H, K, L	—
4. Nacho	—	F, G, J

Realidades A | Nombre ______ | Hora ______

Capítulo 3B | Fecha ______ | AUDIO

Actividad 6

Listen as students in a health class in Costa Rica present a list of the "dos and don'ts" of staying healthy. Which are **consejos lógicos** (*logical advice*) and which are **consejos ridículos** (*ridiculous advice*)? Place a check mark in the appropriate box of the chart. You will hear each set of statements twice.

	1	2	3	4	5	6	7	8	9	10
Consejo lógico		✔	✔				✔	✔		✔
Consejo ridículo	✔			✔	✔	✔			✔	

Actividad 7

A Spanish-speaking telemarketer calls your home to interview you about the food preferences of teens. He must have gotten your name from your Spanish teacher! He asks you to tell him whether you think certain food items are **malo** or **sabroso**. Be sure to listen carefully so that you will be able to use the correct form of the adjective for each item. Write what you would say in the spaces below. You will hear each question twice.

1. Feminine/Singular
2. Masculine/Singular
3. Feminine/Plural
4. Masculine/Plural
5. Masculine/Singular
6. Masculine/Plural
7. Feminine/Plural
8. Masculine/Plural
9. Feminine/Plural
10. Masculine/Singular

Answers will vary between some form of malo/sabroso.

Realidades A | Nombre ______ | Hora ______

Capítulo 3B | Fecha ______ | AUDIO

Actividad 8

In an effort to improve food in the school cafeteria, students are asked to anonymously call in their opinions about school food. You are asked to chart the responses of the Spanish-speaking students. As you listen to their opinions, fill in the grid. If they say something positive about a particular menu item, put a plus sign in the appropriate column; if they say something negative, put a minus sign in the column. You will hear each set of statements twice.

1	–				–			–	+	
2			+	+						–
3	–				+	–				
4		+					+			
5								+	+	

Actividad 9

Listen as people call in to ask Dr. Armando their health questions on his radio program **"Pregunte al doctor Armando."** While you listen to their questions and Dr. Armando's advice (**consejo**), fill in the chart below. Do you agree with his advice? You will hear this conversation twice.

NOMBRE	¿LA PREGUNTA?	EL CONSEJO
1. Beatriz	¿Cuántos minutos debes hacer ejercicio?	Treinta minutos al día.
2. Mauricio	¿Debo comer pasteles?	Debes comer pasteles...y verduras, frutas, pescado y pan también.
3. Loli	¿Es bueno caminar (en el centro comercial)?	Debes ir al gimnasio.
4. Luis	¿Debo comer si no tengo hambre?	Debes hacer ejercicio.

Answers may vary slightly. Some teachers may prefer that students fill in grid with information in English.

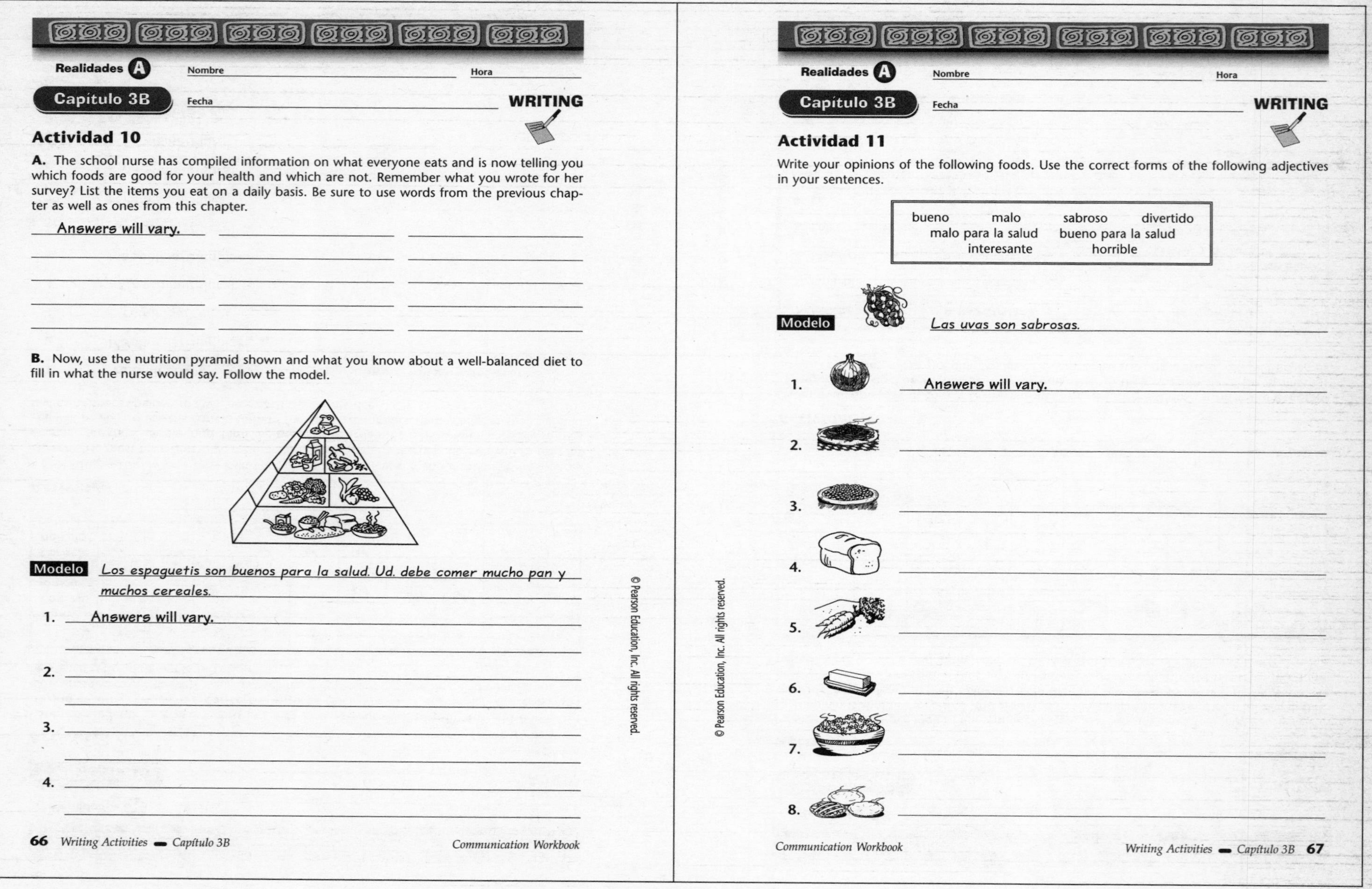

Realidades A Nombre ______ Hora ______

Capítulo 3B Fecha ______ WRITING

Actividad 10

A. The school nurse has compiled information on what everyone eats and is now telling you which foods are good for your health and which are not. Remember what you wrote for her survey? List the items you eat on a daily basis. Be sure to use words from the previous chapter as well as ones from this chapter.

Answers will vary.

B. Now, use the nutrition pyramid shown and what you know about a well-balanced diet to fill in what the nurse would say. Follow the model.

Modelo *Los espaguetis son buenos para la salud. Ud. debe comer mucho pan y muchos cereales.*

1. *Answers will vary.*
2. ______
3. ______
4. ______

Realidades A Nombre ______ Hora ______

Capítulo 3B Fecha ______ WRITING

Actividad 11

Write your opinions of the following foods. Use the correct forms of the following adjectives in your sentences.

bueno	malo	sabroso	divertido
malo para la salud		bueno para la salud	
interesante		horrible	

Modelo *Las uvas son sabrosas.*

1. *Answers will vary.*
2. ______
3. ______
4. ______
5. ______
6. ______
7. ______
8. ______

Realidades A | Nombre ______ | Hora ______

Capítulo 3B | Fecha ______ | WRITING

Actividad 12

Below you see three groups of friends sitting at tables in a cafeteria. Describe the people and items at each table.

1
yo
Pilar
2
tú
3

Mesa 1:

Answers will vary.

Mesa 2:

Answers will vary.

Mesa 3:

Answers will vary.

Realidades A | Nombre ______ | Hora ______

Capítulo 3B | Fecha ______ | WRITING

Actividad 13

Write a letter to your Spanish-speaking pen pal about a restaurant that you and your parents like to go to for dinner. Tell what you and your family members normally eat and drink, what the food is like, and what the waiters (**camareros**) are like.

Estimado(a) ______:

Answers will vary.

Un abrazo,

______

Test Preparation Answers

Reading Skills
p. 145 2. **B**
p. 146 2. **A**

Integrated Performance Assessment
p. 147
Answers will vary.

Practice Test: Pizza, ensaladas y ... helado de fresas
p. 149

1. D
2. H
3. A
4. G
5. Las respuestas variarán, pero los estudiantes deben incluir la comida que han estudiado como, por ejemplo: tocino, salchichas, verduras, pollo, cebolla, guisantes, judías verdes o tomates.
6. Answers will vary, but students should include items from all the food groups and include healthy snacks.

Table of Contents

Tema 4: Los pasatiempos

Capítulo 4A: ¿Adónde vas?

Capítulo 4B: ¿Quieres ir conmigo?

Theme Project

Los pasatiempos
Guía del ocio

Overview:
You will create a weekend entertainment guide, featuring the times and locations of six different events as well as an illustration of each event. Then you will present your guide to the class.

Materials:
Construction paper, magazines, scissors, glue, colored markers

Sequence:

STEP 1. Review the instructions with your teacher.

STEP 2. Look at examples of entertainment guides on the Internet or in your local newspaper. Brainstorm what to include in your guide.

STEP 3. Submit a rough sketch of your guide. Incorporate your teacher's suggestions into your sketch.

STEP 4. Create a layout on construction paper.

STEP 5. Submit a draft of the information in your guide. Use your guide to invite a partner to one of the events.

STEP 6. Complete your guide and present it to the class, describing each of the events featured.

Assessment:
Your teacher will use the rubric on the following page to assess this project.

Theme 4 Project: Guía del ocio

RUBRIC	Score 1	Score 3	Score 5
Evidence of Planning	No written draft or page layout provided.	Draft was written and layout created, but not corrected.	Evidence of corrected draft and layout.
Use of Illustrations	No photos/illustrations included.	Photos/illustrations were included, but layout was unorganized.	Guide was easy to read, complete, and accurate.
Presentation	Includes little of the required information in the guide and presentation.	Includes most of the required information in the guide and presentation.	Includes all of the required information in the guide and presentation.

Realidades A

Capítulo 4A

School-to-Home Connection

Dear Parent or Guardian,

The theme for the chapter is *Los pasatiempos* (Hobbies) and this chapter is called *¿Adónde vas?* (Where are you going?).

Upon completion of this chapter, your child will be able to:

- talk about locations in your community
- discuss leisure activities
- talk about where he or she goes and with whom
- ask questions
- understand cultural perspectives on leisure activities

Also, your child will explore:

- how to determine which syllable to stress in Spanish words
- the origins of the Spanish names for days of the week

Realidades helps with the development of reading, writing, and speaking skills through the use of strategies, process speaking, and process writing. In this chapter, students will:

- read a promotional brochure about a shopping mall
- speak about where a new student is from, activities he or she likes to do and on what days of the week, and where he or she goes and with whom

Remember that additional help is available online at www.realidades.com by using the Web Codes in the Student Edition or in the Leveled Vocabulary and Grammar Workbook.

Check it out! Have your child tell you in Spanish three places he or she goes each week and when he or she goes to these places.

Sincerely,

For: Tips to Parents
Visit: www.realidades.com
Web Code: jce-0010

Capítulo 4A Chapter Resource Checklist

Resources	CO†	APV	VH	MAN	LEC	CV	PO	MH	REP	PREP
Teacher										
Teacher's Resource Book										
Input Script										
Audio Script										
GramActiva BLM										
Communicative Activities BLM										
School-to-Home Connection BLM										
Clip Art										
Situation Cards BLM										
TPR Stories Book										
Fine Art Transparencies Teacher's Guide										
Pre-AP* Resource Book										
Student										
Leveled Vocabulary and Grammar Workbook										
Guided Practice										
Core Practice										
Communication Workbook with Test Preparation										
Writing										
Audio										
Video										
Test Preparation										
RPH Workbook										
Lecturas para hispanohablantes										
Grammar Study Guides										
Transparencies										
Answers on Transparencies										
Vocabulary and Grammar										
Fine Art										
Assessment										
Assessment Program										
Quizzes										
Chapter Test										
realidades.com										
ExamView Test Bank CD-ROM										
QuickTake on PresentationExpress										
MindPoint QuizShow CD-ROM										
Alternate Assessment Program										
Performance-Based Speaking										
Self-Test on realidades.com & CWS										
Assessment Program RPH										
Technology										
realidades.com										
myeBook										
TeacherExpress CD-ROM										
PresentationExpress DVD										
Video Program DVD										
Culture Video DVD										
Audio Program CD 8										
Assessment CD 20										
Song CD 22										
Canciones de hip hop on realidades.com & CWS										

† *See Abbreviation Key on page iv.*

Input Script

Presentation

Input Vocabulary: Place the overhead transparency on the screen. Act out each place or activity and have students guess where you are or what you are doing. Then hand out copies of the Vocabulary Clip Art and have students tear the images into individual places. Review the personality traits from Chapter 1B by describing imaginary people and telling where they like to go: *"Mi amigo Tomás es muy deportista. Le gusta ir al gimnasio."* Have students hold up the Clip Art images of the places you mention.

Input Dialogue 1: Model the first two sentences. Present ***el tiempo libre*** by contrasting it with ***el trabajo.*** Sit at a student desk with a pencil and a piece of paper. Say *"¡El trabajo!"* and pretend to write furiously on the piece of paper. Then say *"¡El tiempo libre!"* and put the pencil down, relax, lean back in the desk, and clasp both your hands behind your head. Then call out both expressions and have students act out the same motions. Then use Alicia's class schedule from Chapter 2A to present ***después de.*** Say *"Me llamo Alicia. Aquí está mi horario. En la primera hora, tengo la clase de tecnología. Después de mi clase de tecnología, tengo…"* and so forth.

Model the next two sentences. Then point to the gymnasium and say *"Voy al gimnasio para levantar pesas. ¿Y tú?"* Point to another masculine place word on the transparency and call on a student to say where he or she is going, for example, *"Voy al parque."* Then ask the student if he or she will do a logical or an illogical activity there *("¿Para montar en bicicleta? ¿Para ver una película?")*. The student will respond *"Sí"* or *"No."* Then do the same with feminine place words, first modeling *"Voy a la ___."*

Finally, model the last two sentences. Point to other places on the transparency and tell where you will not be going since you are going to work *("Hoy voy a mi trabajo. No voy a la playa.")*.

Input Dialogue 2: Before presenting the dialogue, write the names of celebrities on scraps of paper and place them in a paper bag. Also, cut up a copy of the Vocabulary Clip Art into individual places and place them in a separate bag. Model the dialogue. Then have students draw a celebrity name and a place. Ask *"¿Con quién vas al centro commercial?"* He or she will answer with the celebrity and then tell where they will go later using the place they drew, for example, *"Voy con Brad Pitt, y después vamos a la piscina."*

Input Dialogue 3: Read the entire dialogue. Then survey the class by asking *"¿Qué haces los sábados?"* Point to activities and say, for example, *"Voy con mis amigos al cine."* Have students hold up the Clip Art image if a statement is true for them.

Comprehension Check

- Tell students the day and time you plan to do different activities. Have them write the day and time on their Clip Art images and then arrange the images chronologically.
- Make statements such as *"Te gusta nadar. ¿Vas a la piscina o a la biblioteca?"* Have students hold up Clip Art image that shows the appropriate place for the activity.
- Make two copies of the Clip Art images and tear into individual places. Hand each student one of the Clip Art images of a place. Students will circulate around the room and ask questions to find the other person with the same Clip Art image. For example, a student who receives the beach image will ask *"¿Vas a la playa?"* Once students have found their partners, ask individual students *"¿Con quién vas al / a la ___?"*

Audio Script

Audio CD, Capítulo 4A

Track 01: ***A primera vista,*** **Student Book, pp. 208 (2:59)**

¿Adónde vas?

You will hear each word or phrase twice. After the first time there will be a pause so you can pronounce it, then you will hear the word or phrase a second time.

el gimnasio	la lección de piano
el parque	el cine
el centro comercial	ver una película
ir de compras	la biblioteca
el trabajo	la piscina

Read along as you listen to the dialogues.

FEMALE TEEN 1: En tu tiempo libre después de las clases, ¿qué haces?

MALE TEEN 1: Voy al gimnasio para levantar pesas y al parque para correr. ¿Y tú?

FEMALE TEEN 1: Hoy voy a mi trabajo. No voy a mí lección de piano.

MALE TEEN 2: ¿Con quién vas al centro comercial?

FEMALE TEEN 2: Voy con Guillermo, y después vamos al cine. ¿Y tú?

MALE TEEN 2: Voy a la biblioteca para estudiar. Después voy al Café del Mundo con Lucila.

Track 02: ***A primera vista,*** **Student Book, p. 209 (2:06)**

You will hear each word or phrase twice. After the first time there will be a pause so you can pronounce it, then you will hear the word or phrase a second time.

la playa	el campo
el restaurante	las montañas

Read along as you listen to the dialogue.

FEMALE TEEN 3: ¿Qué haces los domingos?

MALE TEEN 3: Voy con mis amigos a la playa. Allí comemos el almuerzo. Hay un restaurante muy bueno. ¿Y tú?

FEMALE TEEN 3: Generalmente, voy al campo o a las montañas.

Más vocabulario

You will hear each word or phrase twice. After the first time there will be a pause so you can pronounce it, then you will hear the word or phrase a second time.

la iglesia	la sinagoga
la mezquita	el templo

Track 03: ***A primera vista:*** **Act. 1, Student Book, p. 209 (1:53)**

¿Estás de acuerdo?

You will hear Elena describe where she does seven activities. If a statement is logical, give a "thumbs-up" sign. If it is not logical, give a "thumbs-down" sign. You will hear each statement twice.

1. Me gusta esquiar en la piscina.
2. Voy a la biblioteca para leer.
3. Bailamos en casa.
4. Practico deportes en el gimnasio.
5. Veo una película en el parque.
6. Nado en el cine.
7. Bebo café en el restaurante.

Track 04: ***A primera vista:*** **Act. 2, Student Book, p. 209 (1:38)**

¡Muchas actividades!

Listen to Antonio describe his weekly list of after-school activities. As he names his activities, touch the corresponding picture(s). You will hear each statement twice.

1. Voy a la biblioteca para estudiar.
2. Me gusta correr en el parque.
3. Voy de compras al centro comercial.
4. El viernes voy al cine con Paco.
5. El sábado voy a mi trabajo en el restaurante.
6. El domingo voy a la playa.

Track 05: ***A primera vista: Videohistoria,*** **Student Book, pp. 210–212 (1:49)**

Un chico reservado

¿Qué pasa cuando Ignacio, Elena y Ana hablan con el estudiante nuevo? Lee la historia.

Read along as you listen to the *Videohistoria.*

See Student Book pages 210–212 for script.

Track 06: ***Manos a la obra,*** **Act. 8, Student Book, p. 215 (1:42)**

Escucha y escribe

Look at the painting of Plaza Morazán in Tegucigalpa, Honduras. On a sheet of paper, write the numbers 1–6. You will hear six statements about the painting. Write what you hear. You will hear each statement twice.

1. Hay muchas personas en la plaza.
2. Hace buen tiempo hoy.
3. ¿Ves la bandera de Honduras?
4. Muchas personas hablan en el parque.
5. Voy a la plaza con mis amigos.
6. Me encanta la iglesia.

Track 07: Audio Act. 5, Writing, Audio & Video Workbook, p. 72 (4:12)

Listen as Lorena talks to Luis and Antonio about where they are going during the week. Under each picture in the grid, write in the name of Luis or Antonio if they tell Lorena they are going to that place. In some cases, you will fill in both of their names. After completing the grid, you will be able to complete the sentences under the grid. You will hear this conversation twice.

LORENA: Hola, Luis. ¿Qué haces esta semana?

Luis: Hola, Lorena. Voy al gimnasio el lunes y el jueves para hacer ejercicio por una hora. Tengo una lección de tenis en el parque el miércoles.
Lorena: ¿Adónde vas el martes?
Luis: El martes generalmente me quedo en casa. Voy a la biblioteca el jueves para estudiar. Tengo un examen el viernes.
Lorena: ¿Qué haces el fin de semana?
Luis: Hmmm. Creo que voy al cine el sábado y el domingo voy al Restaurante Marqués con mi familia.
Lorena: ¡No me digas! Yo voy al Restaurante Marqués con mi familia el domingo también. Nos vemos. Hasta luego, Luis.
Luis: Hasta luego, Lorena.

Lorena: Hola, Antonio.
Antonio: Hola, Lorena. ¿Qué tal?
Lorena: Bien. ¿Qué haces esta semana?
Antonio: El lunes, miércoles y jueves voy a mi trabajo en el centro comercial. El jueves, después del trabajo, voy a la biblioteca.
Lorena: ¿Y el fin de semana?
Antonio: Me encantan las películas de Tom Hanks. Voy al cine el sábado. Hay una película nueva con él. El domingo voy a la iglesia con mi familia.
Lorena: Después de ir a la iglesia, ¿vas a comer en el Restaurante Marqués?
Antonio: No, vamos a comer en casa.
Lorena: Bueno. Hasta luego, Antonio.
Antonio: Adiós, Lorena.

You are going to hear this conversation again.

Track 08: Audio Act. 6, Writing, Audio & Video Workbook, p. 73 (2:44)

You are volunteering as a tour guide during the upcoming Hispanic Arts Festival in your community. To make sure you would be able to understand the following questions if a visitor were to ask them, write the number of the question under the correct picture that would correspond to a logical response. You can check your answers to see if you're ready to answer visitors' questions during the Festival. You will hear each question twice.

1. ¿Adónde vas para esquiar?
2. ¿Adónde vas para levantar pesas?
3. ¿Adónde vas para tomar café y comer un postre?
4. ¿Adónde vas para hacer un picnic con perritos calientes y hamburguesas?
5. ¿Adónde vas para ver las películas de México?
6. ¿Adónde vas para leer libros?
7. ¿Adónde vas para comer espaguetis y ensalada?
8. ¿Adónde vas para ir de compras?
9. ¿Adónde vas para estar solo?
10. ¿Adónde vas para nadar?

Track 09: *Pronunciación*, Stress and accents, Student Book, p. 223 (3:18)

How can you tell which syllable to stress, or emphasize, when you see words written in Spanish? Here are some general rules.

1. When words end in a vowel, *n*, or *s*, place the stress on the next-to-last syllable. Listen to and say these words, making sure you stress the next-to-last syllable.

   You will hear each word twice. After the word is pronounced the first time, there will be a pause so you can pronounce it. Then you will hear the word a second time.

   centro, computadora, mantequilla, pasteles, trabajo, escriben, piscina, parque, generalmente

2. When words end in a consonant (except *n* or *s*), place the stress on the last syllable. Listen to and say these words, making sure you stress the last syllable.

   señor, profesor, español, nariz, reloj, trabajador, escribir, arroz, comer

3. When a word has a written accent, place the stress on the accented syllable. One reason for written accents is to indicate exceptions to the first two rules. Listen to and say these words. Be sure to emphasize the accented syllable.

   café, difícil, fácil, número, película, plátano, teléfono, lápiz, artístico

Track 10: *Pronunciación*, Student Book, p. 223 (4:30)

Try it out! Listen to the first verse of the song "La Bamba" and say each word with the stress on the correct syllable. Then listen to the recording again and see if you can sing along with the first verse.

Para bailar la bamba, para bailar la bamba
se necesita una poca de gracia,
una poca de gracia y otra cosita
y arriba y arriba,
y arriba y arriba y arribe iré,
yo no soy marinero, yo no soy marinero,
por ti seré, por ti seré, por ti seré.

Track 11: Audio Act. 7, Writing, Audio & Video Workbook, p. 73 (2:17)

Your friend Miguel calls his mother from your house to give her an update on his plans for the day. Just from listening to his side of the conversation, you realize that his mother has *LOTS* of questions. What does she ask him, based on Miguel's answers? Choose from the following: A: *¿Adónde vas?* B. *¿Con quiénes vas?* C. *¿Cuándo vas?* D. *¿Cómo es tu amigo?* E. *¿Por qué van?*

You will hear each set of statements twice.

1. *Estoy con mi amigo. Él es muy simpático y … y muy*

estudioso. Está en mi clase de matemáticas y … es de una familia muy grande. Ellos son de Costa Rica.

2. *Voy al centro comercial. Sí, mamá. Usted va a ir al centro comercial el sábado, pero me gusta ir con mis amigos.*
3. *Mi amigo y yo vamos con Elena y Marta. Son amigas de la escuela. Sí. Ellas van con nosotros. A ellas les gusta ir de compras también.*
4. *Porque mi amigo necesita comprar algo en el centro comercial para la bicicleta. A él le gusta montar en bicicleta todos los días.*
5. *Después de ir de compras vamos a la casa de Miguel para comer con la familia de él. Voy a casa después.*

Track 12: Audio Act. 8, Writing, Audio & Video Workbook, p. 74 (5:36)

The yearbook staff is identifying students' pictures for the yearbook. Look at the pictures from the class trip to Mexico. Listen to the conversations and write the names of Arturo, Susi, Gloria, Martín, David, Eugenia, Enrique, and Lucía under the correct pictures. You will hear each dialogue twice.

1. **Adult Female:** Estas chicas van de compras al centro comercial. ¿Quiénes son?
   Adult Male: Son Eugenia y Gloria. A ellas les encanta ir de compras. ¡Es un ejercicio para ellas! ¡No son muy deportistas!
2. **Adult Female:** ¿Quién es el chico en la piscina?
   Adult Male: Es Arturo. Él siempre hace ejercicio: nada, levanta pesas o corre. Le gusta mantener la salud.
3. **Adult Female:** ¿Quiénes son las personas en el restaurante? ¿Qué comen? ¿Pescado?
   Adult Male: Sí. Creo que comen pescado. El chico es Martín. A él le gustan los restaurantes elegantes.
   Adult Female: ¿Con quién está? ¿Quién es la chica?
   Adult Male: Creo que es Lucía.
4. **Adult Female:** ¿Quién es la chica en el café?
   Adult Male: Es Gloria. Ella es muy reservada. A veces prefiere estar sola.
   Adult Female: Hmmm. Yo también. Muchas veces voy sola al café para leer.
5. **Adult Female:** ¿Quién es el chico enfrente del cine?
   Adult Male: Es Enrique. Él va al cine cuando llueve o cuando hace sol. Le encantan las películas mexicanas. Su actor mexicano favorito es Cantinflas. Según Manuel, él es muy gracioso.
6. **Adult Female:** ¿Quiénes son los chicos en la playa?
   Adult Male: Vamos a ver … Creo que son Susi y David.
   Adult Female: Hay tres. ¿Quién es la otra chica?
   Adult Male: Ah, sí. Hay dos chicas y un chico. Las chicas se llaman Susi y Eugenia.

Track 13: Audio Act. 9, Writing, Audio & Video Workbook, p. 74 (3:33)

Listen as a radio interviewer talks to Maricela, a young woman from Spain, about her city that was once home to the *Reyes* Fernando and Isabel. You will learn why it is such a popular tourist spot. After listening, answer the questions below. You will hear this conversation twice.

Locutor: Hola, Maricela. Bienvenida a "Viajes por España."
Maricela: Gracias. Me gusta mucho hablar de mi ciudad.
Locutor: ¿De dónde eres?
Maricela: Soy de Aranjuez, España. Es una ciudad fantástica. Es muy famosa en España.
Locutor: ¿Por qué?
Maricela: Porque es "la capital de las fresas."
Locutor: ¿Las fresas? ¿Es famosa por una fruta?
Maricela: Sí. Los turistas van a Aranjuez para comer fresas.
Locutor: ¿Adónde van los turistas después de comer fresas?
Maricela: Van a los palacios de los Reyes Católicos, y … a un café o restaurante para comer más fresas.
Locutor: ¿Dónde está Aranjuez?
Maricela: Está a treinta minutos de Madrid, más o menos.
Locutor: ¿Cuál es la comida típica? Fresas y… ¿qué más?
Maricela: Somos famosos por las fresas, y los pasteles de manzana también son muy buenos.
Locutor: ¿Adónde vas con tus amigos en Aranjuez?
Maricela: Vamos a los cafés del centro de la ciudad y al parque. También me gusta nadar en la piscina pública. ¡Siempre hace sol en Aranjuez!
Locutor: Mucho gusto de hablar contigo, Maricela. ¡Nos vemos en Aranjuez!

You are going to hear this conversation again.

Track 14: *Cultura en vivo*, Student Book, p. 232 (1:30)

Rimas infantiles

First, listen to the song. Then sing along.

See Student Book page 190 for lyrics to song.

Track 15: *Repaso del capítulo*, Student Book, p. 236 (2:59)

Vocabulario y gramática

Listen to these words and expressions that you have learned in this chapter. You will hear each word or expression once.

See Student Book page 236 for vocabulary list.

Track 16: *Preparación para el examen*, Student Book, p. 237 (1:11)

Escuchar

Practice task.

Two friends are trying to make plans for the weekend. Based on their dialogue, what do they finally agree on? a) Who is going? b) Where are they going? c) When are they going?

Male Teen 1: ¿Adónde vas el fin de semana?
Male Teen 2: El sábado me quedo en casa, pero el domingo voy al cine.
Male Teen 1: ¿A qué hora vas?
Male Teen 2: A las nueve y media. Y tú, ¿qué haces el fin de semana?
Male Teen 1: Yo también voy al cine el domingo.
Male Teen 2: ¿Por qué no vamos a las nueve y media?
Male Teen 1: Yo prefiero ir a las siete.
Male Teen 2: Bien … estoy de acuerdo. ¡A las siete!

Realidades A

Capítulo 4A

Video Script

A primera vista: *Un chico reservado* (4:31)

JAVIER: Ah, es una carta de Esteban.

ESTEBAN: Querido Javier, Hola de tus amigos en San Antonio. ¿Qué tal Madrid? ¿Te gusta tu nueva escuela? …

IGNACIO: Hmmm … El estudiante nuevo es un poco reservado, ¿verdad?

ELENA: ¿Quién?

IGNACIO: Javier. Está allí, solo …

ELENA: Ah, sí.

IGNACIO: ¿Hablamos con él?

ANA: ¿Hablamos con quién?

IGNACIO: Con el estudiante nuevo.

ANA: Ah, sí … Yo también voy a hablar con él.

IGNACIO: Pues … vamos todos a hablar con Javier.

IGNACIO: Hola.

JAVIER: Hola.

ANA: ¿Qué tal? Me llamo Ana, él es Ignacio, y ella, Elena.

JAVIER: Mucho gusto. Me llamo Javier.

ELENA: Encantada … Eres nuevo, ¿verdad?

JAVIER: Sí, soy de Salamanca.

IGNACIO: ¡No me digas!

ANA: Pues, Javier, ¿adónde vas después de las clases?

JAVIER: ¿Yo? A casa.

ELENA: ¿Todos los días?

JAVIER: Pues, sí; pero … ¿adónde van Uds. después de las clases?

ELENA: Los lunes, miércoles y viernes, voy a mi trabajo en el centro comercial.

JAVIER: ¿Y tú?

IGNACIO: Pues, generalmente, voy al gimnasio. A la piscina. Me gusta nadar.

JAVIER: ¿Eres deportista?

IGNACIO: Sí.

JAVIER: ¿Y tú?

ANA: Pues, los lunes voy a mi lección de piano … Hmmm … los martes, miércoles y jueves voy a la biblioteca a estudiar … Los viernes, voy a un café, con mis amigos …

IGNACIO: Y tú, Javier, ¿adónde vas los fines de semana?

JAVIER: Me quedo en casa. No tengo muchos amigos aquí.

ANA: Pues, el sábado, ¿por qué no haces algo con nosotros?

JAVIER: Pues, está bien.

ANA: ¿Te gusta … ir de compras?

JAVIER: ¿La verdad? No …

ELENA: ¿Te gusta ir al cine?

JAVIER: A veces … Me gustan las películas.

ANA: ¿Te gusta bailar?

JAVIER: No, no me gusta bailar.

IGNACIO: Pues, ¿qué te gusta?

JAVIER: Me gusta practicar deportes.

IGNACIO: Bueno, ¿qué deportes te gustan?

JAVIER: ¡Me gusta el fútbol!

ANA: ¡No me digas! Muy bien. Nos vemos el sábado en el parque, a las once, para practicar fútbol.

IGNACIO: ¿Está bien, Javier?

JAVIER: ¡Claro que sí! Está muy bien. Hasta el sábado, en el parque.

ELENA: Pero, Ana, ¿fútbol?

ANA: ¿Por qué no? No tiene muchos amigos, y … le gusta el fútbol …

GramActiva Videos: the verb *ir;* asking questions **(6:31)**

The verb *ir*

HERO: Guess where I am going. I'd love to tell you, but first we'll have to learn about the verb *ir. Ir* isn't like other verbs that end in *-ir.* That's right, it's irregular, just like *ser, estar,* and *hacer.*
To infinitives and beyond!

HOST: *Ir* means "to go somewhere." Here are the endings: *voy, vas, va, vamos, vais, van.* The *yo* form rhymes with *estoy* and the other endings are *-ar* verb endings.
The real mystery remains, why all the forms start with *v.*

HOST: Most of the time that you use the verb *ir* it will be followed by *a,* which means "to." Let's build a sentence. Start with the subject pronoun, *Yo,* then the verb, *Yo voy,* then the preposition *a, Yo voy a,* then the place to where the subject is going. *Yo voy al cine.* But remember, you don't really need to use the word *yo,* so *Voy al cine* will do just fine.

FOREMAN: Look what happens when the place you are going is masculine, like *el cine. A* is followed by *el.* When this happens in Spanish, it gets contracted to *al.*
Voy al cine.

HOST: Let's practice with some examples.
Tú vas a la clase de español.
Nosotros vamos a la biblioteca.
Él va al teatro.
Ustedes van al parque.

SCARECROW: Where are you going?

HOST: You mean, *¿Adónde vas? Voy al parque.*

Quiz

HOST: Let's get going on some review. Match the following pronouns to the correct form of the verb.

Yo voy.
Tú vas.
Usted va.
Nosotras vamos.
Ustedes van.

Asking Questions

Host: *¿Quién?*
Shadow: Who?
Host: *¿Qué?*
Shadow: What?
Host: *¿Cuándo?*
Shadow: When?
Host: *¿Dónde?*
Shadow: Where?
Host: *¿Por qué?*
Shadow: Why?
Host: *¿Cómo?*
Shadow: How?
Host: *¿Adónde?*
Shadow: To where?
Host: *¿Cuántos?*
Shadow: How many?

Host: These are just a few of the mysteries that fill our universe, and textbooks. For both these reasons, we'd better learn how they work.

Host: Our biggest word of the day is *interrogative,* as in interrogative words. Interrogative words are words you use to ask questions. In English they are words like *who, what, when, where, why, how, (to) where,* and *how many.*

Foreman: In Spanish, for a question with an interrogative word, we put this word at the beginning of the sentence and then we place the verb next. Then comes the subject.

Turtle: Whoooooo. Thaaaat waasss toooo faaasst.

Host: Let's go slower. Start the sentence with an upside down question mark and the interrogative word.
¿Cuándo ...
The verb is going to come next.
¿Cuándo come ...
Then the subject will come after the verb.
¿Cuándo come Pedro?
Then add the rest of your sentence if there is any more and end with another question mark.
¿Cuándo come Pedro el almuerzo?

Guy: *¿Qué comen ustedes en el desayuno?*
¿Por qué comes tú mi desayuno?
¿Cuándo comen ustedes el desayuno?
Remember that if the subject is a subject pronoun, you can often drop the pronoun, if it's clear from the verb ending who you're talking about.
¿Cuándo comemos?

Host: Just as in English, you don't need to always use interrogative words to ask a question. Questions that can be answered either yes or no can be asked in other ways.
The first way is to leave the sentence the way it is, but change the sound of the way you say it.

Guy: *¿Tú comes las papas fritas?*

Lesko: The second way is to reverse the order of the subject and the verb.

Guy: *¿Comes tú las papas fritas?*

Lesko: The third way is to use an expression like *verdad.* This is like putting the word *right* at the end of a sentence in English.

Guy: *Tú comes las papas fritas, ¿verdad?*

Foreman: When using *verdad* the first part of the sentence is not a question, it is a statement. Therefore the question marks go before and after *verdad* instead of at the beginning of the sentence, and the two phrases are separated by a comma.

Quiz

Host: Did you get all that? We'll see in a minute. Place these words in order to form questions.
Juan/come/qué
¿Qué come Juan?
trabajas/dónde/tú
¿Dónde trabajas tú?
cuándo/ellos/juegan
¿Cuándo juegan ellos?

Nombre ______________________

Communicative Activity **4A-1**
Estudiante **A**

Fecha ______________________

Your partner will play the role of Eduardo, an exchange student from Chile. Eduardo is very busy going places with his friends in the United States. Ask Eduardo the following questions about his plans for the week. Finally, based on his answers, ask him to go someplace with you on a specific day. Record his answers in the appropriate space on the weekly calendar.

1. ¿Adónde vas el sábado?
2. ¿Con quién vas al parque?
3. ¿Cuándo vas a la playa?
4. ¿Adónde vas el jueves?
5. ¿Con quién vas al cine?
6. ¿Cuándo te gusta ir a la piscina?
7. ¿Adónde vas el lunes?
8. ¿Quieres ir de compras el ________________ ?

lunes	martes	miércoles	jueves	viernes	sábado	domingo

Now, you will play the role of María, an exchange student from Guatemala. Based on the calendar below, answer your partner's questions about your plans for the week. If your partner asks you to join him or her, will you accept? Why or why not?

lunes	martes	miércoles	jueves	viernes	sábado	domingo
 Miguel		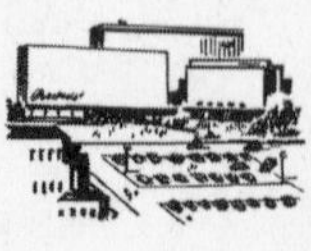			 Fernando	

Nombre ______________________

Fecha ______________________

You will play the role of Eduardo, an exchange student from Chile. Based on the calendar below, answer your partner's questions about your plans for the week. If your partner asks you to join him or her, will you accept? Why or why not?

lunes	martes	miércoles	jueves	viernes	sábado	domingo
	Ramón			**Raquel**		

Now, your partner will play the role of María, an exchange student from Guatemala. María is very busy going places with her friends in the United States. Ask María the following questions about her plans for the week. Finally, based on her answers, ask her to go someplace with you on a specific day. Record her answers in the appropriate space on the weekly calendar.

1. ¿Adónde vas el miércoles?
2. ¿Con quién vas al restaurante?
3. ¿Cuándo vas a la iglesia?
4. ¿Adónde vas el viernes?
5. ¿Con quién vas a las montañas?
6. ¿Cuándo te gusta ir a casa después de las clases?
7. ¿Adónde vas el martes?
8. ¿Quieres ir al campo el ________________ ?

lunes	martes	miércoles	jueves	viernes	sábado	domingo

Realidades **A** | Nombre ____________

Capítulo 4A | Fecha ____________

Communicative Activity **4A-2**
Estudiante **A**

You are discussing with your partner your plans for your free time. Using the chart below, do the following: (1) In the boxes marked *yo* and *mi familia y yo,* write about your plans and your family's plans for your free time. (2) Ask your partner about his or her plans and his or her family's plans and fill in the boxes marked *mi compañero(a)* and *la familia de mi compañero(a).* (3) Ask your partner where your friend is going during his or her free time, when he or she is going, what he or she is going to do, and with whom he or she is going. Follow the model.

¿Adónde va Adriana?

¿Con quién va Adriana (al / a la) ____________ ?

¿Por qué va Adriana (al / a la) ____________ ?

¿Cuándo va Adriana (al / a la) ____________ ?

	Lugar ¿Adónde?	**Día ¿Cuándo?**	**Actividad ¿Qué?**	**Persona ¿Con quién?**
yo				
mi familia y yo				
mi compañero(a)				
la familia de mi compañero(a)				
Adriana				Sergio

Nombre ______________________

Communicative Activity **4A-2**
Estudiante **B**

Fecha ______________________

You are discussing with your partner your plans for your free time. Using the chart below, do the following: (1) In the boxes marked *yo* and *mi familia y yo,* write about your plans and your family's plans for your free time. (2) Ask your partner about his or her plans and his or her family's plans and fill in the boxes marked *mi compañero(a)* and *la familia de mi compañero(a).* (3) Ask your partner where your friend is going during his or her free time, when he or she is going, what he or she is going to do, and with whom he or she is going. Follow the model.

¿Adónde va Adriana?

¿Con quién va Adriana (al / a la)

______________________ *?*

¿Por qué va Adriana (al / a la)

______________________ *?*

¿Cuándo va Adriana (al / a la)

______________________ *?*

	Lugar ¿Adónde?	**Día ¿Cuándo?**	**Actividad ¿Qué?**	**Persona ¿Con quién?**
yo				
mi familia y yo				
mi compañero(a)				
la familia de mi compañero(a)				
Adriana		el sábado		

Realidades A

Capítulo 4A

Situation Cards

Capítulo 4A **Realidades A** **1A**

Talking about leisure activities

You are talking about the weekend with a new student in your school.

— Greet the new student and then introduce yourself.

— Ask the student where he or she goes on weekends.

— Ask whom he or she goes with.

— Say good-bye.

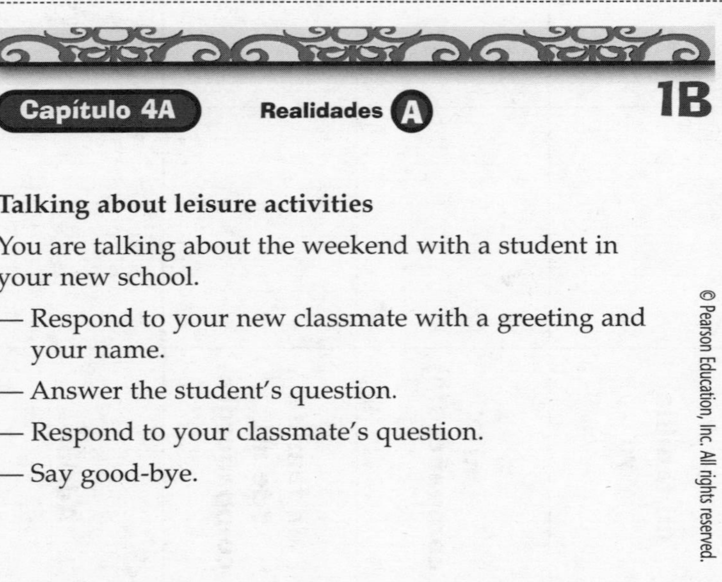

Capítulo 4A **Realidades A** **1B**

Talking about leisure activities

You are talking about the weekend with a student in your new school.

— Respond to your new classmate with a greeting and your name.

— Answer the student's question.

— Respond to your classmate's question.

— Say good-bye.

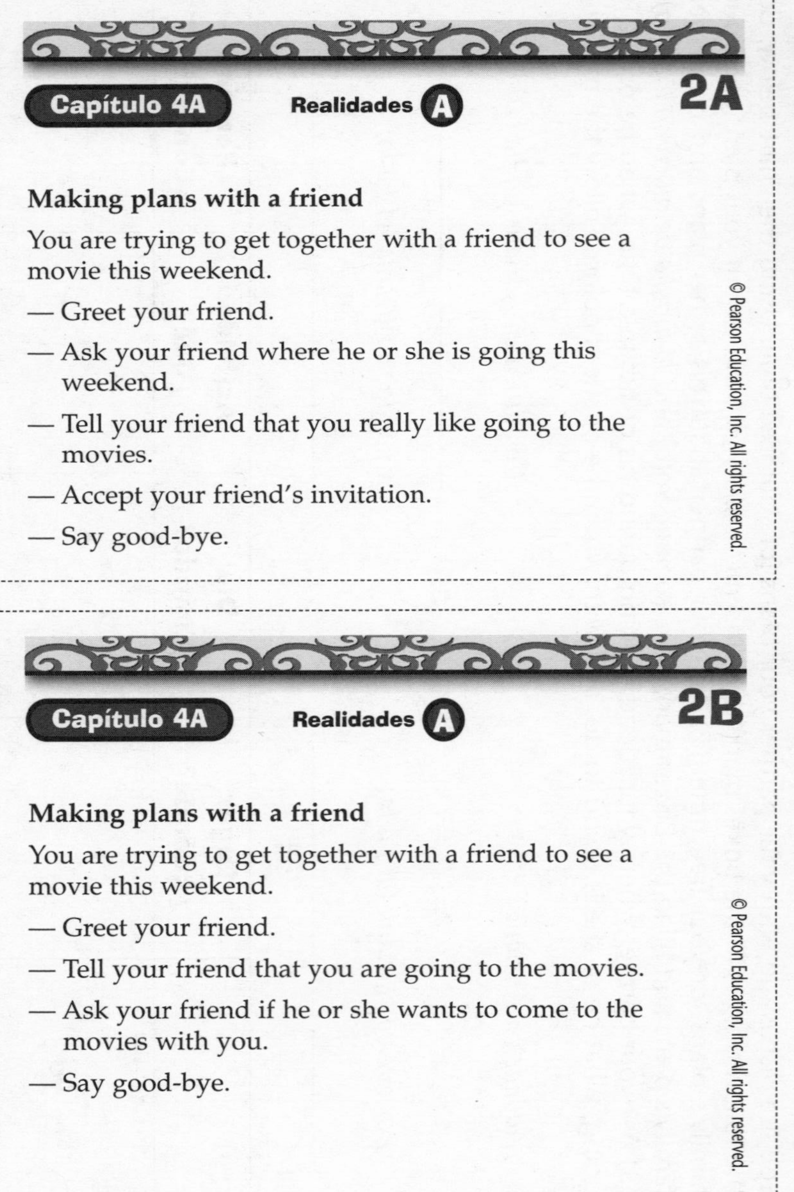

Capítulo 4A **Realidades A** **2A**

Making plans with a friend

You are trying to get together with a friend to see a movie this weekend.

— Greet your friend.

— Ask your friend where he or she is going this weekend.

— Tell your friend that you really like going to the movies.

— Accept your friend's invitation.

— Say good-bye.

Capítulo 4A **Realidades A** **2B**

Making plans with a friend

You are trying to get together with a friend to see a movie this weekend.

— Greet your friend.

— Tell your friend that you are going to the movies.

— Ask your friend if he or she wants to come to the movies with you.

— Say good-bye.

GramActiva

¿Adónde vas?

¿Vas mucho a ...?, p. 214

todos los días

mucho

a veces

nunca

Vocabulary Clip Art

Vocabulary Clip Art

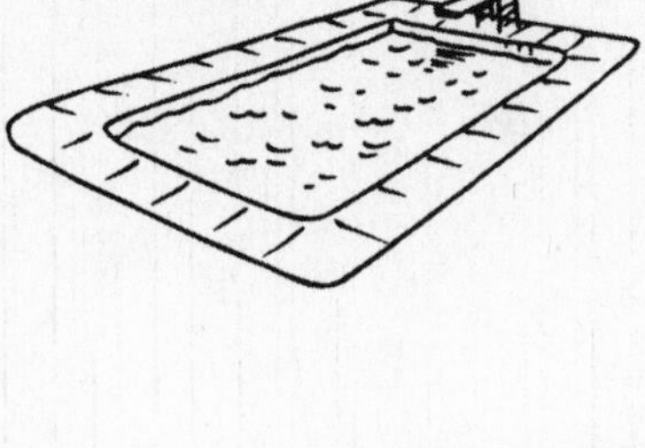

Realidades A

Capítulo 4A

Core Practice Answers

4A-1
1. la biblioteca
2. el gimnasio
3. la lección de piano
4. las montañas (el campo)
5. cine
6. la playa
7. el parque
8. restaurante

4A-2
Answers will vary, but should be structured as follows:
1. Voy al trabajo para trabajar.
2. Voy a la biblioteca para leer y estudiar.
3. Voy a la clase de español para hablar español.
4. Voy al parque para correr y caminar.
5. Voy al centro comercial para ir de compras.
6. Voy a la lección de piano para tocar el piano.
7. Voy al restaurante para comer y beber.
8. Voy al cine para ver una película.
9. Voy a la piscina para nadar.
10. Voy al gimnasio para hacer ejercicio.
11. Voy al centro comercial para estar con amigos.
12. Voy al gimnasio para levantar pesas.

4A-3
1. —estudias
—Voy a la biblioteca
2. —corres
—Voy al parque.
3. —levantas pesas
—Voy al gimnasio
4. —caminas
—Voy a las montañas
5. —vas de compras
—Voy al centro comercial
6. —nadas
—Voy a la piscina

4A-4
1. Tito va al cine los viernes.
2. Tito estudia en la biblioteca los miércoles.
3. Tito hace ejercicio los sábados (y los martes).
4. Generalmente, Tito trabaja los lunes y los jueves.
5. Tito va al gimnasio los sábados.
6. Tito va a la iglesia los domingos.
7. Tito va al gimnasio y a la iglesia los fines de semana.

4A-5
1. LOLIS: voy
ELIA: vamos
LOLIS: va
2. MARTA: vas
JUAN: voy / voy
MARTA: van / voy
JUAN: van
MARTA: vamos
3. RODOLFO: ____
PABLO Y FELIPE: ____
RODOLFO: van
PABLO: voy
FELIPE: voy / Voy
RODOLFO: vamos / va
PABLO: va / van
FELIPE: ir

4A-6
A.
1. Quién
2. Cuándo
3. Cuál
4. Cómo
5. Adónde
6. Dónde
7. Qué
8. Cuántos

B.
Answers will vary. Do not repeat questions from part A.

4A-7
Answers may vary.
TUS PADRES: ¿Adónde vas esta noche?
TUS PADRES: ¿Con quiénes vas?
TUS PADRES: ¿Cómo se llaman ellos?
TUS PADRES: ¿De dónde son?
TUS PADRES: ¿Cómo es Roberto?
TUS PADRES: ¿Y cómo es Ana?
TUS PADRES: ¿Qué van a hacer después de ir al restaurante?
TUS PADRES: ¿Y después?

Crucigrama (4A-8)
Across:
1. templo
4. campo
8. digas
9. mezquita
11. quién
12. lección
14. libre
15. compras
16. después
18. película
19. montañas

Down:
2. playa
3. iglesia
5. parque
6. biblioteca
7. centro
10. gimnasio
13. cine
17. piscina
20. trabajo

Organizer (4A-9)
I. Vocabulary Answers will vary.
II. Grammar
1. **col. 1.** / **col. 2.**
voy / vamos
vas / vais
va / van
2. **A.** quién, qué, dónde, cuándo, por qué, cómo
B. before

Realidades A — Nombre ____ Hora ____

Capítulo 4A — Fecha ____ **Vocabulary Flash Cards, Sheet 1**

Write the Spanish vocabulary word below each picture. If there is a word or phrase, copy it in the space provided. Be sure to include the article for each noun.

la biblioteca	*el parque*	*el cine*
el café	*el trabajo*	*el gimnasio*
el campo	*el centro comercial*	*la iglesia*

Realidades A — Nombre ____ Hora ____

Capítulo 4A — Fecha ____ **Vocabulary Flash Cards, Sheet 2**

ir de compras	*la piscina*	**la mezquita** — *la mezquita*
las montañas	*la playa*	**la sinagoga** — *la sinagoga*
ver una película	*la lección de piano*	**el templo** — *el templo*

Realidades A | Nombre ______ Hora ______

Capítulo 4A | Fecha ______

Vocabulary Flash Cards, Sheet 3

la casa	**Me quedo en casa.**	**¿Adónde?**
la *casa*	*Me* *quedo* *en* *casa.*	*¿Adónde?*
en casa	**a**	**a casa**
en *casa*	*a*	*a* *casa*
el restaurante	**a la, al**	**¿Con quién?**
el *restaurante*	*a la*, *al*	*¿Con* *quién?*

Realidades A | Nombre ______ Hora ______

Capítulo 4A | Fecha ______

Vocabulary Flash Cards, Sheet 4

con mis amigos	**¿Cuándo?**	**los fines de semana**
con *mis* *amigos*	*¿Cuándo?*	*los* *fines* *de* *semana*
con mis/tus amigos	**después**	**los lunes, los martes...**
con *mis/tus* *amigos*	*después*	*los lunes,* *los martes...*
solo, sola	**después de**	**tiempo libre**
solo, *sola*	*después* *de*	*tiempo* *libre*

Realidades A — Capítulo 4A

Nombre ______ Hora ______

Fecha ______

Vocabulary Flash Cards, Sheet 5

de *de*	**¡No me digas!** *¡No me digas!*	
¿De dónde eres? *¿De dónde eres?*	**para** *para*	
generalmente *generalmente*		

Realidades A — Capítulo 4A

Nombre ______ Hora ______

Fecha ______

Vocabulary Flash Cards, Sheet 6

Realidades A | Nombre ______ | Hora ______

Capítulo 4A | Fecha ______

Vocabulary Check, Sheet 1

Tear out this page. Write the English words on the lines. Fold the paper along the dotted line to see the correct answers so you can check your work.

ir de compras	***to go shopping***
ver una película	***to see a movie***
la lección de piano	***piano lesson (class)***
la biblioteca	***library***
el café	***café***
el campo	***countryside***
en casa	***at home***
el centro comercial	***mall***
el cine	***movie theater***
el gimnasio	***gym***
la iglesia	***church***
la mezquita	***mosque***
las montañas	***mountains***
el parque	***park***
la piscina	***swimming pool***
la playa	***beach***
el restaurante	***restaurant***

Fold In ←

Realidades A | Nombre ______ | Hora ______

Capítulo 4A | Fecha ______

Vocabulary Check, Sheet 2

Tear out this page. Write the Spanish words on the lines. Fold the paper along the dotted line to see the correct answers so you can check your work.

to go shopping	***ir de compras***
to see a movie	***ver una película***
piano lesson (class)	***la lección de piano***
library	***la biblioteca***
café	***el café***
countryside	***el campo***
at home	***en casa***
mall	***el centro comercial***
movie theater	***el cine***
gym	***el gimnasio***
church	***la iglesia***
mosque	***la mezquita***
mountains	***las montañas***
park	***el parque***
swimming pool	***la piscina***
beach	***la playa***
restaurant	***el restaurante***

Fold In ←

Realidades A Nombre ____ Hora ____

Capítulo 4A Fecha ____ **Vocabulary Check, Sheet 3**

Tear out this page. Write the English words on the lines. Fold the paper along the dotted line to see the correct answers so you can check your work.

la sinagoga	***synagogue***
el templo	***temple, Protestant church***
el trabajo	***work, job***
solo, sola	***alone***
¿Cuándo?	***When?***
después	***afterwards***
después (de)	***after***
los fines de semana	***on weekends***
los lunes, los martes...	***on Mondays, on Tuesdays...***
tiempo libre	***free time***

Fold In

Realidades A Nombre ____ Hora ____

Capítulo 4A Fecha ____ **Vocabulary Check, Sheet 4**

Tear out this page. Write the Spanish words on the lines. Fold the paper along the dotted line to see the correct answers so you can check your work.

synagogue	***la sinagoga***
temple, Protestant church	***el templo***
work, job	***el trabajo***
alone	***solo, sola***
When?	***¿Cuándo?***
afterwards	***después***
after	***después (de)***
on weekends	***los fines de semana***
on Mondays, on Tuesdays . . .	***los lunes, los martes...***
free time	***tiempo libre***

To hear a complete list of the vocabulary for this chapter, go to www.realidades.com and type in the Web Code jcd-0489. Then click on **Repaso del capítulo.**

Fold In

Realidades A Nombre Hora

Capítulo 4A Fecha **Guided Practice Activities 4A-1**

The verb *ir* (p. 218)

- The verb **ir** means "to go." It is irregular. Here are its forms.

yo	**voy**	nosotros/nosotras	**vamos**
tú	**vas**	vosotros/vosotras	**vais**
usted/él/ella	**va**	ustedes/ellos/ellas	**van**

- **¡Vamos!** means "Let's go!"

A. Choose the correct subject pronoun for each form of **ir** and circle it.

1. (**tú** / **él**) va
2. (**yo** / **usted**) voy
3. (**ellas** / **nosotras**) vamos
4. (**usted** / **ustedes**) va
5. (**ustedes** / **él**) van
6. (**tú** / **yo**) vas
7. (**ellos** / **ella**) van
8. (**yo** / **ella**) va

B. Now, write the correct form of **ir** next to each subject pronoun.

1. ella ***va***
2. ustedes ***van***
3. yo ***voy***
4. nosotros ***vamos***
5. tú ***vas***
6. él ***va***
7. ellos ***van***
8. usted ***va***

C. Complete each sentence by writing in the correct form of **ir**.

1. Yo ***voy*** al cine para ver una película.
2. Ellas ***van*** al parque para correr.
3. Nosotros ***vamos*** al gimnasio para levantar pesas.
4. Tú ***vas*** al restaurante para comer.
5. Ella ***va*** a la piscina para nadar.

realidades.com • Web Code: jcd-0403

Realidades A Nombre Hora

Capítulo 4A Fecha **Guided Practice Activities 4A-2**

The verb *ir* (*continued*)

- When **ir** + **a** is followed by the definite article **el**, **a** + **el** combines to form **al**:

  (vamos a) + (el parque) = Vamos al parque.

D. Complete each sentence by writing a form of **ir** + **al** or **a la**. Remember to use **al** when the noun after the write-on line is masculine. Use **a la** when the noun is feminine. Follow the models.

Modelos Ellos *van al* parque.
Ellos *van a la* oficina.

1. Silvia ***va a la*** casa.
2. Cristina y María ***van al*** café.
3. Tú ***vas a la*** playa.
4. Nosotros ***vamos al*** parque.
5. Usted ***va al*** campo.
6. Yo ***voy a la*** piscina.

- To ask where someone is going, use **¿Adónde?** as in: **¿Adónde vas?**
- To answer, use forms of **ir** + **a** as in: **Voy a la oficina.**

E. Complete the following exchanges by finishing the second sentence with a form of **ir** and the place indicated. Follow the model.

Modelo (el cine)
—¿Adónde vas?
—Yo *voy al cine*.

1. (el parque)
—¿Adónde vamos?
—Nosotros ***vamos al parque***.

2. (el gimnasio)
—¿Adónde van?
—Ellas ***van al gimnasio***.

3. (la piscina)
—¿Adónde va?
—Él ***va a la piscina***.

4. (la iglesia)
—¿Adónde voy?
—Tú ***vas a la iglesia***.

realidades.com • Web Code: jcd-0403

Realidades A | Nombre | Hora
Capítulo 4A | Fecha | **Guided Practice Activities 4A-3**

Asking questions (p. 224)

- Interrogatives are words that you use to ask questions. Here are some Spanish interrogatives.

Categories	Interrogatives		
People	¿Quién?	¿Con quién?	
Location	¿Dónde?	¿Adónde?	¿De dónde?
Things or actions	¿Qué?	¿Cuál?	¿Cuántos? / ¿Cuántas?
Reason	¿Por qué?		
Time	¿Cuándo?		
Description (how)	¿Cómo?		

- You can change a statement into a question by raising your voice at the end:

  ¿Margarita va a la biblioteca? In this case, you do not use an interrogative.
- These kinds of questions expect the answer will be *yes* or *no*. You can add **¿verdad?** (*right?*) to the end to emphasize this: **Margarita va a la biblioteca, ¿verdad?**

A. Each drawing or group of drawings represents a question category in the chart above. Write the interrogatives that go with each group. Follow the model.

Modelo ¿ *Cuándo* ?

1. ***¿Dónde?***
   ¿Adónde?
   ¿De dónde?

2. ***¿Quién?***
   ¿Con quién?

3. ***¿Qué?***
   ¿Cuál?
   ¿Cuántos?
   ¿Cuántas?

Realidades A | Nombre | Hora
Capítulo 4A | Fecha | **Guided Practice Activities 4A-4**

Asking questions (*continued*)

- In Spanish questions with interrogatives, the verb comes before the subject: **¿Adónde va Margarita?**

B. Look at the following groups of exchanges. Write in the correct interrogative to complete each exchange. Use the interrogatives listed for each group.

Location: ¿Dónde? ¿Adónde?

1. —¿ ***Adónde*** van Natalia y Roberto?
   —Van a la biblioteca para estudiar.
2. —¿ ***Dónde*** levantas pesas?
   — Levanto pesas en el gimnasio.

People: ¿Quién? ¿Con quién?

3. —¿ ***Con quién*** hablas mucho por teléfono?
   —Hablo mucho con mi amiga Tina. Ella es muy divertida.
4. —¿ ***Quién*** es su profesor de español?
   — Es la señora Oliveros. Es muy inteligente.

Things: ¿Qué? ¿Cuántos?

5. —¿ ***Cuántos*** libros hay en la biblioteca?
   —¡Hay muchos!
6. —¿ ***Qué*** comes para el desayuno?
   —Como pan tostado y tocino.

Reason and Description: ¿Por qué? ¿Cómo?

7. —¿ ***Por qué*** estudias tanto?
   — Soy muy trabajadora y me gusta leer.
8. —¿ ***Cómo*** es la clase de matemáticas?
   — Es interesante, pero difícil.

Asking questions (*continued*)

C. Look at each group of phrases. Put them in order to form a question by numbering each group 1, 2, or 3. Then write them in order on the write-on line below. Follow the model. You can also look at the questions in **part B** for examples.

Modelo Paulina / adónde / va
3 1 2
¿ *Adónde va Paulina* ?

1. es / el profesor de español / quién
   2 3 1
   ¿Quién es el profesor de español?
2. sillas / hay / cuántas
   2 3 1
   ¿Cuántas sillas hay?
3. Luisa / adónde / va
   3 1 2
   ¿Adónde va Luisa?
4. cómo / ella / es
   1 3 2
   ¿Cómo es ella?
5. corren / dónde / ellos
   2 1 3
   ¿Dónde corren ellos?
6. con quién / habla / Margarita
   1 2 3
   ¿Con quién habla Margarita?

Lectura: Al centro comercial (pp. 230–231)

A. List four events that you think would take place at a special-event week in a shopping center near you.

Answers will vary.

1. ______ 3. ______
2. ______ 4. ______

B. According to the reading in your book, what are the dates for the event week at the Plaza del Sol? Write the answers in English below, next to the days of the week you are given.

Monday, ***January 11*** Friday, ***January 15***
Tuesday, ***January 12*** Saturday, ***January 16***
Wednesday, ***January 13*** Sunday, ***January 17***
Thursday, ***January 14***

C. Look at the word bank below. Choose which expression in English best matches with the words you are given and write it in the spaces provided.

Andean music	Yoga class	Evening of jazz
Evening of tango	Photography show	Yoga performance

1. Música andina ***Andean music***
2. Clase de yoga ***Yoga class***
3. Noche de jazz ***Evening of jazz***
4. Exposición de fotografía ***Photography show***
5. Exhibición de yoga ***Yoga performance***
6. Noche de tango ***Evening of tango***

D. Read the description of Andean music and answer the questions that follow.

El grupo Sol Andino toca música andina fusionada con bossa nova y jazz el lunes a las 8.00 P.M. Abierto al público.

1. Circle the name of the group in the paragraph above.
2. What does this group fuse with its brand of Andean music?
   bossa nova and ***jazz***
3. Can the public attend this show? ***yes***

Realidades A — Nombre ____ Hora ____

Capítulo 4A — Fecha ____ **Guided Practice Activities 4A-7**

Lectura: Al centro comercial (*continued*)

E. Read the description of the yoga class and answer the questions that follow.

> *La práctica de yoga es todos los martes desde las 7.00 hasta las 9.00 P.M. La instructora Lucía Gómez Paloma enseña los secretos de esta disciplina. Inscríbase al teléfono 224-24-16. Vacantes limitadas.*

1. How long does the yoga class last? ***two hours***
2. What does the sequence of numbers 224-24-16 stand for? ***telephone number***
3. Can anyone attend this class? ***no***
   Why or why not? ***limited openings***

F. After looking through the readings in your textbook, you know that four events are explained in detail. These events are listed below. You must choose which event goes with the descriptions you are given. Write the name of the event in the space provided.

Música andina Clase de yoga Sábado flamenco Clase de repostería

1. ***Clase de yoga*** instructora Lucía Gómez Paloma
2. ***Sábado flamenco*** guitarrista Ernesto Hermoza
3. ***Música andina*** grupo Sol Andino
4. ***Clase de repostería*** la Repostería Ideal
5. ***Clase de repostería*** maestro Rudolfo Torres
6. ***Sábado flamenco*** es el sábado a las 8.00 P.M.

Realidades A — Nombre ____ Hora ____

Capítulo 4A — Fecha ____ **Guided Practice Activities 4A-8**

Presentación oral (p. 233) *Answers will vary.*

Task: You and a partner will play the roles of a new student and a student who has been at school for awhile. This student must find out about the new student.

A. You will need to prepare the role of the student who has been at the school for awhile. On a separate sheet of paper, make a list of four questions you have for the new student. Then, think of a greeting to introduce yourself.

First question: Find out where the new student is from.
Second question: Find out what activities the new student likes to do.
Third question: Find out on what days of the week the student likes to do things.
Fourth question: Find out with whom the new student does these activities.

B. You will need to practice your conversation.

1. First, work on the greeting. See below for a model.
   EXPERIENCED STUDENT: ¡Hola, amigo! Soy Ana María. ¿Cómo te llamas?
   NEW STUDENT: Me llamo Miguel Ángel.
2. Now, you will need to put together your questions and answers in a conversation. Use the following as a model:
   EXPERIENCED STUDENT: ¿De dónde eres, Miguel Ángel?
   NEW STUDENT: Soy de Barranquilla, Colombia.
   EXPERIENCED STUDENT: Bien. ¿Qué te gusta hacer en tu tiempo libre?
   NEW STUDENT: Me gusta ir al campo, nadar en el mar y caminar en las montañas.
   EXPERIENCED STUDENT: A mí también me gusta ir al campo. ¿Cuándo vas tú al campo?
   NEW STUDENT: Voy al campo los fines de semana. Me gusta caminar cuando estoy de vacaciones.
   EXPERIENCED STUDENT: ¿Y con quién vas al campo o a las montañas?
   NEW STUDENT: Voy con mi familia.
3. Now work on a closing. Use the following as a model:
   EXPERIENCED STUDENT: ¡Bueno, hasta luego Miguel Ángel!
   NEW STUDENT: ¡Nos vemos, Ana María!

C. You will need to present your conversation. Make sure you do the following in your presentation:

____ provide and obtain all the necessary information
____ have no breaks in the conversation
____ speak clearly

Antes de ver el video

Actividad 1

Think of activities you do at different times during the week. Make a list of four activities you do during the week and then four activities you do during the weekend.

Actividades durante la semana	Actividades durante el fin de semana
Answers will vary.	Answers will vary.

¿Comprendes?

Actividad 2

Javier has just moved to a new high school in Spain, and he is sitting by himself. Ignacio, Elena, and Ana try to find out more about him. What do they do, and what do they learn? Write **cierto** (*true*) or **falso** (*false*) next to each statement.

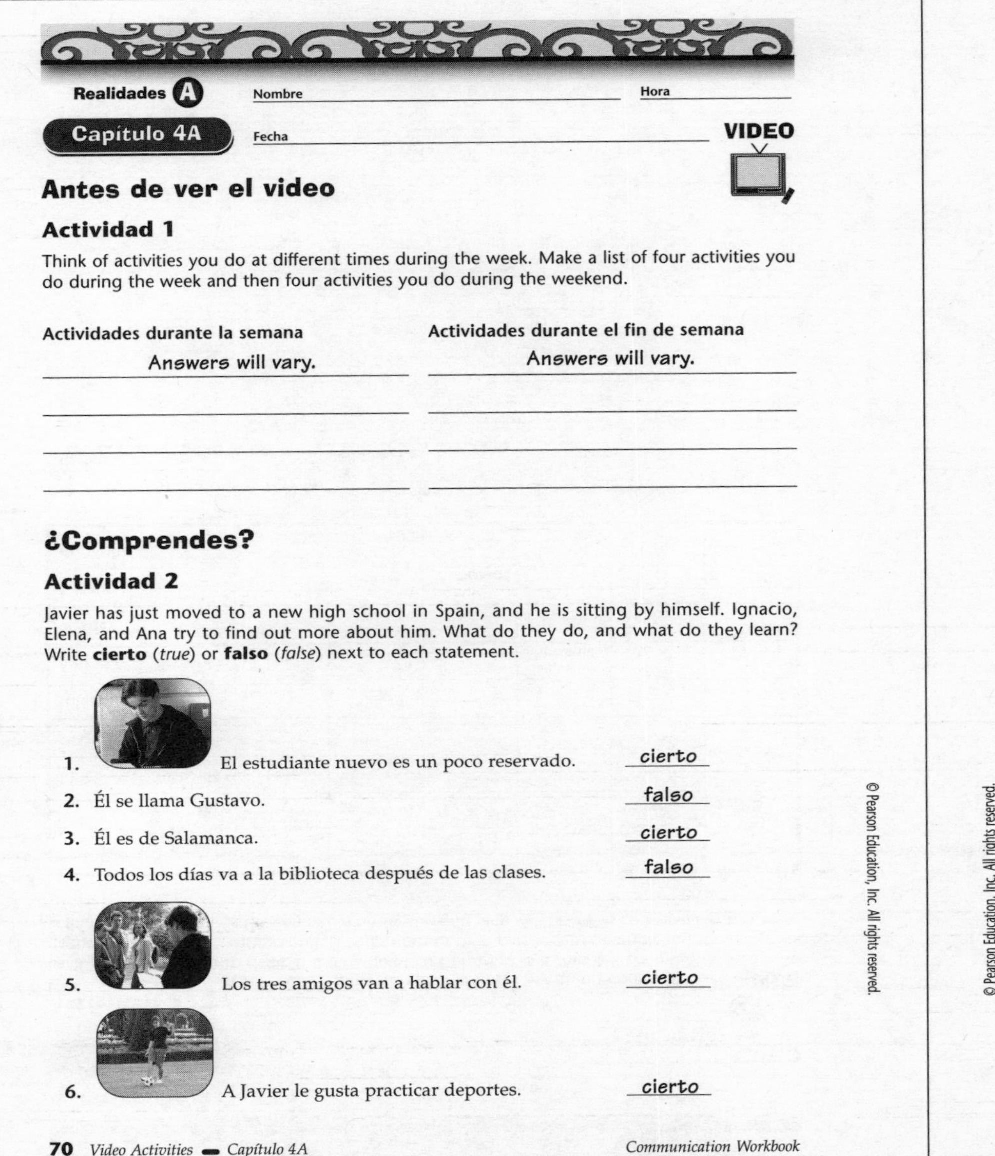

1. El estudiante nuevo es un poco reservado. cierto
2. Él se llama Gustavo. falso
3. Él es de Salamanca. cierto
4. Todos los días va a la biblioteca después de las clases. falso
5. Los tres amigos van a hablar con él. cierto
6. A Javier le gusta practicar deportes. cierto

7. A veces, él prefiere ir al cine a ver películas. cierto
8. A él no le gusta hablar con su amigo Esteban de San Antonio. falso

Actividad 3

What do the new friends do after class? Fill the blanks with complete sentences.

Nuevos amigos	¿Adónde va después de las clases?
1. Javier	Javier va a casa después de la clases.
2. Ignacio	Ignacio va al gimnasio y a la piscina.
3. Elena	Los lunes, miércoles y viernes, Elena va a su trabajo en el centro comercial.
4. Ana	Los lunes, Ana va a su lección de piano, de martes a jueves va a la biblioteca y los viernes va a un café con sus amigos.

Y, ¿qué más?

Actividad 4

What do you do after school every day? What do you sometimes do, and what do you never do at all? Write a short paragraph about your afterschool activities, following the example below.

Modelo *Yo voy a mi trabajo todos los días en el centro comercial. A veces, voy con una amiga al cine después del trabajo. Nunca voy al gimnasio durante la semana.*

Answers will vary.

Realidades A — Nombre ____ Hora ____

Capítulo 4A — Fecha ____ AUDIO

Actividad 5

Listen as Lorena talks to Luis and Antonio about where they are going during the week. Under each picture in the grid, write in the name of Luis or Antonio if they tell Lorena they are going to that place. In some cases, you will fill in both of their names. After completing the grid, you will be able to complete the sentences under the grid. You will hear this conversation twice.

lunes	Antonio	Luis					
martes							
miércoles	Antonio		Luis				
jueves	Antonio	Luis			Luis Antonio		
viernes							
sábado				Luis Antonio			
domingo						Luis	Antonio

1. Luis y Antonio van al (a la) *cine* el *sábado*.
2. También van al (a la) *biblioteca* el *jueves*.

Realidades A — Nombre ____ Hora ____

Capítulo 4A — Fecha ____ AUDIO

Actividad 6

You are volunteering as a tour guide during the upcoming Hispanic Arts Festival in your community. To make sure you would be able to understand the following questions if a visitor were to ask them, write the number of the question under the correct picture that would correspond to a logical response. You can check your answers to see if you're ready to answer visitors' questions during the Festival. You will hear each question twice.

8	9	4	5	7
6	2	3	10	1

Actividad 7

Your friend Miguel calls his mother from your house to give her an update on his plans for the day. Just from listening to his side of the conversation, you realize that his mother has LOTS of questions. What does she ask him, based on Miguel's answers? Choose from the following:

A. ¿Adónde vas?
B. ¿Con quiénes vas?
C. ¿Cuándo vas?
D. ¿Cómo es tu amigo?
E. ¿Por qué van?

You will hear each set of statements twice.

1. D 2. A 3. B 4. E 5. C

Realidades A — Nombre ______ Hora ______

Capítulo 4A — Fecha ______ **AUDIO**

Actividad 8

The yearbook staff is identifying students' pictures for the yearbook. Look at the pictures from the class trip to Mexico. Listen to the conversations and write the names of Arturo, Susi, Gloria, Martín, David, Eugenia, Enrique, and Lucía under the correct pictures. You will hear each dialogue twice.

Arturo

Susi, David y Eugenia

Enrique

Martín y Lucía

Eugenia y Gloria

Gloria

Actividad 9

Listen as a radio interviewer talks to Maricela, a young woman from Spain, about her city that was once home to the **Reyes** Fernando and Isabel. You will learn why it is such a popular tourist spot. After listening, answer the questions below. You will hear this conversation twice.

1. Maricela es de
   a) Madrid. (b) Aranjuez. c) Barcelona.
2. La ciudad es famosa por
   a) el pescado. b) el helado. (c) las fresas.
3. Los turistas van
   (a) al palacio. b) a las montañas. c) a la playa.
4. La ciudad de Maricela está a unos ______ minutos de Madrid.
   a) quince (b) treinta c) cincuenta
5. Las comidas típicas son
   a) pizza y espaguetis. (b) fresas y pasteles de manzana. c) pollo y judías verdes.
6. Maricela va ______ para pasar tiempo con los amigos.
   (a) al parque b) al cine c) a las montañas

Realidades A — Nombre ______ Hora ______

Capítulo 4A — Fecha ______ **WRITING**

Actividad 10

While on a hike one day, you stumble upon a "Wheel of the Future." When you spin this wheel, you will land on a picture of a place. The wheel will send you to that place if you tell it when you want to go and what you plan to do there. Write what you would tell the wheel for each place. Follow the model.

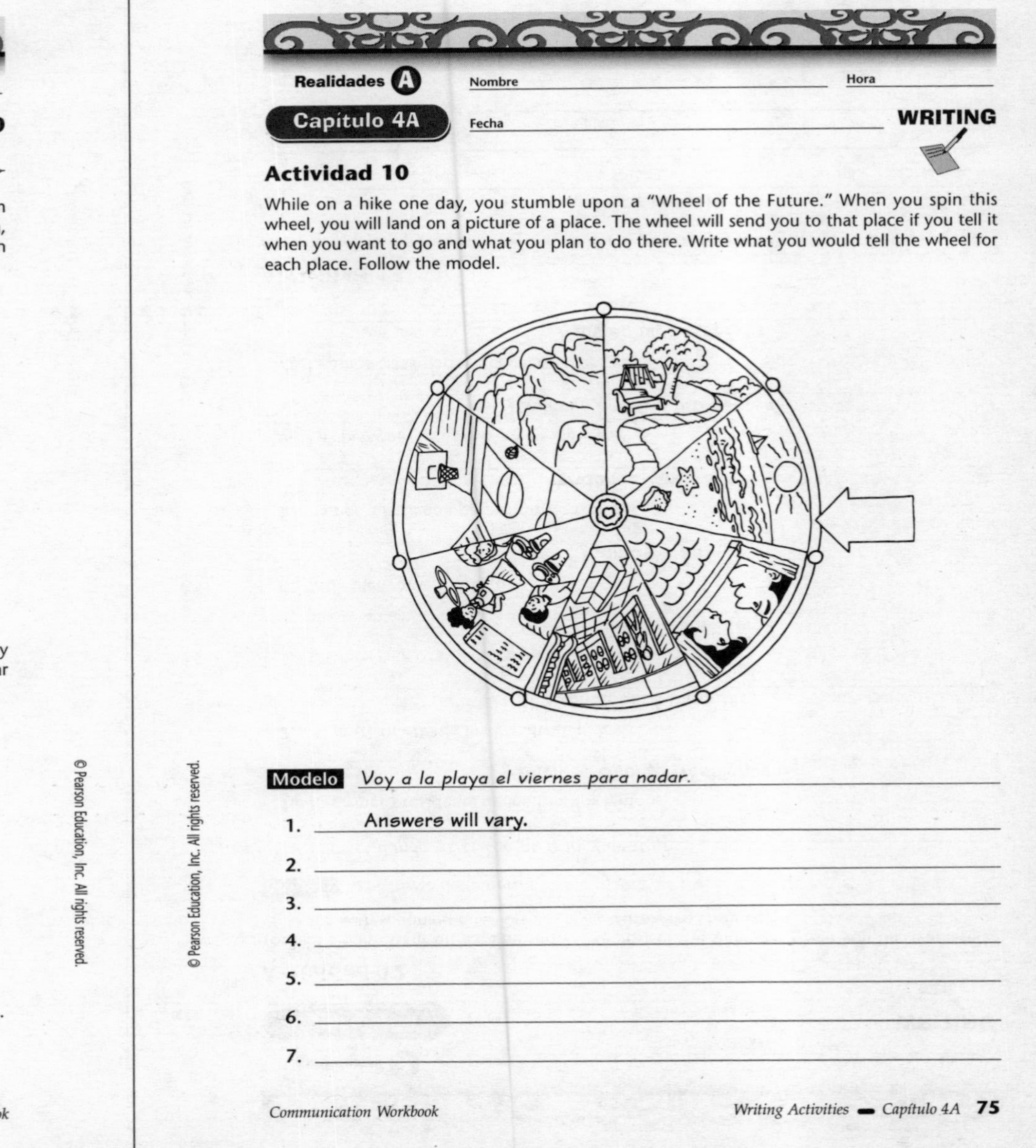

Modelo *Voy a la playa el viernes para nadar.*

1. Answers will vary.
2. ______
3. ______
4. ______
5. ______
6. ______
7. ______

Realidades A Nombre ______ Hora ______

Capítulo 4A Fecha ______ **WRITING**

Actividad 11

You are having a surprise party for your best friend next weekend, and you need to know where your family and friends are going to be this week so that you can get in touch with them to make plans. Below is a planner containing information on everyone's plans for the week. Using the pictures to help you, write where your friends and family will be and what they will be doing on that day. Use the model as a guide.

Modelo (YO) Lunes: *El lunes yo voy a la biblioteca para hacer la tarea.*

Reasons given will vary. Verbs should be as shown.

- Tú — lunes: Tú vas a la lección de piano para... practicar las obras de Chopin.
- Geraldo — martes: Geraldo va al restaurante para... trabajar.
- Mi familia y Yo — miércoles: Mi familia y yo vamos al centro comercial para...comprar ropa nueva.
- Juan y Tú — jueves: Juan y tú van (vais) a la biblioteca para...leer.
- Pedro y Claudia — viernes: Pedro y Claudia van al café para...hablar un poco.
- Mariana — sábado: Mariana va a la piscina para... nadar.
- Anita y Lucita — domingo: Anita y Lucita van al parque para...caminar.

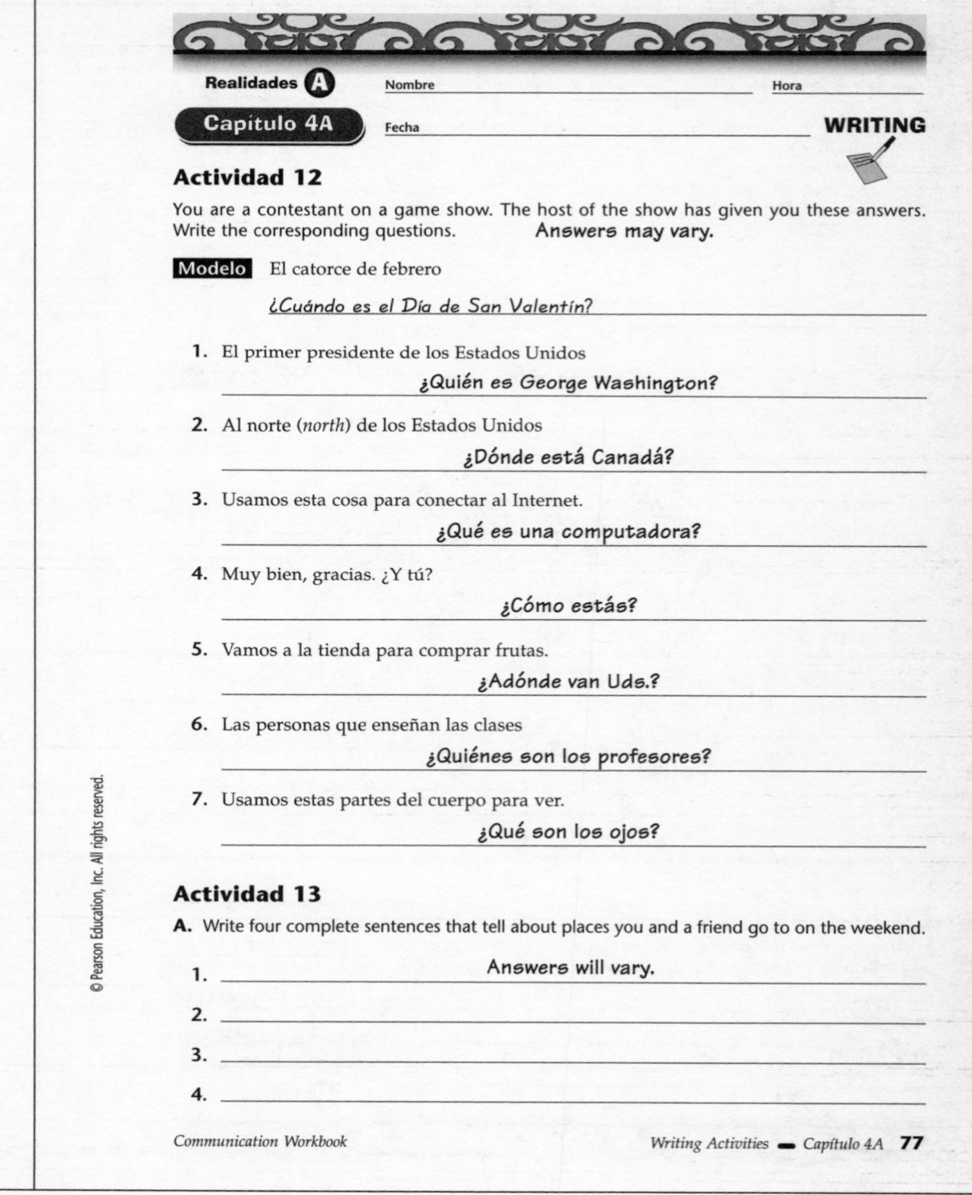

Realidades A Nombre ______ Hora ______

Capítulo 4A Fecha ______ **WRITING**

Actividad 12

You are a contestant on a game show. The host of the show has given you these answers. Write the corresponding questions. **Answers may vary.**

Modelo El catorce de febrero

¿Cuándo es el Día de San Valentín?

1. El primer presidente de los Estados Unidos
   ¿Quién es George Washington?
2. Al norte (*north*) de los Estados Unidos
   ¿Dónde está Canadá?
3. Usamos esta cosa para conectar al Internet.
   ¿Qué es una computadora?
4. Muy bien, gracias. ¿Y tú?
   ¿Cómo estás?
5. Vamos a la tienda para comprar frutas.
   ¿Adónde van Uds.?
6. Las personas que enseñan las clases
   ¿Quiénes son los profesores?
7. Usamos estas partes del cuerpo para ver.
   ¿Qué son los ojos?

Actividad 13

A. Write four complete sentences that tell about places you and a friend go to on the weekend.

1. **Answers will vary.**
2. ______
3. ______
4. ______

WRITING

B. Now, use your sentences from Part A to write a paragraph telling with whom you go to these places, what the places are like, and what you do when you are there.

Answers will vary.

Realidades A

Capítulo 4A

Test Preparation Answers

Reading Skills
p. 151 2. **B**
p. 152 2. **A**

Integrated Performance Assessment
p. 153
Answers will vary.

Practice Test: Aztec Games and Rituals
p. 155

1. D
2. H
3. B
4. H
5. Answers will vary but should draw on factual information from the article as well as from students' imagination.

Realidades 

Capítulo 4B

School-to-Home Connection

Dear Parent or Guardian,

The theme for the chapter is *Los pasatiempos* (Hobbies) and this chapter is called *¿Quieres ir conmigo?* (Do you want to go with me?).

Upon completion of this chapter, your child will be able to:

- talk about after-school activities
- extend, accept, and decline invitations
- tell when an event happens
- understand cultural perspectives on after-school activities

Also, your child will explore:

- the correct pronunciation of the letter *d*
- some Spanish words that are borrowed from English

Realidades helps with the development of reading, writing, and speaking skills through the use of strategies, process speaking, and process writing. In this chapter, students will:

- read about sports cards and information on two golfers
- write an invitation to a special event

Remember that additional help is available online at www.realidades.com by using the Web Codes in the Student Edition or in the Leveled Vocabulary and Grammar Workbook.

Check it out! Have your child write three sentences in Spanish about leisure activities or sports that he or she enjoys. Then ask him or her what each sentence means.

Sincerely,

For: Tips to Parents
Visit: www.realidades.com
Web Code: jce-0010

Realidades **A**

Capítulo 4B

Chapter Resource Checklist

Resources	CO†	APV	VH	MAN	LEC	PER	PE	MH	REP	PREP
Teacher										
Teacher's Resource Book										
Input Script										
Audio Script										
GramActiva BLM										
Communicative Activities BLM										
School-to-Home Connection BLM										
Clip Art										
Situation Cards BLM										
TPR Stories Book										
Fine Art Transparencies Teacher's Guide										
Pre-AP* Resource Book										
Student										
Leveled Vocabulary and Grammar Workbook										
Guided Practice										
Core Practice										
Communication Workbook with Test Preparation										
Writing										
Audio										
Video										
Test Preparation										
RPH Workbook										
Lecturas para hispanohablantes										
Grammar Study Guides										
Transparencies										
Answers on Transparencies										
Vocabulary and Grammar										
Fine Art										
Assessment										
Assessment Program										
Quizzes										
Chapter Test										
realidades.com										
ExamView Test Bank CD-ROM										
QuickTake on PresentationExpress										
MindPoint QuizShow CD-ROM										
Alternate Assessment Program										
Performance-Based Writing										
Self-Test on realidades.com & CWS										
Assessment Program RPH										
Technology										
realidades.com										
myeBook										
TeacherExpress CD-ROM										
PresentationExpress DVD										
Video Program DVD										
Culture Video DVD										
Audio Program CD 9										
Assessment CD 20										
Song CD 22										
Canciones de hip hop on realidades.com & CWS										

† *See Abbreviation Key on page iv.*

Input Script

Presentation

Input Vocabulary 1: Place the transparency on the screen. Announce to students *"Voy al Club Deportivo León este domingo. ¿Quieres ir conmigo?"* Read the text from *Club Deportivo León* to *Hay un deporte para ti.* Then point to each sport on the transparency and ask students if they play the sport *mucho, a veces,* or *nunca.* Ask if they are good or bad at each sport. Say *"Juego bien al fútbol. ¿Y tú? Juegas bien o mal al fútbol?"* Have students respond with a "thumbs-up" or "thumbs-down" sign. Then call out athletes' names and have students hold up the Clip Art image of each athlete's sport.

Input Dialogue 1: Bring to class the ball used in each sport of the *A primera vista.* Read the first five sentences of the dialogue, using gestures to convey the meanings of the sentences. Then ask one student *"¿Qué quieres hacer, jugar al fútbol o al vóleibol?"* and toss that student the soccer ball. Say *"No quiero jugar al fútbol...."* (encourage the student to throw the soccer ball back) *"... Prefiero jugar al vóleibol."* (Toss the student the volleyball.) Repeat with other students and other balls. You might coach students into saying the last two lines themselves. Then use the soccer ball to present the last two lines of the dialogue. Hand out the balls to students. Say *"¿Qué te gustaría hacer esta tarde? Me gustaría jugar al fútbol."* The student with the soccer ball will hold it up. Repeat, substituting other sports.

Input Vocabulary 2: Read each event. Then write two alternatives below each one. For example, under ***el concierto,*** write the name of a musician your students like and the name of a musician they definitely do *not* like. For ***la fiesta,*** write ***Cumpleaños del / de la Señor(a)*** ___ (the name of your principal) and ***Cumpleaños de*** ___ (the name of the musician your students like). For ***el baile,*** write ***polka*** and ***hip-hop.*** For ***el partido,*** write ***el fútbol americano*** and ***el fútbol.*** Then ask students if they would like to go to each event. Have students raise their hand when they do want to go to an event.

Input Dialogue 2: Have the following props ready before presenting the dialogue: a pile of textbooks, an empty fast-food restaurant bag, a thermometer, a flashlight, and a fishing hat, vest, or lure (with the barbs removed). Read through the dialogue, using the props to act out what each person says. Then repeat portions of the dialogue at random and pick up either the correct or an incorrect prop. Have students give a "thumbs-up" sign when you use the correct prop and "thumbs-down" when you use an incorrect prop.

Comprehension Check

- Take a survey of students' opinions about different sports. Ask them to show you the Clip Art image of the sport they think is ***interesante, aburrido, difícil, fácil, bueno para la salud,*** and so forth.
- Describe situations to students and have them tell if you are going to be busy, tired, or sick (for *sick,* you might say *"Voy a comer veinte perritos calientes.)"*
- Set up stations around the room and have students test their skill at putting a golf ball, shooting a basketball, and throwing a football. First, go around the room and have students sign up for each station by telling you *"Quiero jugar* ___*."* or *"Me gustaría jugar* ___*."* Give students a scorecard and let them each have three tries at each station. Then have each student report how he or she did by saying *"Juego bien al* ___*."* or *"Juego mal al* ___*."*

Realidades A

Capítulo 4B

Audio Script

Audio CD, Capítulo 4B

Track 01: *A primera vista,* Student Book, p. 240 (2:44)

¿Quieres ir conmigo?

Read along as you listen to the statements.

Club Deportivo León

Parque de la Independencia

¿Te gustan los deportes? ¡Puedes practicar con uno de nuestros expertos! ¿Juegas bien o juegas mal? ¡No importa! Hay un deporte para ti.

You will hear each word or phrase twice. After the first time there will be a pause so you can pronounce it, then you will hear the word or phrase a second time.

el fútbol
el vóleibol
el golf
el tenis
el béisbol
el básquetbol
el fútbol americano

Read along as you listen to the dialogue.

Male Teen: ¿Qué quieres hacer a las ocho de la mañana, jugar al fútbol o al vóleibol?

Female Teen: A ver ... No quiero jugar al fútbol. Juego muy mal. Prefiero jugar al vóleibol. Necesito practicar más. ¿Y qué te gustaría hacer a las cuatro esta tarde?

Male Teen: Me gustaría jugar al fútbol americano.

Track 02: *A primera vista,* Student Book, p. 241 (2:02)

You will hear each word or phrase twice. After the first time there will be a pause so you can pronounce it, then you will hear the word or phrase a second time.

el concierto
la fiesta
el baile
el partido

Read along as you listen to the dialogues.

Female Teen 1: ¡Hola! Soy Rosa. ¿Quieres hacer algo conmigo este fin de semana? Hay un concierto en el parque.

Male Teen: Lo siento, pero no puedo. Estoy demasiado ocupado y tengo mucha tarea.

Female Teen 2: No puedo porque tengo que trabajar. Trabajo esta noche a las siete y mañana trabajo a la una de la tarde. Voy a estar un poco cansada. ¡Ay! ¡Qué pena!

Female Teen 3: ¡Qué triste! No, no puedo ir contigo. Estoy un poco enferma.

Female Teen 4: ¡Qué buena idea! Pero no me gustan los conciertos. Prefiero ir de cámping. Siempre estoy muy contenta cuando voy de cámping ... ¿A qué hora es el concierto? ¿Mañana a las cinco de la tarde? Entonces, nos vemos.

Track 03: *A primera vista:* Act. 1, Student Book, p. 241 (1:46)

¡Deportemanía!

Marcela is a sports fanatic! As she lists the days on which she will play the various sports, touch the picture of each sport. You will hear each statement twice.

1. El lunes tengo que practicar el golf.
2. El martes hay un partido de básquetbol.
3. El miércoles juego al tenis con Lorenzo.
4. El jueves tengo que jugar al béisbol.
5. El viernes hay un partido de vóleibol.
6. El sábado tengo que jugar al fútbol.

Track 04: *A primera vista:* Act. 2, Student Book, p. 241 (1:32)

¿Cómo estás?

You will hear how five people are feeling. Act out the adjectives that you hear. You will hear each statement twice.

Female 1: ¡Uf! Estoy muy cansada.

Male 1: Lo siento pero estoy muy mal, muy enfermo.

Female 2: No tengo tarea esta noche. Estoy muy contenta.

Male 2: ¿La señora Sánchez no enseña la clase de español? Estoy triste.

Male 3: Tengo mucho que hacer. Estoy ocupado.

Track 05: *A primera vista: Videohistoria,* Student Book, pp. 242–244 (1:57)

¡A jugar!

Ignacio, Javier, Ana y Elena están en el Parque del Retiro en Madrid. ¿Qué van a jugar y hacer? ¿De qué hablan? Lee la historia.

Read along as you listen to the *Videohistoria.*

See Student Book pages 242–244 for script.

Track 06: *A primera vista:* Act. 10, Student Book, p. 248 (1:46)

Escucha y escribe

You will hear three invitations to events and the responses given. On a sheet of paper, write the numbers 1 to 3. As you listen, write down what each invitation is for and whether the person accepted it (write *sí*) or turned it down (write *no*). You will hear each dialogue twice.

1. **Male Teen 1:** ¿Puedes ir conmigo al baile esta noche?
   Female Teen 1: ¡Qué pena! Tengo que trabajar.

2. **Male Teen 2:** ¿Te gustaría ir conmigo al partido esta tarde?
   Female Teen 2: ¡Qué buena idea! Me gustaría mucho.

3. **Female Teen 3:** Voy a jugar al golf el domingo. ¿Quieres jugar?
   Male Teen 3: ¿Contigo? ¡Genial!

Track 07: Audio Act. 5, Writing, Audio & Video Workbook, p. 81 (3:03)

There are not enough hours in the day to do everything we want to do. Listen to the following interviews. What do these people want more time to do? In the blanks provided, write the number of the statement that corresponds to each picture. You will hear each set of statements twice.

1. Quiero más tiempo para ir a los conciertos con mis amigos. Me gustaría ir todos los viernes.
2. Quiero más tiempo para ir de pesca con mi amigo Carlos. ¡Me gustaría comer pescado!
3. Quiero más tiempo para ir de cámping con mis amigos. Es muy divertido.
4. Quiero más tiempo para ir a fiestas con mis amigos. Hay una fiesta en casa de Julia este fin de semana.
5. Quiero más tiempo para ir a los partidos de básquetbol. Me encanta este deporte.
6. Quiero más tiempo para leer en el parque. No me gusta leer en la biblioteca.
7. Quiero más tiempo para jugar al tenis. Juego muy mal ahora. Necesito practicar más.
8. Quiero más tiempo para ir a los bailes de la escuela. No sé bailar bien, pero me gustaría ir con mis amigos.

Track 08: Audio Act. 6, Writing, Audio & Video Workbook, p. 81 (4:08)

After listening to each of the following statements, decide if you think the excuses given are believable or unbelievable. Be prepared to defend your answers with a partner after making your decisions. You will hear each set of statements twice.

1. **Male Teen:** Me gustaría ir a la fiesta contigo, pero no puedo. Necesito estudiar los fines de semana. Soy un estudiante muy serio.
2. **Female Teen:** No puedo ir de compras. Estoy muy ocupada. Después de las clases juego al básquetbol en el gimnasio al lado del centro comercial todos los días.
3. **Female Teen:** Lo siento. No puedo ir de cámping este fin de semana. Tengo que escribir una novela.
4. **Male Teen:** Me gustaría ir al concierto contigo el sábado. ¿A qué hora? ¿A las nueve de la noche? Lo siento. Tengo que estar en casa a las nueve y media para estudiar.
5. **Female Teen:** Me gustaría ir contigo al cine, pero necesito ir a España este fin de semana.
6. **Male Teen:** ¡Qué buena idea! Un baile en el parque. Pero, ¿esta noche? No puedo. Tengo que ir al trabajo a las seis.
7. **Male Teen:** Lo siento. Estoy muy ocupado este fin de semana. Me gustaría ir al partido, pero no puedo. Tengo que practicar el piano para el concierto.
8. **Female Teen:** Me gustaría jugar al tenis contigo, pero estoy enferma. Me quedo en casa hoy.

Track 09: *Manos a la obra:* Act. 17, Student Book, p. 252 (2:17)

Escucha y escribe

Rosario and Pablo have left messages on your answering machine telling you what they are going to do and inviting you to join them. On a sheet of paper, write their names and, under each one, the numbers one to three. As you listen to each message, write down information to answer these three questions:

1. ¿Adónde quiere ir?
2. ¿Qué va a hacer?
3. ¿A qué hora va a ir?

You will hear each statement twice.

Female Teen: ¡Hola! Soy Rosario. ¿Qué pasa? Tomás y yo vamos a patinar esta tarde. ¿Te gustaría ir con nosotros? Vamos a estar en el parque a las cuatro. Hasta luego.

Male Teen: ¡Oye! ¿Cómo estás? Soy Pablo. ¿Puedes ir al gimnasio conmigo? No tengo que trabajar hoy. Muchos estudiantes van a jugar al vóleibol a las siete. Háblame por teléfono si puedes ir.

Track 10: *Pronunciación,* The letter *d*, Student Book, p. 254 (2:57)

In Spanish, the pronunciation of the letter *d* is determined by its location in a word. When *d* is at the beginning of a word, or when it comes after *l* or *n*, it sounds similar to the *d* in *dog*. Listen, then say these words.

You will hear each word twice. After the word is pronounced the first time, there will be a pause so you can pronounce it. Then you will hear the word a second time.

diccionario	calendario
domingo	donde
deportes	día
doce	bandera
desayuno	

When *d* comes between vowels and after any consonant except *l* or *n*, it sounds similar to the *th* of *the*. Listen, then say these words:

cansado	ensalada
idea	puedes
tarde	partido
ocupado	atrevido
sábado	

Try it out! Here is a tongue twister to give you practice in pronouncing the *d*, but also to give you something to think about!

Porque puedo, puedes,
Porque puedes, puedo;
Pero si no puedes,
Yo tampoco puedo.

Track 11: Audio Act. 7, Writing, Audio & Video Workbook, p. 82 (5:27)

Listen to the following couple as they try to decide what they are going to do tonight. Every time an activity is mentioned that one of the two people is going to do, draw

to do that activity, draw an *X* through the picture. The pictures with circles only should represent what both people finally decide to do. You will hear each conversation twice.

1. **Male:** Oye. ¿Adónde vas?
   Female: Pues, voy a un baile.
2. **Male:** No tengo interés en los bailes formales. No sé bailar bien. ¿Vas a hacer algo diferente?
3. **Female:** Claro que sí. Voy a un concierto. Hay uno en el parque esta noche.
   Male: ¿Un concierto en el parque? ¡Qué asco! Un concierto con los insectos. ¡Creo que no! ¿Quieres ir al partido de fútbol americano?
4. **Female:** ¿Esta noche? ¡No! Hace demasiado frío. Bueno. ¿Vas al centro comercial?
   Male: No voy a ir de compras, pero hay un cine en el centro comercial. ¿Vas al cine?
   Female: ¡Por supuesto! Vamos al centro comercial. Vamos a ir de compras y al cine. ¿Estás de acuerdo?
   Male: Sí, estoy de acuerdo.

Track 12: Audio Act. 8, Writing, Audio & Video Workbook, p. 82 (3:52)

Listen as a radio program host interviews a fitness expert, Doctora Benítez, about the best way to get in shape. Listen to the *entrevista* and choose the best answer to the questions below. You will hear this conversation twice.

Locutor: Bienvenidos. Me llamo Miguel Moto y estoy aquí con la doctora Benítez. Ella es experta en ejercicio y nutrición. Buenas tardes, doctora Benítez. Esta tarde en el programa, queremos saber cómo mantener la salud. ¿Qué debemos hacer?

Doctora Benítez: Bueno. Usted debe hacer ejercicio una hora todos los días. Está bien cuando usted camina con la familia, juega al fútbol, baila con una amiga, monta en bicicleta, levanta pesas. Hay muchas actividades buenas.

Locutor: ¡Una hora todos los días! No puedo hacer una hora de ejercicio. Es muy difícil, ¿no? Generalmente, yo estoy muy ocupado y demasiado cansado.

Doctora: En la primera semana, puede hacer quince minutos de ejercicio, nada más. Poco a poco, puede hacer más. No es difícil. Es divertido.

Locutor: Para mí es divertido comer pizza enfrente de la tele.

Doctora: No debe pasar más de dos horas enfrente de la computadora o del televisor. Usted debe jugar al básquetbol, no verlo en la tele.

Locutor: Me gustaría hacer más ejercicio, pero no sé practicar muchos deportes.

Doctora: ¿Usted sabe jugar al tenis o al básquetbol? ¡No tiene que jugar como Shaquille O'Neal! La dieta balanceada es muy importante también. Tiene que comer cereales, frutas y verduras, leche, y pescado o carne. No debe comer pasteles.

Locutor: Juego al golf … Bueno. Mañana voy a hacer ejercicio.

Doctora: Es fácil y muy divertido cuando uno juega con un amigo.

Locutor: Mis amigos y yo jugamos al béisbol mañana.

Doctora: Bien. Es importante jugar con un grupo.

Locutor: Gracias. Encantado de hablar con usted.

You are going to hear this conversation again.

Track 13: Audio Act. 9, Writing, Audio & Video Workbook, p. 83 (3:40)

Your Spanish teacher always encourages you to speak Spanish to your classmates outside of class. In order to do that, you and your friends agreed to talk on the phone and/or leave messages on each other's answering machines for at least a week. Listen to the messages your friends have left on your answering machine today. Based on the messages, decide a) where the person wants to go; b) what the person wants to do; c) what time the person wants to go. Use the chart below to record the information. You will hear each set of statements twice.

1. **Male Teen 1:** Hola. Habla Justo. ¿Quieres ir conmigo al parque esta noche? Vamos a escuchar un concierto a las siete. ¿Nos vemos?
2. **Female Teen 1:** Oye. Soy yo, Eva. ¿Te gustaría ir de compras esta tarde conmigo? Vamos al centro comercial a las cinco. ¿De acuerdo?
3. **Male Teen 2:** ¿Dónde estás? ¿En la biblioteca? ¡Tú estudias demasiado, chica! Soy yo, José. ¿Puedes ir a una fiesta esta noche a las ocho? Vamos a comer pizza y ver un video. ¿Quieres ir con nosotros?
4. **Female Teen 2:** Oye. Habla Margarita. ¿Quieres ir de cámping con mi familia este fin de semana? Vamos de pesca y a caminar en las montañas. Vamos el sábado a las seis de la mañana.
5. **Male Teen 3:** Hola. Soy Pedro. ¿Quieres jugar al básquetbol esta tarde en el gimnasio? Voy a las cinco y media. Creo que Chucho y Andrés van a jugar también.

Track 14: *Repaso del capítulo*, Student Book, p. 266 (4:41)

Listen to these words and expressions that you have learned in this chapter. You will hear each word or expression once.

See Student Book page 266 for vocabulary list.

Track 15: Preparación para el examen, Student Book, p. 267 (0:54)

Escuchar
Practice task.
On your answering machine, you hear your friend asking if you can go somewhere with her this weekend. Based on her message, try to tell a) where she is going, b) what she is going to do, and c) what time she wants to go.

Female Teen: "Hola Toni, soy Susi. Oye. Yo voy al centro comercial después de las clases a las cuatro de la tarde. ¿Te gustaría ir conmigo? Voy a comprar algo para un amigo."

Video Script

A primera vista: *¡A jugar!* (5:23)

Ignacio: ¡Hola! ¿Qué tal?
Javier: Muy bien. Hola, Elena. Hola, Ana.
Girls: Hola, Javier.
Javier: Vamos a jugar al fútbol, ¿no?
Ignacio: Juegas muy bien.
Javier: Pues, sí, pero necesito practicar más. Elena, ¿quieres jugar?
Elena: Vale … pero no juego muy bien.
Javier: ¿Ana?
Ana: Sí, vamos a jugar.
Javier: Oye, Ana, eres muy buena. ¿Puedes jugar mañana?
Ana: Me gustaria, pero no puedo. Mañana juego al tenis con mis primos.
Javier: Bueno, ¿qué tal después de jugar al tenis?
Ana: De verdad, me gustaría, pero voy a estar demasiado ocupada.
Javier: ¡Qué pena!
Elena: Bueno, yo también estoy muy cansada y tengo mucha sed. ¿Por qué no tomamos un refresco?
Ignacio: ¡Qué buena idea!
Elena: ¡Qué deliciosa!
Ana: ¿Juegas esta tarde al vóleibol?
Elena: Sí, a las seis.
Javier: ¿Sabes jugar también al vóleibol?
Elena: … Sí.
Ana: Sí. Elena juega muy bien al vóleibol.
Ignacio: El vóleibol … no sé. Prefiero otros deportes, como el fútbol.
Elena: Ay, Ignacio, por favor.
Ana: Ay, Ignacio. Siempre el fútbol.
Ignacio: No, también me gusta ir de pesca.
Ignacio: Ah, y las fiestas. Me encantan las fiestas.
Ignacio: Oye, esta noche hay una fiesta. Nosotros vamos a ir. ¿Quieres ir a la fiesta con nosotros?
Elena: ¡Ignacio, qué buena idea!
Javier: ¿A qué hora es la fiesta?
Ana: A las nueve de la noche. En la escuela.
Javier: ¿Tengo que bailar?
Ana: Pues, sí. Puedes bailar conmigo y con Elena.
Javier: Lo siento. No sé bailar bien.
Ignacio: Yo tampoco sé bailar, pero las fiestas son divertidas.
Ana: ¡Vamos, Javier!
Javier: Bien, voy.
Ana: Sí, a las nueve.
Elena: La fiesta va a ser muy divertida. Vamos a bailar y a cantar. Y la comida va a ser deliciosa. Voy a preparar un pastel fabuloso.
Javier: Hasta las nueve entonces.
Ignacio: ¡Bien! Hasta más tarde.
Todos: ¡Adiós!

GramActiva Videos: *ir* + *a* + infinitive; the verb *jugar* **(3:57)**

***Ir + a* + infinitive**

Host: Once upon a time we talked about going to class and going to the park.
We used the verb *ir*, which means "to go."
Host: In the very beginning we talked about infinitives, verbs in their purest forms.
Host: Today we're putting them together to make a whole new sentence called the "going to do something sentence"!
Foreman: We'll be taking some of the verb *ir* and joining it in sentences to some infinitives. You might have seen infinitives around and wondered what you use them for … well this is it. The important thing to remember here is that to stick them together with *ir* you're going to need an *a*.
Host: A what?
Foreman: An *a*. Look at this.
Host: *Yo* means "I."
Host: *Yo voy a* means "I am going to."
Host: *Yo voy a comer en el restaurante* means "I go to eat in the restaurant."
Host: *Ella* means "she."
Ella va a means "she is going to."
Ella va a leer un libro means "she is going to read a book."

Quiz

Host: Got it all? Then how about this!
Use what you just learned to complete these sentences.
Host: (going to) Los estudiantes _________ dibujar.
Los estudiantes van a dibujar.
(going to) Yo _________ usar la computadora.
Yo voy a usar la computadora.

The verb *jugar*

Host: We've talked about a lot of different verbs so far. There are three categories of regular verbs: they are *-ar*, *-er*, and *-ir* verbs. There are also a whole host of irregular verbs. The irregular verbs we've studied have a variety of conjugation rules, but today we're going to look at *jugar*, which not only has a new rule, but a new type of rule.
Host: *Jugar* is the first verb we're looking at that is in a category called stem-changing verbs. That means the stem will change.
Host: As you can see, right up front the *yo* form of *jugar* has an added *e*. In fact the *u* in the stem changes to *-ue-*. *Yo juego*. The *-ue-* is in all but the *nosotros* and *vosotros* forms. *Tú juegas*, *usted juega*, and *ellas juegan*. Notice, though, that in every other way it's just like other *-ar* verbs.

Host: It might help you to remember your boots. If you look at a standard conjugation for a stem-changing verb, the forms with stems that change form the shape of a boot. Sometimes they are called "boot" verbs.
Hero: To quizzes and beyond!

Quiz
Host: Quiz yourself on the forms of *jugar.*

Yo juego.
Tú juegas.
Usted juega.
Nosotras jugamos.
Ellas juegan.

Nombre ______________________

Fecha ______________________

Communicative Activity **4B-1**

Estudiante **A**

Your partner would like to do some activities with you but you already have a busy week. Listen to your partner's questions and tell him or her if you can or cannot do certain activities based on your schedule below. Start your response with one of the following phrases:

Sí, me gustaría ... *No. Lo siento. Voy a ...*

Record the time and activity of the things you have planned with your partner in the calendar below.

el lunes	el martes	el miércoles	el jueves	el viernes	el sábado	el domingo
7:00 de la mañana ir de pesca		9:00 de la mañana jugar al vóleibol		5:00 de la tarde jugar al tenis	8:30 de la noche ir a la fiesta	
12:30 de la tarde jugar al básquetbol						

Now, you would like to do some activities with your partner next week, but he or she already has a busy week planned. Ask your partner the questions below to find out what activities you can do together.

1. Este sábado, ¿te gustaría jugar al fútbol a las seis de la tarde?
2. Este martes, ¿te gustaría jugar al tenis a las nueve y media de la mañana?
3. Este lunes, ¿te gustaría jugar al golf a las siete de la mañana?
4. Este miércoles, ¿te gustaría jugar al béisbol a las diez de la mañana?
5. Este jueves, ¿te gustaría ir al partido a las nueve de la mañana?
6. Este jueves, ¿te gustaría jugar al vóleibol a las seis y media de la tarde?
7. Este viernes, ¿te gustaría ir al baile a las nueve de la noche?
8. Este sábado, ¿te gustaría jugar al fútbol americano a las ocho y media de la noche?

Nombre ______________________

Fecha ______________________

You would like to do some activities with your partner this week but he or she already has a busy week. Ask your partner the questions below to find out what you can do together.

1. Este miércoles, ¿te gustaría ir de cámping a las nueve de la mañana?
2. Este martes, ¿te gustaría ir al partido a las ocho de la mañana?
3. Este jueves, ¿te gustaría jugar al béisbol a las diez de la mañana?
4. Este lunes, ¿te gustaría jugar al golf a las siete de la mañana?
5. Este jueves, ¿te gustaría ir al concierto a las tres y media de la tarde?
6. Este viernes, ¿te gustaría jugar al fútbol a las cinco de la tarde?
7. Este viernes, ¿te gustaría jugar al fútbol americano a las diez de la mañana?
8. Este domingo, ¿te gustaría ir al baile a las diez de la noche?

Now, your partner would like to do some activities with you next week but you already have a busy week planned. Listen to your partner's questions and tell him or her if you can or cannot do certain activities based on your schedule below. Start your response with one of the following phrases:

Sí, me gustaría ... *No. Lo siento. Voy a ...*

Record the time and activity of the things you have planned with your partner in the calendar below.

el lunes	el martes	el miércoles	el jueves	el viernes	el sábado	el domingo
	9:30 de la mañana ir de cámping			3:30 de la tarde ir de pesca	8:00 de la noche ir a la fiesta	8:00 de la noche ir al concierto
			1:30 de la tarde jugar al básquetbol			

Nombre ______________________

Fecha ______________________

You and your friends are not playing sports today. Using the chart below, do the following: (1) Think about a sport you cannot play today and complete the boxes marked *yo*. (2) Ask your partner about what sport he or she is not playing today, when, and for a reason why not. Then complete the boxes marked *mi compañero(a)*. (3) Ask your partner what sports your friends are not playing, when, and why not. Follow the model:

¿Qué deporte no practica?

¿A qué hora no juega al vóleibol?

¿De la mañana, de la tarde o de la noche?

¿Por qué no juega al vóleibol?

	¿Qué deporte no practica?	**¿A qué hora?**	**¿Cuándo?**	**¿Por qué no?**
yo				
mi compañero(a)				
Rosario				
Felipe		3:30		ocupado
Anita y Carlos				

Nombre ______________________________

Fecha ______________________________

You and your friends are not playing sports today. Using the chart below, do the following: (1) Think about a sport you cannot play today and complete the boxes marked *yo.* (2) Ask your partner about what sport he or she is not playing today, when, and for a reason why not. Then complete the boxes marked *mi compañero(a).* (3) Ask your partner what sports your friends are not playing, when, and why not. Follow the model:

¿Qué deporte no practica?

¿A qué hora no juega al vóleibol?

¿De la mañana, de la tarde o de la noche?

¿Por qué no juega al vóleibol?

	¿Qué deporte no practica?	**¿A qué hora?**	**¿Cuándo?**	**¿Por qué no?**
yo				
mi compañero(a)				
Rosario		10:00		enferma
Felipe				
Anita y Carlos		8:30		cansados

Situation Cards

Capítulo 4B Realidades A **1A**

Describing leisure activities

You and a new friend are talking about what you do in your free time.

— Greet your new friend.

— Ask your friend what he or she does outside of school.

— Respond to your friend's question and then ask if he or she plays sports.

— Respond to your friend's feeling about a certain sport by agreeing or disagreeing with him or her.

Capítulo 4B Realidades A **1B**

Describing leisure activities

You and a new friend are talking about what you do in your free time.

— Greet your new friend.

— Respond to your friend's question and then ask if he or she plays sports.

— Answer your friend's question and say how a certain sport makes you feel.

Capítulo 4B Realidades A **2A**

Dealing with invitations

You are inviting a friend to go somewhere with you.

— Greet your friend.

— Ask your friend to go to a certain event with you.

— Respond to your friend's question.

— React to your friend's answer.

— Say good-bye.

Capítulo 4B Realidades A **2B**

Dealing with invitations

Your friend is inviting you to go somewhere.

— Greet your friend.

— Ask your friend the day and time of the event.

— Tell your friend why you can or cannot go to the event with him or her.

— Respond to your friend's reaction to your accepting or declining to go.

— Say good-bye.

GramActiva

¿Quieres ir conmigo?

¿Qué vas a hacer?, p. 254

¿Qué?	¿Cuándo?	¿Con quién?

Realidades A

Capítulo 4B

Vocabulary Clip Art

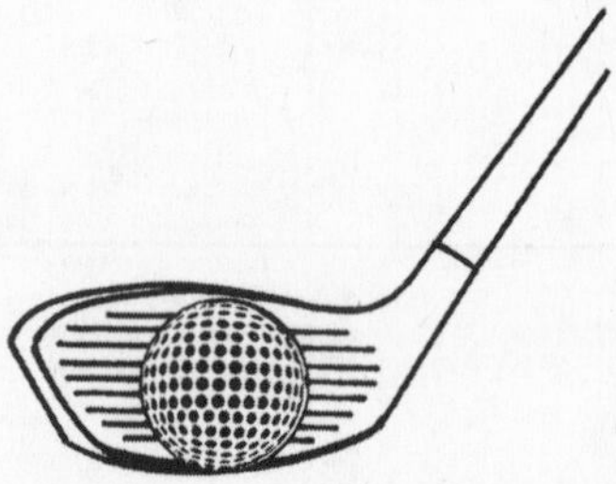

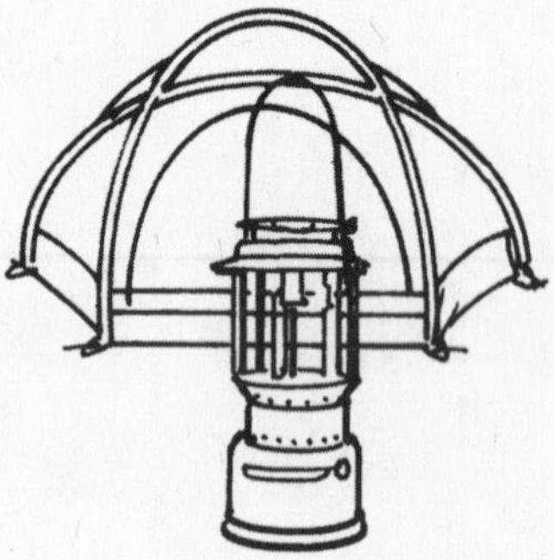

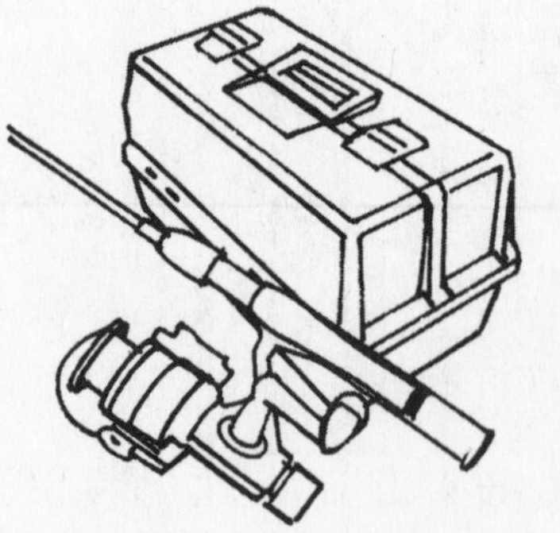

Vocabulary Clip Art

Core Practice Answers

4B-1
1. jugar al tenis (el tenis)
2. jugar al vóleibol (el vóleibol)
3. jugar al básquetbol (el básquetbol)
4. jugar al fútbol americano (el fútbol americano)
5. jugar al golf (el golf)
6. jugar al béisbol (el béisbol)
7. jugar al fútbol (el fútbol)
8. ir de cámping
9. ir de pesca

4B-2
1. —ir de compras
   —Sí, puedo ir de compras
2. —jugar al básquetbol
   —Sí, quiero jugar al básquetbol
3. —ir al restaurante
   —Sí, puedo ir al restaurante
4. —ir a la playa
   —Sí, me gustaría ir a la playa
5. —jugar al tenis
   —Sí, quiero jugar al tenis

4B-3
1. Está enferma
2. Está ocupado
3. Están contentos
4. Están cansadas
5. Están tristes
6. Está cansado

4B-4
1. Lucía tiene que trabajar a la una.
2. Va a casa a las seis de la tarde.
3. Lucía y su amiga corren a las ocho de la mañana.
4. Come la cena a las seis y media de la tarde.
5. Estudian a las diez y cuarto de la mañana.
6. Va al cine esta noche a las nueve y cuarto.

4B-5
1. Ana y yo vamos a estudiar esta noche.
2. Pablo va a jugar videojuegos esta noche.
3. Yo voy a tocar el piano esta tarde.
4. Mis amigos van a correr esta tarde.
5. Tú vas a usar la computadora esta noche.
6. Nosotros vamos a ver una película esta noche.
7. Ud. va a comer el almuerzo esta tarde.
8. Ana y Lorena van a jugar al béisbol esta noche.

4B-6
Answers will vary.
1. No, no quiero. Voy a estar cansado(a)
2. No, no me gustaría. Voy a ir al centro comercial
3. No, no quiero. Voy a jugar al tenis
4. No, no puedo. Voy a ir al templo el viernes
5. No, no me gustaría. Voy a esquiar
6. No, no me gustaría. Voy a ver una película
7. No, no quiero. Voy a comer el almuerzo
8. No, no puedo. Voy a estar ocupado(a)

4B-7
1. juegan
2. juego
3. jugamos
4. juegan
5. Juega
6. Juego
7. Jugamos
8. juega

Crucigrama (4B-8)
Across:
3. demasiado
4. triste
5. fútbol
7. partido
9. sabes
10. siento
12. americano
15. cansado
17. baile
19. genial
20. concierto
21. conmigo

Down:
1. fiesta
2. vóleibol
6. tarde
7. pesca
8. fin
11. ocupada
13. cámping
14. noche
16. oye
17. béisbol
18. mañana

Organizer (4B-9)
I. Vocabulary Answers will vary.
II. Grammar
1.

col. 1.	**col. 2.**
juego	jugamos
juegas	jugáis
juega	juegan

2. conmigo / contigo
3. ir / a

Realidades A

Capítulo 4B

Nombre ______ Hora ______

Fecha ______

Vocabulary Practice, Sheet 1

Write the Spanish vocabulary word below each picture. If there is a word or phrase, copy it in the space provided. Be sure to include the article for each noun.

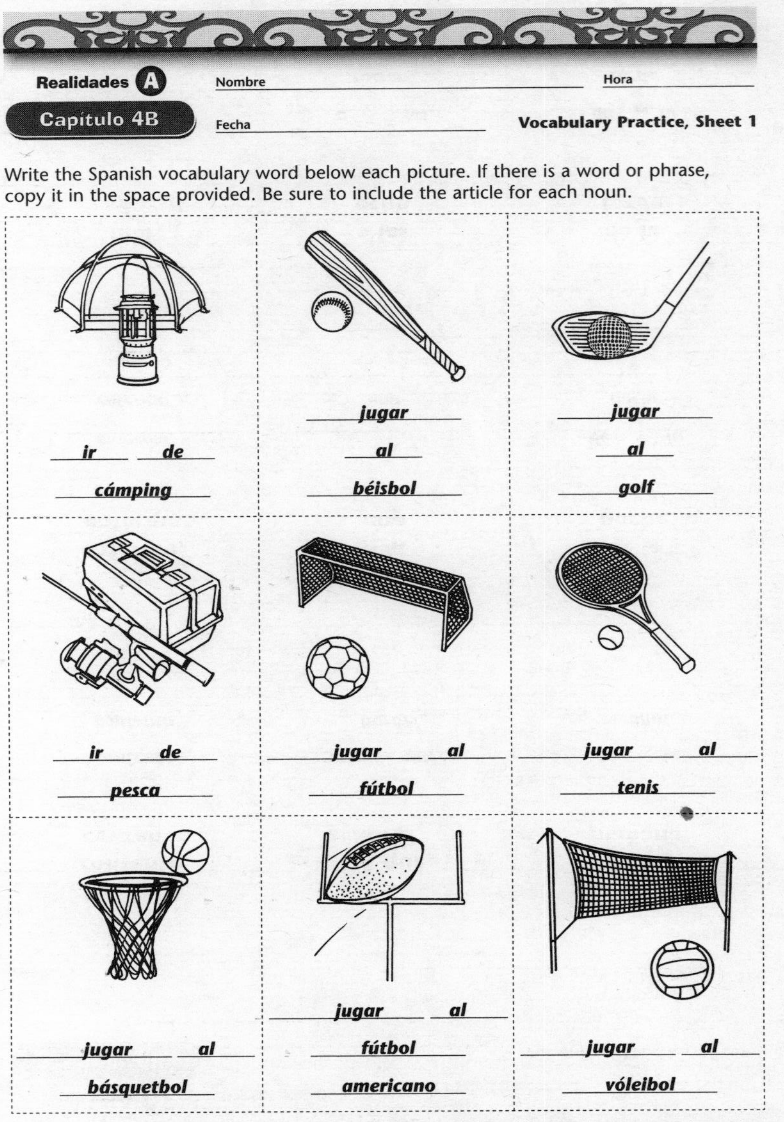

Realidades A

Capítulo 4B

Nombre ______ Hora ______

Fecha ______

Vocabulary Practice, Sheet 2

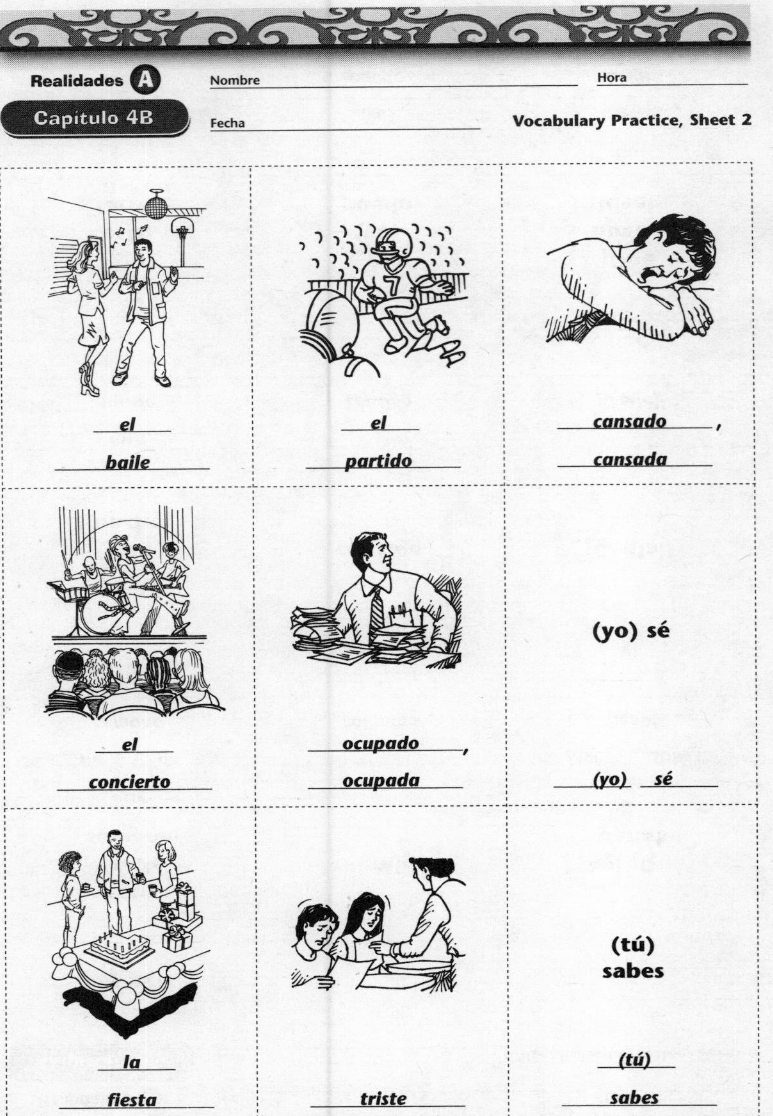

Realidades A — Nombre ______ Hora ______

Capítulo 4B — Fecha ______

Vocabulary Practice, Sheet 3

contento, contenta *contento*, *contenta*	**¿A qué hora?** *¿A* *qué* *hora?*	**de la mañana** *de* *la* *mañana*
enfermo, enferma *enfermo*, *enferma*	**a la una** *a* *la* *una*	**de la noche** *de* *la* *noche*
mal *mal*	**a las ocho** *a* *las* *ocho*	**de la tarde** *de* *la* *tarde*

Realidades A — Nombre ______ Hora ______

Capítulo 4B — Fecha ______

Vocabulary Practice, Sheet 4

este fin de semana *este* *fin* *de* *semana*	**conmigo** *conmigo*	**¡Ay! ¡Qué pena!** *¡Ay!* *¡Qué* *pena!*
esta noche *esta* *noche*	**contigo** *contigo*	**¡Genial!** *¡Genial!*
esta tarde *esta* *tarde*	**(yo) puedo** *(yo)* *puedo*	**¡Qué buena idea!** *¡Qué* *buena* *idea!*

Realidades A Nombre Hora

Capítulo 4B Fecha **Vocabulary Practice, Sheet 5**

¡Oye! ***¡Oye!***	**¿Te gustaría?** ***¿Te gustaría?***	**demasiado** ***demasiado***
lo siento ***lo siento***	**me gustaría** ***me gustaría***	**entonces** ***entonces***
(yo) quiero ***(yo) quiero***	**Tengo que...** ***Tengo que...***	**un poco (de)** ***un poco (de)***

Realidades A Nombre Hora

Capítulo 4B Fecha **Vocabulary Practice, Sheet 6**

(tú) puedes ***(tú) puedes***	**(tú) quieres** ***(tú) quieres***	**ir a + *infinitive*** ***ir a + infinitive***

Realidades A — Capítulo 4B

Nombre ______ Hora ______

Fecha ______ **Vocabulary Check, Sheet 1**

Tear out this page. Write the English words on the lines. Fold the paper along the dotted line to see the correct answers so you can check your work.

el baile	***dance***
el concierto	***concert***
la fiesta	***party***
el partido	***game, match***
ir de cámping	***to go camping***
ir de pesca	***to go fishing***
jugar al básquetbol	***to play basketball***
jugar al béisbol	***to play baseball***
jugar al fútbol	***to play soccer***
jugar al fútbol americano	***to play football***
jugar al golf	***to play golf***
jugar al tenis	***to play tennis***
jugar al vóleibol	***to play volleyball***
cansado, cansada	***tired***
contento, contenta	***happy***

Fold In

Realidades A — Capítulo 4B

Nombre ______ Hora ______

Fecha ______ **Vocabulary Check, Sheet 2**

Tear out this page. Write the Spanish words on the lines. Fold the paper along the dotted line to see the correct answers so you can check your work.

dance	***el baile***
concert	***el concierto***
party	***la fiesta***
game, match	***el partido***
to go camping	***ir de cámping***
to go fishing	***ir de pesca***
to play basketball	***jugar al básquetbol***
to play baseball	***jugar al béisbol***
to play soccer	***jugar al fútbol***
to play football	***jugar al fútbol americano***
to play golf	***jugar al golf***
to play tennis	***jugar al tenis***
to play volleyball	***jugar al vóleibol***
tired	***cansado, cansada***
happy	***contento, contenta***

Fold In

Realidades A — Nombre ______ Hora ______

Capítulo 4B — Fecha ______

Vocabulary Check, Sheet 3

Tear out this page. Write the English words on the lines. Fold the paper along the dotted line to see the correct answers so you can check your work.

enfermo, enferma	***sick***
ocupado, ocupada	***busy***
triste	***sad***
a la una	***at one (o'clock)***
de la mañana	***in the morning***
de la noche	***in the evening, at night***
de la tarde	***in the afternoon***
este fin de semana	***this weekend***
esta noche	***this evening***
esta tarde	***this afternoon***
¡Ay! ¡Qué pena!	***Oh! What a shame!***
¡Genial!	***Great!***
lo siento	***I'm sorry***
¡Qué buena idea!	***What a good idea!***

Fold In

Realidades A — Nombre ______ Hora ______

Capítulo 4B — Fecha ______

Vocabulary Check, Sheet 4

Tear out this page. Write the Spanish words on the lines. Fold the paper along the dotted line to see the correct answers so you can check your work.

sick	***enfermo, enferma***
busy	***ocupado, ocupada***
sad	***triste***
at one (o'clock)	***a la una***
in the morning	***de la mañana***
in the evening, at night	***de la noche***
in the afternoon	***de la tarde***
this weekend	***este fin de semana***
this evening	***esta noche***
this afternoon	***esta tarde***
Oh! What a shame!	***¡Ay! ¡Qué pena!***
Great!	***¡Genial!***
I'm sorry	***lo siento***
What a good idea!	***¡Qué buena idea!***

Fold In

To hear a complete list of the vocabulary for this chapter, go to www.realidades.com and type in the Web Code jcd-0499. Then click on **Repaso del capítulo.**

Realidades A Nombre ______ Hora ______

Capítulo 4B Fecha ______ **Guided Practice Activities 4B-1**

Ir + *a* + infinitive (p. 252)

- You have already learned to use the verb **ir** (*to go*). To review, here are its forms, which are irregular.

yo	voy	nosotros/nosotras	vamos
tú	vas	vosotros/vosotras	vais
usted/él/ella	va	ustedes/ellos/ellas	van

- As you have learned, the infinitive is the basic form of the verb (**hablar, comer, leer,** etc.). It is equivalent to "to . . ." in English: *to talk, to eat, to read.*
- When you use **ir** + a with an infinitive, it means you or others are *going to do something* in the future. It is the same as "I am going to . . ." in English: **Voy a leer el libro. Vamos a ver la película.**

A. Review by writing the correct form of **ir** next to each subject pronoun.

1. tú ***vas***
2. ellos ***van***
3. él ***va***
4. usted ***va***
5. ella ***va***
6. yo ***voy***
7. ustedes ***van***
8. nosotras ***vamos***

B. Now complete each sentence with the correct form of **ir**.

1. Marta y Rosa ***van*** a estudiar esta tarde.
2. Yo ***voy*** a jugar al tenis esta tarde.
3. Tú ***vas*** a montar en monopatín mañana.
4. Nosotras ***vamos*** a bailar mañana.
5. Ustedes ***van*** a correr esta tarde.
6. Serena ***va*** a ir de cámping mañana.

C. Complete the exchanges with the correct form of **ir**.

1. LAURA: ¿Qué ***vas*** a hacer este fin de semana?
   CARLOS: Yo ***voy*** a jugar al golf.
2. ANA: ¿Qué ***van*** a hacer ustedes mañana?
   TOMÁS: Nosotros ***vamos*** a trabajar.
3. ERNESTO: ¿Qué ***va*** a hacer Susana hoy?
   RICARDO: Ella y yo ***vamos*** a ir al cine.

realidades.com • Web Code: jcd-0413

Realidades A Nombre ______ Hora ______

Capítulo 4B Fecha ______ **Guided Practice Activities 4B-2**

Ir + *a* + infinitive *(continued)*

D. Write questions with **ir** + **a** + **hacer**. Follow the models.

Modelos (tú) / hacer hoy
¿Qué *vas a hacer hoy* ?
(ellos) / hacer este fin de semana
¿Qué *van a hacer este fin de semana* ?

1. yo / hacer esta tarde
   ¿Qué ***voy a hacer esta tarde***?
2. nosotros / hacer mañana
   ¿Qué ***vamos a hacer mañana***?
3. ustedes / hacer hoy
   ¿Qué ***van a hacer hoy***?
4. tú / hacer este fin de semana
   ¿Qué ***vas a hacer este fin de semana***?
5. ella / hacer esta mañana
   ¿Qué ***va a hacer esta mañana***?

E. Write sentences to say what the people shown are going to do tomorrow. Follow the model.

Modelo Roberto
Roberto va a jugar al béisbol.

1. Ana
   Ana va a correr.
2. Juan y José
   Juan y José van a jugar al tenis.
3. tú
   Vas a esquiar.
4. yo
   Voy a jugar videojuegos.

realidades.com • Web Code: jcd-0413

Realidades A | Nombre | Hora

Capítulo 4B | Fecha | **Guided Practice Activities 4B-3**

The verb *jugar* (p. 256)

- **Jugar** (*to play a sport or game*) uses the regular **-ar** present tense endings.
- However, **jugar** does not use the same stem in all its forms. **Jugar** is a *stem-changing verb*. In most forms, it uses **jueg-** + the **-ar** endings. But in the **nosotros/nosotras, vosotros/vosotras** forms, it uses **jug-** + the **-ar** endings.
- Here are the forms of **jugar:**

yo	**juego**	nosotros/nosotras	**jugamos**
tú	**juegas**	vosotros/vosotras	**jugáis**
usted/él/ella	**juega**	ustedes/ellos/ellas	**juegan**

A. Circle the forms of **jugar** in each sentence. Underline the stem in each form of **jugar**.

1. Yo (juego) al tenis este fin de semana.
2. Ellos (juegan) al básquetbol esta noche.
3. Nosotros (jugamos) videojuegos mañana.
4. Ustedes (juegan) al golf este fin de semana.
5. Tú y yo (jugamos) al béisbol esta tarde.
6. Tú (juegas) al fútbol americano este fin de semana.
7. Ella (juega) al fútbol esta tarde.
8. Nosotras (jugamos) al vóleibol hoy.

B. Now, write the forms of **jugar** you circled in **part A**. Put them in the corresponding rows of the table. The first one has been done for you.

Subject pronoun	Form of *jugar*
1. yo	*juego*
2. ellos	***juegan***
3. nosotros	***jugamos***
4. ustedes	***juegan***
5. tú y yo	***jugamos***
6. tú	***juegas***
7. ella	***juega***
8. nosotras	***jugamos***

realidades.com
• Web Code: jcd-0414

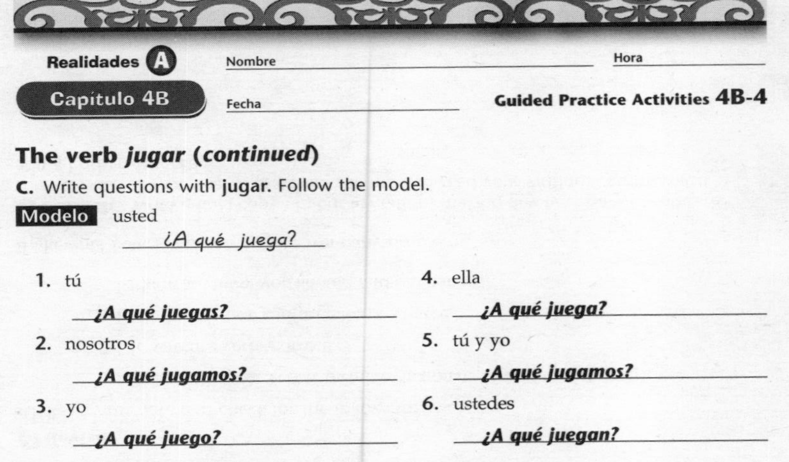

Realidades A | Nombre | Hora

Capítulo 4B | Fecha | **Guided Practice Activities 4B-4**

The verb *jugar* (*continued*)

C. Write questions with **jugar**. Follow the model.

Modelo usted
¿A qué juega?

1. tú
   ¿A qué juegas?
2. nosotros
   ¿A qué jugamos?
3. yo
   ¿A qué juego?
4. ella
   ¿A qué juega?
5. tú y yo
   ¿A qué jugamos?
6. ustedes
   ¿A qué juegan?

D. Now write sentences to say what people are playing. Follow the model.

Modelo Eduardo
Eduardo juega al fútbol.

1. Rosa y Ana
   Rosa y Ana juegan al vóleibol.

2.  nosotros
   Nosotros jugamos al béisbol.

3.  yo
   Yo juego al tenis.

4.  tú
   Tú juegas al básquetbol.

5.  ustedes
   Ustedes juegan al fútbol americano.

realidades.com
• Web Code: jcd-0414

Realidades A — Nombre ______ Hora ______

Capítulo 4B — Fecha ______ **Guided Practice Activities 4B-5**

Lectura: Sergio y Lorena: El futuro de golf (pp. 260–261)

A. A list of personal information is given about each golfer in your textbook reading. Below are several of the categories for each piece of information. Write what you think is the English word for each category below.

1. Nombre — ***name***
2. Fecha de nacimiento — ***date of birth***
3. Lugar de nacimiento — ***place of birth***
4. Su objetivo — ***their objective***
5. Profesional — ***professional***
6. Universidad — ***university***

B. Look at the list of **aficiones** (*interests*) for each golfer below. Then, answer the questions that follow.

SERGIO: Real Madrid, tenis, fútbol, videojuegos

LORENA: básquetbol, tenis, bicicleta de montaña, correr, nadar, comida italiana

1. What one interest do both golfers share? ***tennis***
2. What interest does Sergio have that is not a sport? ***videogames***
3. What interest does Lorena have that is not a sport? ***Italian food***

C. Look at the following sentences from the reading. Circle **S** if they are about Sergio and **L** if they are about Lorena.

1. (S) L Juega para el Club de Campo del Mediterráneo en Borriol.
2. S (L) Es la mejor golfista de México.
3. (S) L Su padre Víctor es golfista profesional.
4. (S) L Juega el golf desde la edad de tres años.
5. S (L) Quiere ser la golfista número uno.
6. (S) L A la edad de 17 años gana su primer torneo de profesionales.

D. Now, answer the questions about the two golfers from the reading. Write in either **Lorena**, **Sergio**, or **both** depending on the best answer.

1. Who was born in 1980? ***Sergio***
2. Who is from Spain? ***Sergio***
3. Who likes soccer? ***Sergio***
4. Who likes tennis? ***both***
5. Who went to the University of Arizona? ***Lorena***
6. Who wants to be the best golfer in the world? ***both***

realidades.com • Web Code: jcd-0415

Realidades A — Nombre ______ Hora ______

Capítulo 4B — Fecha ______ **Guided Practice Activities 4B-6**

Presentación escrita (p. 263) ***Answers will vary.***

Task: Pretend you want to invite a friend to an upcoming special event on your calendar. You will need to write one invitation to that friend and anyone else you want to invite.

1 Prewrite. Think about what event you want to attend. Fill in the information below about the event.

Name of event: ______

When (day and time): ______

Where: ______

Who is going: ______

2 Draft. Use the information from **step 1** to write a first draft of your invitation on a separate sheet of paper. See below for a model.

> *¡Hola amigos!*
> *Quiero invitarlos a una noche de baile caribeño en la sala de reuniones de la iglesia. La fiesta va a ser de las siete de la tarde hasta las once de la noche, el viernes, el cinco de mayo.*
> *Quiero verlos a todos ustedes allí.*
> *Su amiga,*
> *Melisa*

3 Revise.

A. Read your note and check for the following:

_____ Is the spelling correct? (Consult a dictionary if you are not sure.)

_____ Did you use verbs correctly?

_____ Is all the necessary information included?

_____ Is there anything you should add or change?

B. Rewrite your invitation if there were any problems.

4 Publish. Write a final copy of your invitation, making any necessary changes. Be sure to write or type neatly, as others will need to read your writing. You may also add a border decoration.

Realidades A — Capítulo 4B

Nombre ______ Hora ______

Fecha ______ VIDEO

Antes de ver el video

Actividad 1

Think of activities you like to do. Here is a list of six activities. Rank them in order from your favorite to your least favorite, with 1 as your favorite and 6 as your least favorite.

Answers will vary.

_____ ir a bailar

_____ nadar

_____ estudiar en la biblioteca

_____ ir al cine a ver películas

_____ montar en bicicleta

_____ ir de compras al centro comercial

¿Comprendes?

Actividad 2

Ignacio, Javier, Elena, and Ana are playing soccer at the park. Who makes each statement? Write the name of the person who says each item on the line.

1. "Mañana juego al tenis con mis primos." **Ana**
2. "Yo también estoy muy cansada y tengo mucha sed." **Elena**
3. "Prefiero otros deportes, como el fútbol." **Ignacio**
4. "¿Sabes jugar también al vóleibol?" **Javier**
5. "También me gusta ir de pesca." **Ignacio**
6. "Puedes bailar conmigo..." **Ana**
7. "Lo siento. No sé bailar bien." **Javier**
8. "Voy a preparar un pastel fabuloso." **Elena**

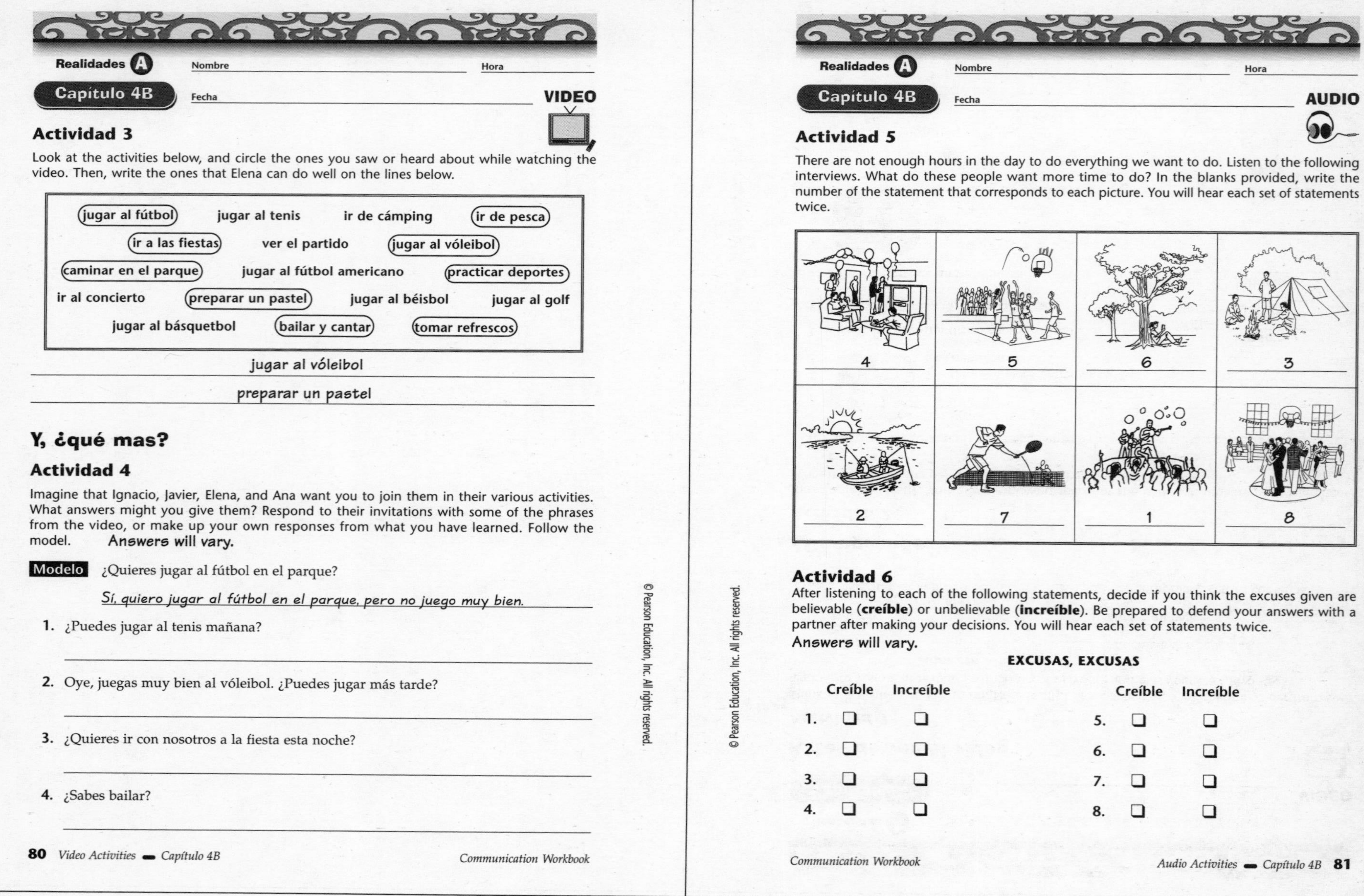

Realidades A | Nombre | Hora

Capítulo 4B | Fecha | **VIDEO**

Actividad 3

Look at the activities below, and circle the ones you saw or heard about while watching the video. Then, write the ones that Elena can do well on the lines below.

(jugar al fútbol)	jugar al tenis	ir de cámping	(ir de pesca)
(ir a las fiestas)	ver el partido	(jugar al vóleibol)	
(caminar en el parque)	jugar al fútbol americano	(practicar deportes)	
ir al concierto	(preparar un pastel)	jugar al béisbol	jugar al golf
jugar al básquetbol	(bailar y cantar)	(tomar refrescos)	

jugar al vóleibol

preparar un pastel

Y, ¿qué mas?

Actividad 4

Imagine that Ignacio, Javier, Elena, and Ana want you to join them in their various activities. What answers might you give them? Respond to their invitations with some of the phrases from the video, or make up your own responses from what you have learned. Follow the model. **Answers will vary.**

Modelo ¿Quieres jugar al fútbol en el parque?

Sí, quiero jugar al fútbol en el parque, pero no juego muy bien.

1. ¿Puedes jugar al tenis mañana?
2. Oye, juegas muy bien al vóleibol. ¿Puedes jugar más tarde?
3. ¿Quieres ir con nosotros a la fiesta esta noche?
4. ¿Sabes bailar?

Realidades A | Nombre | Hora

Capítulo 4B | Fecha | **AUDIO**

Actividad 5

There are not enough hours in the day to do everything we want to do. Listen to the following interviews. What do these people want more time to do? In the blanks provided, write the number of the statement that corresponds to each picture. You will hear each set of statements twice.

4	5	6	3
2	7	1	8

Actividad 6

After listening to each of the following statements, decide if you think the excuses given are believable (**creíble**) or unbelievable (**increíble**). Be prepared to defend your answers with a partner after making your decisions. You will hear each set of statements twice.
Answers will vary.

EXCUSAS, EXCUSAS

	Creíble	Increíble		Creíble	Increíble
1.	❑	❑	5.	❑	❑
2.	❑	❑	6.	❑	❑
3.	❑	❑	7.	❑	❑
4.	❑	❑	8.	❑	❑

Realidades A — Nombre ____ Hora ____

Capítulo 4B — Fecha ____ **AUDIO**

Actividad 7

Listen to the following couple as they try to decide what they are going to do tonight. Every time an activity is mentioned that one of the two people is going to do, draw a circle around the picture. If the other person is NOT going to do that activity, draw an *X* through the picture. The pictures with circles only should represent what both people finally decide to do. You will hear each conversation twice.

Actividad 8

Listen as a radio program host interviews a fitness expert, doctora Benítez, about the best way to get in shape. Listen to the **entrevista** (*interview*), and choose the best answer to the questions below. You will hear this conversation twice.

1. ¿En qué es experta la doctora Benítez?
   a) deportes   b) cocinar   c) música   (d) ejercicio y nutrición
2. Según la doctora, ¿cuántos minutos de ejercicio debes hacer todos los días?
   (a) una hora   b) quince minutos   c) treinta minutos
3. Según Miguel, ¿por qué no puede hacer mucho ejercicio?
   a) Es demasiado perezoso.   (b) Está muy ocupado.   c) Está triste.
4. ¿Qué es divertido para Miguel?
   a) jugar al tenis   (b) ver la tele   c) jugar al fútbol
5. Después de jugar, ¿qué no debemos comer?
   a) cereales   b) frutas y verduras   (c) pasteles

Realidades A — Nombre ____ Hora ____

Capítulo 4B — Fecha ____ **AUDIO**

Actividad 9

Your Spanish teacher always encourages you to speak Spanish to your classmates outside of class. In order to do that, you and your friends agreed to talk on the phone and/or leave messages on each other's answering machines for at least a week. Listen to the messages your friends have left on your answering machine today. Based on the messages, decide a) where the person wants to go; b) what the person wants to do; c) what time the person wants to go. Use the chart below to record the information. You will hear each set of statements twice.

	¿Adónde quiere ir?	¿Qué quiere hacer?	¿A qué hora quiere ir?
Justo	al parque	escuchar un concierto	7:00 P.M.
Eva	al centro comercial	ir de compras	5:00 P.M.
José	a la fiesta	comer pizza y ver un video	8:00 P.M.
Margarita	de cámping	ir de pesca y caminar en las montañas	6:00 A.M.
Pedro	al gimnasio	jugar al básquetbol	5:30 P.M.

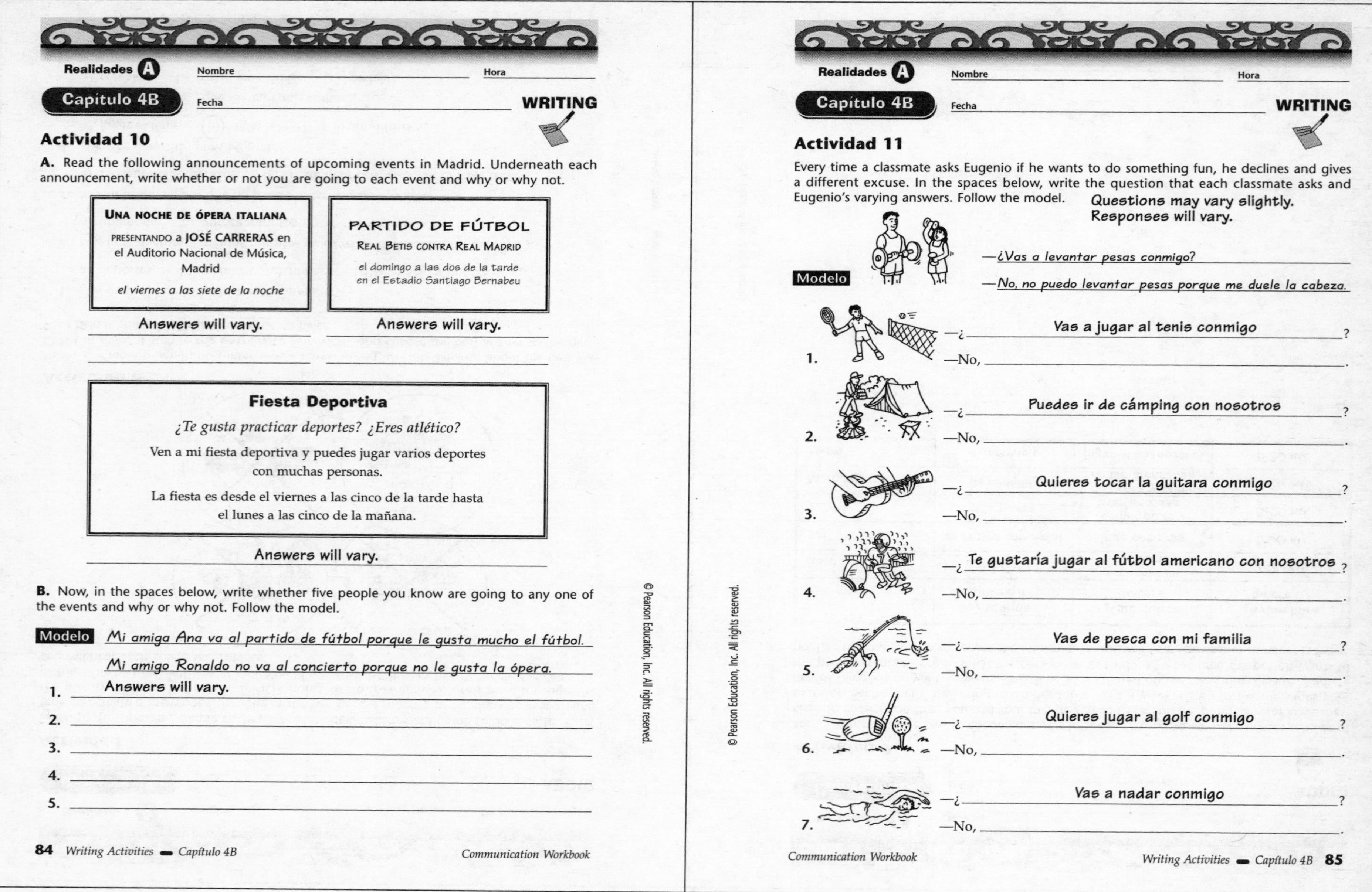

Realidades A Nombre ____ Hora ____

Capítulo 4B Fecha ____ **WRITING**

Actividad 10

A. Read the following announcements of upcoming events in Madrid. Underneath each announcement, write whether or not you are going to each event and why or why not.

UNA NOCHE DE ÓPERA ITALIANA
PRESENTANDO a **JOSÉ CARRERAS** en el Auditorio Nacional de Música, Madrid
el viernes a las siete de la noche

Answers will vary.

PARTIDO DE FÚTBOL
REAL BETIS CONTRA REAL MADRID
el domingo a las dos de la tarde en el Estadio Santiago Bernabeu

Answers will vary.

Fiesta Deportiva
¿Te gusta practicar deportes? ¿Eres atlético?
Ven a mi fiesta deportiva y puedes jugar varios deportes con muchas personas.
La fiesta es desde el viernes a las cinco de la tarde hasta el lunes a las cinco de la mañana.

Answers will vary.

B. Now, in the spaces below, write whether five people you know are going to any one of the events and why or why not. Follow the model.

Modelo *Mi amiga Ana va al partido de fútbol porque le gusta mucho el fútbol.*
Mi amigo Ronaldo no va al concierto porque no le gusta la ópera.

1. Answers will vary.
2. ____
3. ____
4. ____
5. ____

Realidades A Nombre ____ Hora ____

Capítulo 4B Fecha ____ **WRITING**

Actividad 11

Every time a classmate asks Eugenio if he wants to do something fun, he declines and gives a different excuse. In the spaces below, write the question that each classmate asks and Eugenio's varying answers. Follow the model. Questions may vary slightly. Responses will vary.

Modelo —*¿Vas a levantar pesas conmigo?*
—*No, no puedo levantar pesas porque me duele la cabeza.*

1. —¿Vas a jugar al tenis conmigo?
—No, ____.
2. —¿Puedes ir de cámping con nosotros?
—No, ____.
3. —¿Quieres tocar la guitarra conmigo?
—No, ____.
4. —¿Te gustaría jugar al fútbol americano con nosotros?
—No, ____.
5. —¿Vas de pesca con mi familia?
—No, ____.
6. —¿Quieres jugar al golf conmigo?
—No, ____.
7. —¿Vas a nadar conmigo?
—No, ____.

Realidades A | Nombre | Hora

Capítulo 4B | Fecha | WRITING

Actividad 12

When put in the right order, each set of blocks below will ask a question. Unscramble the blocks by writing the contents of each block in the blank boxes. Then, answer the questions in the space provided.

1.

J U E G	D E	E P O R	O S F	U É D	A S L
I N E S	¿ A Q	T E S	N A ?	S E M A	

¿A Q	UÉ D	EPOR	TES	JUEG	AS L
OS F	INES	DE	SEMA	NA?	

Answers will vary.

2.

¿ A Q	M I G O	T E S	U S A	J U E G	U É D
S ?	A N T	E P O R			

¿A Q	UÉ D	EPOR	TES	JUEG	AN T
US A	MIGO	S?			

Answers will vary.

3.

G A ?	L E S	F A V O	¿ C U Á	R I T O	J U E
R T E	U I É N	Y Q	T U	D E P O	

¿CUÁ	L ES	TU	DEPO	RTE	FAVO
RITO	Y Q	UIÉN	JUE	GA?	

Answers will vary.

© Pearson Education, Inc. All rights reserved.

Realidades A | Nombre | Hora

Capítulo 4B | Fecha | WRITING

Actividad 13

You are having a mid-semester party.

A. First, fill in the invitation below with the information about your party. Answers will vary.

FIESTA DE MEDIO SEMESTRE

Lugar: _____

Hora: _____

Comida: _____

RSVP: _____

B. Since you don't have everyone's mailing address, you have to e-mail some people about the party. Write your e-mail below. In addition to inviting them, tell them what activities you will have at the party, and where your house is (**está cerca de la biblioteca,** etc.).

Estimados amigos:

Answers will vary.

¡Me gustaría ver a todos en la fiesta!

Un fuerte abrazo,

Test Preparation Answers

Reading Skills
p. 157 2. **A**
p. 158 2. **D**

Integrated Performance Assessment
p. 159
Answers will vary.

Practice Test: Una conversación difícil
p. 161

1. B
2. J
3. A
4. G
5. C
6. Answers may vary but should include: "It's the thought that counts" means that the intent behind giving a gift is more important than the gift itself. In the story, the fact that Roberto wants to skip spending time with his friends in order to be with his father shows how thoughtful Roberto is. For example: For your friend's birthday, you give her an inexpensive handmade gift because you want to make something especially for her. Even though your gift is not expensive, it is her favorite because she knows that you took the time to make it yourself.

Lecturas Teacher's Guide

Level 1

CAPÍTULO 1

Detesto

Prereading

Answers will vary.

Answers to *¿De qué se trata?*

1. He could be a happy person if he didn't let little things bother him as much. (He can't stand his name, the date of his birth, yogurt, milk, egg yolks, and reading poems.)

2. Answers will vary. Possible answers: He could try to change his name; he could accept what he can't change; he could learn to like the foods mentioned or else try to avoid them.

For further discussion

You may want to ask students the following questions:

1. Using the poem as a guide, write your own poem about the things you can't stand.

2. Write a poem about the things you like and like to do.

3. What are your favorite boy's and girl's names? (You might want to take a poll.) Of the Spanish names you know, which do you like best? Why?

4. Can you think of another first and last name in Spanish as long as Hermenecesto's?

CAPÍTULO 2

Yo

Prereading

Answers will vary.

Answers to *¿De qué se trata?*

1. Answers will vary. Possible answer: She is an average girl, neither tall nor short, fat nor thin, pretty nor ugly, blonde nor brunette.

2. Answers will vary. Possible answers: She means she is just herself; she is an individual with her own identity; she is not like anybody else and can't be put into a category.

3. Answers will vary.

For further discussion

You may want to ask students the following questions:

1. How can you tell that the writer of the poem is a girl? (From the adjectives ending in *-a*.)

2. What do you think the girl in the poem looks like, aside from what the poem says about her?

3. Do you think the poem is applicable to yourself? If not, which words would you change in the poem to describe yourself?

CAPÍTULO 3

Una visita a los indios mayas

Prereading

Answers will vary.

Answers to *¿De qué se trata?*

1. Answers will vary. You might assign this as an extra-credit research project for selected students or for the class as a whole. Possible answers: The Mayas were an American Indian civilization from Central America, and lived mainly in Mexico, Guatemala, and Belize. Their greatest period of development was between A.D. 250 and A.D. 900. They were excellent architects, painters, and sculptors. They were also knowledgeable in astronomy and mathematics, and had a yearly calendar and an advanced form of writing. They may have disappeared due to lack of food, the spread of disease, or a natural disaster.

2. Answers will vary. Possible answers: A piece of glass; a (glass) lens; a piece of mirrored glass; costume jewelry.

For further discussion

You may want to ask students the following questions:

1. Why do you think the guide winks at the end of the story? (Possible answers: He might be amused at the tourists' gullibility; he might have put the "diamond" there himself so the tourists could be happy that they had supposedly discovered a Mayan souvenir by themselves.)

2. The stelae monuments were used by the Mayas to record important dates and events in their rulers' lives. What do you think the *tlachtli* courts were used for? (They were used for ball games; players wore pads to protect

themselves; the object of the game was to pass a solid ball of hardened sap through a stone ring high up on the wall.)
3. Imagine that you are given a choice of visiting some famous Mayan ruins or modern Mexico City. Where would you go and why?
4. Have you ever been on a guided tour? Where? What was it like? What was the guide like?
5. Would you prefer to take a guided tour of a place you have never been to or to try to discover places and things yourself?
6. What type of guided tour would you give of your city? What spots would you point out? What would you tell about your city's or state's history?

CAPÍTULO 4

Equisita—la muchacha sin nombre

Prereading

Answers will vary.

Answers to *¿De qué se trata?*

1. Answers will vary. Possible answers: She should not marry him if she doesn't love him; she is now rich and can do anything or marry anyone she wants.
2. Answers will vary. Possible answers: He could try to start their relationship all over again; he could forget her; he could try to become her friend and wait for her to change her mind about him.
3. Answers will vary. Possible answers: The name "Equisita" comes from *equis—x* in the Spanish alphabet—and since she is described as *la muchacha sin nombre,* i.e., a girl of unknown origin without a name, "Equisita" is the equivalent of "Miss X." (Students may also say that "Equisita" comes from "exquisite.")

For further discussion

You may want to ask students the following questions:
1. What do you think a *radionovela* is? (A radio soap opera, which is very popular in Hispanic countries, especially in rural areas where not every home has a television set.)
2. Why do you think the Italian name Ricaccione was used in the story? (Hispanic *radionovelas* often use the theme of conflicting relationships between the rich and the poor, and the rich are usually given foreign-sounding names.)
3. Why does the narrator of the *radionovela* say near the end: *Señoras y señores, ¡no comprendo! ¡Esto nunca pasa en las radionovelas!*? (Most *radionovelas* end happily with the main character marrying the person he/she loves. In this case the character does something very unusual by not getting married and by talking to the narrator.)
4. Beginning with line 53, do you think that Equisita is reading the lines written for her in the radio script, or has the character (or the person playing her part) suddenly gone berserk?
5. Did you expect this kind of ending when you began the reading?

CAPÍTULO 5

Ocupado y cansado

Prereading

Answers will vary.

Answers to *¿De qué se trata?*

1. Answers will vary. Possible answers: The father probably feels ashamed that he hasn't paid attention to his son before; embarrassed; sad; surprised; pleased.
2. Answers will vary. Possible answers: He might not have a mother; she might also be busy; he might really want very much to spend time with his father, who always seems to be too busy or tired to listen to his son.

For further discussion

You may want to ask students the following questions:
1. How do you think the son feels when he hears his father say: *¡No me digas!*? (Relieved that his father has finally let him finish a sentence; happy that his father might go out with him; happy that he has surprised or pleased his father; pleased that they are communicating.)
2. Can you think of a situation in which you haven't let someone else finish what they were saying or they haven't let you finish? Why do you think this happens?

3. Why do you think it's so hard for some people to communicate?
4. Which feelings or emotions do you think most people find easiest to communicate to others? Which do you think they find hardest to communicate?

CAPÍTULO 6

La voz del fantasma

Prereading

Answers will vary.

If students ask, you might want to present some of the following terminology used in discussing short stories: *ambiente* (atmosphere); *antagonista* (antagonist); *argumento* (plot); *desarrollo* (development); *desenlace* (resolution); *efecto* (effect); *escenario* (setting); *al final* (at the end); *motivo* (motive); *personaje* (character); *personificación* (personification); *al principio* (at the beginning); *protagonista* (protagonist); *punto culminante* (climax); *punto de vista* (point of view); *punto decisivo* (turning point); *representar* (represent); *significado* (meaning); *simbolizar* (symbolize); *símbolo* (symbol); *tema* (theme); *tono* (tone).

Answers to *¿De qué se trata?*

1. Answers will vary.
2. Answers will vary. Possible answers: Ghosts don't exist because you can't see them or hear them; there is always a logical explanation for strange noises or "visions"; your imagination can play tricks on you.

For further discussion

You may want to ask students the following questions:
1. How did Roberto and Susana manage to fool Paquita? (By pretending to be scared and running away from the house with her—lines 31-33.)
2. When do you think Roberto managed to tape his voice? (Possible answers: Before leaving the tape recorder in the abandoned house, or he could have gone back after they had left and taped his voice then.)
3. What do you think the narrator means when she says at the end: *Un día Roberto va a tener una sorpresa también...*? What do you think she could do? (Possible answer: She could try to scare him or give him an unpleasant surprise.)
4. Why do you think ghost stories have always been so popular? (Possible answer: People like mysteries or enjoy being scared.)

CAPÍTULO 7

El periódico del domingo

Prereading

Answers will vary.

Answers to the games

1. muchacha, muchacho (mucha + cho/cha);
2. mi abuela (la esposa del padre del padre de mi hermana);
3. sin coche (5 CH = cinco che);
4. sombrero (s + hombre + ro);
5. correo (correcto con una c y sin t);
6. Elena, César, Irene;
7. pero (una conjunción con una r), perro (tu amigo con una rr);
8. Eres muy antipático;
9. Me encanta el español. (This can be read by tilting the page at a 135° angle from you.)

Answers to *¿De qué se trata?*

1-3. Answers will vary.

For further discussion

You may want to ask students the following question:
Choose the word game or riddle you liked best and make up one similar to it.

CAPÍTULO 8

Izquierda, derecha

Prereading

Answers will vary.

Answers to *¿De qué se trata?*

1. Yes. *Detrás* rhymes with *más* and *encima* rhymes with *rima*.
2. Answers will vary. Possible answers: Before or when they start grade school. The poem teaches them about different (spatial) positions.

For further discussion

You may want to ask students the following questions:
1. Can you remember rhymes or poems that you learned when you were young that had a teaching purpose to them? (Possible answers: The ABC song; One, Two, Buckle My Shoe; Old McDonald)
2. Do you think some things are easier to learn if they are in verse? Why?

CAPÍTULO 9

La carta de David Cisneros

Prereading

Answers will vary.

Make sure students understand the following terminology used in discussing plays: *personaje* (character); *acto* (act); *escena* (scene); *telón* (curtain).

Answers to *¿De qué se trata?*

1. Salvador and David feel sad because Ana María is going so far away; they will both miss her and David would probably like to go with her too.
2. Answers will vary. Possible answers: She might feel embarrassed and angry with her mother for writing the letter; she might feel hopeful about getting a big part in the movie; she might stay away from Pablo Garrido because she's ashamed about possibly getting a part in the movie this way.

For further discussion

You may want to ask students the following questions:
1. Do you think David gets along well with his parents? Explain your answer using examples from the reading. (Possible answers: He probably gets along better with his mother than with his father. His father is preoccupied and doesn't even remember that David goes to the movies every Saturday. His mother acts as a buffer between them—lines 23, 28-29.)
2. Would you have done the same thing that Amelia did for someone you cared about? Why or why not?

CAPÍTULO 10

Las cartas de Ana María Cisneros

Prereading

Answers will vary.

Answers to *¿De qué se trata?*

1. Answers will vary. Possible answer: He gets along well with her and misses her, and would like to be with her in Madrid.
2. Answers will vary. Possible answer: Salvador would probably talk mostly about his play and perhaps mention a few words about David and Amelia.

For further discussion

You may want to ask students the following questions:
1. Imagine that Ana María was not invited to audition for the movie. What do you think Amelia might have done next? (Possible answers: She might have written or called Pablo Garrido again; she might have told Ana María to go ahead and audition for the movie; she might not have done anything else.)
2. Imagine that you are Pablo Garrido and that you are being interviewed about the new movie. What do you think you would say about your new actress and the part she plays in the movie?
3. You might want to ask students to write a two- or three-line review of a movie they have seen recently.

CAPÍTULO 11

El pueblo de tontos

Prereading

Answers will vary.

Answers to *¿De qué se trata?*

1. Answers will vary. Possible answers: Because someone else always fixes things up for them and they don't have to correct things themselves; because they view everything in isolation and don't realize that what they learn

from one experience can be transferred to other situations and help them make better decisions or avoid making the same mistakes.
2. Answers will vary. Possible answer: The Tolencianos might have learned from their mistake and become less foolish.

For further discussion

You may want to ask students the following questions:
1. After reading the title of the story, what did you think it might be about?
2. Why do you think the character of the "fool" is popular in the folk tales of many countries? (Possible answer: The "fool" usually embodies a specific bad trait, and therefore the tale can focus on it and teach a moral about how to deal with that trait. You may also want to tell students that this folk tale is a variant of a Mexican tale called "The Holes of Lagos." These types of anecdotes about fools are found everywhere in the world. Many folk tales from Spanish-speaking countries include *Juan Bobo*—"John Fool"—stories.)
3. When a friend of yours makes a mistake which is obvious to you, do you tell that person what he/she has done wrong? Why or why not?
4. One of the pleasant things about the Tolencianos is that they are not embarrassed by their foolishness. Have you ever done anything really foolish? How did you feel? Were you embarrassed?

CAPÍTULO 12

La caja misteriosa (primera parte)

Prereading

Answers will vary.

Answers to *¿De qué se trata?*

1. Answers will vary. Most likely answer: Curiosity.
2. Answers will vary. Possible answer: The masks have disappeared because someone thought they were valuable and stole them.
3. Answers will vary. Possible answers: They will probably find the masks; the masks might somehow reappear.

For further discussion

You may want to ask students the following questions:
1. Why do you think Elena doesn't open the box right away, even if it means arriving late at the movie? (Possible answer: She might not want to be alone in case the box holds an unpleasant surprise.)
2. Why do you think people write anonymous letters or send anonymous gifts? (Possible answers: Because they are cowardly or insecure; cruel; mischief-makers.) How would you feel if you received one? (Scared; nervous; spied on.)
3. Can you remember something that happened in your life that was unexplainable? What happened?
4. If you write a letter to a newspaper or magazine, you may request them not to print your name, but they will not publish a letter that you have not signed. Why do you think this is so? (If necessary, explain the concept of libel and help students see that there is something cowardly about expressing an opinion that you aren't prepared to stand behind.)

CAPÍTULO 13

La caja misteriosa (segunda parte)

Prereading

Answers will vary. Possible answers: Go to the police; call the Museo de Arte Inca in Cuzco; talk to someone in an art museum or a specialist in Peruvian arts and handicrafts.

You may want to tell students that Viracocha was considered by the Aymaran and Quechuan civilizations of ancient Peru to be the supreme divinity, father of all living beings. It is said that he appeared in a long robe, had a beard, and was leading an unknown animal by the reins. The Indians therefore thought the Spaniards were Viracocha's sons when they first saw them.

Answers to *¿De qué se trata?*

1. Answers will vary. Possible answers: Yes, the police have more connections and more experience in finding solutions to this type of

mystery; no, because the police might think Elena had stolen the masks herself or might become suspicious of her.
2. Answers will vary. Possible answer: I might have helped Elena call the art museum or been with her when she talked to the police and to Sr. Vásquez.

For further discussion

You may want to ask students the following questions:
1. If you were the author of this play, are there any parts that you would have changed? Which ones? Why?
2. If you were Sr. Vásquez, what would you have done about the masks' disappearance? (Possible answer: Go to the police or the government agencies of both the United States and Peru, and get the masks back at all costs.)
3. Have you ever had a dream from which you woke up feeling frustrated because it didn't have a real ending, or because it didn't give you an answer? Can you describe the dream?
4. You might want to assign the following questions as an extra-credit research project for selected students or for the class as a whole: Do you know who the Incas were? Where did they live? (They were an advanced American Indian civilization whose empire reached its peak around A.D.1500. Their empire stretched from southern Colombia to Chile, and included the western regions of Bolivia and Argentina. They were known for their postal service, which consisted of relay runners; their highly developed system of roads and bridges; and their architecture and engineering.)

CAPÍTULO 14

Los números de Juan

Prereading

Answers will vary.

Answers to *¿De qué se trata?*

1. Answers will vary. Possible answers: It is a sad story because Juan did not get the money that he had wanted to win; it is not a sad story because in the end Juan became a more serious, responsible person.
2. Answers will vary. Possible answer: His friend may think that if Juan knows he has won, he might forget about his achievements and become lazy again and not work.

For further discussion

You may want to ask students the following questions:
1. The story deals with two types of success. What are they and which one would you rather have? (Success in work, and success in luck. Answers will vary.)
2. Did you expect this kind of ending to the story? Why or why not?
3. What do you think the moral of the story is? (Possible answer: That one should rely on one's own talents and hard work rather than on luck.)
4. How do you think Juan's life would have changed if he had continued to play the lottery and won? What do you think he might have done with the money? (Possible answers: He might have taken the money and gone to Paris after all, but he would probably have become a serious art student and utilized his talents; he might have gone back to his old ways and spent the money on his friends and on himself.)
5. Do you know someone whose personality was similar to Juan's, but who changed almost overnight? What brought about the change?

CAPÍTULO 15

Manolito y sus amigos

Prereading

Answers will vary.

Answers to *¿De qué se trata?*

1. Answers will vary. Possible answers: He is a determined, resourceful person who knows what he wants and knows how to get it. He doesn't go on vacations just to "get away."
2. Answers will vary.

For further discussion

You may want to ask students the following questions:
1. What do you think of Manolito's idea? Was it a good one? Why or why not? (Possible

answers: Yes, because he worked for something that could be useful for a long time; no, he could have spent his vacation with the others and worked some other time.)
2. Have you ever had a summer job? Did you just spend the money you earned, did you spend it on something specific that you had planned for, or did you save it? Why?

CAPÍTULO 16

Gregorio

Prereading

Answers will vary.

Answers to *¿De qué se trata?*

1. Answers will vary. Possible answers: It depends on what kind of talent you have; writing and drawing require different types of skills; if you don't have imagination you can still draw and write from real life.
2. You might ask students to share their drawings with the rest of the class. You might also ask them to vote for the best drawing.

For further discussion

You may want to ask students the following questions:
1. What line(s) of the story indicate(s) that an unusual event is about to occur? (Lines 27-31.)
2. What do you think of the narrator's solution to the problem of Gregorio's size? What would you have done?
3. What are the advantages and disadvantages of having a vivid imagination? (Possible answer: Imagination can lead to creativity, but you can also get lost in an imaginary world and not be able to deal with reality.)
4. When you are given a writing assignment, do you usually prefer to draw from your own experiences, or do you prefer to make up something? Why? In general, which do you think is easier?
5. Do you sometimes wish you could lead a more exciting life? In what ways do you think this could be accomplished?
6. Do you think everybody has a talent for doing something? If so, why do you think some people are more successful than others at utilizing their talents?
7. What do you think the world would be like if the only thing we knew was reality and none of us had the power to imagine? How would your own life differ? (Possible answers: There would be no inventions; no art or literature; we would be unable to make plans or change things on purpose; we would be powerless and only able to react to events without ever thinking of the possible consequences.)

Notes

Notes

Notes